Oh, Yikes!

HISTORY'S GROSSEST, WACKIEST MOMENTS

BY JOY MASOFF

Illustrated by Terry Sirrell

WORKMAN PUBLISHING · NEW YORK

Library of Congress Cataloging-in-Publication Data

Masoff, Joy, 1951–
Oh, yikes! : history's grossest, wackiest moments / by Joy Masoff.
p. cm.
ISBN-13: 978-0-7611-3684-2 (pbk.)
ISBN-10: 0-7611-3684-3 (pbk.)
1. History—Anecdotes—Encyclopedias, Juvenile. I. Title.

D10.M38 2006
902'.07—dc22   2006045243

Front cover and spine photography by Graham French (www.grahamfrench.com)
Cover design: Lisa Hollander
Interior design: Lisa Hollander and David Riedy
Photo research and editing: Anne Kerman
Illustrations by Terry Sirrell

Workman books are available at special discounts when purchased in bulk for special premiums and sales promotions as well as for fund-raising or educational use.
Special editions or book excerpts also can be created to specification.
For details, contact the Special Sales
Director at the address below.

Workman Publishing Company, Inc.
708 Broadway
New York, NY 10003-9555
www.workman.com

Printed in the
United States of America

First printing July 2006
10 9 8 7 6 5 4 3 2 1

DEDICATED TO THE ONES I LOVE

I'll always remember the night. We were having dinner, and my kids were slumped over their spaghetti moaning about how *booooooor-ing* history was. I looked at them as if they each had two heads! History? Boring? What were they talking about????? How could anything as whacked out, wild, weird, and wonderful as history be dull? Then I looked at their school textbooks. Uh, yeah . . . snoozeville!

This book is dedicated to my bored-with-history kids, Tish and Alex Scolnik, their bored-with-history cousins, Ivan, Miranda, and Serena Levingston,

Eli Townley, and every other girl or boy who has ever yawned through endless dates and unpronounceable battles. I hope this will prove to you that you were wrong, wrong, wrong! Hugs also to my hubby, Lou, who allowed me to discuss unsavory episodes about times gone by at countless dinners, parties, and family gatherings. And a very special hats-off to my former Cub Scouts, Brownies, and Girl Scouts. If we hadn't made those fun-filled field trips to all those hands-on living history sites, I never would have known that it was fashionable to paint your gums black in colonial times!

Just give me one measly minute!

65 MILLION YEARS AGO
Dinosaurs bite the dust after a giant meteor smashes into Earth and changes the climate. Sadly, the only dino to survive is Barney. How cruel!

CRO-MAGNONS (100,000–10,000 YEARS AGO) That's us, baby! Our ancestors start to crop up midway through the Neanderthals' time on Earth. But Cro-Magnons are a little faster and a little smarter. With chow hard to come by 'cause the world is so freezing cold, Cro-Magnons are better at hunting and gathering food. They who eat first, win.
Big contribution: Sharp weapons.

EGYPT (3000–30 B.C.E.) Fun in the sun. Land of the pharaohs, mummies, the river Nile, treasure cities, and cat-gods.
Big contribution: Those amazing Pyramids—5,000 years old and still going strong.

NEANDERTHALS 120,000 to 30,000 YEARS AGO Dumb and hairy? Nope. Neanderthals are smart and strong. They make stone tools, bury their dead with loving care, and build animal-bone houses. But the last great Ice Age zaps them and they slowly die out or mingle with and marry Cro-Magnons.
Big contribution: Fur coats.

END OF THE ICE AGE (10,000 YEARS AGO) Throw out those parkas. Pull on the bikinis! It's warm enough out to start growing crops and stop running after giant hairy elephants. Folks learn to farm and stay put. Towns spring up.
Big contribution: Farming.

MESOPOTAMIA (3500–2000 B.C.E.) More like *messed-up-potamia!* So warlike! So grumpy! Always getting conquered by one group or another. Sumerians, Babylonians, Assyrians, Hittites—sheeesh! Still, these guys are great at math. They invent the decimal system and the 60-second, 60-minute method for keeping time.
Big contribution: An eye for an eye. A tooth for a tooth.

History's Grossest, Wackiest Moments

The entire history of the world can be learned in about 60 seconds. Trust me. Here's how: Just pretend your school is Planet Earth.

There are heroic feats of derring-do, such as sneaking into the science lab to let all the dissection frogs loose. There are natural disasters, like the toilets in the boy's bathroom that keep overflowing. And let's not forget those man-made mishaps—the revolting smell of bean-surprise coming from the cafeteria lunch line.

There are the generals (you might know them as your teachers) always bossing you around, telling you to sit up straight and spit out your gum. And then there is the king or queen, also known as *Your Royal Highness*—the principal. Principals face off against other royals—the principals of other schools. They send in the "troops" to do battle, clad in soccer, baseball, or basketball uniforms. They scream, "Crush them! Beat them! WIN! WIN! WIN!"

CHINA (1800 B.C.E.– 200 C.E.) The world's greatest inventors of all the stuff we love—paper, silk, soccer, noodles, and ice cream—not to mention the compass, kites, rockets, and the umbrella. *Big contribution:* Personally, I want to say ice cream, but really—gunpowder.

ANCIENT GREECE (1500–146 B.C.E) Birthplace of democracy, the column, and the Olympics— home of running the 100-meter dash wearing nothing but a hopeful smile. *Big contribution:* One man = one vote. (Alas, in ancient Greece one woman = diddly squat.)

THE BARBARIANS/ DARK AGES (500–1000 C.E.) Hey! Who turned the lights off in Europe? When the mighty Roman Empire crumbles, no one's in charge anymore. *Big contribution:* Wool socks.

THE PHOENICIANS (1200–332 B.C.E.) No, they didn't invent the phone, silly! They were super sailors, and the Wal-Marters of their time. They imported so much papyrus from Egypt that one of their cities became known as Byblos— the Greek work for papyrus, and the reason we read something called *The Bible* today instead of *The Scrmidfzthyu*. *Big contribution:* Our alphabet (well, at least 22 letters of it).

ROMAN EMPIRE (753 B.C.E.–476 C.E.) Gladiators, crazy Caesars, and one of the biggest empires the world has ever seen. Plus . . . how would we ever know which Super Bowl it is without those nutty Roman numerals? *Big contribution:* The arch (and where would McDonald's be without those?).

THE MESOAMERICANS (1500 B.C.E.–1400 C.E.) Mountaintop cities, powerful kings, sophisticated calendars, and a nifty little thing called the bouncy ball all came from the mid-section of the Americas. The Olmecs, Mayas, and Aztecs had it goin' on—especially when it came to bloodletting! *Big contribution:* Rubber and chocolate.

ix

WANT A WEDGIE?

There are *always* bullies—kids who want stuff that isn't theirs and who won't think twice about grabbing it. There are *always* victims—those poor kids who end up with their underwear on the *outside* of their pants. There are the heroes—kids who are willing to stand up to the bullies. And there are all the rest of us: the geeks, the punks, the jocks, the brains, the artists, the rockers, the comics, the do-gooders, and the goof-offs, who each contribute a little something special to make the day more interesting.

And—bottom line—that's what history is *really* all about. It's not about a whole bunch of boring dates. It's not about the Battle of Watchamacallit and General Who-gives-a-rat's-tail. It's about people who wanted stuff and took it without asking. It's about folks who did wacky things even though people told them they were nuts to even try. It's about volcanoes blowing up and bridges falling down. It's about putrid poxes and muck-filled moats. It's about stupid inventions and pointless pranks. And, of course, it's about heads getting chopped off . . . a *lot* of heads!

GHANA/MALI/ SONGHAY EMPIRES (500–1600) Africa, the Dark Continent? *No,* you big doof! Africa is at its wealthiest in the Middle Ages, with huge deposits of salt, gold, and one of the world's greatest cities of learning and trade.
Big contribution: Universities and libraries.

THE ISLAMIC EMPIRE (570–1260) While Europe stumbles and fumbles, folks in the Middle East have good medicine, fine schools, cool architecture, and the amazing number zero.
Big contribution: Modern mathematics. Thanks *a lot,* guys!

THE MIDDLE AGES (1000–1500) Clanging knights, toothless peasants, kings, queens, and empires galore.
Big contribution: Gothic cathedrals.

THE CRUSADES (1027–1270) There are a zillion stupid, pointless little wars in Europe, so Pope Urban II decides to point everyone in the direction of Jerusalem in the Middle East, guaranteeing hundreds of years of stupid, pointless wars with the nations of Islam.
Big contribution: The Knights Templar.

BYZANTIUM (500–1453) Part of the Roman Empire survives—the part that pokes into Asia. Byzantium (*Biz-ANT-ee-um*) mixes ancient Greek and Roman ways and stirs in a big heaping cup of the Middle East and Asia. But it eventually goes ker-plooie after being invaded one too many times.
Big contribution: Kept Christianity cooking as a religion.

THE VIKINGS (750–1100) Forget readin', writin', and 'rithmatic. Vikings learn sailin', slashin', and stealin'.
Big contribution: Their raids lead to the building of many of Europe's great cities.

AAHHHH!!

THE MONGOLS (1206–1405) Think Greece or Rome were the giants of the empire-biz? Guess again. Mighty Genghis Khan wins the empire size-game.
Big contribution: The post office.

YES, I DID! NO, YOU DIDN'T!

But there is another interesting twist to all these gross goings-on. Think about this: Someone did something. Someone else saw it and told another person about it. Sometimes the person doing the talking didn't know what the heck they were talking about. Sometimes the people hearing the story didn't *quite* remember the story the way they were told—kind of like a giant game of Telephone (you know—you stand in a circle and whisper a phrase into someone's ear and they keep repeating it to the next person until the last person in the circle has to say the phrase and it turns out all screwy and wrong). It makes stories about the past really interesting!

A lot of really horrible, disgusting things have happened since people started writing events down. Some really evil people have done some truly awful, really horrible, no-good, truly terrible things.

BUT THIS ISN'T A BOOK ABOUT THEM!

Instead, this is your chance to poke your nose into some of the freakier, funnier, wackier, wilder parts of our amazing past. Some of it is pretty revolting. All of it is *really* cool. And I promise . . . you won't have to remember a single date (unless you really want to).

THE AGE OF EXPLORATION (1450–1700) The continents are introduced to one another as men like Chris Columbus sail across the seas. Unfortunately for the Native Americans, the meeting does not go so well. They end up getting squished by greedy explorers who bring smallpox and measles with them. Later a steady stream of "settlers" push them off their land.
Big contribution: The Columbian exchange: corn for cows, potatoes for horses.

THE AGE OF REVOLUTION (1776–1917) Don't like being bossed around without having any say in how or why or when? Just throw a little revolution and watch the world's little guys punch the big guys where it hurts.
Big contribution: The Declaration of Independence.

THE SPACE AGE (1950–present) Blast off! Off we go into the wild blue yonder!
Big contribution: Spaceships.

THE RENAISSANCE (1400–1600) Europe wakes up from its long snooze. Art and education flourish. Shakespeare writes, Michaelangelo sculpts, Da Vinci paints and invents. People learn to read, leading to the invention of eyeglasses.
Big contribution: Moveable type.

THE REFORMATION (1517–1648) A lot of people in Europe are beginning to think the Catholic Church has gotten super corrupt! Some popes are stealing, lying, and generally being *very* unholy.
Big contribution: A new religion.

THE AGE OF INVENTION (1800–present) Cars! Planes! Electricity! DVDs and MP3s! What will they think of next? *Big contribution:* Too many to pick from!

THE WORLD WARS (1914–1918, 1939–1945) Some of the world's absolutely worst tyrants make a huge mess of the planet! Just about everybody gets dragged into a big global slug-fest, not once but twice!
Big contribution: Men off fighting brings women into the workforce.

We Can Do It

ATTILA AND THE HUNS

How do you like your meat cooked? Broiled? Grilled? Medium rare? Well, here's a dandy Hun "cooking" idea that adds new meaning to the words "rump roast." Take a slab of raw meat. Get a horse. Remove the saddle. Put the meat on the horse where the saddle should go. Then mount that sirloin and gallop around for six or seven hours. When the meat is squishy from the pounding that your butt has just provided, it'll be ready to eat. No need to cook. Just take a bite. After all . . . it is warm.

And now that you've had a Hun cooking lesson, read on and discover why the Huns were so feared.

HUN-NY BUNCH

Every villain needs a distinctive creepy trait. A sneering cackle, one hideously long fingernail, a piranha pond . . . something along those lines. Attila the Hun—who terrorized folks throughout Europe in the middle of the fifth century C.E.— was no exception. His super-villain trademark was rolling his eyes around and around and around in his head really, really fast. Give it a try. How long can you keep doing it before you need to whip out a barf bag?

Attila was born in 406 C.E. to a powerful family. We are talking about one tough cookie here, even when he was a kid. You think *your* sister or brother is a pain? Get this: Attila's brother, Bleda, was supposed to share the throne with his eye-spinning sibling after their uncle died in 434 C.E. But after a few years of sharing, Attila decided to arrange a hunting "accident" for his poor brother. Bye-bye, Bleda!

What did Attila look like? Written descriptions tell us he had a humongous head, with small deep-set eyes, a very flat nose, and a few scraggly little hairs hanging where a man's beard usually is. Attila had broad shoulders and a short, square, stubby sort of body. He was built like a tree stump and he was mean as an angry bull. His nickname (remember . . . all good villains have nicknames) was "the Scourge of God." Scourge is a fancy word for something that brings misery and death. And when it came to misery, Attila was a master.

THE THREE R'S: RIDING, RAMPAGING, AND RUINING

Attila ruled over the Huns, who originally came from Central Asia. That's the area that sits between China, India, and Russia. The Huns moved westward into Europe in the fourth century C.E. and by the time Attila was spinning his eyes, the Huns had moved as far west as central and southeastern Europe and they were itching to control even more land. In the beginning, about the only thing the Huns had going for them were thousands of miles of fields full of tall grass—not much to build an empire on. But these grasslands, which are sometimes called *steppes,* were great for grazing animals— especially horses.

Beef? It's what's for dinner. Cook it by sitting on it for a day.

HORSING AROUND

The Huns were amazing horsemen—able to actually eat *and* sleep in the saddle. Kids learned to ride at the same time they learned to walk. And to make the men extra-tough, some legends say that newborn boys had their faces cut at birth to get them used to pain. They even drank horse blood—the Hun's equivalent of Gatorade. The result? A lot of really mean guys with buns of steel who could sit in the saddle all day.

Now, a horse is a whole lot bigger than a person. Stick a vicious warrior on top of a half-ton of galloping horseflesh and we're talking serious "uh-oh" here. And the Huns may have had a secret weapon. Some historians think the Huns invented the stirrup—that little loop for your feet to slide into when riding. Stirrups come in really handy when you are galloping full-tilt toward your enemy with a sword swinging in your hands. You can rise up from your seat and throw the weight of your entire body (along with the forward motion of your horse) into knocking off someone's noggin.

Naturally, the Huns thought they were super-cool and generally superior to the rest of the world. After all, they had thousands of horses. They could ride like the wind. Most of the rest of Europe, with their old-fashioned armies of foot soldiers, could only plod along on their aching, smelly feet. So, one by one, tribe after tribe fell to the swarming Huns, who would come galloping through a town, willing to cut down anyone who got in their way. And I do mean anyone—babies, old ladies, sick people. *Everyone.*

Attila was a guy who dreamed big. At that time, Rome was the "big cheese" of the world, controlling big chunks of Europe and North Africa. So Attila pointed his soldiers and horses in the direction of the mighty Roman Empire. Hun warriors, led by Attila (waving a huge rusty sword he claimed once belonged to Mars, the Roman god of war), would gallop in, kill anyone who got in their way, and steal whatever they could. Faced with a thundering horde of screaming, sword-waving, horse-riding warriors, many people decided "if you can't beat them, join them," and pledged allegiance to Attila. (Better than having your head hacked in two.)

HUNSTORY

■ Attila came from a long line of warrior-rulers. The Huns had been beating people up for centuries by the time Attila was born. In fact, some sections of the Great Wall of China were built to keep out the Huns.

■ At the same time Attila was storming across Europe, Rome was hit hard by a run of really bad luck—earthquakes and swarms of crop-destroying bugs. The Bible talks about the Four Horsemen of the Apocalypse, which is a story that describes the end of the world. Some Roman leaders only had to *look* at Attila and his thousands of troops *on horseback* to think that the Bible was right and the end had indeed come.

■ Venice is a beautiful city built on little islands. Instead of riding in cars, people drive boats down streets of water. It was settled by people fleeing from the Huns in the 420s C.E. They figured horses couldn't gallop across miles of H_2O.

■ One group of people, the Magyars, decided that if they gave their country a scary name, no one would bother them. Their rulers decided that they were descended from Attila, so in the 1100s, they began calling their country *Hun*gary (not to be confused with those gross sounds your stomach makes when it needs food).

As word spread of their cruelty, the Huns didn't even have to fight anymore. They just said they were *thinking* of destroying a town and everything in it, unless they were paid huge sums of protection money. Kind of like the school bully who will leave you alone if you give him your Twinkies. Every day. For the rest of your life. People paid up and the Huns grew rich. But oddly, Attila didn't want the riches, only the power. He dressed simply, lived simply, ate simply . . . and lived cruelly.

JUST KIDDING?

Attila *wanted* people to be afraid of him, and stories about his cruelty started flying around. There was even a rumor spread that he actually ate two of his sons. Talk about a mean dad! But it turns out Attila wasn't the only Hun with a serious streak of evil.

Way back then, in many places in the world, it was normal for a man to have more than one wife. Attila had a bunch, and he liked some better than others. Legend has it that one of his grumpier brides was looking for a little revenge, so she cooked up two of his *other* wives' children and served them to Attila for supper, sweetly saying that the tender meat had come from some frisky young mammals. Oh, well . . . she may have been a killer, but at least she was honest.

ATTILA THE DEAD

By 450 C.E., the Huns had been galloping towards Rome for a couple of years, hacking the heads off of anyone who wasn't thrilled to see them coming and extorting money from everyone else. Attila was making a real mess of the Roman Empire. But in the end he couldn't

Anyone got a Kleenex? *A nasty nosebleed meant the end of Attila.*

quite control it. It was hard to feed thousands of horses so far away from the great grazing lands of the steppes, and he soon found himself depending on plain old foot soldiers just like everyone else. On a level playing field, Attila simply didn't have the manpower, and he had to retreat.

What's a fitting end for a cruel and bloodthirsty Hun? Blood, and lots of it. Here's what happened to our dear Scourge. In 453 C.E., Attila decided to get married yet again (to wife number seven!). At his wedding feast he ate and drank a ton. That night he had a bad nosebleed. Could wife number seven have gotten mad at him and slugged him in the schnozzola? Attila was so drunk he didn't realize his nose was bleeding, so he rolled over and went to sleep. By morning the Scourge of God was dead, drowned in his own nasty nose blood. Attila had taken the ultimate nosedive.

Attila's sons took over as rulers, but they bickered all the time. Without Attila, the Hunnish empire soon crumbled. But new cities had been created because of him—and the continent of Europe—sliced up by a short, eye-rolling ruler with a rusty sword—would never be the same.

AZTEC ANTICS

The next time it's Valentine's Day and you find yourself surrounded by all those sappy satin hearts trimmed with lace, think about the ancient Aztecs. They had a thing for hearts, too. But why bother with paper and lace when you can rip the real thing right out of someone's chest?

Hold tight! Hearts are slippery!

THE BEAT-BEAT-BEAT OF YOUR HEART

By the year 1325 C.E. things were really wild down in what is now central Mexico. The Aztecs were in charge and they had some really funky ideas about how to run their empire. And what a magnificent empire it was! Their capital city, Tenochtitlán (*Ten-osh-tit-LAN*), was a gorgeous place in the middle of a huge man-made lake. There were towering pyramids and broad plazas and lovely little canals rimmed with flowers. And there were crowds in those plazas. In the 1400s, about 25 million folks lived in the middle part of the Americas, which is called Meso-America.

The people that lived there called themselves the Mexica (*Me-SHEE-ka*). They had all the goodies of a wealthy civilization: art, music, poetry, science, and lots of cool myths and legends about the gods and goddesses that gave them all that stuff.

Sounds kinda nice, huh? Guess again! Grab a jumbo box of Band-Aids and let's zip back to Aztec times. You're gonna need them!

ON THEIR BEST BEHAVIOR

Naturally, in a place where people could easily see what happened to the emperor's enemies, crime was almost unheard of. From an early age the Mexica had a huge respect for the law. Even little kids faced some pretty tough punishments. Being sent to their rooms? Nuh-uh! They were held over a fire of burning hot peppers, which stung their eyes. They were pricked with cactus thorns. Grown-ups had it even rougher. They could have their lips sliced off for saying something bad about the emperor.

The head priest quickly sliced the victim's chest open with a shiny black obsidian knife. The beating heart was literally torn out of the poor fellow's chest and tossed onto a fire. Then the dead, heartless body was pushed down the steep pyramid steps. (The corpses of really brave warriors were carried down.) Sometimes, the victim's head was sliced off and taken to the central plaza to be displayed on a skull-rack along with the other sacrifice victims' noggins. The rest of the body went to the butcher shop. The lucky person who had captured a sacrifice victim in battle got to go home with three limbs as a souvenir.

Naturally that sort of exciting afternoon called for a feast. A stew of tomatoes, peppers, and human arms and legs was usually served to celebrate Sacrifice Day—the Aztec equivalent of a Thanksgiving turkey.

YOU'RE HEARTLESS!

The Aztecs had a thing for blood—their own or someone else's. That's because they believed that their gods needed human blood to remain happy. The emperors figured the best way to get that sticky red stuff was by attacking their enemies. There were certainly plenty of *those* around since the Aztecs were always grabbing other people's land. As the Aztecs captured enemies in battle, they marched them back to Tenochtitlán. They had plans for their captives. Bloody plans.

They kept their prisoners in wooden cages and fattened them up on corn tortillas while awaiting the big day—Sacrifice Day! Sacrifices were really grisly affairs, but when you grow up with something vile and disgusting, you get used to it. On Sacrifice Day, the priests smeared a special black paint all over their bodies. The paint was made from mind-altering drugs that gave them tons of energy as it was absorbed into their bodies. Then the priests wrapped themselves in cloaks made from the skins of their past human victims. Skin clothing! Ick!

The new victims were dragged to the top of the pyramid and held down by four priests.

Heartlessly we roll along. Sacrifice victims were rolled down the bloody pyramid steps.

PUPPY CHOW

The Mexica had a little problem. There were a lot of people that needed to get fed in their empire and there were hardly any big, juicy animals to eat. No cattle, no horses, no pigs. Most of the large *herbivores* (grass eaters) had long ago become extinct. In South America, there were llamas and alpacas and chubby guinea pigs. But in what is now Mexico, there was a real shortage of protein. The Aztecs tried breeding Chihuahuas, one of the few dogs around, to solve the problem. But we all know there isn't a lot of meat on one of *those* puppies. Some historians and anthropologists believe that the Mexica turned to human sacrifice followed by cannibalism as a way to make their gods happy while keeping their own bellies full.

YIPE! YIPE! YIPE!

WHO'S IN CHARGE AROUND HERE?

Sometimes it's cool to be king. People look up to you. They bring you all sorts of gifts. They have to laugh at your jokes, even if they're totally lame. They have to do *everything* you tell them to. But sometimes it sucks to be a king . . . especially when your entire empire is about to fall apart. And that's what happened to an unlucky fellow named Moctezuma Xocoyotl (*Mock-te-ZOO-ma Zo-ko-YO-til*), the very last emperor of the Aztec empire.

Moctezuma was born around 1480 C.E. He was the baby in his family and even though his dad had once been the ruler, someone outside the family took over when daddy died. Between 1486 and 1502, a really ruthless guy named Ahuitzotl—a bloodthirsty fellow who once sacrificed 20,000 prisoners in one day—ran the show. After Ahuitzotl died, the council of nobles looked for a new emperor and picked Moctezuma to rule because he was the top of his class in Aztec

warrior school. What did that mean? Sure, there was picture-writing, math, and astronomy in Aztec schools. Religion, too. But you also trained to survive for days without eating. You learned how to fight like a wild thing. And then there was everyone's grossest subject—cutting and piercing your own skin. You "graduated" when you captured an enemy alive in battle. You were now a Master of Cuts.

COLD-HEARTED CONQUISTADORES

One of the nastiest groups to ever gallop across the Americas in the 1500s were groups of Spanish soldiers who called themselves *conquistadores* (conquerors). Their motto was "Now that I am here, all your stuff belongs to me, and you have to do everything the way I say, or I'll kill you . . . or better still, make you wish you were dead." These were *not* nice men.

Hernán Cortés was among the conquistadores who conquered Mexico. With a relatively small army, he was able to quickly trash one of the richest empires on Earth. How? Guns. Horses. Snarling attack dogs. Getting the Aztecs' enemies (of which there were plenty) to fight on Spain's side. And, finally, spreading deadly smallpox germs, at first accidentally and later *on purpose*, to wipe out three-quarters of the population. See what I mean? *Not nice.*

IS THAT A GOD ON THE HORIZON?

So Moctezuma took the throne. For a while things went along as usual. Fight. Sacrifice. Fight. Sacrifice. But one day, Moctezuma got some strange news. "Floating islands" carrying people with very pale skin were moving across the waters of the sea to the east of his empire. At the same time up in the sky, a huge comet was streaking past the stars. In those days everyone believed comets were an omen—a sign that something momentous was about to happen.

One of the most beloved (and, naturally, the most feared) of the Aztec gods was Quetzalcoatl (*Ket-zul-coe-AHT-ul*). To the people of Meso-America, he was a lot like Jesus—a real person who, 500 years after his death, became someone to be worshipped and revered. Quetzalcoatl wore white feathers and was linked with the rising sun in the east. His return to Earth from heaven had been foretold for hundreds of years. One of the stories about Quetzalcoatl's return said that a messenger with a beard the color of the sun would come to announce his arrival.

So when Moctezuma looked at the sky and saw a comet, and then saw "islands" floating toward him from the east, he got a little panicky. And when he saw the sun-colored beard of one of the pale-skinned people (a blonde), the strange beasts they had with them (horses), and their flaming fire sticks (guns), he decided that Quetzalcoatl had indeed returned!

Unfortunately, the Aztecs were in for the worst kind of a surprise. The blonde-bearded man definitely wasn't Quetzalcoatl and the "floating islands" were ships from Spain carrying soldiers dead set on conquering the New World. But Moctezuma didn't know that, so he sent out a welcoming committee. It seemed like a good idea at the time—an idea that quickly turned oh-so-bad!

END OF THE LINE

By the time Moctezuma and his royal advisors figured out what the Spanish were up to, it was too late. Mighty Moctezuma was taken captive, and then sent out to tell the Mexica that the Spanish were now in charge. Upon hearing this news, his subjects promptly stoned him to death. A new emperor was named and *finally,* the Mexica started to fight the conquistadores. But, in an odd twist, they fought not to kill, but to take prisoners for future sacrifices—old habits die hard—and in doing so, wasted a huge amount of time and energy.

The Spaniards' game plan was simple. Invite all the Aztecs' enemies—all the other nations the Aztecs had terrorized for so long—to finally get revenge. More than 150,000 Indians joined the Spaniards in the ultimate game of "getting even." On August 13, 1521, the once-beautiful city of Tenochtitlán fell to Hernán Cortés and his gang of big brutes. More than 15,000 Mexica were killed. The city was flattened and the survivors became the property of Spain. Soon, many of those survivors would be dead anyway—victims of terrible plagues of smallpox and measles.

But mighty Moctezuma's memory lives on. Every time a tourist goes to Mexico and comes down with a case of diarrhea, it is said they are suffering from Moctezuma's Revenge.

B

Babies grow in cabbage patches? *Just one of the silly things parents told kids when asked, "Where do babies come from?"*

BEASTLY BABYHOOD

Being a baby is such a cushy job. You get to lie around all day and have people fuss over you. No one ever gets mad if you burp in public. You can drool like a fool and nap all afternoon. And if you want *anything,* all you have to do is open your teeny little mouth and say "waaaaaaaaaah."

Sure, there's the occasional stinky diaper smell to clog your nostrils and Great Aunt Irma, "the Pincher," is a real pain. Other than that, babies have got it easy. But way back when, being an infant was sometimes a crying shame!

OH, BABY, BABY!

Picture yourself with 14 sisters and brothers. Imagine the line for bathroom. And forget about getting to control the TV remote! In the years between 1500 and the early 1900s, across much of Europe and America, it was normal for a mom to have a baby every year. In fact, it wasn't at all uncommon for a woman to pop out 15 or more children in her lifetime.

MAMMA MIA!

Guinness *World Records* swears that a Russian woman named Mme. F. Vassilyev, living in the 1700s, was pregnant 27 times and gave birth to a total of 69 children! This included 16 pairs of twins, seven sets of triplets, and four sets of quadruplets, born over a 30-year period. Another high-yield mom was Leontina Albina, who lived in Chile—mother of 55! How do you rack up numbers like that? Try five sets of triplets for starters! Sadly, only 40 children survived.

Sadly, many of those wee tykes did not survive. Mothers didn't fare much better. Medical care—if there was any—was terrible and often did more harm than good. Doctors never washed their hands or their equipment, and often ended up infecting their patients. Many a mom died in childbirth, or soon after, often leaving a houseful of sad little orphans behind.

Still, with moms pregnant most of the time, lots of babies *did* manage to survive being born. The trick was to live to be a ripe-old toddler. Was there a way to guarantee that a baby would make it to his or her first birthday?

A MUMMY? NO, A BABY!

So let's say you are a baby in Europe or America in colonial times—the years between 1600 and 1800. You managed to survive being born. Now what? No soft little terry stretchies and cushy little crib for you! Many a colonial baby was *swaddled*, which means wrapped up like a little mummy. Feet were tied together. Arms were wrapped tightly to the baby's sides. The baby's little head was held in a cross-cloth. Think baby-sized straitjacket. The idea was to keep those little arms and legs pulled straight as possible for at least two or three months. Why? Many kids born before the 1800s suffered from rickets, a disease that softened and weakened the bones and made them curve. We now know it was caused by a lack of vitamin D, which is found in dairy products and fish oil. But in the 1600s, many a mom believed it was caused by kissing their kids too much. With baby tightly swaddled, parents could smooch their newborns without worrying about bowlegs.

Rickets made little legs bow.

ROCK-A-DRY BABY . . .

In the bad ol' days, mothers didn't get any kind of maternity leave. After the baby was born, Mom was back on her feet and at work, sometimes

Baby on board. *Forget car seats. When mom is your only means of transportation, you might as well ride in style.*

within a few hours. And since Mom had things to do—fields to plant, crops to pick, meals to cook, clothes to make—babies tagged along.

Swaddling helped keep Junior quiet, but how could a mom make baby portable, so her hands were free to do other things? Simple! In many places in Europe and the Americas, mother's little mini-mummy was strapped onto a plank of wood and hung on the wall or swung from a tree limb as Mom worked. Being smooshed into a little baby board wasn't so bad . . . for a few hours. It was kind of fun for a baby to be able to keep an eye on everyone. But now imagine you've been hanging from a peg on the wall most of the day, stewing in your own pee and poop for quite a few hours now. Wow, is your butt sore! No one has bothered to change your diaper all day. Come to think of it, diapers haven't even been invented! So, how *did* they catch number one and number two in the days before Pampers and Huggies?

DID SOMEONE JUST DO A STINKY? THE DIRT ON DIAPERS

Babies have been leaking and squirting since the birth of mankind. And since no parent wants to carry a poo-covered baby in his or her arms, inventing something to catch those baby drippy-bits became a priority. Thank goodness *someone* figured out what to do!

Prehistoric times: Large, soft, fleshy leaves were the perfect thing to wrap around a small, soft, fleshy tushy!

Ancient Egypt: Baby's peeing parts were wrapped in thick layers of linen—round and around and around it went—until there was a mummy-like wad of cloth to absorb those drips.

American Indians, 1300s: The Inuit up in what is now Alaska and northwest Canada packed layers of moss under a slab of sealskin. Furry, blubbery diapers! Down in Peru, the Inca used grass under rabbit skin for the same effect minus the blubber.

England, 1400s: Poor rashy English babes! Their undies were changed only every few days.

In tropical climes worldwide: Baby went bottomless. Moms quickly learned how to tell when the poo-poo train was coming and made sure they swung baby's bottom away from the house.

Pioneer days, 1800s: Wet diapers were rarely washed. They were simply hung by the fire and air-dried, then wrapped back on baby, dried pee and all.

England, 1820s: People start to make a real effort to catch baby squirts. After all, they had houses with nice upholstered furniture. There was a reason to catch the crud.

The late 1800s: The modern diaper, a square of linen or cotton flannel folded into a triangle and held by safety pins, is invented. And diaper rash—that crusty, oozing red gunk that covers babies' private parts—becomes public enemy number one. Moms start boiling dirty diapers to kill bacteria.

World War II: Moms are off working in factories, building bombers as dads go off to fight. No one wants to boil diapers. Companies that pick up pails of dirty diapers and replace them with clean ones are hugely successful.

1946: Marion Donovan invents the first prototype disposable diaper. She calls it the "boater"—layers of absorbent fabric topped with plastic pants made from an old shower curtain. Moms swear it is the greatest invention of all time.

BABY WANT A BOTTLE?

From the 1400s until the late 1700s, many American and European babies were fed from a hollowed-out cow's horn with a tiny hole poked in the pointy end so the milk would drip out slowly. The first glass bottles appeared in the early 1800s.

One brand of bottle was nicknamed the Murder Bottle because so many babies died after sucking on it. Turns out the nipple part was designed in such a way that it trapped bacteria. No one thought of boiling baby bottles in hot water to kill the germs until the end of the 1800s after two really smart guys named Louis Pasteur and Robert Koch proved that it was germs, not evil spirits, that were out to get us. Unlike evil fairies, you actually could do something about germs.

When it was time to add some real food to baby's little menu, the first solid thing a babe ate was called *pap*. Pap was usually made from flour stirred in water (basically the same stuff you make papier-mâché paste with). Many moms used beer or wine to make pap, since the water supplies were dangerously dirty back then. If the pap was too thick, it was considered perfectly okay for a grown-up to spit into the mixture to thin it out a bit.

Another baby delicacy was called *panada*. It was made from flour mixed with butter, milk, and egg yolk. It was basically raw cake batter. Tasty, but not the healthiest thing on the menu. For added protein, moms chewed meat, spit it into a dish, then spooned it into baby's mouth. *Mmmm, yum!*

ROCK-A-BYE BABY

Rocking cradles were a baby must-have, kind of like today's bouncy chairs or strollers. But baby wasn't the only thing in the cradle. For centuries, parents all across Europe and in colonial America believed that placing a piece of iron in the cradle or sprinkling it with salt would help repel evil spirits who might try to snatch the baby away. Cradles were kept quite close to the fireplace, not so much to keep baby warm but well-lit, so moms and dads could see if evil spirits were trying to kidnap their damp, smelly little bundle of joy. Unfortunately, many a child got too hot from the fire and literally cooked to death.

TOUGH LOVE

The ancient Spartans were big, strong warriors who loved to fight. Their city, Sparta, was a tough place to grow up in—that is, if you were lucky enough to actually live long enough *to* grow up. Back in the 400s B.C.E., when a Spartan baby was born, a bunch of soldiers would come marching into the house to check out the child. If the kid didn't look healthy, they'd grab the baby, take it away, and leave it on a mountainside to die. No weaklings allowed in their town!

SICK DAYS, COLONIAL STYLE

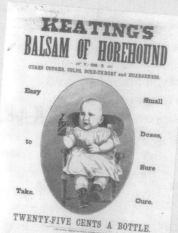

KEATING'S
BALSAM OF HOREHOUND
CURES COUGHS, COLDS, SORE-THROAT and HOARSENESS.

Easy
to
Take.
Small
Doses,
Sure
Cure.
TWENTY-FIVE CENTS A BOTTLE.

Have you ever complained about the yucky taste of medicine? You think *you* have it bad? At least those vile antibiotics are actually saving your life. (Never thought about it that way, did you?) In the past, there were worse remedies, and they didn't even work! Check out some of these remedies from days of yore, and then count "yore" lucky stars.

■ Ever heard someone say they have a frog in their throat? In the 1600s, when kids in parts of Europe and America got sick, one common treatment was to wrap a small live frog in a cloth and place it under the child's tongue until the frog died. The cloth was to keep the poor kid from swallowing the frog. Talk about croaking!

■ For kids who didn't want to take their disgusting medicines, grown-ups had a secret weapon—a special spoon that was designed to forcibly eject all sorts of nasty concoctions down the poor patient's throat at high speed. Colonial kids swallowed powders made from ground crabs' claws mixed with ground-up earthworms and snail shell scrapings. A popular remedy for a sore throat was made from an egg yolk, a powder of white dog's turd, and some honey, which was then smeared on the poor kid's neck.

■ No good mom would be without a jar of leeches. A leech on the nose for sniffles. One on the stomach and one in the butt for diarrhea. And for urinary tract infections? Well, you can probably figure it out.

■ And to keep healthy toddlers from getting sick, there were the dreaded "tonics." In the 1830s many American kids had to drink "steel wine." Two ounces of iron filing were stirred into two pints of sherry—a kind of strong wine—and then taken every day for a month. For those pesky crying babies, a mom could walk into any drugstore and buy an elixir or syrup packed with opium and morphine, heavy-duty drugs. Mother Bailey's Quieting Syrup was a popular choice. Alas, many an overdosed baby stayed quiet permanently.

DRESSED TO KILL

Do you ever get tired of hearing your parents tell you to sit up straight? Well, if you think you have it bad, check this out. Posture was a major obsession in eighteenth- and nineteenth-century England. By the time babies had reached the terrible twos, they were sometimes made to wear *stays*. These thick, corded, quilted garments were tied tightly around a child's middle to make sure the kid's posture would be ramrod straight! And since there was no bending at the waist possible with stays on, slouching was impossible. Some stays were made from whalebone which was as stiff as steel! (You can read all about whalebone by swimming over to WHALE TALES on page 288.)

Other kids were clamped into metal "corrective devices" to keep them from slouching. Wooden backboards were popular, too. These attached to the child with an iron neck collar. Some collars actually had spikes on the inside so the poor kid couldn't even dare relax for a second.

Many toddlers wore a thick roll or pillow around their heads. They were called *pudding caps* and their purpose was to protect a young 'un's soft skull from injury in their frequent crashes onto hard stone floors. After all, both boys and girls were wearing long-skirts and petticoats, making it even easier than it already is for toddlers to trip and fall. Yup. You heard me. Until the late 1800s, in America and parts of Europe, boys wore dresses until about the age of five.

Looking back—to diapers made from seal blubber, opium baby tonics, raw-egg meals and cradles parked so close to the fire that cooked infant was the result—it's a miracle the human race survived. Being a baby was tough going long ago. But surviving childhood was just as difficult. To find out what happened when school bells rang, grab the bus to SCHOOL DAZED on page 234. And for those of you who think school is boring and wish you could get a job, run over to JUNKY JOBS on page 130 and get to work! I promise you . . . you'll be glad you weren't born 200 years ago!

BURIAL CUSTOMS

BAD DAD!

Fathers in ancient Rome had complete power over the lives and deaths of their children. If a new baby got on dad's nerves, the pouting papa could order the baby smothered, starved, devoured by dogs, or simply abandoned. Even as adults, children still had to answer to their father's authority. A father could order an adult child killed if he felt he had been disrespected.

When a bug gets smooshed by a big old hiking boot, do the other bugs get weepy and set off for the nearest Critter Funeral Home? Nu-uh! When a skunk gets slammed by a speeding truck on the highway, do the other skunks paint their white stripes black and then dig a deep hole in which to bury their buddy? Nope! We humans are one of the few species that are capable of feeling sad when someone we love passes away. We are also—at least as far as we know—the only ones who sit around and wonder what happens "next." Is there a heaven? An afterlife? Do we get reincarnated as cockroaches if we are mean to our sisters or brothers? Death sure does bring a lot of questions.

13

BITING THE DUST

For thousands of years, folks have been trying to answer questions about what happens when someone stops breathing permanently. And along the way, we have come up with some pretty weird ideas.

When someone we love dies, we feel awful. We cry buckets. We can't imagine life without that person. It hurts worse than any other hurt there is. And we try to do something special to mark that passing. We might wear black clothes. We put the *deceased* (a fancy word for a dead person) in a beautiful casket before placing that box in a six-foot-deep hole. Some folks choose cremation—ashes to ashes, and all that. Folks who live on or near the water might prefer burial at sea for their loved ones.

Checking out our ancient ancestors' burial grounds is a favorite thing for historians to do. And even though there is a famous saying that dead men tell no tales, how people dispose of their dead tells some pretty far-out stories.

Take the Neanderthals. Even those big galumphs had special rituals to say "bye-bye" to their Neander-dead.

WORD UP!

Funerals are very sad events. But the word *funeral* has to do with something bright. It comes from the Latin *funus*, which means "torch." Many cultures believed that torchlight would help guide the dearly departed to the lands of afterlife. The Romans also started the whole candle thing. They believed that lots of candles around the dead person would frighten away evil spirits (since everyone knows a cranky spirit *hates* bright light).

Archaeologists digging at 50,000-year-old Neanderthal burial sites have found proof that they had torch-lit fires and bouquets of flowers at their funerals.

RIVER OF DEATH

Two ancient civilizations, the Egyptians and the Greeks, agreed that death was a trip. The Egyptians believed you took a lot of luggage. The Greeks believed that you traveled light—just your spirit, ferry fare, and a smile. What to pack for the trip to the next world? That was a question that hung heavy over many an ancient Egyptian. They believed that when you died, you crossed a great river to the next world. And boy, did rich Egyptians pack a lot of stuff for that journey! Games, clothes, makeup, boats, chariots—even a servant or two or three, conveniently killed so they, too, could make the trip! The Pyramids were built so the dead could easily climb to that heavenly river. And mummy-making became a big deal since the Egyptians believed you still would need your old body in the next life. Death was a big part of living. (For more on MUSTY MUMMIES, move to page 166.)

In ancient Greece, the dead were cremated in giant *pyres*—a kind of human bonfire. Just before the torches were lit, a coin was placed on each of the corpse's eyes—carfare for their boat trip across the river Styx to the underworld, where they believed their dead went to dwell.

THE MORE THE MERRIER

The Scythians, who lived in the southern parts of what is now Russia about 6 B.C.E., were real die-hards when it came to death, especially when someone

Forget wallpaper. Try skullpaper. *The Catacombs in Rome are filled with all sorts of decorative decaying bones!*

been resting—sometimes *not* in peace—for almost 2,000 years. Row upon row of rectangular niches, one on top of another like bunk beds for the dead, were the final resting place for the earliest Christians. These Christians did not want to be buried in Rome's Necropolis—the giant pagan cities of the dead—so they dug secret tunnels and carved out "shelves" for their dearly beloved.

Meanwhile, over in Paris, 7 million more skeletons lie stacked in neat piles in another maze of catacombs, moved from the cemeteries in which they once lay. In the 1700 and 1800s, workmen had to empty many of Paris's old burial grounds. Some of the burials had been carried out so hastily that the ground was contaminated. Some bodies came from mass graves that were so overflowing with corpses, that the ground level had risen almost 20 feet in some areas. So all the bones were collected and moved. Today the bones are literally piled to the ceiling in neat piles in various underground chambers. *Mon dieu!*

important, such as a king, died. Scythian royal funerals lasted 40 days. The men would chop off all their hair and slash their ears, foreheads, noses, and arms with sharp knives. Then, after the king was buried along with all his favorite things, folks at the funeral strangled his wives (Scythian kings had lots of wives!) and tossed them into the funeral pile, too. The king's favorite servants were next to get whacked. Finally all his best horses would have their throats slashed. The bodies were neatly placed around the king's and the entire heap of death was covered with a 60-foot mountain of dirt. That's a pile as tall as a six-story building! Talk about going out in style!

CROWDED CATACOMBS

Beneath the city of Rome lies a vast underground world: tunnels that extend for miles and miles. Buried within these walls lie the skeletons of tens of thousands of people who have

14 WAYS TO SAY...

"SHE'S DEAD"

1. Taking a dirt nap
2. Pushing up the daisies
3. Bought the farm
4. Six feet under
5. Belly up
6. Passed away
7. Gone to meet her maker
8. Bit the dust
9. Having the mail delivered by moles
10. Croaked
11. Crossed to the other side
12. The final curtain
13. Game over
14. Kicked the bucket

HIDE AND GO SEEK

Many of today's funeral customs began thousands of years ago because people were afraid that the dead person was going to come back from the "other side" and take them away. Take wearing black clothes. Nowadays that's a sign of respect, but back in ancient times it was sheer terror of death that made people don black. Black clothes, especially with heavy veils, were thought to be a good way to hide from the spirit of a dead person, who might try to creep into the next healthy body he or she saw. In parts of Africa, the exact opposite was true. The darker-skinned Africans also tried to duck the evil spirits, but they smeared white paint all over themselves. Same intent. Same idea. Just different colors.

Dig those skulls! This archaeologist unearthed a bone bonanza.

NAILING THAT COFFIN

In northern Europe, folks went to extreme measures to make sure the dead stayed dead. They often chopped off the head and feet of their dearly departed and tied the corpse's hands together. That was a good start, but they were taking no chances on being haunted, so digging a six-foot-deep hole became standard practice. And coffins with the lid nailed on tightly were added to the burial ceremony—not to protect the corpse, but to keep it from leaping out at one of the mourners. After the box was lowered into the ground, a heavy rock was placed on top. And just to be on the safe side, once the hole was filled with dirt, another big slab of rock was dragged on top of the coffin to keep the buried buried. Ta-da! The first tombstones! It is only in the last 300 or so years that folks have taken to writing the person's name and mini-biography on these slabs.

THE TOMB-INATOR

Some folks went all out when it came time to bury their loved ones. Here are some super-graves.

The Pyramids of Giza, Egypt

Deep within secret tunnels at the center of each pyramid, a pharaoh was laid to rest. Unfortunately, these giant tombs were like arrows pointing the way for grave robbers who knew exactly where to look for the pharaohs' treasures.

The Taj Mahal, Agra, India

When Mumtaz Mahal died in 1630 while giving birth to her fourteenth child, her husband, Shah Jehan, was devastated. He had truly adored her, so he decided to build her the world's most beautiful tomb. It took 22 years and the work of more than 20,000 craftsmen to finish it, making it the most expensive tombstone on Earth.

The Stone Warriors at Xian, China

Can you imagine the look of shock on the face of the peasant who, while digging a well in 1974, accidentally unearthed the first of more than 7,500 life-sized terra-cotta sculpted soldiers? This mammoth clay army had been placed in the tomb of a Chinese emperor named Ch'in Shih Huang-Ti who died in 210 B.C.E. Bet the real soldiers who served the emperor were relieved that they didn't live in Scythia or one of those places where when the king dies, everyone else does, too!

ALBERT EINSTEIN'S BRAIN

Who was one of the smartest men who ever lived? That'd be Albert Einstein. When he died at the age of 76 in April, 1955, scientists wanted to know what made him so smart. They held an *autopsy* (a medical study of a dead body) and his brain was removed just before he was cremated. So far, so good. But somehow, for over twenty years, Einstein's brain got lost. No one was sure where it was. Turns out, the doc who had removed the brain had moved to Wichita, Kansas. Most of the sliced-up brain was in his office, stored in two Mason jars in a beat-up cardboard box labeled "Cider." Finally, in 1996, Einstein's brain came back to Princeton Hospital, where it had begun its weird journey and where it rests in peace (and sliced pieces) to this day.

GOTTA LOVE THAT DEATH

England's Queen Victoria, who ruled England from 1837 to 1901, was one of the world's most famous rulers. When her husband, Albert, died in 1861, she was devastated. She made *mourning* (a period when you do special things to honor a dead person) her entire way of life. She wore black for the rest of her days (which extended for forty years). During her reign, cemeteries became places where families picnicked and children played.

In those days most people died at home. It was pretty common for friends and family to sit with the dead body, stroking the corpse's hands or patting its hair. Children were a part of death ceremonies and many a poor kid had to share a room, and sometimes even a bed, with a dead sibling for a day or two before he or she was buried. Sometimes people had photos taken of their dearly departed. These were called *memento mori* (which means "remember (that you have to) die") and showed the deceased, sleeping peacefully in their coffins, sometimes with living family members gathered around. And after a death, every article of clothing in the mourning family's closets would be dyed black. For the next two years, that was the only color that they could wear.

WAKE UP!!!

Back in the days before fancy medical equipment and sleek hospitals, it was sometimes hard to tell if a person was really dead. Occasionally, some poor dear would be buried only to wake up a day later and find out that they were stuck in a coffin six feet under. So folks started trying to *wake* the dead by sitting with the deceased until it was time to go to the cemetery. That's how the custom of holding a "wake" began—a loud party with lots of noise and tons of friends and family hanging around. It didn't hurt to make extra sure! Here are some people who could have used a good wake:

Oh goody! A funeral! Burials were big social events complete with formal invitations in England.

■ Marjorie Elphinstone died in the early 1600s and was buried in Ardtannies, Scotland. Unfortunately, in those days there were plenty of grave robbers around who waited until dark after a burial, then dug up the coffin and stole all the deceased's jewelry. But when robbers dug up Marge . . . boy . . . did they get a shock! Marge gave a loud groan, scaring the robbers half to death! Then she sat up, walked home, and outlived her husband by six years.

■ In a small town in England in the 1500s, the late Matthew Wall was being carried to his grave when one of the pallbearers tripped. The coffin crashed to the ground, the lid slid off, and the jolt woke up Matthew. He lived for several more years and not only celebrated his birthday, but his "re-birthday" every year.

■ As the dirt was being shoveled on the coffin of a young girl in Belgium in the late 1800s, the child woke up and started *screaming*. This motivated Count Karnice-Karnicki to invent a coffin that would allow someone who was accidentally buried alive to let the world know that he or she was ready to get the heck out of

there! His coffin, which was patented in 1897, had a tube attached to a spring-loaded ball that rested on the corpse's chest. Any breath would release a spring that would let air and light into the coffin. A flag would spring up, and a bell would ring for half an hour. Did it work? There's no record of anyone being saved, but better safe than sorry, right?

WHEN GRANDPOP BECOMES A POPSICLE

After baseball great Ted Williams died in 2002, a big fight broke out in his family. Some of his relatives said that the late ballplayer had wanted to be frozen, so that one day he might come back to life if scientists could figure out how to thaw him out. The rest of the family was horrified at this idea. But on August 12, 2003, Ted's body was sent to the Alcor Life Extension Foundation, a cryonics lab where they freeze human bodies at death to preserve and, possibly, one day revive them. There, his head and body parted company. His head, drilled with holes, is now stored in a steel can filled with liquid nitrogen, and his body stands in a separate nine-foot-tall cylinder. He's one cool guy, literally, frozen to –124°C, a temperature at which all body chemistry simply stops. Ted's got a lot of frozen buddies—60 of them—keeping him company there. And by the way, Walt Disney is not one of them. That's a totally made-up legend!

C

CAVE DUDES

You'd grunt, too, if you had to live in a freezing cold cave wearing nothing but a fur poncho. You'd grunt from sunup to sundown if you had to keep snapping icicles from your nostrils before wiping your drippy nose on your filthy arm. And you'd probably grunt some more if making dinner meant dragging a dead 400-pound animal up a steep cliff.

No doubt about it, living 35,000 years ago in the middle of a great Ice Age was definitely the pits. So grab a sharp rock, pull on your warmest long underwear, and let's go hang with the Neanderthals and Cro-Magnons.

GRUNT!

LAST HOMINID STANDING

Somewhere around 5 to 7 million years ago, our earliest ancestors climbed down from the trees, said bye-bye to the life of an ape, stood up on their back legs, and began to slowly walk off into the world. Because their arms and hands were no longer needed to walk with, they were free to hold onto all sorts of stuff, such as rocks for head bashing and sticks for spearing. Hey, talk about progress! With every passing epoch our ancestors got a little bigger, moved a little faster, and grew a little less furry. Eventually—many millions of years later—*Homo sapiens* (that's us!) appeared. But for about 272,000 years—from about 300,000 to 28,000 years ago—*Homo neanderthalensis* ROCKED the house.

YOU'RE SUCH A NEANDERTHAL!

Naturally, scientists cannot even *begin* to agree on the details of Neanderthal life. They think Neanderthals were parents by the age of 12,

BABY, IT'S COLD OUTSIDE

You think it gets cold in the winter nowadays? Hah! Northern hemisphere winters are nothing compared to the great Ice Ages that have been going on (and off) for about a million and a half years. The last "glacial" hit about 70,000 years ago and lasted for 60,000 years. During that time most of Europe and North America were covered by huge glaciers.

The ice grew to be more than a mile thick in some places. During the Riss Ice Age of 150,000 years ago, ice covered 30 percent of the globe (today only about 10 percent of the world is covered with permafrost). Europe and North America were the hardest hit. How cold was it? In England during the Riss, the temperature never climbed above freezing the entire year, even in the middle of summer. The bitter cold weather forced early humans to figure out new ways to survive—to improvise and become more creative or freeze to death.

old and crotchety by the age of 35, and usually dead by 40. They know they hunted with spears and sharpened rocks, and all too often got gored or trampled doing it. They're pretty sure Neanderthals used their teeth as a kind of third hand to hold stuff. And they know Neanderthals carefully buried their dead and cared for their elderly—even going so far as to chew food for toothless folks.

What about the whole cave-dwelling thing? For some it was cave sweet cave, but others lived inside the giant rib cages

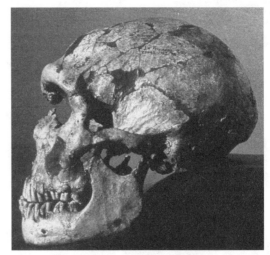

Dumb as dirt? Nah! Neanderthals had a large skull which held a hefty brain.

of dead woolly mammoth carcasses. Neanderthals also made tents from stakes, branches, and animal skins. Some built tents *inside* their clammy, chilly caves to stay extra snug. But that's about all scientists and historians agree on.

It seems like every scientist who studies the Neanderthals has a different opinion. The arguments rage on: Neanderthals could talk. No! They couldn't. They lived in separate male and female groups. No! They lived together as couples and families. They mated with Cro-Magnons, the earliest of the *Homo sapiens.* No! They had nothing to do with Cro-Magnons. They were slow and dumb. No, *no*, NO! They were fast and smart! There has been so much disagreement that scientists have often called other scientists "Neanderthals" when they can't agree.

AN ICE AGE DAY

What was life like for a Neander-kid? Try it!

Breakfast time! Mom's kneeling by a fire built on a bed of very hot rocks. She throws a few hunks of rotting meat on the stones to cook. Neanderthals liked their meat almost raw, so you don't have to wait long. Ripping the meat in pieces using your big teeth and a sharp stone, you gobble down the meat complete with a crunchy coating of ashes.

Neander-school? No books, no reading, no math. For hours at a time, you'll practice throwing spears and rocks at trees and bushes, perfecting your aim. Every once in a while you'll run screaming at that tree as fast as you can, practicing being as fierce and scary as possible.

Hunting time! You have been assigned to the group that waits at the bottom of a big cliff for a day of "cliff driving." Your buddies at the top are going to run like crazy after a herd of reindeer or wild horses and drive them over the edge until they plummet to the bottom and hopefully die. You grunt a prayer that you do not end up on the wrong end of an antler.

Time to drag a dead animal back home. Talk about grunting! It's a good thing you're really strong. The furry skins have to be sliced off the carcasses and the fur scraped off, to be used as clothing and insulation. For the next couple of weeks, everyone will be chewing on the animal skins to soften them up. Think of it as caveman bubblegum.

What's for dinner? The reindeer liver and its fat are the best parts to eat. Brain, kidneys, and lungs, too. For dessert, the partially digested food inside the reindeer's two stomachs will be mixed with blood. And you thought chocolate pudding was yummy!

Bedtime! There are dozens of kids all sleeping together on animal-fur mats around the fire. Pray that Dad doesn't snore too loudly.

FROZEN FOOD

Ice Age animals were huge! Here are some of the most-hunted and tastiest.

■ **Cave Bears**—Bigger than a grizzly at over nine feet tall. Neanderthals thought these creatures had supernatural powers and collected their skulls in stone chests.

■ **Cave Lions**—Take a regular lion and pump it up so it's 25 percent bigger and you'll have these huge European cats.

■ **Cave Hyenas**—Nowadays they only live in Africa, but during the Ice Age these shriekers were one of the most numerous mammals in Europe.

■ **Woolly Rhinos**—Take a regular rhino and wrap it in fur. Add a three-foot-long horn that was perfect for goring a Neanderthal—or shoveling through deep snow looking for food.

■ **Aurochs**—A twelve-foot-long relative of the modern cow. But unlike our gentle mooers, this critter was mean! More like a giant angry bull.

■ **Woolly Mammoths**—Eight tons, 12 feet tall, covered with a shaggy coat and a nice thick layer of fat. The perfect animal for life in the Ice Age! But when the world started to warm up, it simply couldn't adjust to the milder weather. Bye-bye, woolly!

NO-ANDERTHALS

Just under 200,000 years ago, a new breed of human started to make its move up the evolutionary ladder. Scientists are unclear as to how, why, or where exactly it happened. But by 40,000 years ago, *Homo sapiens* (unless you are a cat reading this book, that's you and me, kiddo) were wandering into the Neanderthals' turf. Why did we thrive while the Neanderthals slowly faded away?

Doing wheelies! *Did cave dudes "invent the wheel"? Maybe . . . but they sure didn't invent the bicycle!*

Even though we weren't as strong physically, we *Homo sapiens* were better at just about everything else. We weren't afraid to follow our food to faraway places instead of staying in one spot until there was nothing left to hunt. We had better tools, made out of bone and antlers. We may have had a better ability to communicate. We had a longer lifespan than the typical Neanderthal—living long enough to become grandparents. Long enough to teach our kids and grandkids all sorts of nifty survival tricks.

For a couple thousand years, humans and Neanderthals lived in the same areas. Did the two species mate with each other?

Did they fight with one another? Get along? Ignore each other? Is that really hairy guy at the gas station the descendant of a Neanderthal? It's all still a giant mystery. And a job opportunity for future anthropologists. Interested?

CAVE PAINTINGS AND ROCK CONCERTS

One thing is sure: The first *Homo sapiens,* the Cro-Magnons, were simply more creative than the Neanderthals. They just didn't hang around grunting from reindeer hunt to reindeer hunt; they decorated things while they waited. They built big cooking hearths and had a better mastery of fire than their Neanderthal cousins. They made musical instruments and sang songs. They made art! Some of their most amazing creations are huge cave paintings that were discovered in the twentieth century in France and Spain—walls covered with hundreds of pictures of leaping animals, with hunters closing in.

About 12,000 years ago, the air began to grow a little warmer. The ice began to melt. The frozen tundra gave way to forests. And the era of the cave dwellers drew to a close as people began to wander off to other lands. Now, hunting was not the only way to survive. People could plant crops and stay put and build villages and towns. But the legacy of those fur-wrapped cave dwellers will always stay with us. GRUNT!

Cave-dweller graffiti, *a good way to brag about the 3,000-pound cave bear you just hammered.*

REALLY BAD BREATH

In 1940, four teenagers in Lascaux, France, were cutting school when they stumbled across the mouth of a cave that had been hidden by tree roots. The kids happened on the most amazing art history lesson ever. When they poked their noses inside the cave, they were blown away by what they saw—an amazing collection of cave paintings dating back 15,000 years. For the next 15 years people flocked from all over the world to see the cave paintings. But by 1955, the paintings started to flake away. Turns out bad breath—the carbon dioxide from humans exhaling—was ruining the fragile murals. So the choice was either to not let anyone breathe while they were inside the caves, or to close them.

Lucky for us all, the French government built a replica cave near the original site, where even visitors with the stinkiest breath can inhale and exhale as they gaze upon one of the most amazing works of art in the world.

CIRCUS CLOWNING

You may have heard this famous story. When an elephant named Stefan got "stuck up," his keeper gave him 20 doses of an animal laxative (the stuff that makes you go). Nothing happened. The keeper topped the laxative off with a snack of about seventy pounds of prunes, figs, and berries. Still nothing. Stefan's keeper then decided to try to shoot a little olive oil up the elephant's butt to speed the passage of the backed-up poop. That's when disaster struck: A tidal wave of diarrhea came shooting out of Stefan's big behind with such force it knocked the poor keeper to the ground, where he hit his head, blacked out, and was suffocated under a mountain of dung.

There you have it: a day at the circus. Thrills, chills, and stinky spills. Only problem is, this story is as fake as a clown's red nose. So what's the *real* story about circuses? Wanna know? Read on . . .

GORE GALORE

The ancient Romans were some of the very first circus-goers. They were the ones who gave us the word *circus,* which means a ring or circle. But the typical Roman circus was not exactly a place for family fun. It was a place where people came to cheer for their favorite big, sweaty guys. Think professional wrestling but with one big difference. If a man fighting a man was cool, the Romans thought, a man fighting a lion would be even cooler. And if that lion ripped a man to bloody shreds? Well, that was the coolest yet! Read more about these groovy guys (and gals) in GLADIATORS on page 104.

But bloody death after bloody death could get a little monotonous after a few hours. To liven things up, someone would come out and tell jokes. Tame animals would do funny tricks. Tigers would let clowns kiss them. Elephants (the Romans *loved* elephants) would dance or walk on tightropes. Even 2,000 years ago elephants stole the show!

A LITTLE COMIC RELIEF

After the fall of the Roman Empire at the end of the fifth century C.E., things were pretty bleak in Europe, and traveling shows were just about the only thing to liven up a dull day. Groups of poor entertainers began zipping from one town to another, bringing news from afar, singing songs, and putting on little shows in exchange for food and a place to sleep for a couple of days. There were "gleemen," or minstrels, and jugglers, too. Folks were always happy to see them. By the year 1600, country fairs were common in England and across Europe. They were noisy, rowdy, racy events with acrobats, magicians, and funny men called *jesters* (kind of like our stand-up comics). There were trained bears and dogs that could dance. And there were folks who could ride a horse, standing up and juggling at the same time. Sounds a lot like a circus to me.

WORD UP!

Jumbo fries. Jumbo shrimp. Jumbo sodas. We get the word for our supersized food from an oversized pachyderm named Jumbo the Elephant—P.T. Barnum's prize possession. Jumbo came to America in 1882 and he was a big 'un. He weighed seven tons and was almost 12 feet tall. America went Jumbo crazy and more than 20 million people flocked to see him. Jumbo was a fun-loving critter. He and his keeper used to knock back a six-pack of beer at the end of every show. If his keeper forgot to pop a brew for him, Jumbo would poke him with his trunk until he did.

Alas, tragedy, and a speeding train, struck Jumbo. It took 150 men to drag his corpse off the railroad tracks. But P.T. wasn't fazed. He had Jumbo stuffed (his skin alone weighed almost 1,500 pounds!) and for many years, dead Jumbo drew almost as many visitors as the live version.

Please, please, please . . . Don't drop those jumbo feet on me! Being a circus clown is a dangerous job!

STEP RIGHT UP, FOLKS!

P.T. Barnum invented one of the creepiest creations ever: the sideshow. Sometimes called a peep show, it was home to freaks, fakes, and assorted human weirdos. Soon, every circus worth its salt had a fat man and a bearded lady, a human pincushion, a person who could fit his entire body into a small bowl, a sword swallower, a fire-eater, a three-legged man, and, for good measure, a guy who could eat glass and hammer a spike into his own skull. Here are some of P.T.'s world-famous sideshow celebs.

The Bearded Lady

The Feejee Mermaid An embalmed mermaid from Calcutta . . . my foot! Try a dead monkey's head sewn on to a fish body. Folks loved it, though!

George Washington's Nanny Was that crinkled, wrinkled old lady really 161 years old? Had she really raised our first president? P.T. said she had! Crowds turned out to see her. But after a few months, folks got tired of her, so P.T. said she was an *automaton* . . . an old-fashioned kind of robot. Naturally, everyone came back to see the mechanical woman! After she died, an autopsy proved that Joice Heth was merely a wrinkled eighty-year-old who had never set eyes on George Washington. Humbug!

Chang and Eng Twin babies that are born attached to one another used to be called Siamese twins, named after two brothers born in Siam (a country

The tallest and the shortest

Chang and Eng

now called Thailand). Chang and Eng were born in 1811, joined together at the chest by a five-inch-wide band of flesh. When they were teenagers, the twins left home and began traveling, earning money by exhibiting themselves all over the world. Folks had never seen attached twins before! It was weirdly cool! The brothers were one of Barnum's most famous acts, and to this day many of us are still trying to figure out how they went to the john.

The Tallest, Shortest, Heaviest Barnum loved extremes. He sat the Arabian Giant, at eight feet, two inches and a chunky 590 pounds, next to the French Giant, who was a measly seven feet, eight inches. The two men hated each other and were always fighting. Such fun! He also put Anna Swan who, at eight feet, was "the tallest woman in the world," next to Commodore Nutt, "the shortest man on Earth"—a teeny 29 inches high— that is, until someone even smaller toddled in and stole the show.

Tom Thumb Barnum's greatest treasure was a wee fellow named Charles Stratton. P.T. dubbed him General Tom Thumb. When Tom joined Barnum's circus, he was only 25 inches tall. Everyone went nuts for him. He met Abe Lincoln, and traveled all over the world. He became one of America's most famous people. Over the years he grew to a mighty 35 inches and married Lavinia Warren—a strapping 29-pound, 32-inch third-grade teacher (who had no trouble keeping *her* class in order, by the way). Their 1863 wedding was attended by 2,000 people and was *the* social event of the decade.

A flaming fool. *Juggling is hot stuff for this circus artist.*

HOW TO INVENT A CIRCUS

By the mid-1700s all the ingredients to make a proper circus were in place. Clowns clowned and jugglers juggled. Tightrope walkers wobbled, and caged animals growled as they traveled from town to town. All that was needed was someone to put them all together. That person was a big, brawny guy from England with a booming voice. His name was Philip Astley.

Astley loved horses and decided to teach riding. In order to get clients, he started demonstrating all the cool tricks he could perform—like riding while standing up, or riding two horses at once. Folks gathered to gawk, so Astley began charging folks to watch. In 1761 he bought some land and opened the first modern circus in a round ring with rows of seating.

Calling this kind of entertainment a "circus" came from a copycat rival of Astley's who had opened a riding ring down the road. Maybe the guy was a fan of ancient history, but he borrowed the name from the Romans and called *his* company the Royal Circus. In the meantime, Astley took *his* show on the road, across Europe, and eventually, in 1793, to America. Even George Washington took some time off from being president and went to watch. Because horseback-riding acts were a must for every circus, the ringmaster's job was born. His job was to keep the horses running around the ring as the riders jumped and spun and twirled.

BIG BET AND BAILEY

America added its own twist to the circus when a farmer named Hachaliah Bailey went to Boston in 1804 and came face to face with an elephant named Old Bet. Bet was a big gal—an African elephant that stood almost 12 feet tall. Bailey had never seen an elephant before, let alone a ginormous one. Old Bet made a *big* impression on Bailey.

A few years later, Bailey went to a cattle auction and lo and behold . . . there was Old Bet, for sale. But while everyone else only saw a few thousand pounds of walking deli meat, Bailey saw a business opportunity. He bought Old Bet and began charging folks to see her. Soon Bailey, Old Bet, a trained dog, a few pigs, and a horse were traveling from state to state. Sadly, one cold, dreary July day in 1816, Old Bet was shot and killed by an angry farmer in Maine who decided that in hard times, spending money to see an elephant was a sin.

PRINCE OF HUMBUGS

Phineas Taylor Barnum. Now there's a name to remember. P.T. was the circus king! He began by touring the country with variety shows but his greatest talent was humbugging—scamming and tricking people. In 1841 he opened Barnum's American Museum in the heart of New York City and it soon became one of the most famous places in the world. It

P.T. and T.T! *Barnum and Tom Thumb hangin' out.*

was part circus, part zoo, part exhibition hall, part lecture hall, part theater, and part sleazebag entertainment. And guess what? It was always packed!

The American Museum opened at sunrise and stayed open until ten at night. People lined up for hours to get in. One of the most famous "exhibits" was a sign that directed people *TO THE EGRESS*. Naturally everyone wanted to see what an Egress was, so they pushed open the door that led to it, only to find themselves out on the street. (*Egress* is a fancy word for "exit." What a practical joker ol' P.T. was!)

Packed with "500,000 natural and artificial curiosities from every corner of the globe," Barnum's museum was a disaster waiting to happen, and one day it did. On July 13, 1865, a fire broke out and the museum burned to a crisp. Barnum rebuilt the museum, but it went up in flames a second time three years later. After that, he moved on to a more portable attraction: a traveling circus and sideshow.

SEND IN THE CLOWNS

Clowns have been around even longer than circuses—for thousands of years. But in the beginning, clowns hung around with kings and queens in their royal palaces. Every ancient civilization from the Egyptians to the Chinese to the Aztecs had clowns. Many of those clowns were "little people" (dwarfs and midgets).

In ancient Greece, clowns were bald-headed and wore padded suits that made them look huge! They performed in plays, making fun of the actors, mimicking them, and throwing things at the audience.

Clowns in royal courts were sometimes really smart guys who could get away with saying things that would get anyone else killed. Sometimes they were the only ones who would tell a king or an emperor that they were being stupid. Take Yu Sze, a court jester in Chinese emperor Shih Huang-Ti's palace. The year was about 300 B.C.E. and the Great Wall of China was going up. Thousands of subjects had already died building it when the emperor decided it needed to be painted, too. Yu Sze made so many jokes about painting the wall that the emperor finally decided it was a dumb idea. Yu Sze became a Chinese hero.

In the 1500s, the Italians came up with an improv group called the Commedia dell' Arte, with lots of silly skits about dumb masters and their smart servants . . . and smart masters and their dumb servants. The most famous of the *commedia* clowns was the *harlequin*, a guy in a two-toned suit with a mask. He usually carried a paddle—or slapstick, as it came to be known—which he used to fake-spank people. Nowadays *slapstick* refers to all kinds of physical, falling-down, pie-in-the-face comedy.

CRAFTY CATS

They sleep on your face. Spend the day puking up hair balls. Walk across the kitchen table leaving a trail of pee-dampened, kitty-littery paw prints on the place mats. And they have been at the center of some of history's weirdest events. Or maybe I should say *hissss*-story?

RAINING CATS AND DOGS

Face it. Cats and dogs are usually not the best of friends. But they both are descendents of a weaselly critter called *Miacis*, who began slinking around about 40 or 50 million years ago. Over millions of years, *Miacis* evolved into cats *and* dogs. The cats then split off into three distinct groups. There were the roaring cats—really big pussycats such as lions, tigers, leopards, and jaguars. There were the speed-demon cheetahs, which do not have retractable claws like the other cats. And finally (ta-da!), the *Felis*—our small, stealthy, secretive domestic cats. By the end of the Stone Age, cats were living side-by-side with humans but it took thousands of years for the cat to claw its way to pampered pethood.

Fast-forward to ancient Egypt about 7,000 years ago. The first of the area's settlers were becoming farmers, growing grain along the banks of the Nile. There was a little problem—scads of munching mice and ravenous rats. Thank goodness

cats developed a taste for those rascally rodents— a hungry cat could clear a field of vermin in an evening. They were also surprisingly good swimmers and fine fisher-felines. Before long, cats became *very* important critters in Egypt. Soon, they were even worshipped.

check out Musty Mummies page 166

Fi Fi Fur-Ever

HOLY CAT!

Bastet was an Egyptian goddess with the body of a woman and the head of a kitty. She became one of the most revered of the Egyptian gods— in charge of fertility (making babies), beauty, and motherhood. Egyptians absolutely doted on their cats, which they called *miu*. Stylish Egyptian women wore miu earrings and jeweled miu necklaces, and well-to-do mius wore jewelry, too. Bastet's temple became one of Egypt's most important. Cats had gone from being rat-killers to being sacred!

Cats were so beloved that there were laws protecting them. If your house was burning down, the cat was the first thing you saved. If

A NASTY NOTE

Archaeologists digging in the shadows of the Egyptian Pyramids in the 1800s unearthed a huge cat cemetery filled with more than 300,000 miu mummies!

A-CAT-AMY AWARDS

Some people have very strong feelings when it comes to cats. Some of the most powerful rulers in history used to have absolute hissss-y fits when they saw cats. Julius Caesar, King Henri II, King Charles XI, and Napoléon all had terrible *aelurophobia*—the fear of cats. But other folks just *loved* kitties. Here are just a few of them.

The prophet Muhammad, who started a religion called Islam in the 600s, was a big cat lover. One day, his favorite cat, Muezza, curled up on his sleeve while he was deep in prayer, and promptly fell asleep. When Muhammad finished praying, he realized his cat was snoring away. Muhammad didn't want to disturb his kitty, so he cut off his sleeve, instead. Why was he so kind to his cat? Because a few years earlier, a cat had saved his life by warning him about a dangerous snake.

Cardinal Richelieu, a very powerful adviser to the king in France in the 1600s, was so fond of cats that he lived with 14 of them. He had special servants to look after his cats and when he died, the Cardinal left all his earthly possessions to his furry felines.

Florence Nightingale, the world's most famous nurse, was cat-crazy. She owned more than 60 cats over the course of her lifetime.

Ernest Hemingway was a famous writer who collected cats. He didn't care which breed they were. He just liked the ones with extra toes! In one of his books, he bragged about leaving his infant son with only his cat as a baby-sitter. Good thing Child Welfare wasn't around to follow up on that!

someone accidentally (or worse, deliberately) killed a cat—*whoa*—were they in trouble! That person could be condemned to death. When a cat conked, a high priest had to examine the kitty corpse to make sure it had died from natural causes. Only then was the cat given the full mummy treatment and tucked in a kitty sarcophagus. Tiny mummified mice were provided for the cat's afterlife delight. And when a pet cat died, the entire household went into mourning. People shaved their eyebrows off as a sign of respect for poor dead kitty.

The ancient Egyptians believed that cats could chat with the gods after they were dead and mummified, which led to a very weird kind of business. Dishonest high priests began to run a kind of dead-cat supermarket where folks could go to purchase a former feline. Many of the mummified "cats" weren't even cats. One recently

Cat fight! Catwoman is one of the comic world's most famous fictional female felines.

X-rayed cat mummy revealed a bag of frog bones. Other cats had been clearly killed—necks snapped or strangled, or simply drowned. Cold-blooded *meowdur* indeed.

CAT-TASTROPHES

As travelers from other lands began to visit ancient Egypt, they brought cats back home as souvenirs. Sailors discovered cats kept the decks mice-and rat-free. Traders from ancient Greece, Rome, Japan, and China all returned home from their travels to Egypt with cats. The Japanese fell head-over-heels in love with cats and soon believed that even a painting of one hanging on the wall would keep mice and rats away.

Japanese Buddhists created elaborate ceremonies to honor cats after death, and an entire temple—Gotokuji in Tokyo—is dedicated to the memory of one little good-luck cat owned by a group of poor monks. According to legend, Maneki Neko saved a wealthy samurai warrior from being struck by a bolt of lightning. As a thank-you, the lucky samurai gave piles of money to the monks, who never went hungry again. To this day Maneki Neko is a mega-good-luck symbol throughout Japan.

OH, YIKES!

YUCKY YORE

Here's a tip to make your house a home sweet home. During the Middle Ages it was considered good luck to drop a few live cats inside the walls of new houses and other structures as they were being built. These buried-alive felines were supposed to keep out evil spirits—but instead just smelled up the place.
Pee-eew!!

THE ONLY GOOD CAT IS A DEAD CAT

For 3,000 years, cats were just about the coolest things on Earth. But then something happened to change all that: the Dark Ages, a time when stupidity ruled. Life in most of Europe between 500 and 1000 C.E. was the pits for most folks. Hunger and disease were just about the only things anyone "owned." Everyone had become ultra-superstitious. Learning was suddenly a bad thing. *Everything* that happened—good, or more often, bad—was attributed to God's will.

During this time, the Catholic Church was in charge in Europe, and its leadership was determined to wipe out all traces of the religions of the ancient world. That meant no more cat gods like Bastat. No more praying to the popular Norse goddess Freya who rode around in a cat-drawn chariot. Cats became a big no-no because church leaders began telling people they were the devil's pet.

Most folks died young in those days. But there were some women who knew about herbal medicines and who managed to live past the age of thirty—which was absolutely elderly in those days. So whenever folks saw an "old" woman, especially one with cats, they got a little freaked out.

People decided that cats had magical powers. Magic and godliness did not go together, so the cats—along with their sweet, innocent not-so-old-lady owners—were killed. All across Europe, cats were hunted down, tortured, and killed. And people celebrated religious holidays by first going cat hunting, then attending cat barbecues. (Read more about WICKED WITCHES by hopping on your broomstick and flying over to page 292.)

CAT GOT YOUR TONGUE?

Ever since the Middle Ages, cats and witches have gone hand in hand. And in France in the 1300s, cats were especially hated. Cats had superpowers and everyone knew it. There was only one way to protect yourself from an evil cat. You had to maim it. Cut off its tail. Saw off an ear. Tear out big clumps of fur. Lop off a leg. A maimed cat could not attend the witch's sabbath or cast a proper spell. Soon, cat-bits became popular ingredients in many folk remedies. Here are some surefire cat-cures from the Middle Ages:

Weeds taking over your fields? Bury a live cat or two in the middle of your garden.

Had a bad fall? Suck the blood out of freshly amputated (cut-off) cat tail to ease the pain.

Got pneumonia or the flu? Slice a cat's ear and drain the blood into a glass of wine.

Upset stomach? Add a few lumps of cat excrement into your wine. Stir and sip. Bottoms up!

Want to disappear? In Brittany (a part of France), folks believed that if you ate the brain of a freshly killed cat you would become invisible— but only if the brain was still steaming.

PLAGUE-GROUND

By the 1300s, cat-killing was on the rise. And guess what else was on the rise? That's right, *rodents!* Rats and mice were breathing a big sigh of relief as the cat population began to dwindle. There was only one little teensy problem with all that. Those rats were swarming with fleas that carried bubonic plague, a terrible disease that soon swept through Europe, killing 25 million people—one third of the continent's population (prowl on over to PLAGUES AND POXES on page 194 for all the festering facts!). With hardly any cats around to kill the rats, the plague, known as the Black Death, soon devastated the continent.

By the 1400s, folks began to realize that being stupid and dead just wasn't working for them. They rediscovered a little something called "science." They began to actually think. Beginning in Italy, a new era dawned: the Renaissance (*REN-uh-sahnts*), which means "rebirth." Suddenly cats were cool again, even though they were still the mouse-eating, rat-killing, endearingly furry little critters they always had been.

Let's make **meow-sic!** *Cat concerto, anyone?*

Mee-ouch! Cats were worshipped one minute and tortured the next.

CAT-ATONIC

By the 1600s and 1700s cats were back in style. Life in Europe was getting better, too. People weren't dying from the plague by the millions. There was a new social class of merchants, shopkeepers, and craftspeople. Cats were once again pampered, and in some wealthy households they were treated a whole lot better than the servants. To the folks who lived in poverty—the vast majority of people in those days—it was pretty annoying that cats were eating better than they were. In some cities cats were becoming a hated symbol of class divisions. C-A-T spelled trouble.

In the late 1790s in Paris, workers in a big print shop had enough. They decided to kill all of the master's cats. They held mock trials, and the pampered cats—stand-ins for their cruel boss— were hanged or beheaded. Their master never figured out exactly what happened, but historians now see it as a warning of bad times ahead. A few weeks later the people of France decided they'd had enough of their spoiled-rotten king and queen and all their rich buddies and cut off all their heads.

Since then cats have settled in to our lives as treasured pets. And where would we be without our dear kitties today? We wouldn't have *The Cat in the Hat, Puss in Boots, Catwoman,* or *Garfield!*

CRAZY CALENDARS

Party on the 12th? No school on the 22nd? Think about it! Without a calendar, you wouldn't know what day of the week your dreaded math test was. You wouldn't know what day to bring cupcakes into school for your birthday. You wouldn't know *exactly* when Christmas or Kwanzaa or Chanukah or Ramadan was. And you definitely wouldn't know what day of the year you got to put a whoopee cushion on your teacher's chair, or plastic vomit on his desk—all because it's APRIL FOOL'S DAY!

WHAT DAY IS IT, ANYWAY?

Back in the Ice Age, the first humans marked the passing of the days by notching little marks into grungy old animal bones, counting time that had already passed. As our awareness of the world grew, it started to make sense to measure the

MOONDAY TO FRIGGDAY

Ever wonder where the days of the week got their names? When folks in ancient Babylon (where Iraq is now) split the day into 24 hours, each hour was dedicated to one of the known planets at that time, along with the sun and the moon. The Romans "borrowed" this idea for the days of the week. One theory points to the fact that seven days matched the seven "planets" known to the ancient worlds. Check them out at left.

Moon-day

Mars-day

Mercury-day

Jupiter-day

Venus-day

Saturn-day

Sun-day

You can detect these ancient roots in the names for the days of the week in Latin-based languages, such as French and Spanish. But since the English language and culture were heavily influenced by the Vikings, we ended up with some names drawn from Norse mythology. Thus:

Tiw's Day

(for the Norse god of war)

Wotan's Day

(for the Norse father of all the gods)

Thor's Day

(for the Norse god of thunder)

Freya-Day (for the Norse goddess of marriage and motherhood)

Since both Venus and Freya were the goddesses of smooching, these days Freya-day is sometimes called T.G.I.F., or "Thank God It's Freya-day"—a day devoted to kicking back and blowing off a little steam to mark the end of the week.

passing of days to predict the coming of the seasons. But how you measured them depended on what part of the globe you inhabited. People in places with teeth-chattering winters or soaked-to-the-bone rainy seasons were going to measure things differently than people in places where the weather was the same year-round. Think about it: You couldn't measure by the seasons if you didn't have any. However, there was one thing that people all over the globe had in common that they could use to help them keep track of the time. What was it? Here's a hint: Look up!

MOON MADNESS

Since cave-dude times, folks have been staring at the sky, and by the time the first civilizations started to spring up, some clever folks had figured out how to measure the *day*—how long the Earth needs to complete one 360-degree spin. They worked out the *month*— how long it takes the moon to circle around the Earth. And they determined the *year*—the 365.2424 days that it takes the Earth to spin all the way around the sun. With all these elements figured out, ancient thinkers soon realized they had the beginnings of a calendar.

GIGUNDA-TIME

You think a wall calendar is big? Head off to Mexico and take a look at the Pyramid of Kukulkan (or in Spanish, El Castillo) at Chichén-Itzá, which was built by the Mayas in 1050. The entire pyramid was actually a calendar! There are four flights of stairs, each with 91 steps and a platform at the top, which added up to 365—the number of days in a year. Using this calendar was partly time-measuring, partly Stairmaster!

Just how big is it? You'll get quite an aerobic workout running up the steps of this giant calendar!

The first calendars were kind of hit or miss. Many places measured time by the new moon, others by the sun, and some used a combination of both. In the land of the Aztecs and Mayas (now Mexico), they devised huge, complicated stone tablets. These worked pretty well, but try and hang one of *those* suckers on the wall! There were even tall dunce cap-like calendars made of solid gold that high priests in central Europe got to wear, even though you'd have to have eyes on the top of your skull to be able to read them. Given these complicated ways of tracking time, people were often a little mixed up about exactly what day it was.

Super-sized! This one-ton calendar of stone weighs as much as an elephant and is about the same size.

HAPPY WHATDAY?

Fast-forward to the mighty Roman Empire (you know—gladiators, toga-parties, and those soldiers with the brooms on the top of their helmets). For a really powerful empire, Rome's calendars were a total mess! The high priests who made the calendars had a bad habit of "inventing" months to suit their whims. Imagine this. In America, Election Day is always held on the first Tuesday in November. What if some politician came along and said, "I'm adding a new month, right after October and just before November. Those pesky elections will just have to wait." That's what the high priests in Rome were doing.

One of Rome's greatest rulers, Julius Caesar, was becoming totally bummed out by the high priests' shenanigans. By now so many stray days had been added that the Roman calendar was saying it was still summer when it was clearly getting nippy outside! So Julius decided to get the smartest folks in Rome to invent a whole new calendar, which he named after himself—the Julian calendar. (And for those of you *begging* to know when he did this, the year was 45 B.C.E.) Julius's new calendar was pretty cool. He had just had a mushy love affair with a famous Egyptian queen named Cleopatra, and had learned a lot about Egypt's calendar from her. So he borrowed some Egyptian ideas, such as dividing the year into 12 months with 30 days. But it was still hard to make the days add up to 365.2424. The Egyptians had simply tacked on a five-day holiday at the end of each year, but Julius had a better idea.

He decided that his years would have 365¼ days. And since you can't have one-fourth of a day, he added up the fourths and made a whole extra day every four years. Ta-da! Leap years!

Julius also had to deal with the fact that Romans had only ten months (you can still tell from the names of *Sept, Oct, Nov,* and *Dec,* which mean seven, eight, nine, and ten in Latin, the language of ancient Rome). So he added two new months. He named July for himself and named the second for another emperor, Augustus Caesar.

Julius did a pretty good job of getting things into some kind of working order. Still, it's too bad he couldn't have arranged for a calendar consult with the Mayas and Aztecs. Or the Chinese for that matter. They were all crackerjack calendar-makers who had more accurate calendars.

MY CALENDAR IS BETTER THAN YOURS

Julian's calendar worked pretty well for about 1,400 years. But in 1582, Pope Gregory, a powerful religious leader, decided the calendar needed changing again. At that time, popes were super-important. They even got to boss kings and queens around. Gregory was miffed because the date for Easter—one of the most important holidays on the Christian calendar—was getting all messed up. So Greg set out to create a new calendar that would stick Easter in the right place. Naturally, he named it after himself: the Gregorian calendar.

Greg decided the time had come to get rid of all traces of the old pagan ways that still remained. One of his biggest changes was moving New Year's Day from April 1, where it had been, to January 1. All of a sudden April 1—which up to then had been the final day of a week-long springtime festival of frivolity and fun—was now just a regular dull day in the eyes of the powerful Catholic Church.

But the Gregorian calendar was a little slow to catch on outside of the Catholic countries. And England, a nation whose people got so fed up with the pope that

FOOLED YA!

Since prehistoric times, spring and having fun have always gone hand in hand: There's something about the release from the long, dark, gloomy winter that always seems to bring out the giggles. During the Middle Ages in Europe, a funky little holiday called *Festus Fatuorum*—the Feast of Fools—sprang up as a replacement celebration for the old Roman New Year's holiday that the powerful Catholic Church had banned.

In India, folks frolic during *Holi,* which usually falls sometime between the end of February and the beginning of March. *Holi* is a day when people throw brightly colored powders at one another until everyone is covered with pink, blue, green, yellow, and orange. In France, streams swelled with so many new fish as the weather warmed that one tradition said that even a fool could catch those foolish fish! To this day, some French folks give each other chocolate fish to celebrate *Poisson d'avril*—April Fish Day. And in Scotland, April Fool's Day is so big, it lasts for two days! Day Two is completely devoted to pranks involving the lower cheeks (aka your butt). It's called Taily Day and it was on this most important of holidays that the beloved "kick me" sign was born.

THE DATING GAME

■ There are about 40 different calendars still being used in the world today, and six major ones: the Gregorian (that's the one we use), Hebrew, Islamic, Indian, Chinese, and Julian (still in use by some groups to set church holidays). Some are based on the cycles of the moon, some on the sun, and some on both.

■ Our calendar repeats itself every 400 years. That means that every single day of every single week will fall on exactly the same day as it did 400 years ago.

■ Every 2,500 years, our calendar accumulates an extra day because of the whims of our solar system. But since we've only been using it to measure time for about 500 years, we're cool for the next 2,000 years or so!

■ Since the Gregorian calendar wasn't officially used in England and America until 1752, George Washington always told people he was born on February 11, not February 22. I say we should get both days off!

they started their own big church, refused to use the new calendar until 1750—almost 200 years later! Now remember, at the time there were no TV's to broadcast a big ball dropping in Times Square at midnight. So for a long time, there were still quite a few people—especially country bumpkins in various out-of-the-way parts of Europe—who thought the New Year's holiday still began on March 25 and ended on April 1. But as the years wore on, they began to look a little foolish, partying on a plain old, ordinary day. It wasn't long before city folks started making fun of them.

Pretty soon those uneducated peasant-types were the *only* ones still stuck on the old day. And since the only folks still ringin' in the New Year on the wrong day weren't the sharpest crayons in the box, the day got dubbed April *Fool's* Day. (Wanna find out the best April Fool's pranks ever? Zip over to HUMONGOUS HOAXES on page 121.)

WHAT NEXT?

Nowadays, we live in a world where we are all connected—a world where people in Brazil do business with people in India. It makes sense to use the same calendar no matter where we live. But will our current day-marker stand the test of time? Believe it or not, folks are talking about changing it!

One idea making the rounds is called the Fixed Calendar. It'd have thirteen months (YIKES! Head over to FRIDAY THE 13TH on page 94 to find out why *that* idea might creep some people out). Each month would be exactly four weeks long and every month would start on the same day—say, a Monday, for example. A new month, called Sol, would get tucked in after June and before July. And at the end of every year, there would be one day that belonged to no month—the perfect day for a holiday, don't you think?

BEFORE AND AFTER

Religion was so important to Pope Gregory that he also came up with a whole new way of dividing history into two parts—*before* and *after* Jesus was born. He labeled every year before the very first Christmas B.C. (for Before Christ). Every year after that big birthday was called A.D. (which stood for *Anno Domini*—The Year of Our Lord). Nowadays, in a world filled with people of many religions all working together, it seems unfair to mark time based on one faith. Today historians use C.E. and B.C.E.—for the Common Era and Before the Common Era.

CREEPY COLUMBUS

Row, row, row your boat. Then take over a continent. That's the Chris Columbus way!

In October of 1492, a group of Taino Indians living in what is now known as the Bahamas discovered a bunch of dirty, smelly, hairy Europeans washed up on their shores. Dumb, too! It was 90 degrees out, but the sweaty newcomers were dressed from head to toe in wool and steel armor. Still, the Tainos held their polite noses and did everything they could to make the newcomers feel at home. And were they ever sorry they did!

SPICE CAPADES

Nowadays, we have refrigerators to keep food from spoiling. But back in the olden days, keeping maggots and worms out of the pantry was a real challenge. Spices and salt kept bugs and germs from making a rotten mush of food and also helped mask the taste of food that had started to spoil and now smelled like underpants that hadn't been changed in a week. (Salt is so amazingly cool that it has its own section—SALT ASSAULT on page 225.)

But there was a wee problem getting to those spices. Spices grew in only one part of the known world—way to the east of Europe, in the Indies. There were other cool things to buy in the East, too, like silks, satins, and precious gems. But if you lived in Europe, the Indies were far away! It took *forever* to make the trip, and it cost a small fortune to get there, too. That's where the explorer Christopher Columbus (Cristóbal Colón in Spanish, or Cristoforo Colombo in Italian) pops into the picture.

CHATTY CHRIS

Young Chris was born in 1451. He was a cheery, talkative guy with bright blue eyes and red hair. People liked him. Chris's folk were weavers in Genoa, a town in Italy on the Ligurian Sea. But weaving bored Chris—he preferred waves. So he left home when he was 12 and spent the next 28 years happily sailing up and down the Mediterranean Sea into the Atlantic Ocean—north as far as Iceland, and south along the African coast. Legend has it that he was once even shipwrecked six miles from shore and managed to swim to safety clinging to a timber from the wrecked ship. He became convinced that God had saved him for a special mission.

FLAT? MY FOOT!

As far back as the ancient Greeks and perhaps even earlier, folks knew the world was round. What they didn't know was how big it was. Was it big and round, or *small* and round? Chris became obsessed with proving that the world was teeny. He just *knew* it was little enough so that he could sail west instead of east, and still end up in the Indies. He figured it was about a ten-day sail, tops. But he needed money to prove his theory. So for the next ten years he begged everyone for a chance to prove his point. His

BUT WE WERE HERE FIRST!

More than 18,000 years ago, the first humans began trickling onto the continents of North and South America. Some came on boats from Polynesia and parts of Asia. Some sailed over from Africa. Some may have walked here during the Great Ice Age, when the oceans froze and sea levels dropped, opening up a land bridge from Asia to Alaska.

More than 400 years before Columbus was even *born,* Vikings landed and lived in part of what is now Canada. Archaeologists who are digging up ancient sites are finding that America has been a big melting pot for a very long time—even 10,000 years ago! So Columbus wasn't exactly the first guy to "discover the New World" (nor, for that matter, was it even "new"). He found a place that had already been found, was clueless about where he was when he got there, never figured out where he had been, and then got credit for everything. Go figure!

own country, Italy, turned him down. Portugal, which was the biggest seafaring nation in those days, turned him down, too. Finally, after six years of his nagging, Queen Isabella and King Ferdinand of Spain got tired of listening to Chris and agreed to fork over some boats for a trip.

Chris didn't ask for any money up front. Instead he asked for the title "Admiral of the Seas," along with a measly 10 percent of the wealth with which he just *knew* he would return. Queen Isabella gave Chris a tubby old cargo ship called the *Santa Maria.* Then she commandeered (a fancy word for "took") two ships from smugglers—the *Niña* and the *Pinta*—and found two experienced captains to steer them.

Chris was good to go! Of course, he had never actually commanded a ship before, so he was a little clueless about how to be a leader. But he was a darned good navigator, and that

was what counted. On August 3, 1492, the three boats set off, heading south to the Canary Islands and then due west into the Sea of Gloom, as the Atlantic Ocean was sometimes called in those days.

ARE WE THERE YET?

I'm sure you've asked *that* question a time or two. Columbus's crew was no different. The trip was miserable. The boats stank to high heaven as garbage collected in the *bilge* (the ship's bottom). The drinking water, which had been packed in big wooden buckets, turned funky. No one was happy to be there—except Chris.

One day the ships got stuck in a giant sea of seaweed. For a time, the wind died down and they drifted for days. After being at sea for what seemed like forever, the crew began to get *very* antsy. They started whining that they wanted to go back home. There were whispers of mutiny. But he begged the crew to be patient for just three more days. Boy, did he get lucky!

I SAW IT FIRST!

Before they left Spain, Chris had promised a big reward to the first crewman to spot land. On October 12, after more than two months at sea, Rodrigo de Triana screamed out "LAND! I see land!" But Chris insisted that *he* had seen land the night before and cheated de Triana out of his reward. What a cheater!

The boats dropped anchor. Chris pulled on his finest silk cloak, grabbed a cross and a Spanish flag, and took a landing party ashore. He strode onto the sandy beach on a small island that is part of what is now the Bahamas, jammed his damp flag into the beach, and

I see land! Now give me my money!

NEED A NIBBLE?

The folks who provided the food and drink for Columbus's voyages were cheapskates. The barrels they built were so bad that the crew's water and wine leaked out. The wine was too old and quickly turned into vinegar, and the food was starting to spoil when they set sail. Several barrels exploded from the build-up of toxic gases.

Everyone ate ship biscuits, a recipe that had been around since the time of the ancient Greeks. Made of flour and water, they were very dry and hard, and if you tried to eat one dry, you would most certainly break a tooth. They usually had to be soaked in water or soup, but the heat and high humidity in the Caribbean quickly turned the biscuits into a yucky mush, filled with pulsating black weevils. The salted meat and dried fish soon stank worse than month-old garbage. Most sailors ate in the dark. Do you blame them? At least that way they didn't have to see what was crawling on their plates. But it was either that, or starving to death.

claimed the land for Spain and the Catholic Church. But wait . . . something wasn't quite right.

Where were the pagodas with gold roofs? Where were all the natives dressed in fine silks? These folks standing on the shore, staring wide-eyed, were not dressed in *anything*. They were buck naked! Still, Columbus was convinced he was in the Indies (mainly because that's where he was planning to go), and dubbed the natives "Indians." Those Indians did not know it, but they were now the property of Spain.

MINE! MINE! MINE!

On the day Christopher Columbus planted his flag on that beach in the Bahamas, there were millions of people living in the Americas—at least 25 million in Central and South America and at least another 4 million in North America. Some were gnarly and war-like. Some ate their neighbors. But *many* were generous and peaceful—like the people living on the island where Columbus had made landfall. They welcomed the smelly sailors with open arms

and happily shared everything they had with the Spaniards. It was a great welcome, but Columbus was confused. Where was China? It had to be somewhere nearby! Maybe just a *little* more west? So he set off once again and headed towards what is now Cuba. Along the way, his crew discovered the natives had nifty rope beds called hammocks that would be great for sleeping on the boat—a whole lot better than a wet wooden deck. They also found some funky stuff called tobacco that was smoked in pipes. There were no spices. But there was something even better. *Gold!* Columbus and his crew became crazed about gold . . . willing to kill for gold! They forgot about their spices and on they sailed, looking for "shiny" instead of "spicy."

Off Columbus and crew went to what is now Haiti. Check out what Chris wrote in his journal: "I could overrun these islands . . . [the natives] bear no arms and are all unprotected . . . they are fit to be ordered around and made to work." Is it any wonder that Columbus Day is not exactly a day of celebration for many Native Americans?

39

Retail holiday. Many Americans use Columbus Day as an excuse to go shopping.

IF AT FIRST YOU DON'T SUCCEED . . .

Each of Christopher Columbus's four trips to the Americas had more than its share of gross moments. Here are the highlights (or perhaps I should say *low*lights).

Voyage #1: Oh, Goody! Gold! (1492) Here's the scoop on the rest of that first trip: The *Pinta* sailors are sick of Chris and sneak off. They hope to grab some gold on another island, then rush back to Spain first and get all the glory. On Christmas Eve of 1492, the *Santa Maria* runs onto a reef off Hispaniola and sinks. Chris is now down to one boat, the *Niña,* which is way too small to hold everyone. He has his crew build a fort and leaves 40 of them behind with a promise that he'll be back to get them ASAP. Then he returns to Spain, meets up with the *Pinta* along the way, and tells a big fat lie to the queen. He tells her he has found scads of gold and will need a lot more ships and men to carry it all back.

Voyage #2: I'm Baaaaaa-ck (1493–1496) Seventeen ships, 1,200 men, and 50 giant dogs that have been trained to kill on command—Chris really means business this time. But the little fort he built on his first trip is gone—nothing left but a few rotting corpses. Surprise! The natives have killed all the Spaniards! Of course, they all deserved to die. They had been absolutely dreadful—abused the natives and attacked their women, stolen, and killed. Still, Columbus is furious!

Chris makes himself the governor of Hispaniola. His first act? He ties copper tags to the Indians' necks. Not wearing your tag? Off with your hands! He gives every native over the age of 14 three months to fill a small bell with gold dust. Can't fill it? Too bad . . . you die! Many natives swallow poison rather than live with these crazy Europeans. In two years, the Spaniards manage to kill half the island's residents. After a hurricane in 1495 destroys all of Chris's ships, he has to creep home on two ships that have been patched together from the wreckage of his once-big fleet. He tells his surviving crew that if they tell *anyone* in Spain the truth about what is really going on, he will slice off their tongues.

Voyage #3: From Bad to Worse (1498–1500) By now other explorers are cutting in on Chris's action. The islands are overrun by greedy European adventurers who want to get rich quick. No one in Spain is really buying Chris's "China" story anymore, so he's not exactly getting the cream of the crop for his crews. He sails with eight boatloads of criminals. He leaves some ex-cons in Hispaniola, which has become the home plate of the New World, and then sails all along the top edge of South America searching for gold. By the way, Chris *still* thinks he's in China or Japan.

Back on Hispaniola, things are completely out of control. It's anarchy (*AN-ark-ee*)! That

SO WHY IS IT NAMED AMERICA?

By 1493, the first wave of explorers and fortune hunters were already flocking across the sea. One guy, Amerigo Vespucci, made maps of all the lands he sailed to. Those maps were published by a German fellow who scrawled Amerigo's name across the bottom. The new maps were a big hit and folks became convinced that Amerigo was the name of the new land—not the name of the mapmaker.

WHY LEIF ERIKSSON DOES NOT HAVE A HOLIDAY

When it comes to Europeans "discovering" the Americas, how come Chris ended up with all the parades and the holiday? Why not poor Leif, the Norseman who got here almost 500 years earlier?

VIKINGS
1. Fought with spears and axes
2. News of the discovery told in poems (yawn)
3. Happy to find grapes for wine (hiccup!)
4. Pretty mellow about religion (one God, ten gods, whatever!)

COLUMBUS
1. Fought with guns and vicious dogs
2. Printing press has been invented. Everyone reads the headlines!
3. Europeans happy to find gold and slaves. Gold + slaves = power.
4. Believed that *everyone* should follow his religion, or be killed

means no rules, no order. The Spaniards are just *awful* to the Indians, and the Indians have finally had enough. A bunch of Chris's crew grab some ships and sail back to Spain to complain that Chris is a terrible governor. Soon, a ship is sent from Spain to bring Chris home, and the "Admiral of all the Seas" returns to Queen Isabella's court in chains. Naturally he is pretty steamed and *really* melodramatic about it. He makes a huge scene when he returns!

Voyage #4: Four-get About It (1502–1504) By now Chris is 50 years old, arthritic, and cranky as heck as he sets off with a crew of mostly 12- and 13-year-old lads. He makes landfall in Central America and zips through Honduras, Nicaragua, Costa Rica, and Panama, almost all the way to Mexico. Just a little farther south and he would have found the vast golden fortunes of the Aztecs (don't miss those AZTEC ANTICS on page 4)!

Chris's crummy boats are falling apart because they've been infested by shipworms—a kind of clam, like a giant, watery termite, that has a two-foot-long worm inside. The boats are leaking so badly they have to be abandoned. Chris

Will the real Chris stand up? No portraits of Columbus were ever painted in his lifetime. Every artist had to guess what he looked like.

and his crew make it to the island of Jamaica, where generous natives feed the lazy sailors for almost a year, and in return get treated like pond scum.

In the end, this is Christopher Columbus's legacy to America's native peoples: Find them, enslave them, and go ahead and kill them if they get ornery. Chris returns to Spain for the last time, a bitter old man. To the end of his life he remains stubbornly, defiantly, and completely wrong about what he has "discovered." So Happy Columbus Day, folks!

CIAO, COLUMBUS

Chris may not have been the sweetest guy ever. In fact, he really *was* a creep! But 1492 is one of the most important years in history—one that completely changed the course of life on this planet. Foods from the Americas, such as corn, peanuts, and potatoes, were soon planted in Europe and Africa. Horses and cattle from Europe and Asia now galloped across American soil. People's lives on every continent were forever touched—all because of a bossy, greedy guy with a big mouth.

CRUEL CONSTRUCTION

Check out a modern-day construction worker. Spiffy Day-Glo hard hat. Kickin' steel-toed shoes. Neat-o safety goggles. Now, zip back 5,000 years. If you could spy on a building crew, this is what you might see. Barefoot. Crushed toes and missing fingers, or worse . . . dead on the job. Not only was construction work a tough way to earn a living, it could send a guy to an early grave.

Super-Sphinx! This giant guard-critter has stood for centuries.

CHAMBERS OF DEATH

There are some pretty amazing buildings on planet Earth. Giant pyramids, huge cathedrals, massive canals, enormous dams, towering skyscrapers, and dazzling bridges. But stuff like that doesn't just spring up out of nowhere with the snap of a finger. Building something that humongo takes a ton of work and a lot of luck. Just look at Egypt's Pyramids— some of the oldest, wow-iest "buildings" in the world. Sure, they're awesome, but they were miserable to construct, and sometimes a real "dead" end for the guys who built them.

The Pyramids were *supposed* to be the final resting place for the mighty *pharaohs* (FAY-rowz)—the kings of Egypt. Unfortunately, they also ended up as the final resting place for some of the construction workers! How did the Egyptians build these enormous things with no power tools, no cranes, no bulldozers, and no blueprints? How did they move stones that each weighed up to 15 tons— about the weight of a school bus? And why the heck did they pick that wacky shape?

Step Right Up!

Egypt's first pyramids are called *step pyramids* because they looked like a flight of steps to the sky. Do *you* have a better idea about how to walk up into the heavens? They were based on triangular shapes because that shape looked like the sun's rays shining through the clouds. A pharaoh named Djoser built the most famous step pyramid in 2611 B.C.E. When he died his body was carried deep underground through a complex maze of tunnels and hidden safely away. But why go to all that trouble?

The ancient Egyptians believed that you actually *could* take it with you when you died, so the Pyramids were built not only to hold the dearly departed, but all of that corpse's stuff, too: games, clothing, furniture, chariots. Everything! Robbing a grave was an easy way to get rich quick. And in the end, all of Djoser's fancy tunnels did him no good. When archaeologists dug up his tomb centuries later, all they found was one royal mummified left foot.

Big 'Un Going Up!

In 2550 B.C.E., about 60 years after Djoser died, a powerful pharaoh named Khufu started to build *his* final resting place. It had to be grand; it had to be big. It *had* to be the most amazing thing ever built. He was a flashy kind of guy.

Khufu's high priests picked a good-luck spot, the architects laid out rope lines to mark the foundation, and the workers started to sweat! Working conditions sucked. Laborers worked barefoot, wearing nothing more than wisps of cotton that looked like big, baggy diapers. Needless to say, lots of those bare feet were crushed by the elephant-sized stones. Fingers were smashed too, as the giant stones were rolled up ramps covered in squishy mud to help them slide. It was hot, hot, hot under the scalding desert sun. And plenty of people went to *their* graves helping to *build* graves for Egypt's kings.

How do you build a trio of giant pyramids? Somewhere between 20,000 and 30,000 sweaty workers labored for 80 years! Historians think that almost every able-bodied Egyptian guy came and pitched in on the building for a couple of months at a time every year. Women, too. They all lived in giant work villages with enormous bakeries, butcher shops, breweries, and, naturally, hospitals for the crushed-of-limb.

Huge stones were floated on barges down the Nile River straight to the pyramid's base. There, the stones were pushed and pulled up the mud-slicked ramps by the biggest, strongest men at the work site. The same slippery mud that made it possible to push the giant stones uphill also made it tough to get a foothold. Slipping and falling in ankle-deep mud as a stone the size of six hippos came sliding back down at you had to have been a major "yikes." Some history-guys think the Egyptians also might have used giant levers to lift their big rocks into place.

There are three pyramids at Giza: one for grandpa, one for junior, and one for his grandson. Khufu's pyramid is the biggest with over 2 million blocks of stone. His son, Khafre, knew his old man would get steamed if he built a bigger tomb. That'd be disrespectful, so his tomb was smaller. And Menkaure, Khufu's grandson, built a smaller pyramid still. How many stone blocks are in the three Great Pyramids at Giza? Enough to build a ten-foot-high wall around the entire country of France! For more than 4,300 years, until the start of the twentieth century, Khufu's pyramid was the biggest building on the planet—481 feet tall!

You can't have a pyramid without a decent mummy, so head over to page 166 to unwrap the truth about MUSTY MUMMIES.

When the structures were complete, the pyramids were covered in layers of white limestone so shimmering it was almost impossible to look at them without being blinded. Inside each pointy mountain of stone lay secret chambers and long tunnels that reached deep down below the surface of the Earth. There were false doors and passageways all over the place that led to the burial chambers. Did it work? Did these tricks keep robbers away? Nope! The truth is, those glittery pyramids were giant arrows for grave robbers, marking the exact spot where the king's loot was buried. Just about every pyramid in Egypt was picked clean.

Up, up, up you go. Each giant block in these pyramids is taller than a grown-up.

All fenced in. If the Great Wall were in America it would reach from Washington, D.C., to the California border.

WALL OF FAME, WALL OF SHAME

Let's say your neighbors are loud and noisy. They keep having wild parties and coming over and stealing your lawn furniture. They're always tossing empty soda bottles and chicken bones into your yard and their dog keeps doing his business on your front walk. You're so tired of coming out in the morning and stepping in you-know-what. Building a big, high fence seems like a splendid idea.

The same thing happened on a really gigunda scale in China beginning in the seventh century B.C.E. when the Zhou dynasty started to build a bunch of small walls to keep out invaders. By the third century B.C.E., things had gotten worse. China's neighbors were always fighting and those brawls were spilling over into Chinese lands, with innocent folks getting caught in the crossfire. In 221 B.C.E. a new dynasty, the Qin, came to power, led by a ruthless emperor, Qin Shi Huang Di. He decided to make the wall even bigger and longer. So he began rounding up enemies of the state—peasants, convicts, scholars, and writers with whom he disagreed—and put them all to work

building the Wan Li Chang Cheng—the Great Wall of 10,000 Li (a *li* is a unit of measure similar to a mile). More than 800,000 people began the backbreaking work of making a wall that stretched across most of an entire country—and a huge country at that.

At least the workers laboring in Egypt knew that they had rocks to build with. But as the wall started to grow across China, finding stuff to build it with was often a problem. So what do you build a big, high, strong wall with if you have no rocks? Dirt!

When there were no rocks, workers built huge wooden, rectangular frames and filled them with shovelfuls of dirt. Then they climbed into the frames and start jumping up and down until each layer of dirt was tamped down to exactly four inches thick. It took hours just to do *that*.

Fill, tamp, fill, tamp, fill, tamp, until the wall was tall enough—a wall 16 feet high and built four inches at a time. Chinese stories say that for every block placed in the wall, a worker died. More than a million people perished—from disease, injuries, and the terrible working conditions—during the building of the Great Wall.

Dynasties come and go. After the Qin came the Han Dynasty (206 B.C.E.–8 C.E.). The Han added tall watchtowers to the wall, each spaced within sight range of the next. On the top level of the towers, fires burned 24 hours a day. But they weren't wood-fueled.

MYTH-CONCEPTION

WALLS OF BODIES

You may have heard that the Great Wall is full of the bodies of dead laborers. But using dead bodies to fill the space would have made the wall weaker, since a decomposing body takes up less and less space as flesh-eating critters nibble away at it. And many people believe that the Great Wall is the only man-made structure visible from outer space. But you can tell them that's absolute rubbish. Lies! All lies.

DOIN' WHEELIES

Nowadays, every gardener has a wheelbarrow. The Han were the first to invent this nifty tool (the Europeans didn't figure out how to make wheelbarrows until 1,000 years later). Another Chinese creation was mass-produced bricks, invented during the Ming Dynasty (1368–1644 C.E.). Ming builders made big ovens to bake mud and straw hunks, then loaded the bricks onto men's and donkey's backs. In places where the mountains were super-steep, they would tie bricks to the heads of surefooted mountain goats and chase them up the steep slopes to fortify the wall and strengthen the towers. Goat-barrows?

Instead, they built fires from wolf poop, producing tall, dark columns of smoke that were used to send "smoke signals" from tower to tower. You could see these smoky plumes from great distances and messages were sent via those doo-doo pyres. When there was a lot of fighting going on, writers would describe it as "a rash of wolf-dung bonfires all over the land."

Merciless Ming Men

In 1215 C.E. gallopin' Ghenghis Khan and his Mongol marauders did the seemingly impossible. They managed to fight their way over the Great Wall and soon controlled the northern half of China. But they didn't last long. The Mongol rulers got fat and lazy, and a bunch of natural disasters so angered the Chinese that they finally revolted. The leader of that revolt became the first emperor of a new dynasty—the Ming family. For the next 300 years, Ming rulers were the top bananas. And one of the Ming emperor's first decrees was that the wall get fixed, *fast!*

The wall *had* gotten a little scruffy and was in desperate need of a facelift. Back came the workers as every crumbling brick, stone, or hunk of tamped mud was filled in, and the wall was made even longer. The Great Wall we see today is the wall the Mings built. When they were done,

the wall stretched almost 4,000 miles (6,400 kilometers). Think about it. That's like a wall that reaches from Washington, D.C., to the California state line!

The age of the great emperors in China has come and gone. Two thousand years of rain, sleet, and snow have come and gone, too. But the wall still stands today—amazing, huge, and GREAT!

HOT DIG-ITTY

Isthmus. Sounds like someone talking with a lisp, doesn't it? But actually, an *isthmus* is a narrow neck of land with water all around it that hooks two big hunks of land together. And the Isthmus of Panama was the hunk that attached North America to South America. Back in the nineteenth century, there were lots of people who couldn't help thinking that if only that neck could be chopped off, a ship could get from, say, London to San Francisco in a few weeks instead of the five months it took back in the days when you had to go all the way around the tip of South America.

In 1869, after ten long years of digging in Egypt, the 100-mile-long Suez Canal had opened, making travel from Europe to Asia much faster. Now it was time to do the same thing in the Americas. A French guy named Ferdinand de Lesseps was the brains behind the Suez Canal, and he just knew

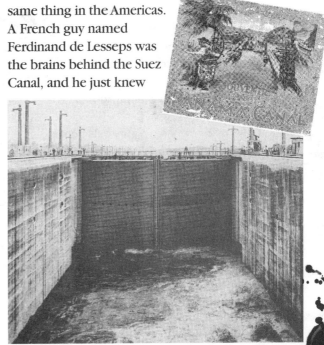

Fill 'er up! The giant locks of the Panama Canal are watery elevators for giant ships.

he could pull off the same engineering miracle in Panama. Boy, was he ever wrong! He understood the engineering challenges, all right. But he was overlooking one teeny, tiny little thing—actually millions of teeny, tiny little things: the pesky mosquitoes that thrived in Panama's hot, steamy jungles.

Itching to Death

"If you try to build this canal there will not be trees enough on the isthmus to make crosses for the graves of your laborers," a Frenchman told de Lesseps. And he was right. Gazillions of mosquitoes bred in the swamps, along the edges of the rivers and streams, and in the puddles that never seemed to dry up in Panama's fierce humidity. And those mosquitoes carried not one, but *two* deadly diseases; yellow fever and malaria. What difference did it make if you had the technological know-how to cut a huge canal, when your entire workforce kept dropping dead? Those mosquitoes eventually took the lives of about 20,000 workers and forced the French to give up on the project.

But U.S. President Teddy Roosevelt wasn't ready to quit. In 1903, after Panama declared its independence from Colombia, the United States offered money and protection to the new country. In exchange, the United States bought the rights to build the canal from the French for 40 million bucks. The first thing Roosevelt did was hire a doc named William Gorgas to zap those mosquitoes.

SKULL BUCKETS

Horrible accidents happened all the time during construction of the Hoover Dam. There were electric lines to get fried on, rocks to fall from, and falling rocks to get knocked out by. There were hard-to-control air hoses that could knock a guy's teeth out. The men on this job decided that their heads needed protecting so they made their very own "hard hats" by putting two baseball caps together, one brim in front, the other facing the back. Then, they dunked the caps in tar a few times and set them out to dry. The result? Heads you could nearly bounce a boulder off.

They could have used a little help from a guy named E.W. Bullard. E.W. had returned from World War I, inspired by the little metal helmets the soldiers wore. His dad owned a company that made mining gear and he figured a metal hat would be a good thing to have in a place where rocks kept crashing down on people's noggins. In 1919 he started selling the "Hard-Boiled Hat" made from steamed canvas, glue, and black paint. It was the granddaddy of today's hard hat, but folks back then called them "skull buckets."

The Swat Team

There were so many mosquitoes on the isthmus that when a person opened his mouth to talk, a slew of skeeters flew in! Gorgas hired thousands of people to search the canal zone and spray oil on top of all the pools of water where the mosquitos laid their eggs. The oil smothered the larvae so new bugs couldn't be born. Gorgas had buildings sprayed with bug-killer and had screens put on all the windows of the dorms where the workers slept. He made sure the grass was kept cut. And he gave quinine to the workers, a drug that kept the disease from killing them.

~~CRUEL~~ COOL CONSTRUCTION

No sissies in sight at these construction sites.

Chartres Cathedral in France is just about the coolest cathedral you can imagine. Back when it was first built, beginning in 1145, there was nothing like it anywhere! At a time when most people lived in mud shacks, everything about Chartres was amazing, from the towering ceilings to the gorgeous stained-glass windows. But one of the neatest things about Chartres is the floor, a giant *labyrinth* (kind of like a maze without the dead-end parts) that leads you right to the heart of the cathedral.

The Leaning Tower of Pisa. And a good place to eat pizza, too! This Italian bell tower was started in 1173, and when it was done, it stood perfectly straight up and down. Soon after it was finished, it began to lean to one side. Was it the architect's fault, or was there something funky about the soil it was built upon? In 1838 it took a sudden turn for the worse and really started to tilt. Finally, in 1988 they closed the tower to the public and started to take steps to make sure the Leaning Tower didn't become the Falling Tower.

The Brooklyn Bridge. Oh, the suspense of building the first suspension bridge! Could John Roebling hang an entire bridge from steel cables attached to two big pillars? Back in 1869 no one believed he could. But 14 years later, folks had changed their tune! Roebling's bridge came with a big price tag in human life, though: about 30 deaths. Some workers developed a brand-new disease called "the bends"—a crippling illness caused by coming from deep below sea level to the surface too quickly. Roebling himself died after his foot was crushed by a ferryboat and tetanus set in.

Mount Rushmore. No offense to all you South Dakota dwellers, but in 1923, a state historian came up with the idea of cutting a giant sculpture into a mountain so people would finally have a reason to come visit his state. He hired a sculptor named Gutzon Borglum. Borglum built a model of the sculpture and then fearlessly used dynamite to blast away rock from a mountainside until there was only a thin layer of granite left. For months he crawled all over the mountain to check out different angles as a team of guys with chisels carved out the heads of four *really big* presidents.

The Empire State Building. Calling King Kong! This granddaddy of the great skyscrapers was begun in 1931. One of the coolest things about it is the men who built it—especially the Mohawk Indians. The Mohawks were completely unafraid of heights and could walk on the steel girders 80 stories up without so much as a safety harness. They had such a terrific sense of balance, they could carry girders in their arms, in high winds, as they walked on the narrowest of steel beams.

The Chunnel. Tunnels have been around for centuries. But not 32-mile-long ones! The English Channel separates Great Britain from the rest of the European continent. In 1994, work started as giant boring machines chewed through the earth hundreds of feet below the Channel. The price tag? $21 billion dollars!

One Step Forward, One Step Back

Finally, with the mosquitoes "offed," the workers could start to cut the canal. The toughest part came at the Culebra (now known as Gaillard) Cut—a nine-mile-long slice in the middle of Culebra Mountain. Drill. Dig. Move. Unload. Drill. Dig. Move. Unload. Oh . . . and sweat buckets with every move 'cause it's hotter than an oven down there!

Using giant steam shovels and railroad flatcars pulled by powerful locomotives, the dirt and rock was slowly hauled away—a pile 4,200 feet high. That's ten times bigger than the biggest pyramid in Egypt! But every time there was heavy rain (which was plenty often), giant mudslides would wash away weeks and weeks of work. Still, they wouldn't quit. Finally, on August 15, 1914, the first boat began its trip along the amazing canal. It took nine hours and 40 minutes, even less time than planners had estimated.

One of the things that's so cool about the Panama Canal is that its highest part is 85 feet above sea level. The engineers had to figure out a way to get a boat to basically go up and down a mountain so they designed huge gates called *locks* that, depending on which way the ship was sailing, could be flooded to raise or lower the water levels. Sort of like watery elevators for mega-big boats.

DAM YOU!

The Great Depression was a tough time in America's history. After the stock market crashed in 1929, many folks who had invested all their life savings found themselves flat broke. Banks also lost all *their* money and closed their doors. Companies went belly-up. To add to the misery, a great *drought* (a time with no rain) turned Oklahoma into a giant "dust bowl." Soon, more than 30 percent of America's workforce was out of work, out of money, and out of luck. So, when word got out about a huge building project out in the

"Look ma, no safety net!" The men who built the Empire State Building had no safety devices at all!

middle of the Nevada desert, thousands of people came looking for a job—any job.

In 1931 Las Vegas was just a little town in the middle of a huge sandbox—a place to get a quickie divorce and then get the heck out of there. In the days before air-conditioning, about the only things that lived happily in this oven-hot part of the country were rattlesnakes, lizards, and tarantulas. About 35 miles from Vegas, in one of the gnarliest places you can imagine, the narrow opening of Black Canyon slowed the waters of the Colorado River (the same river that carved the Grand Canyon). If the waters from the river could be controlled, people figured, the dry desert areas would be more habitable, so the U.S. government made plans to build a giant concrete dam called the Boulder Dam that would divert and control the waters. Best of all, this plan would create jobs for all those people who were out of work.

As word spread about the project, people started coming, some with nothing more than the clothes on their backs. They came by the thousands. Now, imagine thousands of people in the broiling desert sun with no sewage, no houses, no toilets. There was no electricity, no place to buy food. *No nothing* except *bad* water, *bad* sanitation, and *bad* sandstorms, lots of disgusting, germ-carrying flies, and deadly rattlesnakes. About 5,500 men were going to get jobs and their families were going to get regular meals and a roof over their hot little heads. But until they were hired, they slept in their cars. And if they needed a potty, they grabbed a shovel and dug a hole.

Hot, Hot, Hot!

As bad as living near the construction site was, *working* at it was even worse. Bunkhouses built in the canyon were ovens. During the summer of 1931, the temperature averaged 113° Fahrenheit during the day. Drinking water for the workers, pumped in from the river, was stored in uncovered tanks that soon became vats of bacteria-laden hot water. *Dysentery* (a type of *mega*-diarrhea) spread quickly and long lines soon formed at the primitive toilets—hundreds of men vying for a dumping spot on the three (count 'em, three) toilets provided for 5,000 workers in the early days of the project. Then there was the heatstroke: convulsions followed by vomiting, collapse, and soon after, death. It was an hour to the nearest hospital, so if there was going to be any chance for a victim to survive, he had to be packed in ice. Try finding ice in a broiling desert! A local doctor noted on his medical chart that one heatstroke victim had arrived "dead, bloated, and looking like he had been parboiled."

For five solid years, seven days a week, with only Christmas and July 4th off, the men worked on the giant dam. They earned only $4 a day, but back then you could buy a can of salmon and a loaf of bread for a dime. For $1.25 a day they got a roof over their heads and three square meals. At a time when many Americans were so broke that some were willing to eat from a trash can, any food was a blessing, even if that food was cooked before you could open the can.

Blast Me A River

The first years of the project were spent building roads and rail lines so that equipment and supplies could actually get to the canyon. Next came the little task of diverting the river. Have you ever tried to move a river? We're talking major sweat here. Men spent two and a half years digging tunnels with jackhammers, setting off dynamite to blast out the rock, hauling it out, then building a barrier that would redirect the course of the river. Four giant tunnels had to be dug, all at the same time. It was nasty, dangerous, dirty work, especially because the long tunnels had a tendency to fill up with carbon monoxide, a deadly gas. Finally the dam went up—and up and up—to the height of a 70-story building. But concrete gives off a lot of heat as it cures, so it had to be poured in five-foot layers, and giant refrigerators were built to help cool the slabs. Otherwise it would have taken about 125 years to dry!

In 1935, the Boulder Dam, soon renamed after Herbert Hoover—the prez at the time—was finally complete. And a new bit of geography was added to America's maps: Lake Mead, which quickly grew into a 115-mile-long, 550-foot-deep man-made lake. The Colorado River's days of wiping out helpless farms and towns was over. And today, every day, Hoover Dam spits out enough energy to light up the homes of 1.3 million people. Not bad for a project that started with three potties for 5,000 men!

CUSSIN' COWBOYS

Sit on a hard slab of leather until your butt is completely numb. Stick a few cactus thorns in your legs. Inhale clouds of dust all day long. Get soaked by the rain, pelted by snow, smashed by hail, and fried by the sun. Oh, yeah . . . and spend your day in the company of thousands of farting, belching cows and lovesick bulls. Wow, being a cowboy sure is some kind of glamorous!

THE FIRST COWBOYS WERE ACTUALLY INDIANS!

Ever watch a cowboy movie? It's all about wide-open spaces, dusty cattle drives, high-noon shootouts, and those huge golden sunsets. But what was it *really* like? Well, until the first Spanish explorers arrived in the Americas in the 1500s, there wasn't a single horse here. (Come to think of it, there were no cows, either.) Back in Europe, there were cows aplenty, but they were kept penned up, since land was scarce. But America's West was huge. There was no reason to keep cattle crowded in little spaces. No need to spend a lot of time and effort feeding them. Let those lazy moochers get their own food and water!

Spanish settlers began to make themselves at home in what is now Mexico in the 1500s. They soon had scads of horses and longhorn cattle roaming around all over the place. Ta-da! The first ranches were born. The new ranch owners realized they needed help looking after their growing herds, so they taught local groups of

Bet the word *cowboy* doesn't make you think "New York." But that's where the word was first used, during the Revolutionary War when British loyalists rang cow bells just before they pounced on patriot farmers.

Indians to ride and watch over the cattle. The Spaniards started calling the cow herders *vaqueros*. (A *vaca* is a cow, in Spanish.) The Native American *vaqueros* were absolutely amazing riders. They rode barefoot 12 hours a day and could literally leap onto a moving horse. The *vaqueros* learned how to snare a runaway steer with a little braided rawhide rope, which the Spanish called *la reata*—which became the "lariat." By the early 1700s, *vaqueros* were grazing their cattle as far north as modern-day Texas.

GO WEST, YOUNG MEN

By the time the Civil War ended in 1865, there were literally millions of cattle running wild all over the Southwest. Back in the South, the war had pretty much ruined everything. Confederate money was only useful as toilet paper. The great plantations were in ruins. And the men who had fought in the war and survived were pretty fried. A lot of them felt that a change would do them good.

So young, single guys in their teens or early twenties flocked west. Many were illiterate farm workers. Quite a few (in fact, almost a quarter

Woopie-tie-i-yay! Rope tricks were a good way to pass the time on the range.

50

of all cowboys) were freed slaves who wanted to get as far away as they could from the terrible memory of slavery and life in the South. There were also Midwestern farm boys looking for a little adventure. Most of these guys figured life as a cowboy couldn't be much worse than starving and struggling back home. They were all tough guys, and they needed to be, because a day on the range could veer from bored-to-death to scared-to-death in a matter of seconds. Think about it: One minute you're sitting half-asleep in the saddle and the next you're facing a 25,000-cow stampede. Yikes!

SWEET SIXTEEN AND IN THE SADDLE

What was a typical day like for the average teenage cowboy? Let's share his thoughts.

■ Still dark out? Grrr! Brrr! Gotta get in the saddle before sunup! But my darned blanket is frozen. How the heck am I supposed to fold it?

■ Set off riding "flank," "swing" (beside), or "drag" (behind) and get those longhorns moving. Why do I always get stuck with drag? Riding drag *is* a drag. Do you have any idea how much a cow plops every day?

■ Hope that those dark clouds on the horizon don't mean thunder and lightning. Cattle are absolute crybabies when it comes to storms. Was that howling a wolf? Ugh! Wolf + cattle = big stampede. I'm *not* in the mood to be trampled to death!

■ River to cross. Cows like water about as much as I like eating dirt. And it's not like I can swim, either!

■ Stampede! Please don't let me slip out of the saddle! I don't want to know what it feels like to have an entire longhorn stuck in my rump. Gotta catch up with that lead cow and start a cow conga-line.

■ Ten miles in the saddle today. Butt is definitely starting to ache. Time to find a "bedding" ground. Need good grazing and a watering hole for the cattle.

THE DEVIL'S ROPE

So, you've got cattle all over the place. How do you keep 15,000 steer from wandering over to your neighbor's ranch? A plain fence just won't cut it! But some razor-sharp wire with sharp spikes will stop a heifer dead in her tracks! In 1874, a man named Joseph F. Glidden saw a piece of wooden rail with sharp nails sticking through its sides hanging from a plain old fence. Barbed wire was born—stuff so nasty it was called "the work of the devil" by many. Barbed wire changed the way the West worked. Came in handy in the East, too, for keeping criminals in jails—or *out* of places they shouldn't be.

■ Not fair! Stuck with "night herd" again. Now I gotta "ride herd" all night, circling around the cattle and singing stupid lullabies to calm them down 'cause they're afraid of the dark—the big babies!

■ Starving! Hope Cookie is ready with dinner. Sure would love some vinegar pie. Could literally eat a cactus right now.

■ Egads! Is Charlie playing that wretched harmonica again? Sounds like a cat having his guts squeezed out. Guess the guys will start singing soon—can they write any sadder songs? Homesick. Lovesick. Lonely. Dead. Sheesh! Lighten up, guys! I *do* like the songs about loyal horses, though.

■ Sure am sleepy. Better rub some tobacco juice in my eyes. Hopefully the pain will keep me awake.

■ Only six more months of this until we get back to civilization! Yippee-tay-yie-ay!

YUCKY YORE

Go into some 4,000-year-old Egyptian tombs and you will see hieroglyphics of cattle branding. But as recently as 1822, humans were branded, too! Fugitives, galley slaves, gypsies, criminals, and even people with different religious beliefs have been marked with "symbols of shame." During the Civil War, *deserters* (people who just flat-out quit fighting) had big letter D's branded onto their faces for everyone to see.

DRESS LIKE A
BUCKAROO

COWBOY HAT
Made from beaver belly, it cost a month's wages, but that's a small price to pay for shade, an umbrella, a pillow, and a water bucket all rolled up into one! ➝

BANDANNA
Wanna eat dust? Didn't think so! Bandannas made great dust filters and sweat moppers. And you were always ready for a quick game of blind-man's bluff!

GLOVES
Trust me! You don't want to pick up bull droppings with your bare hands.

SHIRT
Long-sleeved wool. Itchy as heck. Big chest pocket for holding a drawstring tobacco sack and cigarette papers.

HOLSTER & SIX-SHOOTER
'Cause just saying "bang-bang" really will not protect you in a duel.

BLANKIE
Even a cowboy needs a little "security."

LARIAT
Can't rope a calf without one.

BOOTS
High heels kept your feet from sliding through the stirrups. They were good for squishing scorpions, too.

HORSE
A cowboy's true love, best friend, and locomotion.

SPURS
Horse napping on the job? A kick with one of these will wake him right up.

CHAPS
Heavy leather keeps you from becoming a human pincushion. Also available in pouffy sheepskin, called "woolies," if you don't mind having fat legs.

BRAND X

Before the Civil War, folks really didn't eat a whole lot of beef. Cattle were raised mostly for leather, and cow fat was used to make *tallow,* the fat that is used in soap and candles. But in the 1870s, new ways to pack meat were being invented. America's heartland became a perfect place for this great meat-massacre to take place. And there were suddenly a whole lot of extra cows. Folks in Chicago, Fort Worth, and St. Louis all built fortunes by killing beefy animals. The 1880s were the peak of the cattle industry. Almost 44 percent of the United States was being used for grazing cattle. That's almost half of the country!

Since it was kind of far for a cow to walk from Texas to Chicago, railroads started carrying the cattle to the slaughterhouses. Cowboys had to drive the cattle from the wide-open ranges to the nearest rail depots. And they needed a way to keep track of which cattle were theirs.

Cattle branding worked like a charm and stopped cattle rustlers from stealing the herd. About 300 calves could be branded in an afternoon. It was a big, messy job. First you'd heat the brand to a dull red so it did not burn too deeply, then, holding the little calf down, give each wee heifer your ranch's stamp. Next, you'd crop the calf's ears or notch them top or bottom. Most young boy calves had their manly parts lopped off. The young bull's cut-off private parts were tossed in one bucket. The ear hunks were tossed in another. One lucky cowpoke got to count all the body bits at the end of the day. Unfortunately raw brand marks and ear cuts attracted blowflies, which laid eggs in the wounds. The blowflies led to screwworms, inch-long maggots that made the cattle miserable. Miserable cattle equals miserable cowboys, so ranch workers always carried carbolic acid and axle grease to help heal the wounds. If your cattle had *mange*—a skin disease—the "cure" was to pour kerosene all over the cow and hope it didn't get too close to a cooking fire. Ever see a cow explode? Very messy!

EAT LIKE A COWBOY, FART LIKE A BULL

Grab a grown-up and cook up some Son-of-a-Gun Stew. It was originally called Son-of-a-*%#*% Stew, and it was a favorite cowboy dish. Everything but a cow's hooves, hair, and horns went into it. Its special ingredient is *margut,* a hunk of intestine from a baby calf that is filled with partially digested milk.

You'll need:

A chunk of suet	Margut (that baby calf intestine hunk)
1 calf heart	
1 piece calf liver (about ⅓ the size of the heart)	Calf brains
	6 cloves garlic, minced
	1 large onion, chopped
2 calf kidneys	Salt
Calf sweetbreads (the thymus gland)	Chopped hot green peppers (optional)

Cut the heart, liver, kidneys, sweetbreads, and margut into bite-size pieces. Sear this on top of the stove in a roaster in which you have melted the suet. Mash the brains and add them. (This makes the whole thing nice and gloppy.) Add garlic, onions, salt to taste, and, if you like, a few finely chopped hot green peppers. Put the cover on the roaster and place in 300°F oven until done—about an hour and a half. Stir once or twice but not too often. Serve with a side of beans, a cup of belly wash (coffee), and a barf bag.

OH, YIKES!

D

DASTARDLY DENTISTRY

Catch a glimpse of a European mouth during the Middle Ages and you'd probably run screaming into the next room. And that's *after* you'd almost passed out from the smell. Teeth need a lot of TLC if you want to keep them healthy—in fact, if you want to keep them at all. And history teaches that when they're gone and all you can eat is soup, a person will go to just about any lengths to get them back—including digging up a corpse, armed with pliers!

TEETH TO DIE FOR

These days we take pretty good care of our teeth. We brush. We're *supposed* to floss. But back in the bad old days, it was a different story. The result? Teeth decayed and cracked. Gums swelled, and teeth fell out or had to be pulled. People soon found out that life was difficult without proper chompers, so false teeth were invented.

By 800 B.C.E. folks in Etruria (a part of what is now Italy) were making false teeth from hippo and whale bone and setting them into lovely gold settings that fit right into a toothless mouth. The Etruscans were the best dentists in the ancient world. When a person died, whatever decent real teeth they had left were extracted from their corpses and fashioned into beautiful Etruscan *dentures*—a fun word for false teeth. Unfortunately, the dental skills of the Etruscans vanished along with their civilization.

MAKE 'EM SHINE!

Barbers were the dentists of the Middle Ages. They also were the teeth whiteners. First they would take a metal file and roughen up the surface of the tooth. They then brushed the tooth with a solution of corrosive nitric acid. Sure, the teeth were white for a little while, but the acid ate away the enamel. When the protective enamel was gone, a mouthful of cavities soon followed. And there you were—toothless as a month-old baby.

By the year 100 C.E. in ancient Rome, people were sticking little metal hunks of wrought iron that had been beaten into fang-like shapes into their jawbones to replace missing teeth. And you thought braces made you look like a metal mouth!

Not surprisingly, during the Dark Ages, between 500 and 1000 C.E., the art of replacing missing teeth was lost. The best thing anyone could figure out was to carve animal bones into toothy shapes and tie them together with silk thread. Dastardly "dentists" then lassoed the fake teeth onto whatever was still left standing in their customer's almost toothless mouth. Trust me. It didn't work.

Medieval and Renaissance folks from the 1300s to the 1500s were clueless as well. They thought cavities—those ouchy holes caused by too many sweets—were the work of tooth worms. The best the toothless rich could hope for was to buy good, strong teeth pulled from the poor, which were then set into fake gums made of ivory.

How did people keep these contraptions securely in their mouths when they ate? It was tricky! In the 1500s, some folks had their gums pierced with hooks, and then wired their false teeth to their jaws. When springs were finally available, the wire wearers gave a sigh of relief. But spring-held dentures could be pretty embarrassing, too. Sometimes they went flying out of the wearer's mouth at the most embarrassing moments.

THE TOOTH FAIRY'S WORST NIGHTMARE

It didn't matter if you were rich or smart. Kings, queens, and most of America's Founding Fathers had serious teeth issues (see page 57).

In the late 1700s, hope for the rotten-toothed arrived! A French dentist and pharmacist invented rot-proof dentures made of porcelain (the same stuff that your toilet bowl is made from). An Italian dentist figured out how to make a single porcelain tooth on a little stickpin that attached to a metal plate in 1808. But the new fake teeth still hurt like heck.

THIS BITES!

During the Middle Ages and right up through the American Civil War in the 1860s, folks would do anything to get new teeth, including stealing them from corpses. Alas, the dead teeth they stole rotted quickly and gave you dragon breath to boot. But that didn't stop the tooth thieves—or the tooth merchants. After the Civil War, barrels of young American soldiers' teeth were shipped to Europe to be made into dentures.

In 1839, a fellow named Charles Goodyear figured out how to take the sap from a rubber tree and make something useful from it: soft flexible rubber. The squishy rubber took a lot of the pain out of wearing dentures.

TIME TO BRUSH

10,000 Years Ago Cave dwellers pried out those annoying hunks of meat caught between their teeth by stabbing at them with branches that had been chewed on, softened, and then frayed at one end. *Voilà!* The first toothbrushes were born.

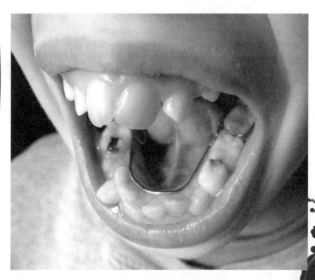

Crooked mouthful. *Until the advent of modern orthodontics in the 19th century, everybody went around with crooked teeth.*

3000 B.C.E.–500 C.E. The ancient Egyptians, Greeks, and Romans all used toothpicks, chewsticks, tree twigs, linen strips, birds' feathers, animal bones, or porcupine quills to poke at the gunk that got caught between their chompers.

250 C.E. Folks in ancient Rome brushed their teeth with human urine. They gargled with it, too. For some reason, rich Romans believed that pee from Portugal was the very best and were willing to pay big bucks for it. You may be surprised to learn that they were actually on to something. Urine is loaded with ammonia, which is a great cleanser.

600 C.E. Over in Africa and the Middle East, they learned by trial and error that one particular small tree—*Salvadore persica*—had a chemical in its branches that kept teeth sparkling and healthy. Many people in the Middle East still chew on the branches for a sweet, bright smile.

YUCKY YORE

In Tudor times (the sixteenth century in England) many wealthy people's teeth turned black from eating too much sugar and not brushing afterwards. So for a while, it was the fashion for women to blacken all their teeth to prove that they could afford plenty of sweets. Those who wanted to keep their original teeth brushed with the favorite toothpaste of the time: a mixture of ground crystal, rock salt, marble, glass, snail shells, and a half quart of white wine. Burp!

900 C.E. A Persian doc named Rhazes figured out how to fill cavities—those pesky holes in your teeth that hurt like heck. The only problem was how to get rid of the decayed part. Rhazes had to hold a metal spike and twist it between his thumb and forefinger, literally screwing the decay away.

1000–1300 C.E. Over in Europe, those who did brush their teeth (and they were few and far between) used horsehair brushes. Badger hair was another popular choice, but most folks just stabbed at their gunk-covered teeth with a metal toothpick.

1500: The always-inventive Chinese were brushing their pearly whites with a brand-new gizmo: the toothbrush. They plucked the very stiff hairs from pigs' necks and stuck them into tiny holes drilled into a bamboo base.

1850: In England about 150 years ago, it was not uncommon for parents of the bride to pay to have all her teeth yanked out so her new hubby wouldn't have to deal with the dentist's bills that were sure to come in the next few years.

Stuck on a desert island without a brush? Make your own!

X-PERIMENT — TRY THIS!

Why didn't wooden dentures work? Try this. Take a small bowl and spit into it until you have about half a cup of saliva. This may take a day or two, but that just adds to the yuck factor. Now drop a wooden toothpick into the spit and cover with plastic wrap. Come back in a few days and your toothpick will be all mushy. That's because there are enzymes in saliva that break down cellulose—the main ingredient in wood.

1938: The first nylon-bristle brushes rolled off the assembly line in America. But the brushes were so stiff, they literally made people's gums gush blood.

1939: It took a war and the United States Army to get people into the habit of taking better care of their teeth. Up until World War II, most folks just didn't brush their teeth regularly. But in the armed forces, every soldier got a toothbrush and toothpaste and a nasty drill sergeant ordered them to use them! When the war was over, they kept up the habit.

PRESI-DENTURES!

It's hard to imagine the signing of the Declaration of Independence being done by a bunch of gummy guys, but it was! The grim truth is, that by the age of 20, some colonial Americans had lost *all* their teeth. Unfortunately, we're talking grown-up snappers here: There aren't any more sets of teeth waiting in the wings. The reason? Americans had a big sweet tooth even back then. They consumed *way* too much sugar and drank sugar-rich apple cider all day instead of water.

Take George Washington. The Father of our Country was never one for a serious twice-a-day brushing, so his teeth troubles started when he was still a teenager. He lost his first tooth at 18, and by age 22, the rest were rotting like year-old fruit. On the day he took the oath of office as the president of the brand-new United States, in 1789, he had exactly one real tooth in his mouth.

His first set of false teeth kind of solved the problem, but not completely. If he tried to smile, the hinges that held the falsies together would fly open. And it was hard to sleep at night with a mouth throbbing with constant pain. (Go grab a one dollar bill. When Washington sat for his official presidential portrait, his teeth were hurting so much he had to take them out. The artist, Gilbert Stuart, had to pack cotton under George's lips and cheeks to plump out his toothless, sunken features.) Desperate to dump his dentures, in 1784, Washington (who was a slave owner) had some of his slaves' teeth transplanted into his own jaw. Unfortunately for both George and his slaves,

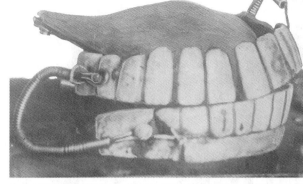

Tusk, tusk! George Washington's dentures were made from elephant tusks!

the operation flopped. But there are some advantages to being the leader of a nation. Washington's last set of dentures, made in 1798, were a masterpiece of colonial dentistry. The upper part had carved ivory teeth screwed to a palate made from a sheet of gold. The bottom denture, a single-carved block of elephant tusk, was attached to the upper by steel springs.

If you don't want to end up like ol' G.W,. brush, brush, brush, and brush some more. Your grown-up teeth are all you've got unless you want eat to mush for the rest of your life!

WHAT TIME IS IT? TOOTH-HURTY!

Up until a hundred years ago, toothaches were an everyday event. One common medieval remedy was to hang the thighbone of a toad off the aching tooth. Another popular cure was applying a paste of burnt rat brains. If the thought of chewing rat brain gum wasn't tempting, you could always gargle with urine.

When the rat's brains and urine gargle failed (as they *always* did), folks had their teeth pulled by whomever was in a pulling mood. It might be the barber or the blacksmith. You never knew and you didn't care. You just wanted the tooth *out. Now!* Unfortunately, until the mid-1800s, if you lost your choppers, that was it. Puréed or mashed food for you, for the rest of your miserable life, since false teeth were *way* too expensive for the average Joe. In fact, peanut butter was invented by a St. Louis dentist as a source of protein for his toothless patients who couldn't chew anymore.

DOG-GONE DOGS

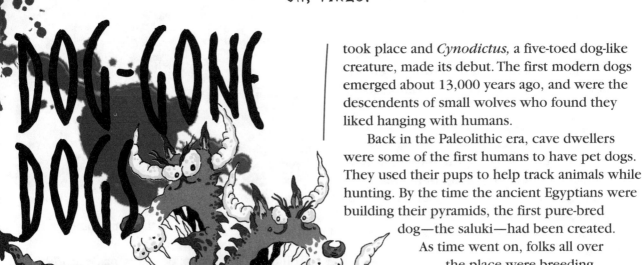

Okay. So dogs have been a big part of human history since the day 13,000 years ago, when the first wolves decided that if they played their cards right, they could train us humans to play catch with a drool-dripping tennis ball for hours on end. But even if they are "man's best friend," you've got to admit they have some pretty gross habits. That whole eating-their-own-puke thing? Definitely not cool! And those room-clearing farts? Disgusting! Not to mention the way their poop litters city streets, suburban yards, and sometimes ends up on the bottom of your shoe. But you gotta admit, they're kind of lovable, and they do have a storied past.

THE DOG WHO CRIED WOLF

Dogs, wolves, and foxes are all descended from the same critter as cats—a small weasely tree-dweller called *Miacis,* which first appeared about 40 million years ago. Around 20 million years ago, another shift

took place and *Cynodictus,* a five-toed dog-like creature, made its debut. The first modern dogs emerged about 13,000 years ago, and were the descendents of small wolves who found they liked hanging with humans.

Back in the Paleolithic era, cave dwellers were some of the first humans to have pet dogs. They used their pups to help track animals while hunting. By the time the ancient Egyptians were building their pyramids, the first pure-bred dog—the saluki—had been created.

As time went on, folks all over the place were breeding superdogs—bigger, stronger, faster, furrier, sometimes sweeter, but more often, more vicious. There were swift greyhounds, spotty dalmations, and huge mastiffs that weighed 250 pounds and could rip a guy's bowels out with one swift snap.

But things weren't all hunky-dory for dogs. Many religions had a way of portraying dogs in a pretty negative light. In Greek mythology, hell was protected by a three-headed dog named Cerberus. Over in Central America, the Mayas believed that dogs were death's messengers and had not one but *two* death-dog spirits, Nahua Xolotl and Pek.

Was this perhaps because dogs had a tendency to go a little nutso when they came upon an animal carcass (think of a dog's reaction to a ratty old bone)? Whatever the reason, in both the Hebrew and Muslim cultures, dogs were thought of as unclean animals. Not exactly a creature you'd want for a pet. People could not even eat an animal that had died of natural causes if it had been licked by a pack of dogs. And considering that back then many dogs carried rabies bacteria, this was probably not such a bad rule.

WORD UP!

Boy, the dog days of summer sure can get hot! But what does heat have to do with dogs? Well, many ancient peoples looked to the stars to find their way around. From July 3rd until August 11th, Sirius, called the dog star, becomes the brightest in the northern hemisphere's heavens. And it is just around then temperatures swell to their stickiest. Hence the name.

A DOG'S LIFE

Still, dogs have always been a lot of fun to hang around with, and in many civilizations, people were major pooch-lovers. By the time of the Roman Empire, dogs were not only workers: they had crossed over to pet status. Of course, the Romans also had their bloodthirsty side. Over at the Coliseum, crowds gathered to watch dogs fight against lions, leopards, gladiators, slaves, and even an elephant or two. (Flip to GLADIATORS on page 104 for more on that.)

In China, dogs lived a double life. There were lucky dogs—such as the chow chow, the shar-pei, and the Pekingese—that were so pampered that some of them even had human servants. The Chinese liked their dogs with smooshed-looking faces, so there were servants whose job it was to rub a dog's snout into a rough surface to literally grind away his face. In the royal courts, pure-bred dogs were treated like precious gems and were the perfect gift for a highly ranked emperor or king. But for the average mutt in China, being the main course at dinner was more like it. To this day, doggie dishes are still eaten in some parts of the world.

By the Middle Ages, bloodhounds were the dog of choice in Europe. They got their real name, blooded-hounds, not because they could smell the red stuff, but because they were of pure blood. Dogs became the ultimate status symbol for royal types. Men liked huge hunting dogs. Women preferred little lap-pups who not only were cute, but could keep a lady's feet warm in those unheated, drafty castles.

DOGS RULE!

Over in Japan, in the mid-1600s, a *shogun* (a powerful military governor) named Tokugawa Tsunayoshi tried to be a compassionate ruler. For example, he passed laws that protected abandoned kids, back in the days when parents often killed any child they could not afford to keep. He opened state-funded hospitals, and improved the conditions of local prisons. But he went a little overboard with his rules protecting dogs. Anyone who injured, harmed, killed, or even ignored a dog in need could be exiled, sent to prison, or put to death. Alas, there were soon hundreds of dogs wandering the streets, fighting for food, and terrorizing people. The sidewalks were soon piled high with pooch-poop. Worse yet, there always seemed to be rotting dog corpses everywhere. People began to become really annoyed about the situation, and secretly, stealthily, when no one was looking, began to kill dogs, usually to protect themselves.

Tsunayoshi went berserk. In one month alone, in 1687, 300 people were killed for being unkind to dogs. In his 30-year reign, more than 60,000 people were executed because they had been unkind to a bow-wow.

YES, YOUR MAJESTY

During the eleventh century over in Norway, a king, angry that his subjects had tried to get rid of him, appointed his dog, Saur, to the throne. For three years Saur was a king of Norway—and not too bad as kings go!

WORK, WORK, WORK

Not all dogs had it easy in the olden days. No sleeping all day long before digging into a big bowl of Alpo. Some dogs worked their little tails off! There were guard dogs who roamed the streets at night, ready to remove a person's vital organs if they did something wrong. There were *turnspits*—little dogs that ran for hours on treadmills turning wheels that spun meat roasting on great big cooking fires. There were hounds to fetch shot-down ducks, and shepherds and sheepdogs to keep moo-ers and baaa-ers well behaved. Some dogs also did the job of horses, pulling carts down narrow streets. Dogs could be paid with a pat on the head, a scratch of the ears, and a grotty old bone.

Of course, there are still plenty of working dogs around these days. Dogs still help with hunting and herding. And Seeing Eye dogs have been helping blind people live full lives since the late 1920s. After World War I ended in 1918, the Germans, who had lost the war, decided to train German shepherds to be the seeing eyes for soldiers who had been blinded in battle. An American woman named Dorothy Harrison heard about the puppies being trained to cross busy streets and stop for red lights, and decided the idea would be wonderful for anyone who couldn't see—not just soldiers.

These days the busiest dogs in town are bomb-sniffing and drug-detecting dogs. That's 'cause a dog's cold, wet nose is up to 10,000 times more sensitive than *your* nose and can pick out a single scent—such as a chemical used to make an explosive device—from a pot full of perfume.

YOU'RE IN THE ARMY NOW

Dogs haven't only worked for civilians; throughout history, they've gone off to war. Those poochy soldiers have played a lot of different roles:

- The ancient Romans were the first to have formations of attack dogs, wearing spiked collars and carrying pots of flaming sulfur and resin (nasty, stinking, eye-tearing stuff) into battle.

MOVE OVER, LASSIE . . .

Sure, there are lots of brave dogs in the movies—Lassies and Benjis and Rin-Tin-Tins galore. But those dogs were just acting. These dogs were the real thing! Here are a few famous critters:

- Where would America be without Abraham Lincoln? And if it hadn't been for his pup, Honey, who rescued him from the deep, dark cave he fell into as an 11-year-old, we might now be the Un-united States of America.

- Balto, the Disney character, is based on a real-life Siberian husky—the lead dog who pulled a sled 674 miles from Nenana to Nome, Alaska, in 1925, carrying diphtheria serum to the victims of a terrible epidemic that struck the city in the dead of winter. It is to honor Balto and his doggie buddies that the Iditarod dog race is run every year.

- Laika, the first dog to fly into outer space aboard *Sputnik II* in 1957, became one of the most famous dogs in the world. Alas, this Russian cosmopooch died a few hours into the flight from overheating—a hot dog and hero all in one.

Peddlin' pooch. Dogs' appeal has helped sell products for decades.

Doing the dirty work. *During World War I, trained dogs helped during attacks of poisonous mustard gas, the most lethal of the poisonous chemicals used during the war.*

■ During the Middle Ages, dogs clad in little suits of armor fought alongside their steel-clad masters.

■ Napoléon, the great French general, *hated* dogs—especially after his wife's pup bit him on his butt on his wedding night! But that didn't keep him from keeping a dog to taste his food to see if it was poisoned—or posting dogs as sentries to warn his troops of sneak attacks.

■ America's first doggie soldiers fought during the Seminole Wars of 1835 and 1842. They were bloodhounds trained to track runaway slaves and Indians who were hiding in the swamps of Florida and Louisiana.

■ Civil War dogs worked as messengers, guard dogs, and company mascots. Many a homesick soldier, on both sides, brought his pet with him to keep him company.

■ In 1884, the Prussian army started the first doggie West Point—a military training school especially for pups.

■ Some of the bravest soldiers in World War I and II were pooches! More than a million dogs fought on both sides. Dogs parachuted behind enemy lines and served as sentries, messengers, ammunition carriers, four-legged meal trays, scouts, sled dogs, ambulance dogs, and ratters. Wearing saddlebags filled with medical supplies, Red Cross dogs were trained to find wounded men. Many a dying soldier went to his final resting place with a cuddly dog curled up beside him. And thousands of soldiers on both sides owe their lives to these plucky puppies.

■ During World War II, soon after the attack on Pearl Harbor, the American Kennel Club asked folks across America to "enlist" their dogs in the Quartermaster Corps. On March 13, 1942, the K-9 Corps began training their four-legged recruits to become soldiers. About 19,000 dogs signed up and about half made it past basic training.

■ The Berlin Wall was a huge concrete barrier that divided East and West Germany at the end of World War II. When the hated wall finally came tumbling down in November 1989, more than 10,000 watchdogs, horse dogs, and patrol dogs found themselves—and their masters—suddenly out of a job.

OLD FOAMY

Dogs are cute. But there's nothing cute about a snarling, vicious, mean dog that's foaming at the mouth and just hankering to take a bit out of your butt. Dogs can get a disease called *rabies*, which messes with the nervous system. Lots of other animals carry the disease, too, but since you are not likely to have a pet raccoon or bat, the chances of catching it are slim. But lots of people have dogs.

Get bit by a rabid dog and you will be in serious trouble. Rabies makes you drool as your body starts to make too much saliva. Pretty soon you start acting crazy and having convulsions. And shortly thereafter you will become paralyzed and unable to breathe. If you don't get a series of special shots, you will be a goner.

DREADFUL DRACULA

Pop in some plastic fangs. Add a trickle of fake blood running down your chin. Pull on your black cape and slick back your hair. Oh . . . and don't forget to crawl back into your coffin before daybreak or you'll crumble into a pile of ashes. It sure is cool being Dracula for Halloween.

But was there ever a *real* Dracula with a *real* spooky castle in Transylvania? Betcha a bite on the neck there was! And, as you're about to discover, the real Dracula was a heck of a lot scarier than that midnight-munching movie vampire.

PRINCE OF DARKNESS

Empires have a way of coming and going. Here today. Gone tomorrow. From the twelfth to the fifteenth centuries, the big-cheese empire was the Ottoman Empire, which got its start in Turkey as the Byzantine Empire was crumbling (and *that* empire got its start when the Roman Empire crumbled). Well, as the saying goes (kind of), that's how the empire crumbles!

But what do vampire tales—necks to nick, blood to chug-a-lug, and a nice comfy coffin to snuggle into for a good day's sleep—have to do with mighty empires?

In medieval central Europe, there were lots of scattered little "states" ruled by tough-as-nails princes. One of those places was called Wallachia, in what is now Romania. In the mid-1400s, the head honcho in Wallachia was a man named Vlad III. Vlad's dad (also named Vlad) had belonged to a secret society called the Order of the Dragon. *Dracul* means "dragon" in Romanian, and *dracula* means "son of a dragon." And Vlad II—or Dracula, as he liked to be called—was as frightening as the worst fire-breathing monster you've ever heard about, in the scariest story you've ever read.

A HERO TO SOME?

No doubt about it, Vlad the Impaler was a card-carrying creep. But in Romania, he does have his defenders. In fact, quite a few folks there actually admire him. He built a strong country and ruled over a kingdom where law and order mattered. And he dared to stand up to the powerful Ottoman rulers—a sort of medieval David facing a mighty Goliath. And some Vlad fans say that he wasn't any crueler than any other ruler of his time period—not that that's saying much!

Neck-Louse? The real "Dracula" probably never actually bit anyone.

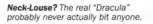

YOU'VE HEARD OF THE COUNT. NOW MEET THE COUNTESS . . .

Countess Erzsébet Báthory (1560–1613) came from a very wealthy, and very crazy, family. She lived on a vast estate at the foot of the Carpathian Mountains in what is now Hungary and married a rather cruel army officer named Nádasdy who was away fighting most of the time. Bored—and, well, let's face it, flat-out insane—Erzsébet decided she needed a hobby.

When the prettiest young women in the surrounding villages began to disappear, at first no one could figure out what was happening. But at night, they could see the Nádasdy carriage, drawn by black horses clattering by, with the terrified faces of young girls pressed to the glass. The girls never came back.

That's because crazy Erzsébet was convinced that bathing in the blood of young women would keep her beautiful. Every day, she would nick the veins of her young prisoners, draining their blood until they were literally bloodless. Then she'd fill a bathtub and soak in her deadly beauty bath—a bloodle bath!

At last, one evening, the families of the missing girls got together and followed Erzsébet from town up to her creepy castle-hideaway. And that was the end of the line for Draculette!

Dracula was determined to keep the Ottomans out of his country. He was also determined to keep his little kingdom free of *any* crime, free of all enemies . . . and, while he was at it, free of anyone who annoyed him for any reason.

BREAD AND BLOOD

Dracula actually was ruler of his country three separate times. He took control for the first time in 1448 but got shoved out by a rival ruler. For the next eight years he plotted ways to get his castle—and his power—back. In 1456 he succeeded, and for the next six years, he went on one of the bloodiest and cruelest rampages imaginable. Ahhh, sweet revenge!

Word spread quickly through Europe about the cruelty of the cold-hearted prince and his evil deeds. By 1463 stories about him were in print all over Germany, with titles like *The Frightening and Truly Extraordinary Story of a Wicked Blood-Drinking Tyrant Called Prince Dracula*—complete with pictures showing the nasty tortures he came up with. And what did Dracula like to do best? Well for starters, folks said he dipped his bread in human blood.

I vant to go to Hollywood. Dracula movies have been some of the scariest horror flicks around.

I'll have a stake, medium rare. *Dining with the dying was a favorite Vlad meal plan.*

A PLEASANT, THEN UNPLEASANT, PEASANT PARTY

Dracula had some pretty weird ideas about how to deal with social issues such as health care and poor people. One of the very first things he did when he became ruler the second time was to throw an enormous banquet. He invited the poorest peasants, beggars, and folks with dreadful diseases and handicaps to his castle for a great banquet. After serving them a hearty dinner, and way too much to drink, he asked his drunken, overstuffed guests if they had enjoyed the meal. "Oh yes!" they shouted happily. He asked if they would like to never be hungry again . . . free of worries and aches and pains . . . never to have another care in the world. Naturally they all said, "Sure!" Then he promised them their wishes would come true. He excused himself, told his soldiers to board up and chain the doors closed, and set fire to the hall— burning all his dinner guests to a crisp. Hmm, guess he kept his promise: After all, if you are dead, you can't possibly be hungry anymore, right?

On another occasion, several ambassadors from Turkey (the heart and head of the Ottoman Empire) came for a visit. They refused to remove their hats upon meeting Dracula, saying it was not their custom to go bareheaded. So Vlad calmly ordered his soldiers to have the hats *nailed* into their heads.

But Dracula's real specialty was torture and his favorite torture device was the wooden stake. He stuck long, sharpened wooden spears through so many people that he became known as Vlad the Impaler. If you can stand to think about it at all, you'll realize that dying with a stake stuck through your body is a pretty horrible way to go. It takes days for the victim to die—and it's a slow, painful death. During his terrible reign, Vlad impaled somewhere between 40,000 and 100,000 people. His idea of a swell dinner was a meal surrounded by his dying subjects, writhing in pain. He also liked to arrange them in patterns, such as from short to tall. He thought of it as his "art."

When the mood struck, for a little variety, he might decide to skin someone alive, or boil his victims, or simply hack them into little pieces. And no one was safe from him: Women and children, even teeny babies, were skewered just as often as men were.

THE STAKES WERE TOO HIGH . . .

In 1462, Dracula decided to get the Turks out of his neck of the woods. Naturally the sultan at the time, Mehmed II, did not like this idea, and he went after Drac with a vengeance. Dracula had no choice but to retreat back to his territory, but as he raced back to his castle, he burned his own villages and poisoned all the drinking water along the way. He also set up traps for the pursuing soldiers.

By the time the sultan reached Dracula's capital city he was greeted with a horrifying

"I VANT TO SUCK YOUR BLOOD..."

The very first vampire story was written by a doctor named John Polidori in 1819. He was the one who coined the term *vampire* and his book *The Vampyre* was a bestseller in the 1800s. But the actual character of Count Dracula was created by a writer named Bram Stoker in 1897. He set his story in Vlad the Impaler's neighborhood, which is sometimes called Transylvania. Stoker *was* going to call his blood-drinker Count Wampyr until he stumbled on a story about Vlad Dracula, the perfect name for a blood-sucking monster.

A FITTING END

Eventually the sultan's forces got a lucky break. Vlad's little brother, Radu, decided *he* wanted to be in power and joined the sultan's side. Radu knew the ins and outs of the land and, after a few fierce battles, managed to kick Dracula out. Dracula died fighting in 1476 and the sultan finally got a little mini-revenge for his 20,000 skewered soldiers. Dracula's dead head was stuck on a pole and displayed in the city of Constantinople. The rest of his body was buried at a monastery on an island called Snagov. But guess what? When archaeologists went to exhume the body in the 1930s, the coffin was empty. Creepy!

So there you have it. The real Dracula did not wear a cape. He did not have fangs. He did not bite necks or suck blood. But he sure liked seeing it! The real Dracula contributed gallons of blood, his scary name, and his misty Transylvanian homeland to all those scary stories of vampires. And just like those creatures of the night, who, legend tells, live forever as long as they have a neck to nick and a coffin to sleep in, it's spooky-fun to think about where Vlad the Impaler—his headless body missing from his final resting place—might actually be.

sight: 20,000 of his soldiers stuck on stakes—a forest of bodies as far as the eye could see. The sultan's surviving forces were too scared to continue—can you blame them?—and got the heck out of there as quickly as they could.

But I'm not dead yet! *Being buried alive used to happen all the time, which gave rise to the story of the undead Dracula.*

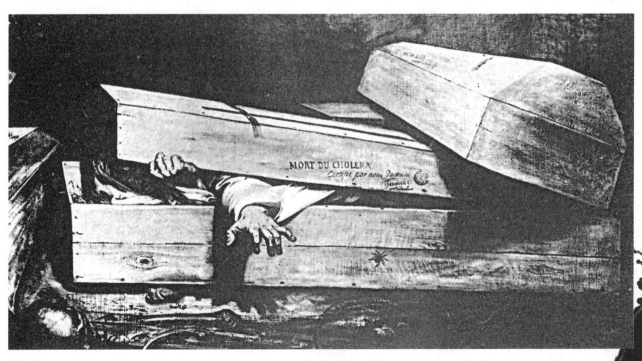

MORT DU CHOLERA

DUMB DUELS

So you're sitting in the cafeteria, eating your PB&J, minding your own business, when suddenly, you feel something wet running down your back. That clumsy kid from two tables over has just tripped and dumped a carton of liquid moo-cow all over you . . . *again!* Now you smell like baby barf. You're steamed! Too bad you didn't live 200 years ago or earlier. You could have slapped his cheek and challenged him to a duel.

MAY THE TOUGHEST GUY WIN . . .

Ever had a school bully grab you by the collar and tell you to meet him outside at three o'clock? Nowadays, you'll get into *big* trouble for fighting. But for centuries, it was considered perfectly okay to challenge someone to a fight with—choose your weapon—fists, daggers, swords, and even guns. This is how it all started.

Let's say somebody has just been clobbered to death with a big old rock and *you* have been accused of doing it. Back in Europe, up until the year 500 C.E., you would go before an altar and swear your innocence. Then your friends and family would swear you didn't do it (even if you did). Next, came the *ordeal.* A high priest would take a heated iron from the fire and sear it onto

your skin. If the burn healed quickly, that was proof that you were innocent. Or you might be asked to grab a ring from the bottom of a bowl of boiling water. If your scalded fingers healed completely? Proof of innocence! A third ordeal involved being tied up and thrown into the water. It was believed that if you were telling the truth, you would sink to the bottom. If you were lying, folks believed that the water would reject you, and you would float to the surface, whereupon you would be swiftly killed. (That one was kind of pointless, wasn't it, since either way you were a dead duck.)

TALK ABOUT THE PITS!

Fact of life. Men are usually physically stronger than women. Men and women sometimes fight. So in the Dark Ages (500–1000 C.E.), to level the playing field when a man and woman dueled (and duel they did!), the man had to stand in a waist-deep pit. He was allowed a club, but no shield. The woman got a giant sack with a five-pound stone block in it. You are probably not surprised to learn that the man often ended up as a dead blockhead.

DUELING BASICS STEP BY STEP

Here are the rules—1700s style—for dueling in Europe and America.

Walk up to someone you don't like. Slap his cheek with your gloves. He will have no choice but to challenge you to a duel.

Pick a good buddy to be your *second*—your helper for the duel.

Decide on the details of the duel. Where? When? Weapons? First blood or to the death?

Deliver a cartel (a written challenge).

Get in shape for the duel. Go to fencing school for a couple of weeks and work out with a fencing master. Not a good idea to fight a duel with a big beer gut in your way.

Meet at sunrise, on the day of the duel. Bring your second. Bring a doctor, too. You may be needing one.

Look bored. Look uninterested. Look invincible. Do not show the slightest hint of nerves. Be unbelievably polite to your opponent.

Swish your *rapier* (a popular kind of sword) around to freak the other guy out.

On your mark. Get set. *Duel!*

Draw blood. If the duel is *not* to the death, go hang out with your opponent after one of you has "drawn first blood." Dueling often brought people closer together. (If one of them wasn't dead, that is.) If the duel is to the death, pray *hard* that you are the one to win.

MIGHT MAKES RIGHT . . .

In 501 C.E. a German king named Gundebald came up with a new "Judgment of God." He decided that "might meant right." So people started fighting each other to settle their disagreements. If you lost the fight, it was believed that you were guilty and deserved to lose (and hence to die). There were no courts of law, no TV reporters to report injustice. This was the way to settle a dispute.

The rules of these "judicial duels" were simple. A time and place were set. A "ref" was appointed. The public was invited to watch, but had to be absolutely silent. If someone in the crowd spoke up or tried to interfere, he could have his right hand sliced off.

FIGHTIN' WORDS

By the year 1000, Europe was beginning to crawl out of the Dark Ages. The Catholic Church was growing increasingly powerful and since one of its biggest rules was "Thou Shalt Not Kill," a different system of justice was put into place. There were laws and public punishments. But a man's reputation was mighty important, so duels kept on happening. Some duels, over really minor matters, were fought only to "first blood," or as the poets prettily called it, "red bloom." There were also duels that were fought to the death, over matters of honor. In those days, you might not have a roof

ON SECOND THOUGHT ...

One day Frederick the Great, the king of Prussia from 1740 to 1786, had a bright idea. When two of his officers asked for permission to duel, he asked them where the duel was to take place. He then had a gallows set up at the same spot. When the officers arrived to duel, they found Frederick the Great sitting next to the gallows, smiling. They asked him what the gallows was for. Frederick answered, "The winner of this duel." The two duelists quickly said, "Never mind!" and called it quits.

over your head, or enough food to eat. But by golly, you had your family name to defend. Someone might say you were a coward or a liar and ZAP!—out came the swords.

Naturally everyone wanted to be able to protect themselves. In the fifteenth century, when swords became the weapon of choice, fencing schools opened all over Europe. Students were graded on their ability to fight to "red bloom" or to the first wet or dry blow. Dripping red blood might be a C+. A big, ugly, red welt was a grade A! Fencing school had its rules and you'd get expelled for such no-nos as arm breaks, leg breaks, groin thrusts, murder thrusts, knee thrusts, finger holds, or eye gouges. But when it came to an actual duel there were *no* rules. By the 1500s, there were no longer judges or church officials present at a duel. And no onlookers either. Folks decided that a duel was a private gig. Showing up to fight proved that you were fearless and dying was better than being thought of as a big old coward.

KINGS DO IT!

In 1550 King Henry II of France said "STOP THE MADNESS!" and outlawed dueling. He did not, however, ban tournaments and jousting (which is just a duel fought with really, really long sticks). In 1559 he was jousting with the Earl of Montgomery when the earl's lance slipped through his helmet and skewered his skull. He died ten days later. And, despite King Henry's edict, in the late sixteenth and early seventeenth centuries in France, dueling became a national craze. Thousands of noblemen died believing that honor and courage were more important than life. Silly duelers! Still, it was true that in those days if you lost your honor, your life was no picnic: you could not own land or even buy bread in some places. You could be banished or hunted down. And you could end up dead anyway.

Bucking for a fight? Don't have a sword? Antlers make dandy weapons.

ALL-AMERICAN DUELS

When the first settlers came to America from Europe in the 1600s, they brought dueling with them. Nothing had changed in the New World— a man's honor was still his most valuable possession. The first recorded duel in America took place at Plymouth Rock on June 18, 1621, when two servants decided to have a go at each other. They were only mildly injured, but both were punished—not because they had engaged in violence, but because duels were for gentlemen only, not lowly servants.

By the time of the American Revolution, dueling was still considered a very cool thing to do. Even one of the signers of the Declaration of Independence, Button Gwinnett, fought a duel to defend his honor! Alas, he did not survive. But the most famous duel in American history was fought in 1804 between Alexander Hamilton and Aaron Burr. Hamilton had been our very first Secretary of the Treasury (check him out—he's the guy on our $10 bills). Aaron Burr was the Vice President of the United States under Thomas Jefferson.

Burr and Hamilton had been political enemies for 15 years, fighting over how much power the new American government should possess. Hamilton felt that Burr could not be trusted and wrote a bunch of letters to this effect. The letters fell into the public's hands and Burr got so mad he demanded a duel. Hamilton didn't want to fight because three years earlier, his own son, Philip, had been killed in a duel because of advice dad had given to his son. When Philip had asked his father for guidance about fighting, Hamilton had told his son that a good Christian does not take another man's life. So Philip showed up at the duel but wouldn't fire his pistol (clearly, his opponent had no qualms about doing so). Now Hamilton had to make a choice. To *not* show up would make him a laughingstock. But how could *he* pull the trigger on Burr after what he had told his son?

Hamilton and Burr met on a cliff in Weehawken, New Jersey, overlooking the Hudson River. Burr's pistol fired first and found its target. Hamilton's did not. Hamilton dropped to the ground, mortally wounded, and died the next day. So who won the duel? Well, today we remember Alexander Hamilton every time we spend ten bucks. And Aaron Burr? Even though he continued on as Vice President, his political career was over. He died, flat broke and generally disliked, in 1836.

THE FINE ART OF DUELING

By the early 1800s, swords were no longer used at dueling time. Pistols made dueling easier—a lot less work than all that thrusting and parrying and waving around a heavy sword.

Dueling was now only an upper-class sport. Everyone else had figured out that it was just plain STOOOOOPID! But the rich folk believed that dueling was glamorous. Dueling was classy. A duel proved that you were a nobleman in heart and spirit. Now you could duel with someone because you disagreed with his politics. People would duel because someone stared at them for too long without blinking, or because they didn't say hello. Plenty of duels were over pointless, dumb things. Dueling was a sport. Sometimes, if folks got bored with pistols, they would duel with bizarre things like pitchforks, or on bicycles. Ah, the life of the idle rich!

DOO-DOO AT DAWN

In 1842, Abraham Lincoln wrote a series of mocking, anonymous letters to a well-known politician, James Shields. Shields found out that Lincoln was behind the letters and guess what? Yup! He challenged him to a duel! Since Shields was the challenger, Lincoln got to pick the weapon. He decided on clumps of cow manure.

Shields was furious! How dare Lincoln make fun of his challenge! So he insisted that Lincoln pick a different weapon. This time Honest Abe chose "Cavalry broad swords of the largest size," and stipulated that the duel be fought while standing in a square ten feet wide and twelve feet

DUEL PERSONALITIES

■ Andrew Jackson, the founder of the Democratic Party and our seventh President, was also a champion dueler. By the time he became the prez in 1829, he had fought in 14 duels and killed a man who had said something unkind about Mrs. Jackson.

■ At the dueling ground, the attending doctor would place his surgical instruments on the ground with the hope that the duelists would look at the bag of medical torture devices, smarten up, and call it quits. In the nineteenth century even a slight wound could be lethal. Germs were everywhere. Cleanliness was not.

■ In 1836 a surgeon had been sucked into the horror of having to fight a duel. He knew that deadly infections could be caused by even a small piece of fabric being forced into the body. His solution was to show up for the duel buck naked. His opponent flat-out refused to shoot a man in his birthday suit.

■ A very famous actress named Lola Montez received a bad review, so she decided to challenge the newspaper's editor to a duel—with pills! One pill was poisonous. The other identical-looking pill was filled with sugar. Both pills would be placed in a box. One person would die and one would live based on his or her choice. The editor declined the offer.

deep. Shields was a whole lot shorter than Lincoln, and Lincoln had hoped Shields would realize how silly the whole thing was getting, but the petite politician would not back down. So both men went ahead with their preparations for the duel until their very smart seconds managed to arrange a peaceable settlement at the last minute. No dueling doo-doo at dawn after all.

"HE DESERVED TO DIE"

The Western gunfight was just another kind of duel. When miners struck gold in California in 1849, people flocked west to get rich. For the next ten years, people poured into the territory. And practically every man who went to California during the Gold Rush went there with a gun in his belt or hip holster.

The handgun (see WACKY WARFARE on page 282 for more) was as much a part of the West as a ten-gallon hat and a pair of cowboy boots. Spinning a gun around on your index finger was a great way to prove a point. Give a bully a gun (and permission to use it), and pretty soon you end up with a lot of guys lying face down in the dirt in front of the local saloon. But in those days, as long as "the other guy drew first," it was considered perfectly okay to shoot someone. Many people of

the time felt that the varmints killed in gunfights probably "needed shooting anyway." Between 1850 and 1890, approximately 20,000 men dueled their lives away in the Wild West.

Why did the duel die? Did someone challenge *it* to a duel? As governments got stronger and better laws were made, it somehow seemed silly to stand shivering in the wet dew of dawn with a pistol in your hand. You could go to a court of law and perhaps get money by suing someone instead. Rich and alive, or broke and dead? Which do *you* think won?

Meet me in front of the saloon at high noon. *All sorts of arguments in the Wild West were settled with gunfire.*

E

ELECTRIC SHOCKS

Ever gotten dressed and gone to school only to discover that you have a stray sock and your mom's underpants clinging to the back of your shirt? Ever combed your hair only to see it stand up so straight that you look like you just saw eight ghosts? You have electricity to thank both for your bad hair and clinging laundry day.

Electricity is amazing stuff. Deadly, too. So flip a switch and find out how the first sparks flew. And along the way discover the *shocking* truth about Thomas Edison and his sneaky little secret.

WORD UP!

Electric. That's such a zippy word. So modern-sounding, too. But it comes from the ancient Greek name for hunks of fossilized tree sap: amber. The Greek word for amber is *elektron*.

I AM SHOCKED! SHOCKED!

Where, oh where would we be without electricity? Sitting in the dark, whittling sticks for entertainment, that's where! There'd be no TV. No computers. No microwave popcorn. No freak-out electrical storms. In a word, boring!

Electricity, and the tale of how it was invented, is pretty cool. Ever rub a balloon on your sleeve and then hold it over your hair? The ancient Greeks were the first folks to notice that when they rubbed a piece of *amber* (a clump of fossilized resin from conifer trees) on their togas, feathers would stick to it. Something magical was at work here, but no one knew what it was, or what to do with it. It was just a neat party trick. What the Greeks had discovered was static electricity— the stuff that sparks off your fingertips when you walk across carpeting and then shake hands with someone. The stuff that leaps off of the TV screen or the car door and zaps you when you're least expecting it. *That* stuff!

SIZZLIN' IN SOUTH AMERICA

Gold is gorgeous. Gold is rare. How to make a little of it go a long way? Between 200 B.C.E. and 600 C.E., the Moche people, who lived in what is now Peru, figured out how to make electricity by using water and naturally occurring chemicals. One of the things the Moche had in ready supply was copper, one of nature's basic elements. And when copper comes into contact with an acid, it gives off electricity. The Moche used their electricity to deposit thin coats of gorgeous, shiny gold on the surfaces of other, duller metals. The electricity made the metals permanently "stick" to each other.

"Magical" may be a good enough explanation for a lot of folks. But it's never enough for science dudes.

By 1660 a German guy named Otto von Guericke had figured out how to make a machine that made static. That machine was the first step towards that fab video gaming system of yours, and plenty of other electronic gizmos as well. In the years that followed von Guericke's discovery, scientists kept studying the sparks and trying to figure out how to capture them. In 1746, a fellow in Holland wrapped a glass jar filled with water in a sheet of metal. His jar—the Leydon Jar, named after the town he lived in— could store the energy from the static machine. But now what?

DON'T TRY THIS ONE, PLEASE!

Today everyone knows you'd have to be a total dimwit to run outside in the middle of an electrical storm holding a piece of metal in your hands. So why would one of America's smartest, cleverest men—Benjamin Franklin—head out into a storm with a metal key tied to a kite?

Franklin knew all about the Leydon Jar. In fact, he even had one. Big Ben suspected that lightning was a form of static electricity. So, as the legend goes, one evening in 1752, as a storm drew near, Franklin grabbed his kite, tied a house key to it and went for a kite-fly.

But in fact, a legend is exactly what that is. Franklin never really flew the kite in an actual storm. That would have been stupid! In fact, many folks suspect he never actually even went outside with it. He just *knew*, even before he allegedly flew his kite, that lightning was a form of electricity.

DEAD FROGS, ITALIAN-STYLE

By the 1780s, scientists were getting really juiced about all the things they were discovering about electricity. An Italian named Luigi Galvani took a damp, dead frog and applied a little electric current to it with a metal probe. The legs moved! Galvani became convinced that dead amphibians were an electrical source and that, just maybe, our souls were electric, too. Galvani was a little off, but soon folks figured out that when metal mixed with certain chemicals, it gave off electricity. Don't believe me? Check out a little thing called a battery.

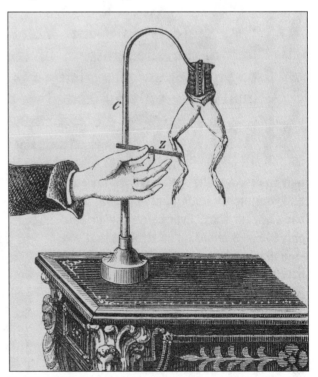

Feel like croaking? Sending an electric current through a metal probe into a dead frog's leg will make it move.

STUCK ON YOU

Figuring out static electricity was a big piece of the how-to-harness-electricity puzzle. But there was another piece to figure out, and that had to do with magnets. Turns out, electricity and magnetism were best buddies—and the reason why your mom's underpants stick to your fleece sweatshirt in the dryer.

In the 1830s in England, a fellow named Michael Faraday figured out how to make electricity jump from one wire to another by using magnets and built the first electric generator. Suddenly all kinds of regular people, not just scientists, began to realize that this sparky stuff was really useful.

Maybe you really *didn't* need a horse to pull something. Maybe an electric machine could push a cart or carriage. Electric machines didn't have to be fed. They didn't leave steaming piles of poop on the streets! And electricity wasn't just for machines. . . .

THE SHOCK DOCS

Doctors found uses for electricity, too. By 1748, Swiss doctors were experimenting with electric zaps to the muscles of their paralyzed patients. One doc reported that he had cured people by repeatedly doing this! But zapping bodies was one thing, zapping brains was another. . . .

In 1848, an explosion drove an iron rod through the cheek and out the top of the brain of Phineas Gage, a railroad worker. *Ouch!* Before this accident, Gage

WORD UP!

Ever hear talk of how many *volts* something has? Thank Alessandro Volta, an Italian sci-guy from the early 1800s for giving his name to that good cause. Drawing on Volta's discoveries, he made the first battery, except his was the size of a stack of two hundred pancakes.

And in the 1820s a French math-whiz named André Ampère figured out how to measure exactly how much electricity was flowing through a wire. He called his measurements amperes, which we now call *amps* for short.

had been a very soft-spoken, very religious man. But afterwards, when the rod was removed from his head, Gage became a real potty-mouth. *Something* had happened!

Doctors were fascinated! It seemed pretty obvious that driving a metal rod into a guy's skull could cause some pretty big changes. So docs started poking around in mentally ill people's brains to see if cutting, pushing, or prodding certain parts would end their mental illness. And one of the things they tried was zapping brain parts with electricity.

In 1938, an Italian doctor named Ugo Cerletti learned that butchers in Rome's slaughterhouses used an electric shock to the head to paralyze pigs just before killing them. He decided to try electric-shock treatments on humans. Alas, people woke up from their "shocking" experiments unable to talk or walk, or shuffling around like zombies.

These days some *psychiatrists* (docs who treat mental illnesses) believe that electrical zaps to the brain can make a super-sad person feel better. Do shock treatments really help people with severe depression? Some say yes, others say no. The debate sizzles on.

THEN A LIGHT BULB WENT OFF . . .

You probably think that until Thomas Alva Edison threw the switch on his lightbulb, the world sat around in flickering candle- or gaslight. Naturally, you would be wrong, wrong, wrong. Check this out! Thomas Edison really *didn't* invent the lightbulb. Long before Edison was born, in

1802, an English guy named Humphry Davy made an arc lamp. By 1844—three years before Edison was even born—the Place de la Concorde in Paris, France, was bathed in electric light, thanks to Jean Foucault's improvements on Davy's lamp. (That's why they call it the "City of Light.") And in 1878, ten months before Edison flipped the switch on his "invention," William Swan had made a carbon filament lamp in England. Edison's claim to fame was that his filament lasted longer.

Still, Edison really was an invention powerhouse: He thought of all kinds of new ways to use electricity, from recording music to making movies. And—a more dubious honor—without the "Wizard of Menlo Park" as he was called, we wouldn't have the electric chair.

THE FRY GUY

Back in the 1880s, criminals were put to death by hanging. But hanging was a hit-or-miss way to die. Sometimes it didn't quite work. Sometimes it took forever. So in 1886, a group of men got together to see if they could think of another way to kill people in a "nicer," less painful way.

At around the same time, Thomas Edison was trying to make himself the master of all things electrical. He had come up with a system called Direct Current (DC), which used copper wire to conduct electricity. But copper was expensive, and Edison's system had other big flaws, too. His system needed giant power stations every few miles and sometimes gave off dangerous sparks and short-circuited. And to make matters worse, Edison had business rivals. George Westinghouse was one of them.

Westinghouse had come up with a system called Alternating Current (AC). It was better than DC—with none of the dangers, and much cheaper, too.

But Thomas Edison was a great inventor, so he invented a devious plan to stop his rival in his tracks.

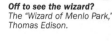

Off to see the wizard? The "Wizard of Menlo Park," Thomas Edison.

Electric Chair, Sing Sing Prison, N.Y.

The original hot seat. The spot to fry, then die.

CRISPY CRITTERS

Edison started spreading rumors. "Pssssst. AC current is dangerous! Pass it on." He got Harold P. Brown, a fellow who secretly worked for him, to rig up a 1,000-volt Westinghouse AC generator. Then Brown invited the newspapers in, hooked the generator to a piece of metal and then, one after another, connected dogs, cats and assorted other animals to the metal plate, threw the switch, and fried them to a crisp. The press went wild, and a new word was born. *Electrocution* (*ee-lek-tro-CUE-shun*): the quick and easy way to kill someone. People started talking about using electricity as a form of capital punishment, which is the official way of saying, "You're guilty, now you die." So have a seat—the electric chair was born.

Edison pushed, and pushed hard, for AC current (Westinghouse's invention) to be used for the electric chair. Look at what it had done to those poor animals! Sizzled to a crisp! But secretly, Edison's plan was this: Would *you* want to use the same electricity in your house that was used to fry folks in prison? AC was for killing. DC was for nice, bright reading lamps.

RARE OR WELL DONE?

So the folks at Edison's lab got busy. They began running public experiments on dogs, cows, and horses, torturing the poor animals with deliberately low dosages of DC current that left the poor critters howling in pain. (Too bad PETA wasn't around to stop him.) Then, to show the difference, they would send a quick zap of AC current through the poor beasts, killing them instantly . . . "proof" that AC was indeed the superior killer. Edison made sure there were always plenty of news reporters on hand to watch these

experiments. He also made sure that one of his scientists was on the government committee to decide which electrical system to use. And gosh . . . can you believe it? The committee chose Westinghouse's "killer" AC voltage to win the prize. I, for one, am *shocked!*

New Year's Day of 1889 saw the electrical execution law go into effect in America. Poor Mr. Westinghouse was horrified at this use of electricity, and refused to have anything to do with developing an electric chair. But Edison and his pals managed to find some old AC generators, and supplied them to the prison executioners. Westinghouse tried to fight the idea of "the chair," claiming that it was barbaric. But Edison's team convinced the courts and the press that it was a swift, painless way to die. For years after, being electrocuted in the chair was called being "Westinghoused." Unfair, but true!

"OLD SPARKY"

Edison's evil plan to crush Westinghouse didn't exactly work in the long run. The truth is, AC current (which we use in our homes now) is much safer than DC, and Edison knew it. But the electric chair stuck around for more than 100 years, as America's weapon of choice when it came to permanently punishing criminals. How did it work? Take one condemned convict. Strap into chair. Attach one electrode to the head, another to a leg. Send one quick round of 2,000 volts—enough to cause instant unconsciousness. Then send a longer jolt, which causes the body to heat up to 138 degrees Fahrenheit, cooking the internal organs. Sounds nice and neat, doesn't it? But after many a convict's head *caught fire* and their eyeballs popped out, even the most die-hard supporters of the chair had to agree that "Old Sparky" had its flaws.

Nowadays, 38 states still have a death penalty, but lethal injection has taken the place of the sizzlin' seat in all but one. But that's another story, just waiting round the bend in EVERYDAY EXECUTIONS!

EVERYDAY EXECUTIONS

Looking for something to do on a sunny summer Saturday? Forget the swimming hole. Pass on that softball game. Why not pack a picnic and take the whole family off to the nearest execution. What the . . . ? Yup! For almost 5,000 years, folks thought that watching someone have their head whacked off with an axe, or get hung by their neck from a swinging rope until dead, was a perfect way to pass the day. Families came to watch, with overflowing picnic hampers, old grannies, and little babies in tow. The bigger the crowd, the better. In fact, that was the whole point.

Misbehave and prepare to pay the ultimate price!

TROUBLEMAKERS, BEWARE!

From day one, people have found ways of getting into trouble. (Remember Adam and Eve and the mess they made in the Garden of Eden?) And from day one, some people have been better than others at getting into serious Big Trouble.

As long as there have been people living together in communities, there have been rules to try to keep people from becoming troublemakers; sometimes it works, sometimes it doesn't. As people became more "civilized," it became common to take the life of the lawbreaker, and to use his or her execution as an example of what happens when you have been *very, very* bad. Now, this may have made some sense when it was first thought up, but it didn't always work so well. And a whole lot of people who hadn't done anything wrong found themselves on the sharp end of an axe, at the end of a noose, or with a sharp stone stuck in their skull. Talk about unfair!

CAUGHT BETWEEN A ROCK AND A HARD PLACE

Back in biblical times, pelting someone with rocks was the preferred way to execute him. Stoning pops up in the Bible in dozens of places, and though you may think that's because back then people were a lot worse than they are today, the truth is that nowadays we'd probably all end up getting stoned to death. The rules back then were super-strict! If someone used the name of the Lord in vain? Stone 'em! Told a lie? Pile on the rocks! Picked up some firewood on the Sabbath? Yup, you got it . . . tie the guy to a post and get the whole town to throw rocks at him until he's dead. Yikes!

X MARKS THE SPOT

Back in 1000 B.C.E. the Phoenicians (who lived along the Mediterranean Sea, east of Greece) invented a new way to get rid of the enemies of their state. They made a big **X** out of wood, tied their victims to it, and left them hanging there without food and water. Death and a flock of vultures circling overhead both followed shortly.

The ancient Romans took the Phoenicians' simple cross, turned it on its side so it made a †, and developed an even crueler way to kill a person, which they called *crucifixion*. Being crucified was reserved for the lowest of the low (at least in a Roman ruler's eyes): runaway slaves, the skeeviest criminals, and—starting with Jesus of Nazareth—Christians. Always looking for a way to do things bigger and better, the Romans made the condemned person drag his own heavy wooden cross to the execution site. That doomed soul was then nailed up by the hands and feet and left to die a slow and painful death.

In the years following Jesus' death, Roman leaders were determined to squash the growing Christian faith. They thought that if they kept killing the faithful, they'd eventually extinguish the new religion. Makes sense, right? So all across the Roman Empire, Christians were hoisted up on crosses, or dropped onto beds of sharp metal spikes. They were tossed into vats of boiling oil or smeared with honey and left to be devoured by swarms of insects. But despite all this, Christianity grew stronger and more and more people joined the church. So there!

OFF WITH THEIR HEADS

When the Normans (folks from what is now a part of northern France) invaded England in 1066, they brought a little something with them: the fine art of beheading, which had been passed down to them from the Greeks and Romans. Of course, the Normans weren't the only ones with such a clever idea. Over in China, heads had been rolling for all sorts of reasons, millennia

YUCKY YORE

The Celts, who hung out in what is now the British Isles, had a unique way of executing their enemies. They followed the Druid faith—a nature-based religion that considers trees and rivers to be symbols of the great spirits. Pity the poor Celt who offended a Druid priest. If you had been accused of doing something sinful, you were tossed into a huge wooden cage built in the shape of a giant god, and locked up. Then the whole thing was set on fire as priests stood by, supervising the blazing event. These crispy-criminal offerings were somehow supposed to make the gods happy, although the priests were a little vague on the details of how that part worked.

before the Normans started chopping noggins.

You could get your head removed from your body for all sorts of odd reasons in China. For example, in 2300 B.C.E. two Chinese astrologers were beheaded for having failed to predict a solar eclipse. The Chinese executioners took great pride in their work. The best ones boasted of being able to decapitate a prisoner without spilling a single drop of blood on their royal yellow silk execution aprons.

Chopping off a head was hard work. It took a strong man with a strong stomach to do the job. The *decapitation (dee-cap-ib-TAY-shun)*—the official big word for head-cutting-off—was usually done on a raised platform so that the crowds

Chop! Chop! What to do on a boring afternoon? Go to town and watch the heads roll!

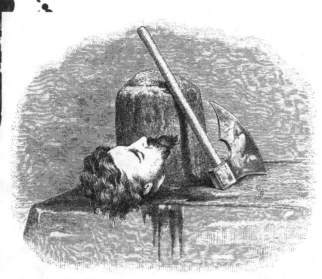

I've lost my head. Literally!

about a thousand years after Jesus was crucified, many leaders of the Catholic Church, now a wealthy and powerful force across Europe, turned just plain ugly—and brutal. And in an odd twist of history, Christians, the very people who had at one time been hunted down and killed for practicing their faith, now began killing others in God's name. Does this make any sense at all?

"Hate Thy Neighbor"

Starting in the 1200s, some leaders of the Roman Catholic Church decided that *everyone* should be a member of the Church . . . whether or not they wanted to be. "Kill them all. God will know His own." Can you believe that a pious Christian monk (and grade-A creep) named Brother Cesaire actually said that? Throughout the Middle Ages, Dominican and Franciscan monks swept across the countryside of France, Spain, and Portugal, rounding up anyone who dared to say anything bad against the Church. But, as if that wasn't bad enough, things took an even deadlier turn.

Let's say someone had a grudge against you. That person could go to an *inquisitor* (a word which means "question-asker") and rat on you, claiming that you were a *heretic (HER-it-ick)*—a non-believer. Being a non-believer in those days was a *big* no-no. Then, based on a flimsy little accusation, you would be taken away in chains, asked a bunch of questions, and tortured. And we're talking major torture here: being burned with hot coals, strapped to a rack until your joints pulled apart, or having your fingers and toes

could get a good view. The prisoner placed his or her neck on a block of wood and prayed, prayed, prayed. As if watching the head fly off wasn't a good enough lesson for the people watching, the severed head was then parboiled in salt and spices, stuck on a pole, and displayed in the town square as a reminder to always *behave!*

WHAT WAS THAT ABOUT "DOING UNTO OTHERS?"

All religions teach some form of the Golden Rule—that we should treat others as *we* would want to be treated. But, sad but true, religion has also been one of the biggest reasons for people to kill each other in the past—and to this day, is one of the biggest causes of death worldwide. For centuries, people have been slaughtered because of *what* they believed . . . or killed because they *didn't* believe in what others wanted them to. You just can't win sometimes!

So, whatever happened to "love thy neighbor," anyway? Well,

A NASTY NOTE

Know that old nursery rhyme about London Bridge? "Take the key and lock 'em up"? For a typical Brit in the mid-1600s, the words "London Bridge" meant just one thing: a vision of severed heads stuck on poles, displayed for months on end. After someone was beheaded, the head was tossed into a kettle and boiled with bay salt and cumin seed to keep the flesh from rotting and to keep birds from pecking at the flesh. The severed-heads-on-a-stick would last for months, thanks to this dandy preservation trick.

Then there was gibbeting. A gibbet was a wire cage, the size of a person. The corpse was stuffed into the cage and then hung from chains along the Main Street in town for all to see. Nothing like a rotting corpse in a cage hanging over your head to make a shopping trip memorable!

LAST DANCE

The folks who gathered to watch Mary, Queen of Scots, lose her head on a nippy February day in 1587 were terrified when her headless body began jerking around all over the platform. Turns out she had brought her little terrier, Geddon, with her. The pup had been Mary's companion during her long years in prison, and she had carried it with her, hidden under her voluminous gown, to her execution. The poor little dog, who had gotten stuck in her clenched arms, was trying to get out, and his frantic movements caused Mary's grisly last dance. Poor dead Mary had to suffer one other final embarrassment, too. When the executioner went to hold up her dead head to display to the crowd, the head slipped out of his hands, and literally bounced on the ground when it hit. He didn't realize that Mary had been wearing a wig, and that all of her own hair had fallen out. Truly a bad hair day for Mary.

crushed one by one—until you confessed to your guilt, whether you were guilty or not. You *had* to confess 'cause that was the only way to get them to stop! Then, because you had "confessed," it was off to be burned at the stake for working against the faith. Kind of a lose-lose situation.

NO NOOSE IS GOOD NOOSE

Hanging, which was reserved for common criminals, was a less glamorous way to die than being beheaded. It could take as long as one excruciating, suffocating hour for a person to expire. The Persians (who lived in what is now Iran) were the first to think of tying a rope around a guy's neck and dangling him from a tree, but the method soon spread across Europe. And, just to make sure the end of the victim's life was as unpleasant as could be, in northern Europe in the 1500s, prisoners were hanged upside down with a hungry dog or wolf snapping at their skulls—kind of like a human piñata!

Women weren't hanged because it wasn't considered proper for folks to be able to look under a woman's dress in the days before underpants were invented. Instead, they were usually burned at the stake. (Much more polite!) Of course, their clothes quickly burned off anyway, so there were still problems with the method. Considered better still was burying a

THE TORQ-MONSTER!

The most evil of all the evil Inquisitors who ever lived was a *mega*-creepy guy named Tomas de Torquemada, who lived in Spain in the 1400s. He believed that torturing thousands of people of different faiths would save them from ending up in hell. (How thoughtful of him!) Using the usual "torture until they confess" method, he tried to get people of the Jewish and Muslim faiths to give up their religions and choose his. Thousands of people were burned to death at his *auto-da-fé* (which means "act of faith"). Many more, realizing that they were already living in "hell" in the terrifying streets of Spain and Portugal, packed up their families and left the country while they still could.

woman alive, out of respect for her modesty. Up until the late 1500s, an uncovered coffin with metal bars imprisoning the victim was lowered into the ground and dirt was thrown in until the poor victim suffocated.

THREE TIMES THE FUN

Oh, how the English loved their execution days! The spot to go if you wanted to see a convict swinging was a place called Tyburn Tree. But one tree was simply not enough for all the criminals packed away in jail, so in time, three posts were raised, linked by a beam that could hold 24 necks at a time. Hanging Days at Tyburn Tree were a big social event in London in the 1600s to 1700s. Huge crowds came out to watch the day's criminals go for a final swing.

SLICE AND DICE

We think of the guillotine as a French invention, but Monsieur Guillotine was certainly not the first to devise a human head–chopping block. Over in Italy, the neat and tidy Italians had invented a machine for cutting heads off by the 1200s. After all, why get your hands dirty? And starting in 1564, Scottish criminals got a kiss on the neck from the Scottish Maiden, a giant beheading device with a falling blade that could sever a spinal column in seconds. But it was the French who perfected the slice-and-dice machine in the late 1700s, with a contraption that became known as the "Widow"—a device so ghoulishly gory it has its very own section, GUILLOTINES on page 108.

JUSTICE, AMERICAN STYLE

When Williamsburg, Virginia, was being restored as a kind of early American historical theme park in the 1950s, archaeologists were stunned to discover a site with literally thousands of chicken bones in it. Turns out, they had come upon the local hanging spot in the 1700s; the chicken bones had been left by hungry hanging-watchers who liked their death scenes accompanied by a feast of spicy wings.

The first poor soul to meet his death on Williamsburg's gallows—the wooden frame that holds a hanging noose—was a guy named Daniel Frank, who was put to death in 1622 for stealing. And for the next 200 years, hanging was the all-American way to be executed. But America did not want to be left out of the execution-invention business, so in 1889, we gave the world the electric chair (you can read all about this shocking creation in ELECTRIC SHOCKS on page 71).

PONDERING THE DEATH PENALTY

Should really evil criminals be killed? That's a hot topic everywhere. Sadly, plenty of innocent people have been killed by mistake. Some of the people sentenced to die had serious mental deficiencies and couldn't even understand what they had done and why they were being punished. When it comes to executions, no one wants to say, "Whoops, I goofed. It wasn't you!" And so the debate about the death penalty rages on. Still, it's nice to know we've come a long way from the days when weekends were made for beheadings. At least we don't have to walk past a half dozen heads on stakes when we go to the store. And thank goodness it's against the law to string people up from the nearest tree branch, just because we don't like them. Yup—we've learned a lot of important lessons from a *very* ugly past. But let's face it, we've still got a long way to go.

F

FARFETCHED FASHIONS

Can you imagine how bizarre it would be if everyone went to school in their birthday suits? Picture the principal wagging a finger in some spitballer's face with nary a stitch on. How about the bus drivers bouncing down the road in the buff? Or the lunch ladies ladling out chili, wearing hairnets and nothing else? All I can do is shudder and say, "Thank goodness someone invented clothes!"

THE FAST AND THE FUR-IOUS

Back in the Stone Age, it was pretty darn chilly outside. From 100,000 to 10,000 B.C.E., a lot of the planet was covered with ice. Walking around in a blizzard in the buff is a dumb idea, and our Neanderthal and Cro-Magnon ancestors knew it. They looked at the shaggy bears and woolly mammoths and decided that a fur coat was just the thing to take the sting out of the bitter cold. So they sharpened some rocks and learned how to slice the fur off the animals that they had just hunted for food. Clever!

Now they were warmer, but the skins always got stiff as a board as they dried up. And who wants to walk around wearing wooden shorts? After a while, folks discovered that chewing on the animal skin softened it. So after skinning an

DIRTY DRESSING

Of course, it wasn't cold everywhere on the planet, but even in warmer climates, people had other reasons to cover up. In some places, folks slopped handfuls of mud all over them to protect their skin from the burning sun, or to keep beastly bugs from biting them. But just plain mud was awfully dull, so artsy types began drawing swirly patterns onto their muddy bodies. And over in parts of Oceania (the islands of Polynesia), clothing grew on trees: People there stripped the bark off tree trunks and tied the pieces together to make outfits.

animal, they would spend the next couple of weeks sucking and slurping on the bloody hides until their saliva broke down the enzymes in the skins.

In the beginning, men and women wore the same thing: basically ponchos made of one piece of fabric, with a hole for a head to fit through. In time, they learned to lace two pieces of fur together to make a *tunic* (basically a big T-shirt). It sure made deciding what to wear in the morning a snap.

By 10,000 B.C.E., after being stabbed by sharp pieces of animal over and over and over, folks began to figure out how to make sewing needles from mammoth bones and tusks, or bird and fish bones. Then, using thread made from animal tendons (the strong, stretchy parts of a body that hold muscle to bone), they began to sew bits and pieces of fur and critter-skin together.

FEELING HOT, HOT, HOT

The world's first great civilizations popped up in places where the weather was nice. With a pleasant climate and rich soil, folks could stay in one place and grow their food instead of always having to (pant . . . pant . . . pant) run after it. Soon, they figured out how to make fibers—things like linen and flax—from the plants they grew. They started raising animals and learned how to give their sheep, goats, and llamas buzz cuts, and then spin the wool into yarn. Then they watched how spiders make webs, and figured out how to weave yarn into cloth.

Over the next 6,000 years, people would wear all

WORD UP!

Dirty diapers . . . such nasty things! But around 1100 C.E. in Byzantium, a new kind of white silk was produced. It was so snowy white that they named the stuff *diaper* from the Greek word *diapros*, which means "pure white." Soon all white cloth was called diaper. But, if you've ever been on the wrong end of a baby poop, you know that diapers may start out as pure white, but they sure don't end up that way.

sorts of ridiculous-looking, incredibly uncomfortable things. Here are some of the funkiest moments and weirdest fashions of all time.

BOILED WORM SHIRTS

One of ancient China's neatest finds happened by accident, or so the story goes.

Around 2600 B.C.E. an empress named Xilingshi (*Zhee-ling-she*) was sipping a cup of steaming tea in the shade of a mulberry tree. Suddenly, a silkworm cocoon dropped from a leaf and plopped into her hot water. Within seconds . . . POOF! Shimmery strands were floating in her cup. She pulled the glop out to discover a long, shiny strand—almost 800 yards (that's the length of eight football fields), all from that one single cocoon. The empress had her master weaver quickly weave the giant thread into some cloth—and *wow!* So amazingly soft and . . . well . . . silky! Silk had been discovered! The Chinese loved silk. They made enormous robes with huge sleeves from it, and then embroidered the robes with gorgeous colorful designs.

ONE, TWO, BUTTON MY . . . SLEEVE

Some clothes kept people warm; others kept them cool. They also protected them when they went off to fight. But clothing didn't stay purely practical for long.

Fast-forward to the year 1200 and an important clothing innovation.

After 800 years of Dark Ages designs—

A FUNKY FACT

Silkworm moths will only eat mulberry leaves. They spin their cocoons from a single thread—a thread that can be up to half a mile long! But the poor little critters! After all that hard work, their fate is to end up boiled and made into a necktie. It takes about 112 silkworm cocoons to make a man's tie—a cool factoid to dazzle dads or granddads with next Father's Day. If you feel sorry for those poor, dead silkworms, choose raw silk instead. It's made from used cocoons after the moth has emerged.

Smooth and light as a feather. You can carry a mile of silk on your head without breaking a sweat.

dirty, putrid, lice-ridden clothes—things started to get a little better for Europe's wealthy. Buttons started to appear on clothing. Francis I, a French king in the 1500s, had one suit with 13,600 totally useless gold buttons sewn to it. Some historians say buttons were first sewn on sleeves to discourage people from wiping their runny noses on their arms. Another fun thing to sew onto clothes were bells. Men and women tinkled (no . . . not *that* kind of tinkle, you silly thing) whenever they moved.

FASHION GOD

One of the weirdest fashion no-no's of all during the Middle Ages had to do with ears. The Catholic Church pretty much ruled all over Europe, and it decided that women's ears were way too sexy and needed to be covered at all times. Funky looking hats with big chin straps to keep ears concealed became a must-have. The wealthier you were, the wider the chin strap.

Folks in the Middle Ages were super-religious. They believed that God wanted them to be miserable and uncomfortable on Earth to earn eternal happiness in heaven. So instead of an undershirt, many pious folks wore *hair shirts*—very painful reminders to always think about God. These were made of horsehair, which is very stiff and prickly. (Kind of like wearing a cactus.) Hair shirts were also breeding grounds for fleas, who lived between the hair shirt and human skin—biting for blood.

YOU CUT-UP, YOU!

One of the wildest styles of the Middle Ages was a passion for slashes. Coats, pants . . . even shoes had cut marks in them, to show off the layers underneath. It started as a sign of toughness—an "I survived a knife fight . . . that's how brave I am" kind of look. But soon, even the most chicken-hearted fellows wore slashed styles.

And in the 1500s in Europe, no well-dressed person of either sex left home without a big ruff. It was a style imported from India, where men wore stiff collars to protect their silk clothes from the oils in their hair. But in Europe collars soon grew to the size of wagon wheels—so big that spoons had to be made with really long handles in order to reach a person's mouth.

Ruff-stuff. Collars, called ruffs, reached epic sizes.

THE 6,000-YEAR-OLD CLOSET

Ancient Egypt: Life was good—and the afterlife was even better. Egyptians liked showing off their bodies and wore light wraps of fine sheer fabric. They learned how to make linen from the flax plants that grew along the Nile River, and then made tons of the stuff to wrap the bodies of their dearly beloved dead—their mummies.

Ancient Greece: Toga party! Togas were white, woolen robed garments usually worn over clothes by important men for ceremonial purposes. Women wore *chitons* (close-fitting, floor-length T-shirt–style dresses).

Mesopotamia: What do you wear when all you want to do is fight? The very first armor is made from small, thick leather squares linked together. When the Persians galloped over in 450 B.C.E., they brought something new and comfy with them: PANTS! After all, who wants to bounce around on a horse without protection for those delicate private parts?

Roman Empire: More togas, but only the rich were allowed to wear them. And the richer you were, the more material you merited.

The Dark Ages: If you were lucky, you had one smelly, scratchy woolen tunic that you wore every day. Barbarian men always looked like something the cat dragged in—their long, dirty hair tied into scraggly ponytails, their droopy moustaches littered with chunks of food and dirt. Women didn't look much better. But the Barbarians, who lived where it could get mighty cold in the winter, had something totally cool that folks to the south had never seen before—WOOL SOCKS!

The Middle Ages: Pssst. Wanna buy some silk? News of this closely guarded Chinese secret gets out. By the 1200s, Middle Eastern traders, traveling on what came to be known as the Silk Road, were bringing the amazing fabric along with another wonder—cotton—to the royal courts of Europe. At last—clothing that didn't feel like wearing a box of thumb tacks!

BIGGER. WIDER. MORE UNCOMFORTABLE!

Come the Renaissance, folks were pulling their heads out of the Middle Ages' clouds of superstition. They wanted to learn about the world. Oh . . . and they LOVED clothes—the wilder, the better.

Imagine a six-pound pillow made from rags, horsehair, cotton, and bran (BRAN? . . . The cereal stuff? . . . Yup!). Guys began stuffing their jackets with this concoction, which was called *bombast*—it made them all kind of look like Santa Claus, with really skinny legs. Only problem was, if you got into a knife fight (which they were *always* doing back then), your bombast leaked cereal! Beneath your bombast-stuffed jacket, you wore breeches that looked like two jack-o'-lanterns. Belts were cinched super-tight, to keep your pumpkin breeches up and your bombast from slipping out.

Women had their own ridiculous fashion trend. It all began when a powerful queen tried to hide the fact that she was expecting a baby (her husband was a bedridden invalid and definitely *not* the father). The queen decreed that the new fashion was a giant fabric-covered birdcage. Soon women everywhere decided that they, too, wanted to have hippo-hips. This new style, the *farthingale* (*FAR-thing-ail*), made women a good two feet wider.

THE PETITE KING

By the middle of the 1600s, France had a new ruler, Louis XIV. He called himself the Sun King, but he really should have been called Louis the Short because he was a really little guy. Kings were supposed to be big, powerful men. So Louis started wearing towering wigs and really high heels. And he made clothes a big deal in his court: He figured if his court was busy worrying about what to wear, they wouldn't have time to plot to overthrow him.

Now there were no more ruffs, bombasts, or farthingales (thank goodness). Instead, everything was decorated to within an inch of its life. Men and women wore yards and yards of ribbons and bows. Everything was dripping with lace. And wigs, an ancient Egyptian style, made a comeback (read more about them in HEINOUS HAIR on page 110).

TALKIN' 'BOUT A REVOLUTION

By the mid 1700s, King Louis's lacy, ribbony style was in full tilt. At the same time women decided it would be cool to look like a walking sofa, so *panniers,* bulky frames which stuck out 'neath a skirt from the hip to ankle (for more information, see UGH! UNDERWEAR on page 272), were invented. As you can well imagine, fitting through the average door was impossible. And forget about sitting.

WORD UP!

Ever tell a lie? Oh c'mon . . . not even a teeny fib? You and I both know *that* is a *falsehood*—a fancy word for a lie.

Back in the Middle Ages, folks wore cloaks with hoods in lots of different styles, from pointy to double-pointy to a hood that looked like a grocery bag stuck on a head. Different professions had their own hood styles. Doctors wore a different type of hood than lawyers; city officials had different hoods than priests. But sometimes, sneaky criminal types snuck around pretending to be someone they were not—wearing a false hood. Telling a lie came to be known as a falsehood.

Over in England, there were the oh-so-silly Macaronis— young Englishmen who dressed in the most ridiculous styles imaginable. One of their favorite "looks" was huge mounds of pouffy hair, topped with teeny tiny hats. (They're the ones who stuck feathers in their caps in the song "Yankee Doodle Dandy.")

But revolution was in the air. The days of kings and queens doing whatever they felt like, and spending buckets of money while the people starved, were coming to an end. In 1776, America said bye-bye to Britain, and the French Revolution began in 1789, with royal heads beginning to roll in 1793. Now no one wanted to look like a king or queen anymore. It turned out that fancy clothes really were "to die for."

LOOPY HOOPS

In the early 1800s, clothing went plain jane. No silk, no velvet, no frills, no wigs, no plumage—just plain muslins and woolens. Men discovered wide, floppy long trousers. Women looked like women,

Well, hoop-dee-doo. *This woman is going to need a lot of help to get dressed.*

not furniture. Are you seeing a pattern here? Plain. Fancy. Plain. Fancy. Weird. Normal. Weird. Normal.

And the pattern continued: By the mid-1800s, weirdly shaped women were back in style and this time the *crinoline* was the culprit. These giant hoops made skirts stick out so far, that the average woman looked like a circus tent. Women wearing crinolines on buses had to pay more because they took up so much room! And forget giving Mom a hug—you couldn't get anywhere near her! By the end of the 1800s, women were wearing so many extra petticoats and hoops and bustles (wire frames that made their booties stick out extra-far) that their clothing could weigh 30 pounds!

There *was* one comfy moment in the 1800s, and it had to do with a new sport—bicycle riding. How the heck do you ride a bike in a hoop skirt? In the 1850s a woman named Amanda Bloomer shocked everyone when she went out for a ride wearing extremely baggy pants. The newspapers named the baggy pants after her, and pretty soon *bloomers* were all the rage with biking ladies.

LONG. SHORT. TIGHT. LOOSE. MAKE UP YOUR MIND!!!

In the 1900s, two big world wars—the biggest and bloodiest in history—changed everything, including the way we dress. The steel from all those silly hoops and bustles got collected and turned into two battleships during World War I. And with men gone, fighting overseas during World War II, women went to work in factories. You couldn't build an airplane wearing high heels and pouffy dresses,

Ever tried to ride a bike in a dress? Don't! That's why these baggy shorts, called bloomers, were invented.

so gals pulled on pants. And once you've been really comfortable, it's hard to go back to being pinched, poked, and suffocated.

FROM ROCKS TO ROCK STARS

You probably own something that was first invented in the mid-1800s: blue jeans! When news of a big gold strike was made in California, Levi Strauss, a 20-year-old immigrant, headed west to sell canvas for tents and covered wagons. One day, a miner came up to him and said that what he *really* needed was pants—pants with lots of pockets.

Strauss sewed up some of his canvas into a couple of pairs of pants. He called them waist overalls. All the miners liked the pants, but the canvas made their thighs chafe. So, Strauss decided to try another fabric: a twilled, dark blue cotton called Serge de Nimes, that got shortened to *denim*.

Meanwhile, over in Nevada, a hard-drinking miner named Alkali Ike kept complaining to the local tailor, Jacob Davis, that his pockets were always pulling off from the weight of the rocks stuffed in them. Davis got tired of Ike's complaints and finally riveted the pockets on with copper wire. Ike loved them, so Davis wrote to Strauss and suggested they apply for a patent (see IDIOTIC INVENTIONS on page 127 for the scoop on those) together—his rivets and Levi's pants. On May 20, 1873, the two men got their patent, and the most popular pants in the history of the world were born. Why are they called jeans? A popular brand of denim was made in Genoa, Italy—*gen* for short. And that sounds a whole lot cooler than waist overalls.

FREAKY FLYERS

Go ahead. Flap your arms up and down as hard as you can for as long as you can. Did you fly? Didn't think so! But for thousands of years, quite a few people believed that if they strapped wing-like things onto their arms they would be able to soar like a bird. Instead, all they did was prove that they were total birdbrains!

It's been a long ride from our first attempts to fly to our zippy trips to the moon. So buckle up for a flight through the story of flying. It's gonna be a bumpy ride!

I'M MELTING!

Almost every ancient culture has legends and tales of people who tried to fly. And who wouldn't want to? With wings you could fly up to the heavens. You could zip up to the places where the gods lived and join them for tea. Only problem was, it was really hard to do!

As you read the legends of those ancient flyers, all sorts of interesting flying ideas pop up. There was the Chinese emperor Shun in 2200 B.C.E., who jumped from a burning tower and was able to float over his realm because he was wearing two huge straw hats (the first parachute). There was the African warrior Kibaga, who soared through the clouds dropping sharp rocks on his enemies' heads (the first bomber pilot).

But the most famous early flying legend comes from ancient Greece. Daedalus was a super-genius—an engineer and inventor who could build almost anything. He decided to make a flying machine. He was living on an island off Greece called Crete, which has high cliffs that plunge into the sea. He started hanging around the cliffs, watching the gulls that soared and glided on the strong winds that blew there.

Daedalus tried all sorts of materials for wings. Sail canvas was too heavy. Silk was too light. One day, while watching some eagles flying at the cliffs, he had a brilliant idea. *Feathers!* Daedalus and his son, Icarus, went on an eagle-hunting spree and killed enough birds to make huge feathered wings held together with beeswax.

They were about to do some more experiments when enemy soldiers came galloping in to take Daedalus prisoner. There was no time for experiments, so Daedalus and Icarus strapped on the untested wings. Dad said, "Stay somewhere at a middle altitude. Don't go too low or the sea will wet the wings. Don't go too high or the sun will melt the wax." Naturally Icarus didn't listen to his father, and in the ultimate case of being grounded—permanently—he ended up flying too close to the sun. His wings melted, and this fearless flyer plunged into the sea and drowned.

FLYING BEEF

Here's an interesting idea for a flying machine: Take a chair and attach four poles to it, then stick big hunks of meat on the top ends of the poles. Chain four hungry eagles to the bottoms of the poles. Those famished birds will try to fly up to the meat, flapping their wings like crazy—and up you'll go. A 3,000-year-old story from ancient Persia describes this weird flying gizmo. Alas, the passenger, King Kai Kawus, flew away in this bizarre bird-restaurant, then ended up plunging to his death when the eagles got sick and tired of flapping.

FLYING MONKS

There was something about flying that was just so cool, people couldn't resist trying. One group of hopeful flyers was called the tower jumpers. You know. Strap on some wing-like things, find a cliff or a church steeple, and leap. Most of them ended up flying into the afterlife. But around 1010, a monk named Eilmer of Malmesbury actually managed to glide about 250 yards before hitting the dirt and breaking both legs. The story of Eilmer's flight kept the dream alive.

In 1260, another monk (monks were just about the *only* people who knew how to read or write in those days) learned about Eilmer's leap. The monk's name was Roger Bacon and he was a great thinker. His motto was basically, "If I can think of it, I can do it." He had two ideas about flight. One was for an *ornithopter*. Picture an airplane with wings that flap up and down and you'll get the idea behind this funky flying machine. Bacon's other idea was for a giant globe filled with "ethereal air," stuff like helium. Five hundred years would pass before that dream came true.

WHEN SHEEP FLY

Ever tossed a piece of paper into a fire and seen bits of it go floating up? In the mid-1770s, two brothers, Joseph Michel and Jacques-Étienne Montgolfier, were working in their dad's paper factory in France. There was a huge chimney in the factory and every so often they'd see bits of paper go spiraling up the flue. One day, so the story goes, an opened paper bag filled with the hot air, went up the flue and kept on flying. The brothers thought this was "trés cool," so they began experimenting, filling silk bags with heated air and watching the bags fly. The bags got bigger and bigger until June 1783, when the Montgolfiers gave their

LEAPIN' LEONARDO

If you had to make a list of the most amazing people that ever lived, Leonardo da Vinci (1452–1519) would be at the top. He was a brilliant painter, but he was also a great architect, engineer, inventor, and scientist. He, too, was obsessed with flying and made hundreds of drawings of birds' wings. But his most amazing idea was a prototype helicopter. He built a small model of his helicopter but wrote in his notes that until there was a power source that was a lot lighter than a person, it would just have to wait to fly.

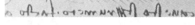

Leonardo was a whiz at whirling.

BLOW-UP BLIMPS

Nowadays, no major sporting event occurs without a giant blimp floating overhead. But not so long ago, people used to travel across the ocean in those lighter-than-air flying machines. Balloons could take people aloft, but it took the work of Henri Giffard to give people the ability to decide exactly where they were going. Giffard's first successful airship or *dirigible* (from the French word "to steer") flight, in 1852, was powered by a cigar-shaped balloon filled with hydrogen. It used a steam engine with a propeller and rudders just like a boat's to steer. By 1884, the *LaFrance* airship could be steered in any direction regardless of the wind. And Count Ferdinand von Zeppelin of Germany gave us rigid dirigibles that were used during World War I to drop bombs.

The *Hindenburg* was the world's biggest and fanciest zeppelin—a super-luxury floating hotel that was the largest thing to ever fly. It was bigger than seven football fields in length! But on May 6, 1937, while coming in for a landing in New Jersey, it caught fire and exploded. Because its arrival had been so eagerly anticipated, a radio announcer was broadcasting and hundreds of folks had gathered to watch it land. In a matter of seconds, the entire zeppelin was devoured by flames as stunned onlookers watched in horror. Thirty-six people died and that day marked the end of the zeppelin as a way to get from here to there.

But blimps never really went away. The Goodyear tire company has been making blimps for more than 80 years. During World War II those blimps were used for aerial surveillance, and helped save lots of lives. And nowadays the Super Bowl or World Series wouldn't be complete without those giant floating markers high above the screaming fans.

first public demo of a model hot-air balloon. The big balloon was made of linen, lined with paper, and coated with alum (think liquid aluminum foil) to keep it from bursting into flames. This whole thing was made of panels held together with about 2,000 buttons. And it worked!

In September, it was time for a manned flight—or in this case, an "animaled" flight. Another Montgolfier balloon was sent aloft holding a sheep, a duck, and a member of the poultry family. The critters lived, proving that you would not die instantly if you left the ground, although, upon landing, the chicken *did* look flustered because the sheep had sat on it.

The brothers did get one thing wrong, however. They thought it was the smoke from the wool and straw fires they were building that made their balloons fly, not the hot air. But it wasn't long before people figured this out and got on the balloon bandwagon. And within 11 years of that first animal flight, balloons were being used to fight wars. We were on our way to flyin' high.

Barf Bag

OH, YIKES!

GLIDE RIDE

Fast-forward to the year 1796. George Cayley (1773–1857), a math and science whiz, was beginning to chip away at the barriers to human flight. He started building model gliders that actually flew. He experimented with all sorts of different things, such as a wing with camber (a curved surface) and a tail that would keep the glider stable. In 1849, Cayley built a large glider, and in need of a live volunteer to go up in it, sent a 10-year-old boy. Four years later, with an even bigger machine to test, he ordered his coachman to hop on board, but after *his* first flight, the rattled coachman said he'd been hired to drive, not fly, and refused to ever fly again.

Throughout the 1800s, dozens of folks developed all sorts of wild flyers. There was the Mechanical Bird, the Aerial Steamer, and the Artificial Albatross. There were bags of gas attached to bicycles that pushed propellers. There were planes that looked like giant bats and ones with wings the length of the entire plane. Some of the contraptions actually got off the ground, but only by hopping. And hopping and bouncing are not flying.

Almost 100 years after Cayley's soaring gliders, a German engineer, Otto Lilienthal (*LIL-ee-in-thal*),

took another stab at the glider idea and ended up performing more than 2,500 test flights. Without Lilienthal's work, the Wright brothers would have been the Wrong brothers. Lilienthal figured out how to steer a plane while it was aloft. He built himself a 45-foot-high launch pad and kept experimenting, then wrote a book about it, *Bird Flight as the Basis of Aviation,* which Orville and Wilbur Wright read fanatically. But sadly, Lilienthal did not glide so well one day in 1896. A sudden strong wind flipped him into the ground and that was the end of Otto.

IT'S ALL WRIGHT

On a windy December day in 1903, after centuries and centuries of trying, human beings finally flew under their own power. You've probably heard a little about Orville and Wilbur Wright—two brothers who *very slowly and carefully* set out to build a proper airplane. They read everything they could find about flying, and tested kites and balloons. They studied the wind. They built gliders. They made a wind tunnel to test wing shapes, and finally designed a glider that flew beautifully. Then,

Wright on! *Orville and Wilbur Wright built the first successful airplane.*

FOUR FAB FLYERS

1. Amelia Earhart (1897–1937) was an *aviatrix*—a

female pilot. She had always been a tomboy, the kind of girl who hunted rats with a rifle for fun. After a barnstormer dive-bombed a plane right at her, she knew flying was for her. Earhart was fearless. During her all-too-brief flying career, she broke all sorts of speed, altitude, and distance records. But she still believed a lady should look like a lady, so she always flew in dresses or neat little suits. She and her copilot, Ted Noonan, were flying around the world when her plane vanished in the Pacific. The search was one of the biggest in history, but Earhart was never found.

2. Eddie Rickenbacker (1890–1973) was a mother's

nightmare—a grade-school dropout, daredevil driver, and World War I flying ace. Eddie shot down 22 airplanes, four observation balloons, and earned every decoration possible, including the Medal of Honor, which he got for taking on seven German planes by himself in 1918. In 1942, during World War II, Eddie was flying over to the Pacific to inspect air bases when his plane crashed at sea. He and seven others bobbed around in a lifeboat for 23 days. A story from the time said that at one point, a seagull landed on Eddie's head. Without moving his head, he reached up and grabbed the gull by the legs. That night the men dined on raw seagull—a nice change from weeks of raw fish and rainwater. He said "Courage is doing what you're afraid to do. There can be no courage unless you're scared." But considering he had no fear of Germany's best war pilots or snapping a live bird in two, you've got to wonder if he was ever scared.

3. Wrong Way Corrigan (1907–1995). Douglas

Corrigan was a pilot who helped build Lindbergh's *Spirit of St. Louis*. After Lindbergh's flight, Corrigan wanted to do the same thing, too—fly across the ocean. Since he was Irish, he decided to fly from New York to Dublin, but he couldn't get permission to go. To top it all off, Corrigan lost his pilot's license.

Finally, in 1938 he got the okay to fly as long as he stayed in the U.S.A. On July 17, he filed a flight plan for New York to California, threw some candy bars into his cockpit, and snuck extra tanks of gas onto his plane. The plane was so heavy it could barely take off before it headed east into a dense fog. East? California is west! Ten hours into the flight over the Atlantic, his feet suddenly felt cold. He looked down to see gasoline leaking over his shoes, filling the cockpit. The only tool he had handy was a screwdriver, which he used to punch a hole in the aircraft floor to drain the fuel. Then he flew straight on praying he'd have enough gas to reach land. Lucky guy. He did. The first person to greet him when he landed in Ireland was an Irish policeman. Corrigan had some explaining to do! For most of the rest of his life he insisted that he had goofed. But everyone knew that Wrong Way Corrigan knew *exactly* where he was going all along!

4. Chuck Yeager (b. 1921). So what if he grew up

dirt-poor in the hills of West Virginia? Chuck Yeager had rich dreams. He joined the Air Force and quickly proved that he could fly just about anything with wings. During World War II, Yeager was a fearless ace. He had 20/10 eyesight and said he could "see forever." He was fearless! After the war he ended up as a test pilot, flying higher and faster than anyone else. In October of 1947, Yeager became the first person to try to fly faster than the speed of sound in the rocket-powered Bell X-1—zipping along at more than 700 mph. The newspapers said it was the greatest aviation achievement since the Wright Brothers' flight. For the next few years, Chuck was the guy every airplane designer wanted testing his plane. He was cool in crisis, and even if he was plummeting to the ground, always managed to figure out what to do to save the day. By 1953, he was flying at 1,650 miles per hour. And by the time America was ready to start sending people into outer space, Chuck was a role model for every astronaut to blast off into space.

as a final step, they built and mounted a 12-horsepower engine to power the whole thing.

The Wright brothers' first attempt at propelled flight began at Big Kill Devil Hill, North Carolina, on Monday, December 14, 1903. Lucky Wilbur won the coin toss, and got to pilot the 650-pound plane. Five out-of-work-for-the-winter lifeguards dragged the plane a quarter of a mile up a hill along a 60-foot monorail. Wilbur hopped in and Orville gave the plane a wee push. Orville was supposed to run alongside it, holding up a wing to keep the whole thing from tilting to one side, but he couldn't keep up. Then Wilbur turned the rudder too sharply and the whole thing nosed up, hit a sandy hillside, and broke into pieces.

Two days later, having patched the plane up, they tried again but the wind wasn't quite right. On the third day a brisk wind blew. They set their monorail track up on flat ground. It was Orville's turn to be the pilot this time. And this time it worked! That first flight only lasted 12 seconds and went a whopping 120 feet, but by the end of the day, the brothers had stayed aloft for almost one whole minute and flown 852 amazing feet. On that windy day, December 17, 1903, the Wright brothers discovered that they had the "Wright" stuff.

FLIGHT FACTOID

The flight controls that the Wright brothers devised to change the angle of their plane's tail and wings are still in use in the aircraft of the 21st century.

POO-POO PLANE

If you think it's cramped on a commercial airline, try squishing into a plane called *Voyager*. In 1981, two flight-obsessed brothers, Burt Rutan and Dick Rutan, and friend Jeana Yeager, decided to design and build a plane that could fly all the way around the Earth without refueling. *Voyager* was made of carbon graphite, had a 110-foot wingspan, and held a crew of two. However, pilots Dick and Jeana couldn't stand for the duration of the flight and had to trade off sitting upright; the resting pilot only had enough room to lie down.

On December 14, 1986, the plane finally took off. During that 25,000-mile-long journey, the pilots ate cold meals, slept on the floor, and went potty in plastic bags that sat there in the cockpit with them. *Voyager* landed safely, nine days, three minutes, and 45 seconds worth of poo later, and is now proudly displayed at the Smithsonian National Air and Space Museum in Washington, D.C. The plane that is. The poo has since been flushed.

TENNIS ON THE WINGS

The Wright brothers' flights opened a door—well, actually more like an airplane hangar. Within a few short years, flyers were everywhere. By 1916, at the height of World War I, planes were dropping deadly bombs across Europe. Germany's Baron Manfred von Richtofen and his flying circus became famous (or infamous, depending on what side of the war you were on) flying their bright red Fokker planes in circles and zigzags—impossible to hit because they were so small. Thankfully we had our own air aces up our sleeves. After World War I ended, all those skilled pilots needed something to do, so they began stunt-flying and wing-walking. Suddenly there were people tap dancing on moving airplanes high above the ground—or even, in one 1924 stunt, playing tennis! Pilots called barnstormers flew loop-de-loops, made death-defying nosedives, and flew upside down. Flying was the ultimate thrill ride.

Tennis, anyone? Accuracy is key to finishing the game.

A HAM SANDWICH AND A THERMOS OF COFFEE

Distance was the next great barrier. Charles "Lucky Lindy" Lindbergh became the guy who would change all that. In 1927, when he was 25 years old, he set off from Long Island, New York, in a tiny silver monoplane called *The Spirit of St. Louis*—a plane with just one set of wings, no barf bag, and zero bathrooms. His solo flight to Paris, France, lasted 33 hours and 30 minutes, and his only meal was a sandwich and a Thermos of coffee. There was no in-flight movie. When he landed in Paris, the world went nuts, and Lindbergh, who went on to become a huge hero, could finally pee.

ROCKIN' ROCKETS

Ten . . . nine . . . eight . . . The clouds of puffy smoke start billowing. Seven . . . six . . . five . . . four . . . Things are really heating up. Three . . . two . . . one . . . LIFT OFF! Rockets are so cool, so Space Age. But the truth is, they have been around for thousands of years.

The Chinese invented the kite. And they were also the first folks to stumble upon the recipe for making explosive powder. By 100 B.C.E. they had learned to use that kabooming powder to make fireworks. But their fireworks weren't picnic-in-the-park-on-a-holiday fireworks. They were used in warfare.

Could the Chinese have strapped a mess of rockets to someone's back and sent him sky high? There is a story told about Wan-Hoo, who was perhaps the world's first

astronaut. Either that or the world's first completely pulverized person. Supposedly, early in the 16th century, Wan built a chair with 47 rockets attached. Wearing his finest silk robes, Wan settled into his rocket chair as 47 servants lit the fuses and *ran!* There was a huge BANG and billows of smoke filled the air. When the dust settled, Wan-Hoo had disappeared. NASA honored this early fly-boy by naming a crater on the moon the Wan-Hoo Crater.

In 1232 Mongols used arrows with rockets on them. By the 1300s, Arabs took the Mongol rockets and made them even better—developing flame-throwers and the like. For the next 500 years, rockets kept getting bigger and better, but no one thought to use them for manned flight until the late 1880s, when Konstantin Tsiolkolvsky, a starry-eyed Russian, began drawing pictures of rockets with a crewed cockpit in the nose cone. And in the next century, his countrymen and the Americans would square off over who would be the first to send a man into space in one of those capsules.

FLYIN' HIGH

There have been all sorts of changes since those really freaky early days of flight—when dreamers flapped and flipped and frequently fell. We've come a long way—from ornithopters to spaceships that can blast a man to the moon, and I could fill three books with flying feats. But since this is a book filled with mishaps, missteps, and muddles, it's time to fly on to the next section. So return your tray tables to the upright position and stow away your personal belongings. We're coming in for a landing!

93

FRIDAY THE 13TH

Wednesday the 11th? Not scary! Saturday the 14th? Nope . . . Not even a teensy bit afraid. But mention Friday the 13th to some people and you can practically see the goosebumps grow. Why does a simple little number strike fear in people's hearts? How come most airplanes don't have a thirteenth row? Why don't apartments have a thirteenth floor? How did this and other spooky superstitions get started? The answer lies (yup . . . you guessed it . . .) in the past.

FREYA'S DAY

Friday's bad rap goes way back. Eve and Adam were booted from the Garden of Eden on a Friday. Noah's flood started on a Friday (talk about a rainy weekend!). And remember the story of the Tower of Babel? Yup—happened on a Friday. King Solomon's temple fell on a Friday and Jesus was nailed to the cross on a Friday. In ancient Rome, Friday was execution day. Clearly Friday was not a day to be messed with.

But there was another reason some places didn't like Fridays. Friday was named after the Norse goddess Freya. Freya, who is also sometimes called Frigg, was the goddess of love and having babies. During the Middle Ages, the folks who ran the Catholic Church did not want people to honor Freya by getting all smoochy. They didn't want to honor Freya at all. So they told everyone that Freya was a witch and Friday was the witch's Sabbath. Friday had became a creepy, not-very-much-fun day.

So that explains Friday, but what about the number 13?

MOON GOONS

What made 13 a target? Simple: a religious battle. As the new Christian faith gained more and more followers, their leaders started to speak out against the old pagan religions—the ones that encouraged the worship of many gods and goddesses. Many pagan religions believed the number 13 to be special. After all, there were 13 full moons in a year and the number 13 was associated with *fertility* (the ability to have lots of healthy babies).

At a time when so many infants died, being fertile was a big deal for a woman. Pagans cherished their carvings of fertility goddesses, some of which showed plump female figures holding crescent-shaped horns with 13 notches. With the rise of the one-God, guy-centered religions and the triumph of the solar calendar

WHO'S AFRAID OF THE NUMBER THIRTEEN?

Not America's founders. They were men of reason, so they decided to thumb their noses at superstition and build a nation that *loved* the number 13. For starters, we had 13 original colonies. Thirteen men signed the Declaration of Independence. We designed a flag with 13 stripes. Now grab a one-dollar bill and check out the back. There are all sorts of "13" things.

❶ 13 steps on the pyramid

❷ 13 letters in the Latin words above it *(Annuit Coeptis)*

❸ 13 letters in *E Pluribus Unum,* our nation's motto

❹ 13 stars above the eagle's head

❺ 13 bars on the eagle's shield

❻ 13 leaves on the olive branch

❼ 13 fruits

❽ 13 arrows in the eagle's talon

over the lunar one, it wasn't long before the number 13 became the odd number out.

Over in India, the number 13 was considered a little funky, too. Hindus believed that it was unlucky for 13 people to be together in any one place. The Vikings in Scandinavia also had a legend about a dinner party for 12 gods that did not end well when it was crashed by an uninvited guest—Loki, the god of mischief. And probably the worst-luck dinner ever held was the Last Supper, when Jesus sat down with his 12 disciples—a meal for 13 that ended very, *very* badly.

BAD NEWS TRAVELS FAST

So, there you have it. By the Middle Ages, Fridays were iffy. And people were superstitious about the number 13. But until the early 1900s, the notion of Friday the 13th as something scary simply didn't exist. What changed? We have newspapers, the radio, and TV to thank for pointing out all the things that can go wrong when the calendar flips open to Friday the 13th. News articles reported tales of over-crowded emergency rooms, terrible storms, and case after case of plain old bad luck. Hollywood didn't help with the story of a hockey-masked psycho named Jason Voorhees in the 1980 movie *Friday the 13th* and the nine sequels that followed.

As the myth of bad things happening on Friday the 13th spread in the media, some not-very-nice folks decided it was the perfect day for a little mayhem. One of the worst computer viruses in history was spawned on that not-so-lucky day. Nowadays, people *expect* things to go wrong.

13 FREAKY FRIDAY THE 13TH FACTS

1. The Egyptians believed that life had 12 "steps" to it. Death was Step 13. Now, the Egyptians thought that death was totally cool—just another part of life. But other civilizations missed that part of the message and simply put 13 and death together.

2. Members of the Friday 13 Club in Philadelphia break mirrors, walk under ladders, and cross the paths of as many black cats as they can on Friday the 13th.

3. In 1993, the *British Medical Journal* ran an article called "Is Friday the 13th Bad for Your Health?" The author compared car-crash statistics from Friday the 6th and Friday the 13th over a period of several years. The results? Fewer people drove on the 13th, but they had far more accidents. But other medical studies have proved that it's just an ordinary day, accident-wise.

4. The Chinese consider the number 13 lucky.

5. In Turkey, the number 13 is so hated that at one time, it was completely removed from the dictionary.

6. Some of the most evil mass murderers in history have had 13 letters in their name— guys like Jack the Ripper, Charles Manson, Theodore Bundy, and Jeffrey Dahmer. Coincidence?

7. Between 8 to 15 percent of Americans think twice about doing certain things on Friday the 13th. The Stress Management Center and Phobia Institute in Asheville, N.C., says that American businesses lose millions of dollars each year because of paraskevidekatriaphobes.

8. There is at least one Friday the 13th every year. There can be as many as three.

9. The 13th of any month is statistically more likely to be a Friday than any other day of the week. Mondays come in second.

10. At Colgate University, having triskaidekaphobia will get you a big red F. They *love* Friday the 13th

Your *un* lucky day.

HOUSTON, WE'VE GOT A PROBLEM

People of Science tend to laugh at People of Superstition. So when the folks at NASA were getting ready to send up a moon mission, they decided it would be dumb to avoid the number 13 simply because it was "unlucky." On April 11, 1970, at 2:13 P.M., *Apollo 13* lifted off toward the moon. The next day, after a routine maintenance procedure, the crew heard a loud ka-boom. Wires had shorted and the insulation in the fuel tanks had caught fire. On April 13th, oxygen tank #2 exploded, damaging another tank and blowing off a bay cover. The mission was suddenly in grave danger. It took a lot of luck and a ton of pluck to get the astronauts back. And people all over the world looked at the number 13 with a wary eye once again. After all sorts of trouble, the spacecraft safely splashed down the 17th of April. Boy—did the men of science get lucky, or what!

there, since the school was started by 13 men with 13 prayers and 13 dollars.

11. Franklin Delano Roosevelt was America's most superstitious president. He would not attend an event in which there were 13 people at the table. Sometimes FDR had his secretary join the guests to make an even 14. If he had to travel somewhere, he'd leave at 11:50 P.M. on the 12th or wait until the wee hours of the 14th.

12. Winston Churchill, prime minister of Great Britain during World War II and a pal of FDR's, also refused to travel by air or car on Friday the 13th.

13. Number 13's biggest bit of bad luck probably stems from the fact that it comes right after 12—one of the most loved numbers in the entire world. There are 12 months of the year, 12 zodiac signs, 12 tribes of Israel, 12 animal signs in the Chinese calendar, and 12 gods of Olympus. And let's not forget 12 eggs, donuts, or bagels in a dozen.

G

GHASTLY GAMES

Jump some rope. Spin a yo-yo. Play a little hopscotch. Fly a kite. Innocent kid stuff, right? Nu-uh! In the olden days this kind of fooling around would have helped launch a sailing fleet, killed a couple of animals, trained for battle, and scared the poop out of your enemy.

Hard to believe, but true. Your favorite goof-offs may look innocent, but some were once dangerous weapons.

THE GAMES OF WAR

So many of the things we play with these days got their start because people were always fighting with one another. Take kites. They're a hoot on a windy day at the beach. But the Chinese invented them around 1200 B.C.E. for a very different reason. They used them in battle as military signaling devices—a way to send secret coded messages from one group of soldiers to another.

And how about hopscotch? The name originates from the old French word *escocher,* which means to cut or scratch, since players scratched lines into the dirt which they then jumped over. Travel back almost 2,000 years, and you'd see Roman foot soldiers—in full armor and field packs—hopping up and down on giant hopscotch courts to improve their footwork. Their hopscotch courts were as long as a football field and the typical Roman soldier's pack could weigh 40 pounds. Try hopping around with that on your back.

And let's not forget jump rope—a game for burly, bearded sailors? Huh? The Phoenicians were great seamen who ruled the Mediterranean in the years 1200 to 332 B.C.E. Ships depend upon sturdy ropes for hoisting sails and tying up at port, so the Phoenicians developed really strong braided ropes. They made them by twisting great lengths of hemp over and over and over until they had very thick lines. As the rope spinners twisted, other workers brought them more hemp. The hemp-bringers spent all day jumping over long lengths of swinging ropes. Getting caught in the twirling ropes could cost a man his neck, so rope makers all were master jump-ropers.

YO! YOU WITH THE YO-YO!

What could be more innocent than a yo-yo? Right? Well, maybe at first. The ancient Chinese were the first creators of a twirling toy with two spinning discs and a string in the center. But by the 1500s in the Philippines, hunters were carving large wooden discs with razor-sharp, spiked edges. They then tied about 20 feet of strong twine to the discs and gave a mighty heave-ho. The discs spun out into the rain forests and wrapped around the innocent legs of a mammal soon to be called "dinner." The hunters named this deadly little device the *yo-yo,* which

One, two, three, wheeee. *This hopscotch move has got to hurt!*

means "come-back" in Tagalog, the local language. In the 1920s, an American named Donald Duncan saw a Philippine yo-yo take down a small critter. He thought it could make a cool toy, but since he didn't want something that could kill a kid, he made his discs a lot smaller and rounder. But he kept the awesome name.

HEY, BONE-HEAD

So the tools of war and fighting in one era became a lot of cool games in another. But how did the very first just-for-fun games get invented? Boredom and a pile of animal bones, that's how! All across the planet—from Africa, to Asia, to Europe, to the Americas—prehistoric people played bone games, especially with the knucklebones, neck bones, or ankle bones of sheep, horses, and dogs. But with the birth of religion, those bones soon took on new meaning.

Five thousand years ago, in Mesopotamia, bones were used by high priests to predict the future. They would gather their collection of bones and give them a little roll. Depending on what side the bones landed on, the priests would decide the empire's future. This manner of tossing and catching bones soon filtered down to ordinary folk. Over in ancient Egypt folks used their bones

Ready. Aim. Walk the dog. *Did European soldiers really use yo-yos in warfare? Probably not, but they were a great way to blow off steam.*

YOU'VE GOT GAME

4500 B.C.E. Have you lost your marbles? By now, kids all over the world had learned to roll little round things at one another. Some used olives. Some used nuts. Some rolled balls of mud. The ancient Egyptians were the first to make polished stone sets.

3000 B.C.E. The royal game of Ur, un-"ur"thed in what is now Iraq by a British archaeologist, is the oldest existing board game ever found. Over in Egypt at about the same time, folks play Senet, a game similar to backgammon.

2000 B.C.E. The Chinese invent paper, then shuffle up the first sets of playing cards. They also invent a diabolical board game that the Japanese call Go (which is a whole lot catchier than the Chinese name for the game, "Board Game of Surrounding One's Opponent").

1400 B.C.E. Africans are the masters of counting-games. They develop all sorts of devious and challenging variations of Mancala or Wari, depending on which part of Africa you come from. Think of it as speed adding.

700 B.C.E. Cubed dice, courtesy of those math wizards the Greeks, start letting you know how many spaces to move your game piece.

35 B.C.E. The first Backgammon games are invented in ancient Rome.

700 C.E. Folks in India learn to master a devilishly hard game called Shatranj. It's like chess with four sets of warriors, kings, and those very expendable pawns instead of today's two warring sides.

1100s The first Tic-Tac-Toe games pop up in Europe. Other in-a-row games like Nine-Man Morris follow. But games are frowned upon by that superpower, the Catholic Church.

1400s Hearts, clubs, diamonds, and spades start gracing playing cards in France after arriving from the Middle East via traders. Gin Rummy follows soon after.

1500s The game of Goose, the great-granddaddy of every kid's chase board game ever made, becomes a favorite.

1800s By the 1830s, Poker has become the new "hip" card game.

1904 The Landlord's Game—the game that Monopoly was "stolen" from—is created by a Virginia teacher, complete with "Get Out of Jail" cards.

1931 You may know it as Scrabble, but it was originally called Lexico. And you got eight points for using the X!

as "dice" for their much-loved board games. And by the year 1000, the Chinese were using *their* grungy old animal bones to make dominos, those little dotted slabs that are so much fun to set up and knock down.

PIGBALL

Long ago, there were no toy stores. And up until about 50 years ago, kids didn't even have a whole lot of time to play games. They were too busy working (read about child labor in JUNKY JOBS on page 130). But kids will be kids, so when children *did* get

a chance to relax, they rolled hoops made of thin strips of wood. They made dolls from corn husks. They played ring toss and tag. And naturally, they played ball—but "way back when," it sometimes had an icky twist.

You're living in the 1300s. You have a few spare moments and you and your buddies have decided to go play a little ball. You head out to the village square and start a game of soccer, or football, as it's called in Europe. Except in this case, the ball is a severed hog's head. So messy! And the snout makes it bounce funny, too.

Today we take our bouncy ball for granted, but until contact with the Americas in the late 1400s— and the very slow arrival of rubber from South America—

HANDS ON THE PAST: DO-IT-YOURSELF BONES!

TRY THIS!

"Knucklebones" was played with a part of the dried ankle or foot bones of sheep. These bones have four different sides: one flat, one concave, one convex, and one curvy. Point values were assigned to each side. Players took turns tossing them in the air, and catching them on the backs of their hands. Less talented players let them fall to the ground. You can make your very own set of ancient knucklebones and have a gross old time doing it! Here's how:

■ Ask your butcher or the supermarket's butcher to save some leg-of-lamb foot bones for you. You're looking for the phalanx bones—two bones that are longer than they are wide, with uniform edges about two inches in length and about as wide as a finger.

■ Get a grown-up to help you pull off the grungy bits of meat and then boil the bones in a pot of water for about a half hour.

■ Get a grown-up to help you pour some bleach into a laundry tub and place bones into it. Leave them overnight.

■ Rinse and pour hydrogen peroxide over the bones. Such foamy, fizzy fun! Keep pouring peroxide on the bones until they stop foaming.

■ If you prefer to let nature take its course, you can can skip the last three steps and put the bones in a large glass jar with a screw-on lid. Poke several holes in the lid so bugs can crawl in. Leave the jar outside for a month or two and let those flesh-eating insects do their thing! Make sure dogs and wild animals can't get at the jar or that'll be the last you see of your bones.

■ Pull out the phalanx bones. Look for the four distinct sides on each that can be landed on if they are rolled or tossed. Use a permanent marker to mark each of the four sides with one, two, three, or four dots.

■ Now take turns tossing the bones into the air and seeing how many you can catch on the back of your hand. Tally up the points for each of the four sides. High score wins.

POKER ALICE

One of the Old West's greatest poker players ever was a little cigar-puffing lady named Alice Ivers (1851–1930). Alice's hubby, Frank, loved to play the game, and Alice often sat and watched while he played. After Frank was blown to bits in an explosion, Alice took his seat at the card table and quickly began to win. Soon she began to play for a living, moving from town to town and eventually becoming a card dealer in Deadwood, South Dakota. Alice fell in love with another dealer and got married a second time, determined to quit cards and become a stay-at-home wife. But her new hubby got pneumonia and died in 1910 in the middle of a raging blizzard. Alice loaded his corpse onto a sled and drove it 48 miles through the storm to the nearest town, pawned her wedding ring to pay for his funeral, and promptly slid back into a poker game to make enough to reclaim her ring!

people made their balls from animal bladders. Kids used to blow up the bladders from dead sheep and knot them off—kind of like big meat balloons. These "balls" were a little better than the pig heads, but they still nicked easily and sprang leaks. So someone decided to encase the bladder in a leather sack, sewn from strips kind of like those brightly colored beach balls we have today. And for the next 500 years, that's what people in Europe used for balls. How'd you like to catch a cow bladder? Sure hope they got all the pee out first!

POKER-FACES

The ancient Chinese, the inventors of paper, were the first folks to play card games way back around 1000 C.E. Silk traders from the lands of the Islamic empire—which stretched from North Africa to the Middle East

to Spain—thought the cards were cool and made their own versions. Their decks had 52 cards and used fancy geometric shapes for their royalty, and their suits were swords, batons, cups, and coins.

By about 1370, the Italians and Spanish began printing cards that showed a bunch of royal-looking dudes—12 different guys, one per card, all wearing different colors. Some men sat; some rode horses. Some were in profile. Some were servants. It was kind of complicated.

When the first cards were printed in Europe in the 1400s, they were all male: a king on a throne, a knight atop his horse, and a servant, who was called a *knave*. The French took a crack at card design and gave us red hearts and diamonds, and black spades and clubs. And in the 1500s, they replaced the knight with a queen. Their cards were beautiful but a lot of really bad printing and mediocre artists copying them eventually led to the pretty weird-looking royals we have today. Those early cards only worked in one direction—not like our upside-down, downside-up cards.

The cards we play with today were designed in England with a king, queen, and jack. But what the heck is a jack? In the middle of the 1800s, someone decided to add the little initial letters and numbers to the corners of each card. Suddenly, there was a K for king, a Q for queen, and another K for knave. Very confusing. So *jack*, a slangy term for a common servant-type of guy, replaced knave.

WORD UP!

How did poker get its name? No one can agree. Some say it comes from a French card game called *poque*. Others point to a German game called *pochspiel*, which, like poker, involved bluffing. People would rap their cards on the table and say, *"Ich poche."* And yet another group thinks the game was named after a British pickpocket term that describes a sucker as a "poke." And many a "poke" has lost his shirt playing poker.

DEAD-MAN'S HAND

There are all sorts of fun things to do with a deck of cards. Gin Rummy. Whist. Bridge. Games of strategy and games of chance. These days, Texas Hold 'Em Poker is one of the hottest games around. Big guys with sunglasses and absolutely expressionless faces (called—guess what?—"poker faces") sit around a green table for hours on end, betting huge wads of cash.

Poker brings out the greed in most folks. And it has since the early 1800s when gamblers started playing the game on riverboats on the Mississippi River. But it wasn't called poker back then. It was known as the Cheating Game— the place where a deck of cards, a pile of money, steady nerves, skill, and the occasional gunfight, all met.

Betting and bluffing. Soldiers played poker to pass the time.

As folks moved out West, their cards went with them. And one of the reasons you sometimes hear people talking about the "Wild West" was because every little dusty cow town with a saloon had a poker game a-playin'. By the late 1850s poker was being played everywhere. America's Civil War (1861–1865) helped spread the game's fame as soldiers in both the North and South played endlessly to pass the time between battles. Being a gambler in the West was a respectable job—as respectable as being a doctor or lawyer back then.

Which brings us to the dead-man's hand. Poker was a game based on *bluffing* (a bluff is when you lie about what cards you have), a game in which people could easily cheat, and a game that went hand-in-hand with whiskey drinking. Naturally, a lot of fights broke out. A fellow named "Wild Bill" Hickok (1837–1876) was one of the true legends of the West. He was amazingly strong and incredibly fearless. He had been a spy for the North during the Civil War, and became a much-feared U.S. marshal. He once fought a bear almost bare-handed and won. He could shoot faster and straighter than any man alive. And he loved to play poker.

One night, in Deadwood, South Dakota (the Las Vegas of its time when it came to gambling), Wild Bill was playing cards at the Number 10 Saloon when a man named Jack McCall saw Bill and tightened his fingers around his gun. Jack believed that Wild Bill had killed his brother in a duel a few years earlier and decided to get revenge. (Dash over to DUMB DUELS, page 66, for more on this.) As Bill studied his poker hand, McCall lifted his gun, aimed at the back of Wild Bill's skull, and pulled the trigger. Wild Bill's hand—a pair of black eights and a pair of black aces (a great hand, by the way)—became forever known as a "dead-man's hand."

I'M BORED. THINK I'LL INVENT A BOARD GAME.

Board games have been around for 5,000 years. There are war strategy games and chase games, matching games and in-a-row games. Parcheesi was originally a game played in India in the 1570s that let the average guy pretend to be King Akbar the Great, luring women through his gardens into his harem.

Two of today's most popular games are Monopoly and Scrabble. Both were "created" in the early 1930s, during a

Gamesapalooza! Those 1700s dudes knew how to have a good time!

time in America called the Great Depression. During the Depression a lot of folks lost their jobs. Times were really rough. Alfred Butts was one of those folks who could not find a job. He was bored to tears. He liked doing crossword puzzles, so one day he started puttering with a make-it-yourself crossword game. For the next few years he experimented. Everyday he read the front page of *The New York Times*—a very word-packed newspaper with a lot of teeny, tiny print—and counted *every single letter,* keeping a chart of how often each letter was used. That way he would know how many letter tiles his game would need. Try making a chart of how many times each letter of the alphabet appears on just this page alone, and you'll truly understand the meaning of the word *bored.*

For ten years, Butts tried to sell his game, first called Lexico, then Criss Cross Words. Finally, Butts met a guy named James Brunot, who loved the game and gave Butts money to develop it. Together they made a few changes and came up with the name Scrabble, which means to frantically grope around. In 1948, Scrabble made its debut and after a slow start, went on to become the second-biggest-selling game ever.

What was number one? Monopoly! Another game born during the Great Depression, it has a slightly sinister story behind it. A lot of people will tell you that an out-of-work engineer from Pennsylvania named Charles Darrow invented the game, inspired by stories of banks taking away people's homes, and the general lack of money all around. But Charles Darrow had a dark secret. He stole his game from a 1904 game called The Landlord's Game, which had been created by a writer named Elizabeth Magie. The older game had a square board, 40 spaces, 22 properties, four railroads, a jail, and a "Go to Jail" space. It had a luxury tax and water and electric utilities. You got out of jail by rolling doubles or paying $50. Sound familiar?

For 30 years, people played Lizzie's game. One of the people who ended up playing it was Charles Darrow. Darrow made a few little changes, like setting the game in Atlantic City, New Jersey, and in 1934 he managed to sell the game to the Parker Brothers, who were just about the biggest game makers of the time. Today, more than 150 million copies later, I'll bet poor Lizzie Magie is rolling over in her grave!

CHECK IT OUT

Checkers may be a straightforward game, but it has a complicated history that stretches back some 5,000 years. About 3000 B.C.E. in Mesopotamia, folks began pushing little discs across a crisscrossed board. Over in ancient Egypt, a similar game, called Alquerque, was used by high priests to predict what was going to happen in battle—all the advances, captures, and retreats that were to come. One pharaoh's palace had an entire roof that was an Alquerque board! Folks in the lands of the Islamic empire called their version of the game El-Quirkat and began to play it for amusement. When Muslims invaders reached Spain in the 1200s, they brought the game with them, and it soon spread to neighboring France. The French were the first to play checkers on a chess board, which they borrowed from India's chess-like game Shatranj. But the French added a new twist called "kinging." By the 1500s, the English, who were always having rumpuses with the French, had discovered the game. They liked playing but they hated anything French, so they renamed the game Draughts. And finally, in the 1800s, we Americans figured that since the game was played on a checkered board, it might as well just be called plain old Checkers.

103

MORE WAR GAMES

World War II (1939-1945) was quite possibly the worst war the world ever saw. But we have two of our favorite playthings because of those terrible days. During the war, rubber became very scarce. How can you make Jeep tires without rubber? The government asked companies to try to invent a synthetic rubber. Over at General Electric, an engineer named James Wright mixed boric acid with silicone oil and came up with some stuff he thought did the trick. It stretched 25 percent more than rubber, bounced higher, didn't get funky if the temperature got too hot or too cold, and best of all, copied comics from the Sunday funny papers. But the army rejected the stuff. No one knew what to do with it. The company sent blobs of the goop to engineers around the world. It took a toy marketer named James Hodgson to see the real use of the nutty putty. In 1950, Hodgson bought $147 worth of the goo, packed one-ounce balls of it in empty plastic Easter eggs, and named it Silly Putty. Everyone told Hodgson it'd be a huge failure. But today, more than 300 million eggs filled with Silly Putty have been sold.

Many World War II battles were fought at sea. Big waves often made the ships' instruments get a little kerplooie. A Navy engineer named Richard James was trying to find a way to stabilize them when he accidentally knocked over a spring he was working with, which "walked" from his shelf to a pile of books, to his desk, to the floor. James showed the trick to his wife that night on a flight of stairs in his house. Betty James knew a good toy when she saw one. She convinced him it could be a huge seller. She named the toy Slinky—a Swedish word that means "stealthy"—and convinced a big New York City department store to give the toy a try. Four hundred Slinkys were sold in 90 minutes, making it an instant hit!

In an interesting twist, Slinky eventually *did* go off to war. During the Vietnam War (1954-1975), soldiers used Slinkys as radio antennas in the dense jungles by tossing them into tree branches. A Slinky even went into outer space to test the effects of zero gravity on springs.

GLADIATORS

You think televised professional wrestling, with its fake blood and staged fights, looks tough? Well those guys with necks like tree trunks wouldn't have lasted *one second* in Rome's Colosseum.

TO THE DEATH

When a couple of gladiators fought, the performance usually ended with one of them dead. So it's kind of twisted that the very first gladiator games were staged in ancient Rome in honor of someone who had just died. Back in ancient times, in some parts of the world it was common to sacrifice a few living, breathing humans (usually a slave or three or ten) when someone died. This generous gesture supposedly fed the blood of the living to the dead so they would have enough energy to make it to the next world. But when Decimus Junius Brutus's dad conked in 264 B.C.E., he took this ritual to another level and decided to hold a funeral with a little something extra—entertainment. The emperor had three pairs of his slaves fight, fight, fight 'til they were all lying in a bloody, panting heap. The mourners thought it was great fun!

As fights-to-the-death began to replace sacrifices, the slaves who would have been sacrificed breathed a little sigh of relief— at least *some* of them would have a chance to make it out alive.

From the very first, the ancient Romans got a big kick out of gladiator fights—the brawny sweating men, the shiny weapons, and especially the spurting blood. Dead bodies were an extra-added bonus. As the games' fame grew and started to spread across the huge Roman Empire, great sporting arenas cropped up, soon to be packed with cheering, screaming people—ready for a bloody good time.

BEASTLY BREAKFASTS

One of Rome's (and the world's) greatest sites is a giant round building called the Colosseum, which was built between the years 75 and 80 C.E. It was here that the best of the best went to fight and . . . die. So, what was a typical day at the Colosseum like?

The fun and games began at breakfast time with the animal vs. animal fights. Rome was a huge empire in those days and stretched far into Asia and south into Africa. Animals were collected from all over and brought to the Colosseum. Imagine a zoo where the animals aren't behind bars—bears, bulls, lions, panthers, rhinos, and elephants, all roaring, snarling, growling, and attacking one another. Sometimes animals of equal strength were pitted against one another— a lion against a tiger. A bull against a bear. Sometimes, for cruel fun, wild dogs would tear a helpless deer into bits. The Romans might pit hippos against hyenas . . . a huge slithery python against a panther . . . lions versus crocodiles. Sometimes, they even "handcuffed" one beast to

another—like the time they chained a seal to a bear.

After pairs of animals had mauled each other into bloody pulp, it was time for the first gladiators—whom the Romans called *bestiarii* or *venatores,* that is, "hunters"—to come out and face the beasts. Some *venatores* had weapons like spears or harpoons and wore protective armor. Others fought with nothing but their bare hands. By the end of the morning, there would be an enormous heap of dead animals. In fact, on the opening day of the Colosseum, 5,000 animals were killed. When the powerful Emperor Trajan came to power, 9,000 animals were killed in his honor! That's a lot of dead meat!

THE LUNCH BUNCH

By lunch hour, the tone shifted at the Colosseum. It was execution time! Criminals condemned to die were paraded out into the stadium. But before they were killed, each took a kind of demented "victory lap" around the arena, carrying a large sign that told the audience what crime they had committed. Some were murderers. Others were thieves. But the unluckiest victims were innocent Christians, sentenced to death for refusing to

YUCK! I CAN'T LOOK!

There were marble statues of Roman gods surrounding the Colosseum. At execution time, the statues' "eyes" were covered with veils so they wouldn't have to see the carnage. Of course, mere mortals like the Emperor Claudius enjoyed a hearty meal while watching the executions take place.

worship Rome's gods. Some condemned criminals would fight one another. One man's sudden death was another's victory—hence our expression "sudden death" for a contest that is settled really quickly.

Some unfortunate folks, such as rebellious slaves, were crucified. Other criminals were forced to fight each other. But the worst way to die was to face the beast of the day—usually a lion, but sometimes a rhino or panther. Some victims didn't have a fighting chance. They were tied to posts, where they waited, praying like crazy, until that rhino or lion would pick up their scent—and came lunging.

AFTERNOON DELIGHT

With a nice lunch in their bellies, the crowds were ready to return for the main event: the Battle of the Gladiators. Some of Rome's first gladiators were prisoners of war from other lands who became slaves—usually big, strong soldiers. A few were criminals. At first gladiators were looked down upon. But over time, even free men decided that being a gladiator might be cool. Dangerous? Sure! But considering that the average life expectancy back then was only about 30 years, being a gladiator seemed like a pretty glamorous "way to go."

If you decided to become a gladiator, you began by selling yourself to a *lanista* (an owner and trainer of gladiators) who got to make all sorts of life-or-death decisions for you. You had to swear to endure "the whip, the branding iron, and death by the sword." But there were also some perks to being a gladiator. You had to train for a few years before you could compete,

SMALL PARTS MAY BE A CHOKING HAZARD

So what's the best way to fight off a lion? The trick, as several clever gladiators discovered, was to wait for the beast to roar, and then quickly shove their entire arm down the lion's throat, causing it to choke and die.

On the other hand, some *venatores* would do almost anything to avoid combat with a raging beast. One *venatore* chose to end his life by taking the sponge-on-a-stick butt wiper that was kept next to every Roman toilet and shoving it down his own throat until he suffocated.

Grrrrrr-acious me! Facing a lion armed only with a knife can scare the pants off a gladiator!

and in "gladiator school" you got three square meals a day. You had access to a doctor at a time when people were swallowing pigeon poop for whatever ailed them (for more on that, pop over to MISERABLE MEDICINES on page 155). And if you won, you received money and prizes. Considering that every gladiator had a 50–50 chance of living, it seemed like a decent career choice.

ADMIT ONE
0813022
081

In time, gladiators became Rome's rock stars—their sports idols, their superheroes. Women loved them. Kids idolized them. Most men secretly wanted to be one. In fact, some women loved the gladiators a little too much. When the wife of Emperor Marcus Aurelius fell madly in love with a gladiator, the emperor ordered her gladiator killed, then forced his wife to take a bath in the poor guy's blood.

MANO A MANO

So when they finally got to square off, what were these fights like? Armed and oh-so-dangerous, the gladiators would rise up to the Colosseum floor in little elevators and get set to face off against one another.

When a gladiator was hurt, the crowd would start whooping and shouting "*Habet, hoc, habet!*" That means "He's had it!" An injured gladiator who didn't think he could fight anymore would raise his left hand with one finger pointing up. It was now up to the crowd to decide if he should be spared or finished off.

If the audience thought the gladiator had fought bravely and well, he might be spared. But if everyone voted for death, the injured man would grasp the thigh of the guy who had beaten him and the victor would slit the loser's throat. Then, two people would come out dressed in costumes. One was dressed as Charon, the ferryboat driver who took people across a great river to the land of the dead. The other man was dressed as Mercury, the god of speed, wearing a little winged hat and shoes. The Charon-guy would pound the dead gladiator's head with a hammer, and the Mercury-man would poke the corpse with a red-hot poker disguised as a wand, to make sure the loser was truly dead.

IF I COULD BE A GLADIATOR I WOULD BE A . . .

Originally gladiators fought in the style of the lands from which they came. For example, Thracians came from the Greek island of Thrace. But in time they could pick from several styles. There were pros and cons to each. Here are a few. Which do you think is YOUR style?

Retarius. Like to fish? Then this is the gladiator style for you. Wrap a skimpy *loin cloth* (a grown-up diaper, basically) around your mid-section and strap a metal shoulder protector on your left arm. You get to carry a big net, a dagger, and a trident or harpoon—very King Neptune-y.

Secutor. Feel like hiding behind a whole lot of armor? These guys were the most heavily metal-plated. They carried a man-sized shield, a sword, *and* a dagger. You get one shin guard on your left leg and a metal or leather sleeve on your right. Top it off with a rounded helmet that covered your face except for two round eye-holes. The pros? You're pretty protected. The cons? You're lugging around enough metal to feel like you're chained to the ground.

Samnite. You get to carry a man-sized shield called a *scutum.* On your left leg, you'll strap on a metal *grieve* (a lot like a steel soccer shin guard). Pull on a visored helmet with a bunch of colorful plumes and grab your *gladius*—a super-sharp little sword.

Thracian. Two thigh-high soccer shin guards for you! But you only get carry a teeny shield. Your helmet might be visored or open-faced with a wide brim and your sword has a broad curving blade that's perfect for peeking around your opponent's shield. These were the coolest of the gladiators.

GUILLOTINES

Ahhh . . . the bad old days! Days when chopping a guy's head off in front of a cheering crowd was a favorite way to execute someone. But it was sooooooo messy! Not to mention that it took a lot of brute strength to part a head from its neck. A good executioner was hard to find. If only there was a machine that could do the trick . . .

HEADS UP?

Chopping people's heads off was long considered the "best" way to execute a bad guy. But it was a lot of work and pretty grisly for all involved. So new solutions were sought. The Italians were one of the first to invent a mechanical beheader in the 1200s, and over in Scotland they had a version by the 1500s. But in the late 1700s, a Frenchman, Dr. Antoine Louis, was the mastermind who refined the Italian head-slicer, giving us that oh-so-efficient guillotine (*GEE-oh-teen*).

PRACTICE MAKES PERFECT

On April 11, 1792, the very first proper guillotine was rolled out onto a French plaza. The first victims were brought out to have the sharp razor blade dropped on them—a sheep and cow. Three days later, the guillotine was moved to a hospital/prison/old people's home and as a sort of dry run, three *cadavers* (a fancy word for dead bodies) were separated from their heads. The machine was working like a charm. But Dr. Louis was still not happy. Further testing was deemed necessary and

more corpses were produced, including a huge muscular man, and a chubster with a fat neck.

On April 25, 1792, the first real, live person, a soon-to-be-dead fellow named Nicholas-Jacques Pelletier climbed the scaffold toward the guillotine. A large crowd gathered to watch. Within seconds, his head dropped in a handy, free leather tote bag!

The guillotine worked beautifully (but alas, the leather bag was a bit leaky). Still, the crowd was sad. It had all happened too fast! "Bring me back my wooden gallows!" they chanted.

THOUSANDS OF DEAD HEADS

The guillotine got its most famous workout during the French Revolution. Inspired, in part, by America's tossing out England's crazy King George in 1776, French folks decided they too were fed up with their raving royals. (See KILLER KINGS on page 135 for more, more, more!) So in 1789 they said, "Enough already!" French royals had been growing richer and richer, the middle classes had no real say in how they were governed, and the poor were literally starving—so hungry that a rat seemed liked a Thanksgiving Day turkey to many people. After a particularly bad harvest in 1788, the government announced that it was raising taxes. That did not make the people who had to *pay* the taxes happy, especially since many of them couldn't afford to put food on their tables. When someone told Queen Marie-Antoinette that the peasants had no bread, legend has it that she said, "Then . . . let them eat cake." That famous line (which she never actually said) proved to be the last straw.

On July 14, 1789, armies of angry citizens stormed the Bastille—a big, bad jail—and released all the prisoners. Now the nobles felt helpless! In August, King Louis XVI was presented with a declaration that demanded liberty and equality for all.

Things were shaky in France for the next few years as a new revolutionary government tried to get France settled down. In September of 1793, things got really ugly. For the next nine months, France lived under a "Reign of Terror," led by a Committee of Public Safety with a guy named Robespierre at the helm.

During those months, 300,000 people were accused of all sorts of crimes, and 17,000 heads

YUCKY YORE

Folks in France went crazy for guillotines. People had guillotine tattoos; women wore guillotine earrings and pins. Kids had toy versions and many a little "executioner" used his to behead live mice.

rolled—including those of King Louis XVI and his spoiled-rotten, cake-loving wife, Marie-Antoinette.

Day after day, people died beneath the "Patriotic Razor," the "National Abbreviator," or simply the "widow maker." The daily papers were filled with "the list of winners of the Lottery of St. Guillotine." If you think that the guillotine went out with the end of the French Revolution, think again. For the next 182 years it kept busy. The last person to officially have his head removed by a guillotine died in 1977.

NOT QUITE DEAD YET?

Was the guillotine a more humane form of execution? You decide!

■ After Charlotte Corday stabbed revolutionary leader Paul Marat in his bathtub, she was sentenced to the guillotine. After her head was removed from her body, the executioner's aide picked it up by the hair and slapped it. Witnesses swear that her cheeks blushed and her mouth curved into a sneer. Paris went wild! The aide was sent to prison for his bad manners!

■ For 200 years, several French doctors devoted their careers to studying the effects of the guillotine. In 1905, Dr. Beauriex decided to run a few tests on a recently severed head. He noted that the victim had walked calmly to his death and that the chopped-off head had landed upright. When he yelled the dead man's name loudly in one ear, the dead eyes opened wide! Dr. Beauriex wrote, "I was dealing with undeniably living eyes which were looking at me. After several seconds, the eyelids closed again, slowly and evenly, and the head took on the same appearance as it had had before I called out. I called out again and, once more, without any spasm, slowly, the eyelids lifted and undeniably living eyes fixed themselves on mine . . ."

A BLADE BY ANY OTHER NAME

Dr. Joseph-Ignace Guillotin, the man whose name graces the gruesome machine, did NOT invent it. He was simply looking for a kinder, gentler way to execute a criminal and suggested that Dr. Louis's machine might do the trick. In fact, poor Dr. Guillotin was freaked out by the whole "Reign of Terror" thing and was horrified when the giant blade got HIS name. When he died in 1814, his children changed their name so as not to be associated with the death machine.

Next? Would you like a little off the neck? The guillotine was one efficient little head-slicer!

H

HELLA... HAIR

Next time you're in a crowd, check out people's hair. There sure are a lot of wacky things going on atop folks' skulls! Some folks have curls, some have hair as straight as uncooked spaghetti. Some have tresses in colors hair simply does not come in. And there's always one guy who has more hair growing out of his ears and nostrils than he does from his scalp.

From the get-go, hair has been a big deal for us humans. Some of us had lots. Some were bald as a bowling ball. For thousands of years, styling decisions were pretty much to cut it short, wear it long, or shave it off. But before long, hair found its way into all kinds of hair-raising "dos" or got covered with bizarre, stinky globs.

HAIR TODAY, GONE TOMORROW

No doubt, Neanderthal and Cro-Magnon hair was a big mess of tangles with twigs, leaves, and creepy-crawly things lurking inside. And the first combs were fingers, tugged through the snarls. But someone noticed that combed hair was kind of cool-looking.

People began tying hunks of hair to get it out of their eyes when they went hunting. Hairstyles were here to stay.

About 10,000 to 12,000 years ago, the first real combs were being carved out of wood. And it wasn't long before people realized that you could do all sorts of fun things with combed hair—braid it, curl it, style it. Hair rocked! But sometimes, no hair was even better.

Bizarro-beard. This Russian peasant had to carry his beard to keep from tripping.

THE MOST BEAUTIFUL BALDIE IN THE WORLD

It's hot in Egypt. Really hot. One of the things the ancient Egyptians did to stay cool was to shave their heads. And not only did men do this, but many women did, too. Queen Nefertiti—known as the most beautiful woman in the world—was bald as a watermelon. Still, Egyptians were very fussy when it came to the look and style of hair. The best hair was very thick, almost blue-black . . . and easily removable when it got too hot.

The solution? Wigs. Every Egyptian beauty wanted a fabulous, gorgeous, flowing wig. There were styles reserved for royalty, short curly wigs, and long wavy wigs with strands twisted into spirals. Wigs were made of real hair if you were rich. And for the money-challenged, there were wigs made of shredded palm-leaves, straw, or sheep's wool (good for those chilly desert nights).

We also have the Egyptians to thank for the perm. One day, a bored woman lounging along the banks of the Nile started wrapping her hair around sticks and slathering them in mud. When her hair dried, she had a head full of (muddy) ringlets. Turns out it wasn't the mud or the sticks that did the trick. It was the heat. Wigmakers quickly discovered that to make hair curl, all you had to do was wind it around something rod-shaped, and then boil it in water. Now, since you cannot dip a human head into a vat of 212°F water, creative folks tried to come up with some other way to heat things up. Several thousand years later the "perm" was invented.

HAIRY ARMPITS? YUCK!

The ancient Greeks hated body hair. They liked their beautiful bodies to be completely hairless. But how to get all that hair off without leaving a mess of shaving stubble? They needed a way to "melt" the hair so it fell out at the root, so they experimented with a bunch of putrid potions and came up with the first *depilatories* (*du-PILL-uh-tor-eez*)—a fancy word for hair remover. One popular recipe called for ivy gum extract, the fat of an ass, bat's blood, she-goat's gall, and pulverized viper. Slather it on, dab with a strip of linen, pull, scream, and ta-da! Smooth-as-marble skin! But Greece's gold standard for hair-removal was a stew of *orpiment* (yellow arsenic sulfide that dissolves hair and is used nowadays as a weed killer and rat poison), quicklime (a crucial ingredient in the making of cement), and starch.

HOW MANY BLONDES DOES IT TAKE TO CHANGE A LIGHTBULB?

There is blonde. And then there is *blonde*—a color that's like wearing a lighthouse on the top of your head. Gleaming golden hair has had a *very* long history. Long before it was the punch line of a zillion blonde jokes, it was a symbol of love.

The cult of the blonde was born when hot-to-trot, golden-haired Aphrodite, the goddess of love, rose to the top of the Greek goddess charts, way back in 1000 B.C.E. Soon Greek women began copying the gilded-headed goddess by powdering their hair with crushed yellow flower petals topped with mashed plant pollen. Dark-haired ladies discovered that sitting in the sun for hours with a thick coating of lye on their hair turned it golden. Golden hair meant romance.

When ancient Rome rose to power, they, too, hopped on the blonde bandwagon. In fact, the word *blonde* comes from the Latin word for yellow—*blondus*. At first, it was

Rugrat. Nothing's rattier than a gross old toupee—especially when it comes off!

Fried hair! *Bleached blonde screen star Jean Harlow had hair that glowed. Too bad it all broke off!*

blonde. Wealthy Roman women employed special hair-dye servants. If the servants got the color wrong, it was perfectly acceptable to stab them with a long, sharp pin.

With the fall of Rome, the hair tables turned. As the Catholic Church rose to power, blondeness became a bad thing. Since having fun was frowned upon by the stern monks who now ruled the roost, being blonde was a no-no. Natural blondes covered their hair with hats . . . or better still, dyed it dark with potions made from puréed leeches and animal guts stewed in a vinegar solution. And so it was for centuries, until the day the first moving pictures began to flicker across screens in the early 1900s.

Blindingly blonde hair looked glorious on the silver screen, so lots of actresses decided to hit the bottle—the peroxide bottle, that is. America's women quickly followed suit. Alas, it turns out that being a blonde in the 1920s was more dangerous than playing with knives in traffic. The chemicals inflicted scalp burns and the fumes caused blinding headaches. Jean Harlow was the woman for whom they invented the phrase "blonde bombshell." Harlow was a natural blonde—but since you could not be *too* blonde, her trademark platinum locks were the result of once-a-week bleaching sessions using a mixture of peroxide, ammonia, Clorox, and soap flakes. By the time she was 22, her real hair was so damaged, she had to wear wigs.

kind of sleazy to have blonde hair in Rome, but when Emperor Claudius's third wife, Messalina, took to prancing around Rome in a yellow wig, the fashion for golden hair swiftly spread. Blonde was now not only about love, but about power, too.

Pigeon dung, arsenic, burning acids—women would stop at nothing in the pursuit of golden hair, undeterred by smell, injury, or pain. And it was dangerous not only for the woman going

TEASE, PLEASE

1900: Tie it!

1920: Bob it!

1940: Roll it!

1950: Tease it!

1960: Beehive it!

1970: Fro it!

GOOD RED

As popular as blonde hair is now, red hair was at the top of the color charts for many, many years, especially because of one woman: Queen Elizabeth I, ruler of the British in the 1500s and a real style-setter. Her gorgeous coppery red hair inspired many a beauty wannabe to mix up dyes of lead, sulfur, quicklime, and water. You have to wonder. Was it called dye because that was what happened after using it?

As Elizabeth got older and grayer, she too, took to dying her hair, which naturally began to fall out from the toxic chemicals she was

Liz-locks. Redder than hair could ever be naturally.

dabbing on it. Her forehead grew taller and taller. But that became a hair-craze as well. Soon, it took pluck to be a beauty in the 1500s in Europe—plucked eyebrows, foreheads, even eyelashes! Women spent hours tweezing their temples and hacking away at hairlines. Just take a look at the Mona Lisa. No eyebrows for her! (You can read more about Elizabeth I in QUIRKY QUEENS on page 214.)

BAD RED!

By the late 1600s, red had become the color of the devil in Europe. And when it came to the subject of red hair? Well . . . speak of the devil . . .

Ancient myths claimed that Thor, the ancient Germanic god of thunder, was a redhead, and it was said that bolts of lightning were discharged whenever he blew into his red beard. Woton, the god of the hunt, had red eyes to go with his red hair. Christian priests in the early Middle Ages knew people were still praying to pagan gods, so they seized on the "redness" of these powerful deities and began to wage a huge public relations campaign to transform them from powerful to simply evil. Woton became Lucifer, the prince of darkness, clad in red from toe to head.

By the seventeenth and eighteenth centuries in England, France, Germany, Spain, and

1980: Poof it!

1990: Straighten it!

2000: Anything goes!

I CANNOT TELL A LIE

Crime scene investigators *love* hair. Hair is a great witness. It always tells the truth, so help it God. Each growing strand traps all the gunk that is present in our sweat and blood—traces of everything that has made the trip through a body in recent months; including the food you have eaten and the medicines you have taken. So not only can your hair tell the world that you're a brunette—it can also tell the world that you secretly stuff yourself with Skittles and Choco-Tacos.

America, red hair was seen as the mark of the devil. Red-hair phobia was spread by fiery preachers who decided that Judas Iscariot, betrayer of Jesus, was a carrot-top. And a woman with red hair was judged, in all likelihood, to be a witch, deserving of death. (Hop on your broomstick and fly over to WICKED WITCHES on page 292.) In some parts of France in the 1600s, if you had red hair, you had to wear a wig or dye your hair a color other than red if you wanted to survive. It was that simple.

OOEY GOOEY "DO"

Until the 1700s and the reign of Louis XIV in France, there was no such thing as a hairdresser. No one to gossip with while wearing a large plastic sheet draped round your neck.

We have one woman to thank for the invention of that job. Her name was Madame de Pompadour. She was Louis's girlfriend, and the only woman ever to have a pouffy hairdo named after her. Madame had a thing for hair, along with

A 100-pound head. Or so it felt like with the huge hairstyles of the 1700s.

a thing for parties—especially theme parties. And one way to get into the swing of things was to have hair styled to match the event. Society women started hiring artists to design their hairdos.

First a frame was built out of wire and wood, stuffed with cotton, straw, and balls of wool. Hair was then draped over the frame and cemented with a paste of beef lard and bear grease. The hair was then powdered and "decorated." The sky was the limit. There were dos that featured live birds in hair cages. Styles that presented famous naval battles, complete with ships and smoke. One sad widow even had a model of her husband's tombstone erected in her hair.

The desire for mighty hair soon swept across the channel to England, and then across the ocean to America. Ah . . . but as always, there were problems with all that hair. For starters, it weighed a ton. Women endured neck and back pain from the strain of toting an entire zoo atop their skulls. Just getting to a party meant kneeling in one's carriage, because the hair simply would not fit any other way.

When you put that much energy (and cash) into a hairdo, you want it to last. The average party-head kept her diorama-do for at least a week . . . often two. But as anyone who has ever left butter out for a week will tell you, it gets yucky. And just because it's spread on hair, it's no different. Soon, along with her hubby snoring happily on the next pillow, vermin of all matter were snoring happily in Madame's hairdo.

For every modern-day woman who has referred to her hair as a "rat's nest," you have France's big-haired court ladies to thank for that expression. The only difference is, their hair literally *did* have rats.

GETTING WIGGY WITH IT

By the 1600s wigs were big. Everyone wore them, especially men. Regular folks wore little wigs. Rich, important fellows wore big wigs. (Ever wonder where the term "bigwigs" came

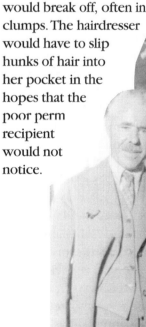

from? Now you know.) The whole wig trend started because the French king, Louis XIII, was bald. He started the fake-hair craze and things just went wild from there. Louis liked his wigs long and curly, with hair that dipped to the waist. His son, Louis XIV, kept ten wigmakers busy working for him.

Soon there were wig thieves who snuck around in the middle of the night and stole people's "hair." Wigs grew so enormous that people had to carry their hats instead of wearing them. Their arms probably weren't long enough to reach the tops of their heads!

It wasn't easy to get hair to make wigs. Poor women sold their hair. One popular source was hair hacked off the heads of dead bodies. Children were sometimes kidnapped, just to slice their shiny locks off. And in a weird twist, men routinely shaved their heads before pulling on their itchy, often lice-infested wigs.

By the 1700s, the styles changed. Guys began tying their wig hair back into ponytails and sometimes that ponytail was tucked into a bag or tied with a huge bow. Cheaper wigs, made of horsehair, goat hair, and even string, were available. And everyone was mortified if a man "flipped his wig." That happened when a poor-fitting wig slipped off as a man bowed in polite company.

RATTY HAIR

Hairstyles, like fashion, have a way of falling out of favor and then back in. At the start of the 1900s, towering hairdos were back. They were the signature of the "Gibson Girl," the girl every woman wanted to be. But a Mt. Everest of hair needs a little help. Women kept little jars on their night tables and dropped their stray strands into them whenever they brushed. When the jar was full, they would take the wad, affectionately

dubbed a *ratt* (no doubt because it was as disgusting as one), and use it to boost their droopy dos. But, as always, beauty comes with a price. So widespread was the use of extra hair that *Godey's Lady's Book,* the fashion how-to book of the time, offered this bit of advice: "When a lady is in danger of drowning, raise her by the dress and not by the hair, which may remain in your grasp."

CURLY-TOP

Fact: People often want what they don't have— and curly hair, if you have straight, was no exception.

But not everyone is born with cascading ringlets. Enter a man named Karl Ludwig Nessler, aka Charles Nestle, who, in 1905, unveiled a machine that looked like something straight out of Dr. Frankenstein's laboratory. Nessler's gizmo supplied electrical current to metal rods around which a woman's hair was wound. Each curler weighed two pounds and it took six hours—six long, unable-to-get-up-and-go-to-the-bathroom hours—for the curls to set. Hairstylists had a pet name for the process: the pocket perm. Why? Nestle's perm was so harmful that the hair would break off, often in clumps. The hairdresser would have to slip hunks of hair into her pocket in the hopes that the poor perm recipient would not notice.

Perm-machine. 1926's Miss America wanted curly locks—and after six hours hooked up to this ghastly gizmo, she got them!

HORRIBLE HENRY THE 8TH

Henry VIII, who ruled England from 1509 to 1547, was a big guy. Everything he did, he did big. He was a big spender. He had a big appetite (and a big gut to prove it). And alas, he also had a big mouth. Being a typical king (see KILLER KINGS for lots more on page 135), Henry figured that rules and laws were for other people. He had six wives during a time when divorce was unheard of; because he felt above the law, he caused one of the biggest shake-ups in world history. Big Hank ruled England for 38 years and during his kingship, he changed things in a *big* way.

EVERYONE'S OUT TO GET ME!

When Henry Tudor was a kid, he was a super athlete, especially when it came to horseback riding. Boy, could that guy joust! He was a good student, a fine singer, and an all-around sharp cookie. But Henry wasn't supposed to be the king. His older brother Arthur was. When Arthur died in 1502, Henry found himself not only being crowned king, but getting stuck with his dead brother's leftover wife.

Catherine of Aragon—first his sister-in-law, and then his bride—was really high up there in the royal pecking order. She was the daughter of the very same Ferdinand and Isabella who had helped Christopher Columbus scoot across the ocean (see page 37). She was very rich and came to England with a huge dowry. (A dowry is what very rich folks used to pay to get someone to marry their daughters—basically trunks and trunks full of jewels and money and

deeds to land.) When Henry's brother died, their dad wanted to figure out a way to keep Catherine's dowry, since he'd already spent a chunk of it. A nifty solution: Have Henry and Catherine marry! The trouble was, Henry VIII's marriage to his brother's widow went against church law, which decreed that you could not marry your deceased brother's wife. Henry's

THOSE TOUCHY TUDORS

What was life like in Europe when Henry Tudor (Henry's given name) came to the throne? For one thing, girls were married at age 12, boys at 14. You didn't pick your own wife or husband. Your folks did. A "good wife" cleaned the house; set the table; milked the cows; dressed the kids; washed the clothes; cooked the meals; brewed the ale; baked the bread; sent corn to the mill; made butter and cheese; cared for the pigs chickens, and cows; collected the eggs; and sold the butter, cheese, milk, and eggs at the market. A "good wife" never nagged or scolded. If she did, she was punished—right in the middle of the town square for all to see.

dad had to make sure that Catherine's marriage to his son could not be challenged. So he wrote to the pope in Rome and after months of waiting, the pope wrote back and said Catherine and Henry could wed.

WELCOME TO HENRY'S PLACE

You might think that a king's castle would be a really fancy, regal sort of place. But for all his fabulous wealth, Henry's castles were real skin-crawlers. Most of the floors were covered with straw because they were frequently used as public restrooms. Henry had endless streams of visitors coming to see him—visitors who peed in the corners of the rooms. There were, of course, rules against peeing in public. But court reports show that everyone did it anyway. When the stink got unbearable, everyone would simply move on to the next castle and send in the clean-up crews.

Henry built palace after palace. He gave huge feasts and hosted lavish tournaments. But as he got older, his personality began to change. He could be great fun to be around at one moment, then fly off the handle and become an absolute creep the next. A friend of Henry's wrote that when the king got mad, he became "the most dangerous and cruel man in the world."

Irritate Henry in any way, and you were a dead dog.

Don't believe me? Take the Bishop of Rochester's cook. The poor cook was being treated terribly by the not-so-nice bishop, so he decided to get a little revenge by ruining a dinner that the bishop was hosting. The cook added a special herb in the bishop's dinner that would give everyone who ate the dish a bad case of the squirts. Unfortunately, two guests liked the dish so much they had extra portions and got such bad cases of diarrhea that they died. The cook was charged with murder and sentenced to be hanged. But Henry stepped in and said that was too nice a way to die, and ordered the cook boiled to death in his own pot.

From king of the hill to oozing old codger. *Henry went from a dazzling athlete to a disgusting relic.*

MY LAND'S BETTER THAN YOUR LAND

Henry *loved* being king. And one thing kings did back then was go to war. France and England were always at each other's throats. Henry's arch-nemesis was the French king, Francis. There was also a third super-power king in Europe, Charles V, who ruled over the Holy Roman Empire—what is now Germany, Switzerland, Hungary, Austria, and the Netherlands.

Henry, no slouch at math, realized that two were stronger than one and decided to get Francis to form an alliance with him, even though he loathed the guy. The two kings agreed to meet and in 1520 threw a huge get-together called the Field of the Cloth of Gold. Each king was determined to outdo the other in terms of displays of wealth. They built a temporary city with temporary palaces, banquet halls, and pavilions covered with actual gold cloth and studded with precious gems. There was a huge golden fountain that spouted two kinds of wine. And they ate and ate. In three

WAVE BYE-BYE TO HENRY'S WIVES

Henry VIII was as famous for his many wives as he was for abandoning the Catholic Church. Three Catherines, two Annes, and a Jane . . . they all married Henry and lived (or died) to regret it.

WIFE NUMBER **1**
Catherine of Aragon (lasted 15 years)

We've discussed her—she was the daughter of Ferdinand and Isabella of Spain—and queen from 1509 to 1533. She and Henry had one daughter, Mary, but no sons. Henry wanted a son really badly. And besides, there was another woman who drove him wild. In 1533 he ditched Catherine, got a divorce from the newly founded Church of England and married . . .

WIFE NUMBER **2**
Anne Boleyn (lasted three years)

Ah, saucy, spicy Anne. Legend has it she had a six-fingered hand. But she, too, only produced a daughter, Elizabeth. Henry quickly lost interest when no boys were born. He'd gotten away with one divorce. Two was pushing it. Anne had turned into a royal pain in the neck. So he decided it was time for a pain in *her* neck and ordered her to be sent to the chopping block for "treason."

Henry, out of "kindness," agreed to hire a French executioner. Everyone knew the French had a gentler touch with head-chopping. But he would not pay for a coffin. Anne's friends had to scrounge around and finally found an empty arrow box in the palace cellar. It was too short for an adult person, but worked perfectly for a lady with her head tucked alongside her body.

But Henry still needed a son, which sent him to the altar ten days later with . . .

WIFE NUMBER **3**
Jane Seymour (lasted 18 months)

Jane did it! The son Henry wanted so badly was finally born in 1537. Sadly, Jane did not survive the birth (and the son would die as a child). Henry was genuinely gloomy, and for two years ate constantly to fill his loneliness. But two years later, the now-very-pudgy monarch decided it was time for . . .

WIFE NUMBER

Anne of Cleves (lasted a couple of months)

Henry needed an ally in Germany (remember the Holy Roman Empire?), and Anne was a German duchess. This wasn't a love match, but a cash deal. Alas, Anne was so ugly that Henry could barely look at her. And not only was she ugly, she smelled! The marriage lasted six months and then everyone pretended it had never happened. Anne of Cleves went away and Henry married . . .

WIFE NUMBER

Catherine Howard (lasted five years)

Henry was almost 50. Catherine was 17. Henry had become a very chubby hubby indeed—with oozing sores on his legs that would not heal from a hunting accident. He didn't exactly make Catherine's heart go pitter-pat. So she started hanging around with guys closer to her own age. This was not fitting for the wife of a king and she was sentenced to death. And she didn't even get a sharp swordsman from France. She got "exed" with a plain old axe. Which leads to . . .

WIFE NUMBER 6

Catherine Parr (lasted four years)

Henry was still lonely, so he married once again. She may have been the queen of England, but wife number six had to deal with the pus-filled wound in his leg, which would not heal and smelled like dirty gym socks. Henry was always in pain, and given to fits of blind rage. He was not a fun person to be around. Would Catherine have met the same end as some of Henry's other wives? He died before that could happen.

weeks, Henry and his group gobbled down more than 2,200 sheep alone!

Queen Catherine sat in a tent completely lined with pearls, and watched as Henry and Francis jousted with one another. The two countries spent so much trying to one-up each other that they ran out of money. And after all that, Henry decided to dump Francis and signed a treaty with Charles V. Within a month, France and England went to war and stayed at war, on and off, for the next 200 years.

I WANT A SON!

After 15 years of marriage to Catherine, Henry only had one daughter, Mary, to show for it. He wanted a boy to keep the Tudor name alive. Catherine was so sad. She had prayed and prayed for a son; she even wore a hair shirt, which left her skin raw and bloody to prove her devotion to God. Henry began to think his marriage was cursed. Maybe it *had* been a sin to marry Catherine after all. He had a brilliant idea and wrote to the pope asking for the marriage to be *annulled*—a fancy word for pretending something never really happened. The pope said, "No way."

People at the time were starting to get fed up with the guys who were running the Roman Catholic Church. A lot of people felt the pope and his bishops had gotten too greedy. Everything seemed to be about money! The Church controlled great riches and vast amounts of land. Henry found an old law that said that the king was the highest authority in the land. So Henry basically said to the pope, "You're not the boss of me. I, the king, am the boss of *you*."

The pope said Henry would go to hell. Henry's advisors said, "The pope can't send you to hell. He can kick you out of the Holy Roman Church, but not from the love of God. Besides, you should be the head of the Church anyway."

About the same time that all this was happening, all across Europe people were getting fed up with the pope and his corrupt ways. In 1532, Sir Thomas Cromwell, one of Henry's closest advisors, decided the time was right to do something dramatic. He turned to the anti-clerical

Henry goes to Hollywood. *There's been a ton of movies about Hank.*

(meaning anti–Catholic Church) Parliament and got them to pass a bunch of acts that cut back on the pope's power. On top of that, Henry appointed Thomas Cranmer as the new Archbishop of Canterbury, head Church guy in England, and Cranmer gave Henry his divorce. This made the pope in Rome very angry, but Henry didn't care. He decided he didn't want to be Catholic anyway. He created his own church called the Church of England, one of the earliest Protestant churches. The churches and all their golden treasures now belonged to Henry.

LONG LIVE THE KING?

The last year of Henry's life was a terrible one. He could barely walk, so he was carried everywhere. He also weighed almost 300 pounds, so the chair carriers had their work cut out for them. He literally rotted to death from his leg wound.

And what end befits England's most famous king? Henry was placed in a lead coffin, which somehow burst open during the funeral procession. An oozy slime dripped from the coffin onto the floor, and stories tell of a dog darting out to lick up the pool of putrefaction.

And so we have met Henry the king, Henry the man, and Henry the husband. In later life he was actively cruel to his daughters but the people of England loved him. He attacked the Church and the pope and changed the way people prayed. His son, Edward VI, became king at the ripe old age of nine and died six years later. His daughter from his first marriage, Mary, an ardent Catholic, became queen for five years and went on a bit of a rampage, killing hundreds of Protestants by burning them at the stake. And then there was red-haired Elizabeth, who reigned for 45 years. (For more on these royal gals, turn to page 214.) Ironically, Henry didn't need a male heir after all. Elizabeth I became one of the best monarchs England ever had.

JUST CALL ME RING-O

Henry loved jewelry. He owned 234 rings, 365 jeweled brooches, and a vast collection of glittering diamond stickpins that he used just to pick the gunk out of his teeth.

It's hard to be a glutton. *Henry sure could pack away a meal, as this scene from a movie-version of his life shows.*

HUMONGOUS HOAXES

A hoax is a giant "gotcha!" People have always loved to fool other people. Sometimes their pranks are harmless. Some are downright hilarious. But sometimes, they can get a little out of hand.

THE LADY THAT GAVE BIRTH TO RABBITS

The 1700s are sometimes called the Age of Enlightenment. You know those pictures of a lightbulb going off over someone's head? That was what was happening all over. People were supposed to be getting smarter. Superstition was supposed to be making way for science. Yet some of the greatest hoaxes ever were born in that era.

Try this one on for size: In 1726, newspapers and town criers everywhere shared the amazing news about Mary Toft. She had gotten pregnant, but instead of giving birth to a baby, she had given birth to a rabbit. In London, Mary became a huge celebrity. She convinced everyone— even the city's best doctors, which doesn't say much for the state of medical knowledge at that time—that she was the mom of a bunny.

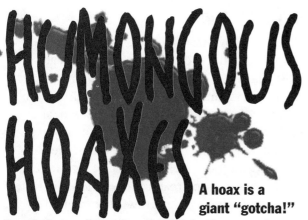

Eventually, when surgeons wanted to hack her open to take a closer look, she was forced to confess that in fact the "baby" was rabbit parts— actually dead rabbit parts—and her fame hippity-hopped away.

BRRR-NING HOT!

Newspapers were a never-ending source of made-up stories. Take this one from an 1874 issue of Nevada's *Territorial Enterprise* that was soon printed in papers around the world.

It told the amazing tale of an inventor who had designed a special suit that would keep him from frying up in the heat of the Nevada desert—even in the dead of summer when temperatures can reach upwards of 120°F. The man had invented solar armor—a suit made of sponges dipped in an amazing "frigorific mixture" that kept him cool as it evaporated. Who would have guessed that the solar armor was so good that it was *too* effective against the blazing desert sun? According to the *Enterprise*, the inventor was discovered in the middle of the blazing desert completely frozen to death, with huge icicles dripping from his nose. For months, the Popsicle guy in the desert was headline news all around the world. Only problem was, the suit never existed, nor did the inventor. The newspaper made the story up to sell more copies.

LOOK WHAT I JUST DUG UP!

On October 16, 1869, a group of well-diggers in the little town of Cardiff, New York, struck something hard with their shovels. Soon they had revealed a giant foot. And there was more. The petrified body they unearthed was over 10 feet tall! Was it a giant from biblical times? A lot of people thought so! Soon people were flocking from all over to see it, paying 50 cents a person for a chance to take a peek. That was a lot of money back in 1869!

The Cardiff Giant was one of the greatest hoaxes ever. The giant was a fake—the brainchild of a guy named George Hull, who had been trying to think of a way to get rich quick. The giant would have been hoax enough, but a group of investors didn't know it was a fake and just *had* to own the Cardiff Giant. They paid $37,500 to the farmer (Hull's partner in crime) who owned the property where the creature was found, and had the giant moved to Syracuse, where it was proudly displayed. Of course, it was promptly dismissed as a fake by a Yale professor, who pointed out the chisel marks all over the body.

But that made the Cardiff Giant even *more* popular. P.T. Barnum—the greatest huckster ever (so great, you have to go to CIRCUS CLOWNING on page 23 to read about him)—just *had* to own him, but the owners would not sell. So Barnum made his own Cardiff Giant and soon his fake of a fake was drawing bigger crowds than the real fake!

A somber moment. Unearthing the Cardiff Giant.

FISH WITH FUR?

Americans love stories of strange animals—so much so that they don't care if they really exist. Have you ever seen a rabbit with antlers? A rabbit with antlers that likes to get drunk on whiskey? Just head to Douglas, Colorado, and you'll be greeted by a big statue of the mysterious "jackalope." Plenty of folks believed in the existence of these weird, whistling wonders. Other trumped-up creatures over the years have included fur-covered trout, who developed a thick coat of fuzz to stay warm in chilly waters, and chirping ice worms that crawled out of the glaciers in Alaska.

EXTRA! EXTRA! READ ALL ABOUT IT!

The great Central Park Zoo escape on November 9, 1874, was front-page news in *The New York Herald*. The paper breathlessly reported that all the animals had escaped during the night and were now roaming the streets of New York City. A lion had been heard roaring inside a church. A rhino has fallen into a sewer. More than 25 people were dead and hundreds injured. Readers were terrified and armed men ran through the streets waving guns. Too bad those panicky people hadn't finished reading the article. At the very bottom, it revealed that the story had been fabricated—in order to point out the terrible conditions at the zoo!

THE MISSING LINK?

As scientists began to unearth real dinosaur bones, folks wondered if there were still dinos roaming the Earth. Soon there were expeditions searching all over the place for them. One afternoon, while digging in England, scientists excitedly uncovered a bizarre-looking skull. It appeared to be half-man, half-ape. They called it the Piltdown Man. Was it the missing link between the great apes and we humans? Everyone was sure it was—everyone except the prankster who had taken the jaw of an orangutan and stained it to look as old as the 50,000-year-old skullcap he'd attached it to.

And when news leaked about a huge serpent swimming in the frigid waters of Loch Ness in Scotland, the world had its next marvel. For hundreds of years, folks in Scotland had told tales of a creature that lived at the bottom of the deep lake. So, in 1933, a London newspaper hired a world-famous big-game hunter and sent him off to find Nessie, the supposed prehistoric sea creature. He didn't see anything in the water. But what were those giant footprints on the shore? They were huge! Everyone went nuts!

Turns out the prints had been made by a coatrack with a base made from a dead hippo's foot—a popular style at the time.

A few years later, a well-respected doctor, while on a drive around the lake, spotted something in the water and happened to have his camera with him. He quickly snapped a picture of it! It was the monster! Or was it? On his deathbed at the age of 90, a fellow named Christian Spurling confessed he'd rigged the whole monster thing using a toy submarine topped with a fake sea-serpent head. The esteemed doc was in on the hoax, too. But he wasn't the mastermind behind it. That big-game hunter, whose hippo footprints had made him the laughingstock of a nation, was the one who organized *this* elaborate hoax.

DON'T MAKE A HEE-HAW OF YOURSELF

Sure, you know who's running for president of the United States. Maybe even governor of your state,

or mayor of your city. But do people *really* know who they're voting for in local elections? What the heck is a town selectman, anyway? The mayor of a small village in Washington State decided that most people didn't have a clue, and were simply choosing a Republican or a Democrat. To prove his point, in 1936, he took his mule down to the county courthouse and registered it to run for office in the next election as Republican precinct committeeman. At the next election, Boston Curtis won resoundingly, 52–0. But Boston Curtis was the mayor's mule. The town's Republicans had just voted into office an animal that is the symbol of the Democratic party!

THE GREATEST HOAX EVER

It all began in 1926 in England on a radio broadcast on the BBC. Folks had tuned in to listen to a comedy show. Unfortunately, it was so scary that people forgot it was a comedy as they heard the news that unemployed workers had begun running wild in the streets of London and had just blown up the House of Parliament and Big Ben (a landmark clock).

Listeners began panicking—running into the streets, trying to get the heck out of London. Phone lines were jammed with calls to the police, who kept insisting that nothing was happening. But the callers kept insisting that it *had* to be happening because they were hearing it on the radio, for gosh sakes!

A young American named Orson Welles was inspired by the BBC broadcast to create a radio show of his own. On the night before Halloween in 1938, CBS was broadcasting some dance music when they interrupted the broadcast to announce that the government had just detected giant blue flames erupting on Mars. Back to the tacky music. Soon another interruption. A giant meteor had just plunged into New Jersey! Back to the music. Soon there was another interruption. Wait! No! Not a meteor! It's a spaceship! And there was a giant tentacled creature that was now heading for New York City shooting out clouds of noxious black gas!

SEVEN GREAT APRIL FOOL'S PRANKS

Sure it's fun to set all the clocks back in your house on April 1, aka April Fool's Day, so your folks think you have another two hours until school starts, but here, in chronological order, are some April Fool's pranks that fooled thousands and thousands!

1. Spaghetti Trees: April 1, 1957

England's largest TV network is the BBC, and folks take it *very* seriously. So when the BBC aired film footage of Swiss farmers plucking spaghetti from trees, the phone lines were flooded by viewers wanting to know how they, too, could grow pasta. The BBC operators were instructed to tell them to stick a sprig of spaghetti in a can of tomato sauce and "hope for the best."

Picking pasta

2. She's Gonna Blow!: April 1, 1974

Folks in Sitka, Alaska, were alarmed when they looked up at the cone of the long-dormant volcano, Mount Edgecumbe, on the morning of April 1, and there was thick black smoke coming from the top! Had the volcano suddenly thundered to life? Turns out a local prankster named Porky Bickar had dumped hundreds of old tires into the volcano's crater and set fire to them.

3. Australia's Iceberg: April 1, 1978

When a millionaire from Sydney announced plans to tow an iceberg from Antarctica to Australia, everybody laughed. But lo and behold, there it was, being towed by a barge into the harbor. Local radio stations gave minute-by-minute updates. Crowds gathered. Only after the iceberg was well into the harbor was it revealed that the "iceberg" was really a mountain of white plastic sheets atop a barge of garbage, covered with shaving cream and firefighting foam.

4. Big Bad Bras: April 1, 1982

A newspaper in England ran a headline that said that 10,000 "rogue bras" had been sold that were causing TV's and radios to get bad reception because the wrong kind of underwire had been used. When the chief engineer of a big television company sent a memo to all his female employees requesting that they identify what brand of bra they were wearing, the newspaper got to yell "Gotcha."

5. Baseball's Super-Pitcher: April 1, 1985

Baseball fans went gaga when they read about a guy named Sidd Finch in *Sports Illustrated*. Sidd had just been signed as a pitcher for the New York Mets. According to the article, he could throw a fastball at an astounding 168 miles per hour—60 miles faster than anyone else on record. Even more incredibly, he had never played baseball before, but had learned to throw in a monastery in Tibet! Mets fans were jumping for joy . . . until they realized they'd been April-fooled.

6. The Taco Liberty Bell: April 1, 1996

You may have heard of a fast-food chain called Taco Bell. And you probably have heard of the Liberty Bell. When Taco Bell ran full-page ads in America's newspapers announcing that they had *purchased* the Liberty Bell and were changing its name to the Taco Liberty Bell, thousands dialed Independence National Historic Park in Philadelphia to complain!

7. The Left-Handed Whopper: April 1, 1998

Burger King ran an ad in *USA Today* announcing a Whopper specially designed for the 32 million left-handed Americans. It bragged that the special sauce had been rotated 180 degrees. Thousands of people visited Burger Kings across the country and tried to order one!

More than 6 million people were listening to the radio that night and supposedly more than a million people panicked and went screaming into the streets. A million people fleeing their homes, folks panicking and in tears! The Martians were coming!

But did millions really panic like the news media reported? In a hoax upon a hoax, the truth is this: Not that many people actually were scared to death. In fact, hardly anyone was. Four times during the broadcast Welles clearly said, "Hey folks—this is a play." Once again, the media hyped the hype of the event way out of proportion.

MY, WHAT BIG FEET YOU HAVE!

There's one hoax that refuses to go away: the legend of the giant ape man who lives in the Pacific Northwest. It's Bigfoot, aka Sasquatch! Is there really a 10-foot-tall, 500-pound creature with 17-inch feet running through the forests? Giant footprints found in Humboldt, California, sure made people think so. In October of 1967, two brave filmmakers even got a glimpse of a hairy beast running through the forests of the Six Rivers National Forest. A leading anthropologist studied the film and declared the beast to be a giant prehistoric ape.

Turns out, Bigfoot was the creation of a practical joker named Ray Wallace. He had a wood-carver friend make some 17-inch feet and stomped around with them to play a joke on his workers. But since then, Sasquatch sightings have been reported hundreds of times, mostly in the Pacific Northwest. Old hoaxes die hard.

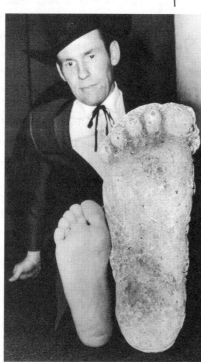

I'd like to see a sneaker in a size 23. Bigfoot meets a regular foot!

Over in Asia, Bigfoot has a fuzzy buddy. In the miles-high peaks of the Himalaya mountains a creature called *Metohkang-mi, mirka,* or *sogpa* darts through the woodlands. You might know it as a *yeti*—the dreaded Abominable Snowman. Actually, its name is "filthy snowman." (Someone goofed while translating from the Tibetan.) And rather than being abominable, folks who claim to have had encounters with the beast describe it as gentle and shy. Somehow "Gentle Beast" just doesn't cut it in terms of scariness. And the truth is, the yeti is probably some sort of rare bear. A filthy rare bear.

THE BOSTON BULLET

Winning a famous race must be pretty cool. But why go to the bother of actually doing all that sweaty running? On April 21, 1980, Rosie Ruiz had another idea. She literally burst out of nowhere to streak across the finish line in the third-fastest time ever recorded by a woman at the Boston Marathon, one of the most famous races in the world. And she wasn't even panting! Turns out she had only run the last mile. She had qualified for the Boston race by finishing the New York Marathon with a most impressive time (achieved by taking the subway for an 11-mile leg of the course). Suspicions grew when she didn't appear in any photographs taken during the race. Finally, a few members of the crowd volunteered that they had seen her jump into the race during its final half-mile.

CROP CIRCLES

In the late 1980s a new phenomena began to catch people's attentions. Strange, circular patterns were appearing in the middle of the wheat fields in southern England. They seemed to spring up from nowhere overnight. Word got out that they were made by space aliens, and soon people were camping out on hillsides trying to get a glimpse of spaceships spinning circles in the middle of the night.

Did space aliens make pretty patterns in the grass? Nah! Two drinking buddies,

Doug Bower and Dave Chorley, decided to have a little laugh. Back in the 1970s, they took an iron bar and some string and went out and flattened circles in big wheat fields. For the next couple of years, they kept perfecting their technique and finally, one day, they created a masterpiece in the middle of a field called the Devil's Punchbowl—a place easily seen from a fairly major road. Everyone went nuts. Folks called "cerealogists" came to study the circles. No one could figure them out. And even after Doug and Dave confessed in 1991, folks still would not believe that a space alien hadn't planted the patterns with a UFO.

MEGA-CAT

Nowadays, the Internet is the perfect place to launch a thousand hoaxes. And a whole lot of what you read online just might be make-believe. But one of the most astounding Internet hoaxes ever involved a kitty cat. And not just your typical hair ball–spewing meower. According to rumor, a worker at a Canadian nuclear research facility named Roger Degagne found two kitty cats hanging around the labs and brought them home. A couple of years later, the cats had kittens. Degagne and his family kept one: Snowball, who allegedly snowballed into one heck of a cat! She grew to 87 pounds! There was even a photo of

Purr-fectly real? Snowball the mega-kitty was a computer creation.

Degagne holding his fluffy little, er, big pet in his arms. Millions of people saw, and fell for, this supercat.

So whaddya think? Real? A hoax? Have you not learned *anything at all* from this section? The truth was, a man named Cordell Haughlie took a picture of his perfectly normal cat and used a computer program to doctor a picture of himself so it looked like he was holding a cat as big as a pony! He sent it to his daughter as a joke, and she sent it to her friends, and soon it was in millions of homes with a hilarious story to go with it.

So here's a word to the wise. Don't believe everything you read, or even everything you see.

I

IDIOTIC INVENTIONS

A DEADLY INVENTION

In the year 30 C.E. in ancient Rome, a gentleman proudly showed the emperor Tiberius Claudius an amazing invention— an unbreakable glass beaker. Tiberius studied the glass, then handed it back to the inventor, who hurled it down, as hard as he could, on the stone floor as the emperor gasped in horror. Amazingly, the glass didn't break! It was only dented.

Picking up a little mallet, the inventor hammered out the dent and smiled proudly. Tiberius asked if anyone else knew about this secret way of making glass. The inventor smugly replied that no one else had figured it out. And with that, Tiberius had the man beheaded. Jealous Tiberius didn't want anyone that smart hanging around *his* court.

Being an inventor is not without its risks.

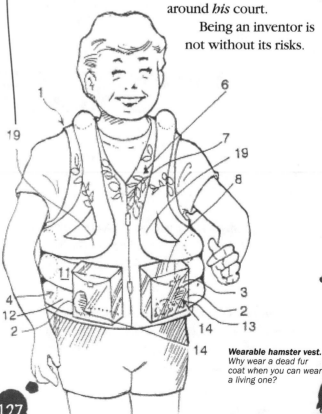

Wearable hamster vest. Why wear a dead fur coat when you can wear a living one?

Love your hamsters so much that you hate to leave them home when you go to school? Thanks to United States Patent number 5,901,666, you can stroll into math class "wearing" your pet in a vest cage. Do dogs keep peeing on your mom's prize petunias? U.S. Patent number 922,956 will take care of that by sending an electric shock through any dog that dares to lift a hind leg near them. Or how about U.S. Patent number 11,942? Get rid of those nasty intestinal parasites with a swallowable bait trap, complete with string to pull it out of your guts, and back through your mouth when the worm has been caught.

127

I THOUGHT OF IT FIRST!

Throughout history, a lot of inventors have kept their discoveries secret because they were afraid their ideas would be stolen by others. Take the famous Italian architect Filippo Brunelleschi. In 1421, he thought of way to greatly increase the amount of weight a boat could carry. He just knew everyone would try to nab his idea, so he kept his lips zipped, but dropped heavy hints that he had a great idea up his sleeve.

The town government knew he was up to something, so they got together and ruled that for three whole years Brunelleschi would be the only one in Italy who would be allowed to use this new invention. If anyone else copied him, they'd be in big trouble. And now a brand-new idea had been "invented"—the patent—a way to protect inventors, and make sure that the profits from their inventions would end up in their wallets.

PATENT THIS!

Long before protected patents, there were some amazing inventions. Take the wheel, which has been around since 5500 B.C.E. The wheel led to the cart, which led to the wheelbarrow, the carriage, and eventually the invention of the car. Thanks to inventors we have lightbulbs,

I caught a spaghetti, mom! Keeping pasta on a fork is such a chore, so an inventor came up with a way to reel in those slippery strands.

televisions, computers, and the iPod. Still, for every amazing, wonderful, life-changing idea (disposable diapers leap to mind!), there have been a thousand useless, pointless, and downright just plain icky ones.

Fortunately, some of the stupidest inventions ever are on file in one of our government offices for all to see. Like Brunelleschi, no one wants to do all the work of inventing, only to see someone else get rich. So how does it work? Let's say you invent hamster dental floss. You make diagrams, draw pictures, build a prototype, and then go to the government and explain exactly what your idea is.

A LIGHTBULB DID NOT GO OFF ATOP THESE HEADS

■ Thomas Edison did NOT invent the lightbulb. About 50 years before Edison was born, in 1802, a guy named Humphry Davy made an arc lamp. By 1844 the Place de la Concorde in France was bathed in electric light thanks to Jean Foucault. And in 1878, ten months before Edison flipped the switch on his "invention," William Swan demo'd a carbon filament lamp in England.

■ Robert Fulton ought to be ashamed! Twenty years before he "invented" the steamboat, John Fitch and James Rumsey were chugging along America's rivers on their own steam. In 1790, Fitch even had a regular steam-propelled boat service crossing the Delaware River between Philadelphia and Trenton, New Jersey.

■ Say cheese! Louis Jacques Daguerre (*Da-gair*) was another invention thief. He's widely known as the inventor of photography, and he named an early kind of photograph (the daguerreotype) for himself. But in fact, the first camera was invented by a French dude named Joseph Niepce who took the world's first photo in 1826. When Niepce died in 1833, Daguerre made one small change to his invention, and took the credit.

BOOM?

In 1867, a Swedish-born inventor named Alfred Nobel got U.S. Patent number 78,317 for the invention of dynamite. Ironically, Nobel went on to found the Nobel Prize, which gives money to scientists, as well as great people of peace, such as Martin Luther King Jr. and Nelson Mandela. Think maybe Alfred was feeling a little guilty about his deadly invention?

If you get a patent for it, no one else can sell hamster dental floss for a certain, set period of years—unless they come up with a completely different way of cleaning the gunk from a rodent's tiny teeth.

The Italians thought up the idea of protecting inventors, but in 1449 the English began to officially keep track of patents. America got into the patent act in 1790, when the United States Patent and Trademark Office was opened to register and protect inventions. And back then, by "inventions" they meant an item that you could physically hold in your hands. The very first patent went to Sam Hopkins for a new and improved fertilizer (although I for one would rather *not* hold fertilizer in my hands).

Reading the list of people who have applied for patents and received them is a quickie course in human creativity. Otis elevators, Colt rifles, Singer sewing machines. Birdseye Frozen Foods. Folks have patented rockets, bras, and televisions. The list is pretty amazing. But there is a funky side to all those patents granted. Some of them are so incredibly stupid as to make a person's jaw drop a foot. So here are:

THE 5 DUMBEST PATENTS EVER GRANTED

1. Chewing Gum Locket. U.S. Patent number 395,515, issued in 1889.

Why stick your used gum on the underside of your desk, when you can wear it? The inventor of this dubious invention bragged, "Chewing gum may be carried conveniently upon the person and is not left around carelessly to become dirty or fall into the hands of persons to whom it does not belong, and be used by ulcerous or diseased mouths by which infection would be communicated by subsequent use to the owner. . . ." You have to wonder—were people in the habit of sharing their used chewing gum in the 1800s?

2. Combined Clothes Brush, Flask, & Drinking Cup. U.S. Patent number 490,964, issued in 1893.

Cleaning the lint from your clothes is a thirsty business. So why be caught dry? This thoughtful invention allows you to gulp while you groom.

3. Chicken Eye Glasses. U.S. Patent number 730,918, issued in 1903.

No more beaks in the eyeballs for your favorite chickens. These sporty specs will protect your poultry's peepers from other chickens in the yard.

4. Human Hat Rack. U.S. Patent number 1,045,060, issued in 1912.

Is your hat too heavy? This little wire hat rack rests on your shoulders, extends up over your ears and distributes the weight of your hat onto your body, not your neck.

5. Dimple Drill. U.S. Patent number 560,351, issued in 1896.

Do you wish you had those cute dimples? Those little round dents in cheeks that some people find charming were a beauty "wanna-have" a hundred years ago. This drill was supposed to dig little holes in your face!

J

Royal Flush

JUNKY JOBS

The next time one of your parents' friends comes over to you, pinches your cheek, and asks you what you want to be when you grow up, calmly announce that it's a toss-up between a *groom of the stool* and a *costermonger.*

Just what does a groom of the stool do to get that hard-earned paycheck? Read on and check out the Help Wanted sections of times gone by.

WANTED: PERKY PEE-STIRRER

Oh, to have been a job hunter in the olden days. So many grossly wonderful occupations to choose from! The Middle Ages (c'mon, kids—you should know these dates by now: 1000 to 1500) were a time when work was pretty disgusting. So, let's pretend there's an employment agency just down the street. Here are some of the positions being offered to boys. You could be a *spitboy,* which had nothing to do with spitting. Instead, picture a huge fire as tall as you. A metal spit with a handle on one end would be yours to turn *and turn*—for hours on end, as roast pigs, sides of beef, and other assorted meats cooked for the king and his gazillion guests. But not only did the meat cook, you did, too! Job perks? Leftover meat scraps after everyone else had been fed!

Spit, spit, spit your roast. Arms sure did get tired from all the turning.

130

THE HOUSE THAT POOP BUILT

Working construction sounds pretty fun, right? Even in the Dark Ages (500–1000 C.E.), you got to build all those cool castles and fierce forts and such. But one of the main construction tasks back then was being a *wattle and daub applier*. The typical little hovel was built by weaving bendy tree branches in and out of stakes (the *wattle* part), and then filling in the spaces with daub. How do you make *daub*? Collect a whole mess of animal dung and mix it with water, straw, and mud. Toss your ingredients into a big bucket and hop in—bare feet and all—to mix the muddy, poopy mess. Repeat every few weeks, because those dabs of daub just don't last.

Or perhaps you might choose the job of a *woad dyer. Woad* is a kind of weed that made a beautiful blue dye. But in order to make the dye, you had to stir in a few other ingredients: cat pee, a dash of excrement, and a dusting of wheat bran. Mmmmmm, such a heavenly aroma!

But probably one of the top "worst" jobs was being a *fuller.* During the Middle Ages, everybody wore wool. But wool could be really scratchy and stiff. Fullers made sure the wool was soft and not so itchy. How? If you were a fuller, you'd spend the day waltzing around in vats filled knee-deep with stale urine. Why? That really old pee is full of ammonia, which helps to pull the lanolin out of the wool. The lanolin helps to close up the fibers, making them soft. Getting the smell off your legs was impossible. But you did have the cleanest feet in town. And your pants didn't itch, to boot!

Girls and women had job opportunities, too. They could be leech collectors. *Leeches* are a kind of worm that were used by long-ago doctors to suck blood from ailing patients. Docs back then believed that too much blood was the cause of many diseases. But collecting leeches was a tough task. You basically had to be leech bait. Up in the Lake District in England, many women would walk barefoot into the reed beds where the leeches lived and wade through the water, waiting for the leeches to attach to their calves. Then they'd peel the bloodsucking critters off, load them into jars, and take them to the nearest doctor's office.

HI, HO, HI, HO! IT'S OFF TO WIPE I GO

Wondering what the "groom of the stool" mentioned earlier is? He lived in England in the 1500s. On the plus side, he got to work in the royal castle, and hang out with the king. His main job was to make sure that "the house of easement be sweet and clear." But the "house of easement" wasn't one of the branches of government. It was the polite way of saying the toilet. He had to keep it clean. But wait, it gets better! The stool groom was also the official butt-wiper of the king. Of course, there was no toilet paper in the 1500s. To clean the royal rump, the groom of the stool used his hands.

Another bathroom-related job in the Middle Ages was that of a *gong scourer* or *gong farmer.* Being a farmer doesn't sound half bad until you realize that what you are farming are solid blocks of compacted doo-doo that filled people's cesspits and latrines. The gong farmer had to use a pick and a shovel to break up the crud and then remove it.

About the same time, some folks found themselves employed as *pure collectors.* Any idea what "pure" is? Doggie doo, dear reader! Bet you thought it was useless. Well, surprise! It was used as a softener in the leather-making process. Bet you didn't think such awesome job opportunities existed!

FOR MUSIC LOVERS

Those beautiful Stradivarius violins from the 1700s make awesome music. But a violin without strings is pretty useless. Somebody had to make those strings. And a few centuries ago, it took guts. Literally. String makers had the honor of working in an *abattoir* (*ab-uh-TWAR*)—a place where animals are slaughtered prior to being turned into neat little packages of meat. In this nasty place, the string maker began by pulling about 30 feet (10 yards) of intestine from a recently deceased sheep.

The next step was to separate the still-steaming guts from the bits of fat that clung to the intestines. Finally, the entire length of gut

It takes guts to fiddle . . . The guts of an animal, like a sheep or cat.

had to be kneaded to squeeze out any poop that was still stuck inside. The cleaned gut was then soaked in cold water, crushed, and fumigated by bathing it in a sulfur bath before the entire thing was twisted into strings. Time needed to make one set of strings? Twelve solid hours of gut-twisting fun!

THE MACHINE AGE

Remember the Mad Hatter from *Alice in Wonderland*? In the 1800s, *hatting* was a real job! But it in fact *did* make you mad. Not angry mad, but cr-aaaaazy mad. To turn fur into felt hats, folks used mercury—a toxin—and the people who handled and inhaled the stuff ended up going totally nuts.

Another dangerous job was being a *match maker*—and I'm not talking about your Aunt Rose introducing Cousin George to the pretty redhead at the bowling alley. I'm talking about making those little sticks that ignite. Back in the 1800s, matches were made by dipping slivers of wood into white *phosphorus,* a dangerous chemical that catches on fire with just a wee bit of friction. Alas, the people who made matches developed something called "phossy jaw" because phosphorus dust filled the workplace. It began with a toothache, then a swiftly swelling jaw that would eventually rot away. The only cure was to surgically remove the jawbone, which left behind a person with a very lopsided face.

WATER WORKS

Life by the water. Doesn't that sound cool? Think again.

Back in the late 1800s in London, you could be a *dredgerman,* and help out the police. What did you do? Troll the Thames River, which was so littered with corpses that it needed regular body removal. Dredgermen were paid by the corpse, but many of them added

L'IL SPINNERS

In America's early days, there was need for lots of workers. Those first colonists needed cheap labor, so in the mid-1600s, a boatload of 100 orphans—referred to as "friendless boys and girls"—were sent over from England to work. All the grown-ups back then were really proud of all this. They thought it was very charitable of them, believing that it kept kids out of trouble.

In 1790, America's first cotton-spinning factory began hiring kids from ages 7 to 12 to do the work. Thirty years later, half the people working in the textile mills in New England were kids your age. If a kid even looked like he was thinking of slacking off a teensy bit, a foreman was waiting in the wings, armed with a stick, a strap, or a whip made of 14-inch-long leather strips studded with tacks (in the style of one Rhode Island factory) to make sure that child couldn't sit down for a week. The factory noise was overwhelming and many kids went deaf from the constant racket. Many lost their little hands to the quick and vicious machinery.

Surely there were laws to protect children? Yeah—well, there was the one that said kids under the age of 14 could ONLY work 12 hours a days, not more. And in 1906, the poster child for the National Labor Committee was an eight-year-old who worked the 12-hour night shift in a Georgia cotton mill. It wasn't until 1938 that the first child labor laws were signed in America. But millions of little kids in other parts of the world are still heading off to work instead of school in countries like India, Bangladesh, Malaysia, Thailand, Portugal, Turkey, the Philippines, and Mexico.

Picky, picky! Even four-year-olds were put to work.

to their income by emptying the dripping pockets of the dead before turning the bloated bodies over to the authorities.

Even very young kids worked at water's edge. Their job was called *mudlarking*. Mudlarks waded into the cold, rocky waters of the river and pulled out crud—any old bits they could find: shoes, old bits of rope, and nails. Was it fun? Well, for one thing, the London sewers all emptied into the river, so there was usually a layer of excrement floating on the water. And one mudlark, too poor to afford footwear, told a newspaper writer, "It is very cold in winter to stand in the mud without shoes."

Out at sea, young boys served in the navy as *loblolly boys*. Don't worry about equal rights, girls; you wouldn't want them in this case. *Loblolly* is a disgusting, thick stew that was fed to sick sailors. The loblolly boy's main job was to spoon-feed this slop to sick crewmen. But there were additional responsibilities—especially helping the ship's doctor. During naval battles, many a seaman had an arm or a leg blown to bits. Doctors routinely chopped off an injured limb instead of trying to repair it. The loblolly boy's job was to heat irons and hot tar. The hot iron was used to sear the stump closed and the hot tar was applied to keep the victim from bleeding to death. Then the loblolly gathered the chopped off limbs and tossed them overboard. But the good news is, it was too far at sea for the mudlarks to have to collect them.

TANNING SALON

Ever think about what goes into making a leather jacket or a pair of leather shoes?

Someone had to take a live cow and turn it into a dead piece of leather—no easy feat. In the days before machines, folks called *tanners* did the dirty deed.

Tanning a hide is tough work. After the cow was slaughtered and skinned, the hide had to be bathed in a pool of a lime solution—and I'm not talking about those tart little green fruits. *This* lime is a strong *alkali* (the opposite of an acid) with a sickly sweet stench. After a weeklong bath, the hides were pulled out and the tanner scraped off the excess flesh, fat, hair, and other assorted goopy bits. The next step was a bath in a pool of *bate*—basically a soup of warm dog or chicken poop, which removed the lime and broke down and softened the stiff hides to make them wearable. For months, the hides were soaked and washed until they were finally finished.

Naturally, this was not a work environment that smelled very pleasant. And in an era when everyday baths were rare, when the day was done, it was hard to shake the smell of chicken poop!

So there you have it. So many jobs . . . so little time! Lesson learned? Unless you want to wade in pee for the rest of your life you just might want to pay attention in school.

CHIM-CHIM-CHIR-OOOO

In the movie *Mary Poppins,* the Chimney Sweeps, dancing on London's rooftops, looked like they were having sooooo much fun. Wanna know the real truth? Kids started working as sweeps as young as age five and were over the hill by age 16. That's because a grown-up can't fit into a seven-inch-square chimney.

To prepare for the job, knees and elbows had to be hardened by rubbing those parts with *brine* (gritty saltwater) near a hot fire, rubbing the skin over and over until a hard callous formed. When knees and elbows were sufficiently tough, it was time to get those little brushes and wriggle down a sometimes twisting fireplace flue. Many a child ended up getting stuck and then roasted to a crisp when the unsuspecting homeowner tossed a couple of logs into the grate and lit a match.

LEAVING
INC. 1809
LAND OF OPPORTUNITY

K

KILLER KINGS

Wouldn't it be cool to be in charge? Have people bow down to you and call you Your Majesty? Bring you stuff whenever you snap your fingers? Just imagine the fun! Don't like what's for dinner? Send the servants out for pizza, cake, and ice cream! Don't want to do homework? Get a royal chamberlain to do it for you! Teacher gives you detention? Off with her head! Yeah . . . being king sounds like some kind of great.

There's only one little problem, as tales of the past have shown us again and again. Many a motley monarch has ended up skewered by his loyal subjects!

THE BEST OF THE WORST

In the beginning of recorded history, people became leaders because they actually could lead. They were braver, smarter, stronger, bigger, or sometimes just plain luckier than the average person. Naturally, folks believed that these fabulous people would have children with the same talents. So *hereditary* (*her-ED-it-ter-ry*) thrones, set up so that a son (or sometimes a daughter) inherits the crown, came to be. This meant that sometimes you had baby kings who weren't even toilet-trained being "advised" by unsavory, power-hungry relatives or other folks angling to get that jeweled crown away.

Being "better" than everyone else meant you had to marry someone who was *also* "better" than everyone else. But who? Lots of royal families ended up marrying their own cousins and sometimes even their own sisters and brothers! *Ick!* This is not a good thing! It can lead to all sorts of genetic defects in the body and brain. As a result, more than one person with the IQ of a box of rocks got to be king. And besides—as time has shown us, again and again—some people are just plain, flat-out nasty. There have been some pretty cruddy kings, stupid shahs, evil emperors, and flat-out crazy Caesars. In fact, there have been so many awful and deranged monarchs that I could write a book the size of a castle and not get to tell you about all of them!

RAVING ROYALS

These days, most kings and queens are just for decoration. Sure, they get to live in palaces and wear crowns on fancy occasions, but mostly they are for show. Until relatively recently (the last couple hundred years), it wasn't like that.

What exactly is a *monarch?* It's a nation's ruler or head, who usually gets that job because he or she was born into it. Kings are not picked by registered voters. They don't have to step down after a few years. And they don't have to listen to the average person, because they never have to run for reelection. The job is theirs for life.

PRINCE FOR A DAY

Think being a prince or princess sounds like fun? I'm sure there were king dads and queen moms who were loving parents. But when you are busy running (or ruining) your country, there's not a lot of time to give Junior piggyback rides. So many little princes and princesses were raised by a fleet of servants and tutors.

Take Pu Yi, the last emperor of China before their monarchy was overthrown. He was born in 1906 and was chosen to rule by his grandmother, who died when he was three. Now, of course a

Why should kings have all the fun? Don't miss QUIRKY QUEENS on page 214.

YUCKY YORE

One of the real perks of being a king-to-be was that no one could really spank you or send you to your room. But still, there were times when grown-ups wanted to make a point. Many princes had whipping boys—some poor kid who had to take a beating for the king-to-be if the prince goofed up in his studies. Wonder if having someone else take their punishment helped keep rascally monarchs in line.

three-year-old can't run a country, so a regent—in Pu Yi's case his father, but often an uncle—did the job.

Pu Yi's playground was in a huge palace called the Forbidden City. Thick 35-foot-high walls kept regular folks out. If they *did* get in, they were killed. Yellow was the official color of the emperor, so little Pu was always surrounded with yellow *everything*—clothes, blankets, dishes, and even floor tiles. Inside the Forbidden City, everything was done by *eunuchs*. These were grown men that had some of their private parts cut off so they could not father any children. These big guys were Pu's playmates. He didn't meet another actual kid until he was seven years old. Everyone—grown-ups, and even his own mother—had to bow down to the little guy when they saw him. There was even a servant to study his poop every day—to sniff it and tell

Trust me, emperors in diapers do not make great rulers. China's Pu Yi is proof.

the cooks to add more of "this or that" to what he was eating if the poop smelled funky.

Wherever Pu went, a large group of servants followed, always carrying food, clothing, and medicines. When the little emperor was hungry, he would yell, "Bring the food"—and poof! Eunuchs would run in with six tables full of food—25 different dishes to choose from. Cooks in the palace cooked 24 hours a day so that there was always food waiting just in case the little emperor got hungry.

What happened to Pu Yi? When he was a teenager, China's monarchy fell apart. Pu Yi, who had grown up being treated like a god when he was a boy, ended up in prison for a time, and then vanished into the vast crowds of his country. But at least no one ever sniffed his poop again.

KING FOR A DAY

Grown-up rulers didn't have it much better. For one thing, they never had any privacy.

Take Louis XIV, the Sun King. For many years, this French ruler would wake up to find dozens of people standing behind a little fence that surrounded his bed. A typical day began with him going number two while his advisors chatted away. He had people to bathe him and dress him—about 100 servants and advisors clustered around as he brushed his teeth.

Every day, between 3,000 and 10,000 people came to Louis's castle at Versailles, hoping to get a chance to talk to the

A KING BY ANY OTHER NAME...

Kings go by different names depending on where in the world they are doing their ruling. Let's check some of these out.

■ In some Islamic countries, such as Oman in the Middle East, a king is called a *sultan*.

■ In ancient Persia (now modern-day Iran) and Afghanistan, their kings were called *shahs*. Up until the 1970s, there was a shah of Iran.

■ Over in Russia, kings were called *tsars*, or *czars*, depending on who was translating Russian into English.

■ In Germany and Austria, *kaisers* wore the crowns until the early 1900s.

■ In India, *moghuls* ruled the country for centuries.

■ In many Asian countries, such as Mongolia, the head honcho was called a *khan*.

■ And in parts of Africa, *mansas* were who you bowed down to.

But it all boils down to the same thing: one guy telling everyone else what to do and, all too often, doing very bad things just because they could.

king or one of his ministers. Every minute of the day was planned. There were advisors to listen to and endless decisions to be made. Church services every morning at 10 A.M. Meetings. A little hunting or a walk to keep the king fit. More meetings. At 10 P.M. supper was served and the public was allowed

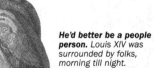

He'd better be a people person. Louis XIV was surrounded by folks, morning till night.

to come and watch the royal family eat—kind of like feeding time at the zoo.

At 11:30 P.M. came the *couchée* (*coo-SHAY*)—bedtime, again with a crowd standing behind the little bed-fence, watching the king get tucked in for the night until the bed curtains were finally drawn.

What a life!

END OF THE LINE

Let's say you are a rich and powerful king. That's another big problem. You usually have enemies. Lots of them, if you have been an unkind king. Being top dog means always having to be on your toes. You have to hope your own trusted friends and advisors aren't going to stab you to death. That's what his buddies did to Roman emperor Julius Caesar in 44 B.C.E. Being head guy meant you always had to be looking over your shoulder before you did everything—even going to the john.

You could never let your guard down, like England's Edmund Ironside did in 1016 C.E., only to get speared in the butt while taking a royal dump one night. You have to hope your soup isn't full of arsenic like Sweden's Eric XIV's was in 1577. And you especially have to pray that your sister or brother (who you did something mean to years ago) isn't waiting to have you beheaded.

KING BOB, THE REALLY UGLY

You know how kings always have those confusing Roman numerals after them? The countries of Europe—especially England, France, and Germany—had a lot of really strange kings, all with the *same* half-dozen names! There have been nine King Edwards, eight King Henrys, 12 kings named Charles, and a whopping 18 kings name Louis. So instead of trying to memorize those numbers, let's remember a few choice rulers for their stunning accomplishments.

1. Ethelred the Unready *(ruled from 978 to 1016)*
Way back in 978, when baby Ethelred, heir to the throne in England, peed in the holy water during

PLAYPALS

What did every king want in his court? Diamonds? Rubies? Nah! Dwarves! For some reason, having a dwarf or two was considered the absolute coolest! Some dwarves were court jesters, telling jokes and juggling. But a few actually became trusted advisors. The ancient Egyptian pharaohs had dwarves. The Aztec kings had 'em, too. Over in China, a dwarf-to-the-emperor was the only one who could speak the truth about dumb things the emperor was doing and not get hacked in half. European kings in the Middle Ages wouldn't be caught dead without a dwarf sitting at his feet. Talk about weird, huh?

The real "Mini-Me." Every court wanted a dwarf.

his baptism, all the assembled guests gasped in horror. The terrified fortune-tellers decided that because of this horrible omen, the entire English population would be slaughtered during Ethelred's reign.

Folks started calling the leaky little baby Ethelred the *Unraed* (which means "ill-advised" in the old language of the Saxons). Nowadays he's known as Ethelred the Unready. Ethelred was indeed unready. Unready to rule. And unready to make good decisions. During his reign, helmet-headed Vikings were always swooping down from Denmark, making everyone miserable (you can read all about VICIOUS VIKINGS on page 277).

By the time he was 24 years old, King Ethelred had turned over *his* lunch money to the Vikings one too many times. One day, after paying over a particularly huge amount of gold, Ethelred cracked. He ordered every person of

Danish extraction living in England killed—men, women, and even babies. Babies were swung by their feet and bashed against walls. Women were buried up to their waists (so they could not escape) and then attacked by wild dogs. Not nice! Still, nothing Ethelred did seemed to work. He abandoned his throne to a Viking king in 1013, grabbed it back a year later, and died—still unready to rule—at the age of 38.

CRACKED-UP CAESARS

Ancient Rome was a magnificent civilization. But when it came to its rulers—aye-yi-yi! There was so much insanity running in the royal families that it's no wonder the empire cracked. Here are the worst.

1. Caligula (ruled from 37 C.E. to 41 C.E.): This tall, spindly, pale, prematurely bald dude was so obsessed with his baldness that if he saw someone with a fine head of hair, he'd order that person's hair shaved on the spot! He tried to have his horse made a senator and liked to roll around naked in piles of gold. He had so many people tortured and killed that his own soldiers assassinated him.

2. Nero (ruled from 54 C.E. to 68 C.E.): Nero Claudius Caesar was one of Rome's worst emperors. Part of the blame goes to his mom, Agrippina, who killed her uncle to get her son the throne. That doesn't exactly set a good example for a kid. Nero figured it was okay to kill anyone he didn't like and eventually he murdered his own bossy, pushy mother— along with anyone who was

better looking, more talented, or who dared to say anything even a teensy bit critical to him. But he is most famous for "fiddling while Rome burned"—failing to act while a great blaze scorched much of the city, conveniently clearing a large space for a new palace for him. Finally, everyone had enough of Nero and demanded he be executed. When soldiers came to arrest him, he tried to kill himself by stabbing himself in the neck, but did a bad job of it. In the end, his secretary had to officially "nick" Nero's nasty neck.

3. Vitellius (ruled in 69 C.E.): Boy could he pack a meal away! This guy literally ate all day long. He'd eat, use a long feather to make himself vomit, then eat some more. His favorite snacks were pheasant brains and flamingo tongues.

4. Domitian (ruled from 81 C.E. to 96 C.E.): Sometimes it's boring to be king. Domitian's hobby was catching flies, stabbing them, and tearing their wings out. Unfortunately, he liked to do the same thing to people (minus the wing ripping).

A stable table. Caligula's favorite pony, Swift, ate like a horse off a golden plate at chowtime.

2. William the Really Fat
(ruled from 1066 to 1087)

Most people know big Bill as William the Conqueror, because as head of the Normans (Normandy is part of France), he conquered the English in 1066. A ruthless ruler, he was the man who gave us beheading as a way to get rid of anyone who happened to annoy him. William was the ultimate control freak, but there was one thing he couldn't control: his appetite. He was a *big* eater and people were always snickering behind his back that he looked like a pregnant woman. A lot of folks probably thought Bill should be known as William the Really Fat.

In 1087, tired of all his subjects making fat jokes, he set off for France to go to a diet spa. He never made it. Along the way, he decided to fight a quickie battle. While celebrating the victory, his horse was spooked by a burning ember and Big Bill's big gut was thrust onto the iron pommel of his saddle. His intestines soon burst, and five weeks later he died.

The funeral was on a very hot day and dead Bill's chubby body swelled so much it didn't fit into the stone sarcophagus. The lid wouldn't close and when the funeral guys pushed on Bill's swollen belly, it burst open, like a balloon. Green pus spewed out, soaking his clothes as a "gag-me" stench filled the chapel. Now there's a regal end!

3. Ivan the Truly Terrible
(ruled from 1547 to 1584)

Russia in the 1500s was a wild place, and Ivan IV was a wild man. In Russia he is called Ivan Grozny, which means Ivan the Awesome. But the rest of the world knows him as Ivan the Terrible. "Terrible" isn't a bad enough word to describe him. Ivan had a miserable childhood, caught in the middle of feuding relatives who all wanted the throne after his dad's death. Ignored and beaten, he started to take his rage out on innocent birds that he caught, plucked, and blinded.

Ivan became tsar of Russia when he was 17. As he got older he drank too much, romanced too much, and just for fun, beat people up. Then he'd feel guilty and run off to church, where he would bang his head against the floor so much that he developed a thick callous on his forehead. After his dear wife died, he became even nuttier. He formed a secret police force called the Oprichniki, who rode off to kill anyone Ivan didn't like. Ivan *always* had a metal staff with him that he used to hit people with. He held target practice on real, live (soon to be dead) people. He trusted no one, even his dearest friends—and even had his closest advisor boiled to death in a cauldron.

In 1570 Ivan and his armies stormed into the city of Novgorod on the basis of a stupid rumor and pretty much killed *everyone* in town, dragging them into the freezing waters of the Volkhov River. And to top it off, one night he got into a fight with his son and hit him with that nasty metal spike, killing him. They don't come more terrible than that, eh?

4. Shah Abbas the Sneaky

(ruled from 1588 to 1629)

Sometimes a king just wants to be an ordinary guy. People treat you differently, and you can listen in on people's conversations and find out what they're really thinking and doing. So Persia's Shah Abbas would sneak out of his palace dressed in beggar's clothes to really see what was going on in town. This was a cute story in *The Prince and the Pauper.* But when the shah did it, it led to cruel punishments: Among the people he met were a dishonest baker, whom he then ordered baked to death in his own oven, and a cheating butcher, who was ordered roasted upon his own spit.

5. George the Drunken Hair Collector

(ruled from 1820 to 1830)

George IV became king of England when his dad, George III, went crazy. Mad King George, as dad was known, was the king who had so pissed off the American colonists that they went to war to get away from him. Was George IV better? Not much. He spent his entire kingship chasing after women and getting drunk. Even though he was married, he had scads of girlfriends. Every time he started hanging out with a new woman, he asked for a lock of her hair. When he died, his aides found more than 7,000 envelopes containing locks of ladies' hair—enough to stuff a mattress! He was also an alcoholic who typically drank three bottles of wine with dinner every night. He would then fall flat on his face and often had to be rolled out of his own puke.

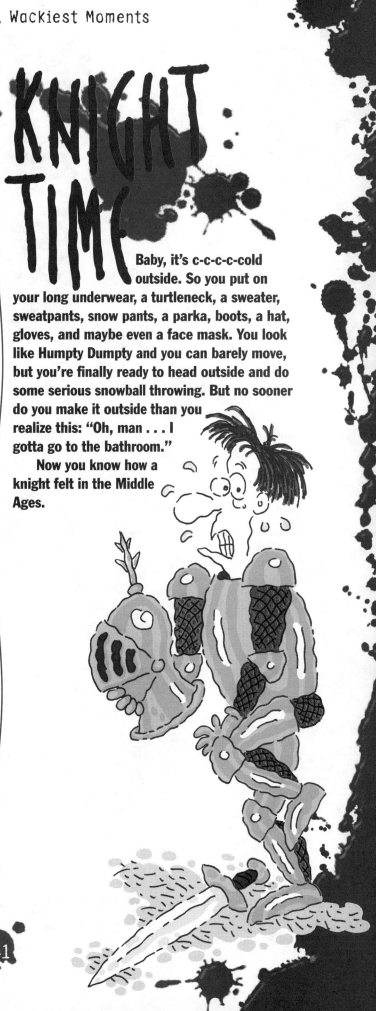

KNIGHT TIME

Baby, it's c-c-c-c-cold outside. So you put on your long underwear, a turtleneck, a sweater, sweatpants, snow pants, a parka, boots, a hat, gloves, and maybe even a face mask. You look like Humpty Dumpty and you can barely move, but you're finally ready to head outside and do some serious snowball throwing. But no sooner do you make it outside than you realize this: "Oh, man . . . I gotta go to the bathroom."

Now you know how a knight felt in the Middle Ages.

MINE, ALL MINE!

After the fall of Rome in the late 400s, Europe was a mess. There was no central government and you never knew when a violent gang was going to come around slicing and hacking at everything in their way. Food was for stealing, livestock for seizing. No one went to school. Hardly anyone could read or write. Staying alive was everyone's main job. So anyone with enough land and money to build a little castle got to be a ruler. But because there were no real laws, these wealthy dudes had to hire men to protect their stuff—kind of like the private security guards you see at the mall these days, only minus the beer belly and walkie talkie. Instead they were equipped with a giant sword, an axe, a horse, and a suit of heavy metal. Enter the age of the knight!

OH, YIKES!

WORD UP!

Lighten up. The word *knight* has nothing to do with the dark. It's from an Anglo Saxon word, *cniht,* which means simply "boy." Back then, a "boy" was a servant. And that's exactly what knights originally did—served their masters. In time, only well-born men could become knights, and it eventually became a term of honor.

THE ROYAL PECKING ORDER

Over the next 800 years, knights became the street gangs, big bullies, kindly policemen, and soldiers in a world gone whacko. The first knights got their start in France. Then the idea rode over to Germany, Spain, Italy, and England, where the legend of King Arthur and his Knights of the Round Table took root.

Knights were part of a system called *feudalism (FEW-duh-liz-um)*. At the top, there was a rich king with thousands of miles of land, hanging out in a big castle. Beneath him were groups of lords who promised to fight for the king in exchange for acres and acres and acres of his land. The lords didn't want to get their hands dirty, so they hired knights to do their dirty work, and gave the knights a couple of acres of their lordly land as payment. And holding the whole pyramid up were hundreds of thousands of smelly, overworked peasants called *serfs,* who farmed the land and made sure everyone was well-fed, except themselves.

SERF'S UP!

Pity the poor (and I do mean poor) serf at the bottom of Europe's feudal system. Nine out of every ten people in the Middle Ages was a peasant working on a lord's farm. Almost everything a serf grew went straight to the lords on whose land they lived. They had to pay taxes to the king on top of this. If they were *very* lucky, they might end up with a teeny bit of wool and flax, or a few extra grains at the end of the year to sell at the village market. They lived in huts made of sticks and mud and barely had enough to eat, yet they were surrounded by thick forests full of animals—deer, wild pigs, and game birds. But touch one deer, catch one fish from the royal pond, and they'd be dead. Everything

DRESS LIKE A
KNIGHT

BEVOIR & VISOR
Saving face is only possible if you *have* a face.

PIKE POLE →
An oldie, but goodie. Half spear, half axe, all dangerous.

GORGET
Want to keep your neck attached to your body? This will help.

BREASTPLATE
Want to have a heart? Protect it with a thick layer of steel.

PALDRONS
If someone hacks off your arms, you can't fight. These protect your shoulders.

GAUNTLET
If you want to still have five fingers at the end of a joust, you'll need these.

HAUBERK
An under-layer of maille was a knight must-have. A split up the front made getting on a horse possible.

SHIELD
Made of heavy oak rimmed in iron with a big stud in the center, called the "boss." At 25 pounds, it's like carrying a big sack of dog food around all day.

GREAVE
Soccer shin guards, but made of steel.

SABATONS
Steel shoes slid into stirrups easily. Of course, you sounded like a walking junkyard and you could never sneak up on someone and surprise them. Oh well.

143

belonged to the king and his lords. Even the guppies. And who was going to protect all this stuff? Call in the knights!

ALL IN A KNIGHT'S WORK

A knight was basically a tough guy with horse, whose job was to protect his master's stuff and make sure it was safe for the serfs to farm. He also had to protect the priests, monks, and nuns who were busy praying that the next life was better than the one they were currently stuck

Architecture that says "Keep Out!" No welcome mats at a castle-door. No door, either.

in. But sometimes, a knight's job was to get *more* stuff for his lord. He did this by killing another lord's peasants, setting fire to the other guy's crops, destroying his tools, and trampling his vineyards. Get in the way of a marauding knight and be prepared to have your eyes gouged out or your feet hacked off. Knights could be very nasty.

STORM THE CASTLE

The knight's home base was his lord's castle. Since the odds were pretty good that another lord was going to come and try to attack, castles were built super-strong to keep the bad guys out.

KNIGHT SCHOOL

So you want to be a knight? Here's what your youth might be like.

■ Kiss your family bye-bye. You may be only eight years old, but you're going to live with a stranger. You'll become a knight's *squire*—a cool word for an assistant. You'll take care of his armor and weapons, feed and groom his horse, and help him get suited up when it's time to do battle.

■ After a year or two has passed, you'll start learning the ropes, including how to ride and use those wicked weapons. Prepare to fall off your horse a lot. Expect to be *very* black and blue.

■ When you turn 13, it's time to become an *arming squire*. You'll spend the next few years running into the middle of battle to replace your knight's broken armor. After the battle, all the muddy, bloody, and dung-filled armor has to be removed from your mangled master, while you wash the armor and scour it with sand, vinegar, and urine so that it's nice and shiny for the next blood fest.

■ Sweet 16? You've reached fighting age. In the next few years, you can look forward to becoming a real knight. You'll become a master of all the knight's deadliest toys: swords, lances, axes, and the morning star (a metal ball with sharp spikes on the end of a chain).

■ Knight time! The king has dropped his sword on your shoulder. You now are a full-time servant of your liege lord. Your job is to do everything you are asked to. You might have to guard the king's castle, be a lord's bodyguard, or hack a few limbs in battle. If you do well, you'll get paid in land.

■ Sometimes you get to play judge and jury as part of an *assize,* a medieval kind of court. You also have to manage your own land (and your very own peasants, lucky you).

■ Got to stay in shape. You have to keep fit and keep practicing your fighting skills. No paunchy, out-of-shape knights at the joust! Shoving a big belly into a too-tight suit of armor is very uncomfortable.

YOU'VE GOT MAILLE

Maille was a must for every knight. It was made from chains with tiny links that's put together like fabric. A maille shirt took hundreds and hundreds of hours to make and cost a small fortune, but it was one thing no knight could do without. A whack with a sword couldn't break the rings, and the little holes were usually too small for a sword blade to pierce.

Shirts weren't the only item made of maille. There were maille hoods, called *coifs,* which gave a guy the worst case of hat-hair imaginable. There were even maille mittens with leather palms. The typical maille layer weighed in at about 31 pounds.

Maille was good protection, but it wasn't perfect. If someone came at you with a mace, a flail (a stick with a heavy chain and ball attached to it), or a hammer, the maille could pop apart. And then you'd be in deep doo-doo.

Maille-Man. This knight has a maille shirt to protect his neck.

For starters, castles were always built on high spots—all the better to see enemies coming. The walls were very high and smooth. Rounded towers offered 360-degree views. A giant deep ditch called a *moat* was dug around the entire building, then filled with yummy things like the contents of the castle's chamber pots (and we all know what was in *those*). Depending on which way the wind was blowing, a castle could smell pretty darn funky.

There was a drawbridge to get over the moat that could be pulled up quickly and a giant iron gate called a *portcullis* that could be dropped down in a flash. Many castles had teeth-shaped things at the top called *crenellations* (*kren-uh-LAY-shunz*) and they were the perfect place for archers, armed with longbows and flaming arrows, to duck behind for protection.

Knights fought on horseback. But the lords had other soldiers to call upon. Foot soldiers guarded the castle. They were the ones who stood on the roof, longbows in hand, arrows at the ready. They were the ones who heated the vats of boiling oil to toss on the other guy's armies. Without their support, the knights would have been goners. (Shoot over to WACKY WARFARE on page 282 for more.)

SURELY YOU JOUST

To prove that you had the "knight stuff," you had to do a lot of fighting. Even when there weren't any wars to be fought or peasants to be trampled, knights had to keep on strutting their stuff. One way they did it was with a *melee*—an itty-bitty mini-war, fought between teams of knights. Think soccer with swords, balls and chains, and no

Oy! My achin' head! A swing from a mace could split a skull!

referees. The trick was merely to hurt your opponent, not kill him. But sometimes, things got a little out of hand and in one melee in 1240, 60 knights "accidentally" died.

Soon the team sports became one-on-one events. And one of the coolest ways to fight was to *joust*—two guys galloping toward each other aiming a 40-pound pole with a sharpened tip at his opponent's eyeballs! The winner got all kinds of goodies: land, ladies, and loot. The loser had to turn over his horse, armor, and all his clothes—usually in front of a hooting, hollering crowd of spectators.

Who put the "ow" in jousting? Once a knight was de-horsed he was dead.

KNIGHT NECESSITIES

What did a knight need to fight? Most important of all was a big sword, broad enough to hack and slice but with a more tapered point so it could find the occasional hole in the armor and draw some serious blood. Armpits were one of the most vulnerable spots, because knights had to lift their arms to use their weapons and a sword could easily travel from underarm to lungs or heart without a lot of effort. Another handy weapon was the poleaxe. *Pole* was the medieval word for head. A poleaxe was

WHAT'S OLD IS NEW

Think maille's gone forever? Not so! Butchers and oyster shuckers wear maille gloves to keep from stabbing themselves. And shark divers wouldn't be caught dead without their maille suits—or else they *would* be dead.

designed to batter a guy's skull. And the axe had a spike that worked a lot like a giant can opener and could pierce armor!

Just as a knight needed his armor to survive, so did his horse. After all, sometimes it was easier for an attacking knight to hack his opponent's horse to bits so the other knight fell off. Once a knight was de-horsed, he was a sitting duck. And a sitting duck often ended up a dead one, so horses got suits of armor, too—*big* suits!

A WALKING TANK

Beginning in the 1400s, a new layer was added to the knight's arsenal: plate armor. Imagine encasing yourself in a big can. That's what armor was. It was strong and smooth, made of wrought iron or steel so that arrows just bounced right off it.

There were three types. Combat armor was designed so that a knight could actually move in it fairly easily. It weighed in at about 45 to 70 pounds. When a knight wanted to get a little fancier, he could pull on his parade armor—that was the tuxedo of armor. It usually had lots of decorations, but it was too weak to actually deflect a weapon and way too fussy to wear in battle. Jousting armor was 80 pounds of heavy-duty steel—the perfect thing to wear when someone was about to come galloping at you at 60 miles an hour waving a seven-foot-long lance with a metal tip. Jousting armor had extra protection on the left side, since the side that got lanced-at the most. There was also a little shelf on the armor-shoulder where you could rest your lance, but it was almost impossible to move around in.

As you can imagine, all this steel came with a whopping price tag—up to a quarter of a knight's yearly earnings. Many beginning knights permanently "borrowed" pieces of armor from dead or wounded knights on the battlefield.

I'M DRESSING MYSELF

Getting dressed was no easy task for a knight. You simply could not put all that metal on by yourself. A servant was a must. And as for the absolutely most important question any of you will have about knights— how *did* they go to the bathroom?— here's the

answer: They made sure they "went" before they galloped anywhere. If, for some reason a knight had to "go" in the middle of a battle, he just "went" in the saddle. Charming, I'm sure.

A knight only pulled on his armor when he absolutely had to. It wasn't like he got out of bed in the morning and the first thing he pulled on was a pair of steel shorts. Jousting armor was so bulky that a knight put his leg pieces on before hopping on his horse, then finished getting dressed in the saddle.

Surprisingly, armor was not that uncomfortable, but it was hot. The padding underneath, topped with a layer of steel, caused many a knight to topple over from heatstroke, especially in battle.

KNIGHTY KNIGHT

The age of knights and chivalry faded away in the 1600s. Why? Bang, bang, you're dead! The one thing that could make a hole in a suit of armor was a gun. Why bother messing with all that metal when a bullet could zip right through? The rules of war changed completely with the arrival of guns. But the image of a knight in shining armor, galloping in to save the damsel in distress, still endures.

L

LEWIS AND CLARK

You know how grown-ups are always nagging you to eat vegetables? Hiding zucchini in perfectly good food? Threatening no dessert if you don't eat your spinach? And how you're always figuring out ways not to comply? But if you could ask explorers Meriwether Lewis and William Clark how they felt about a tub of lima beans topped with a gallon of Brussels sprouts, they probably would have drooled. Read on to find out why.

PASS ME A THUNDERCLAPPER AND MAKE IT SNAPPY

For 28 long months beginning in 1804, Lewis and Clark and the Corps of Discovery—30 brave men, one gutsy woman, her wee baby, and a big shaggy dog named Seaman—trudged 8,000 miles. The Corps' job was to head west from St. Louis, Missouri, and make maps of America's newly purchased, uncharted western territories for President Thomas Jefferson. They planned to follow the course of the Missouri River, which heads west from the Mississippi. They *hoped* it would reach all the way to the Pacific Ocean. And they were also supposed to leave markers along the way, so that others could follow in their footsteps. Little did they know that 200 years after their amazing trip, the paths they left behind came marked with the leftovers of their poop! On their journey, there was nothing to eat but beaver tail, buffalo hump, prairie dog, and porcupine. When you eat no vegetables for weeks on end as they did, your personal plumbing can get a little messed up, if you get my drift.

It's hard to be adventurous when you need to go number two and can't.

Before setting off on this wild road trip, Captain Lewis had to take a crash course in

Did someone say lunch? What? I'm lunch?

Prairie dog was just one of the delicious things the Corps of Discovery ate on their journey.

medicine, along with botany, astronomy, and navigation. One of the most important things in his field kit was a box of 50 dozen Dr. Rush's Bilious Pills, which the Corps quickly named "thunderclappers." Thunderclappers were basically laxatives. When the

"going" was tough, a thunderclapper got a guy's guts gushing. Thunderclappers were 60 percent mercury, which is enough to kill a person. But the laxative pushed everything out so fast the mercury didn't have a chance to get absorbed in the bloodstream. Thanks to those mercury-filled pills, we can trace much of the Corps of Discovery's actual path because traces of mercury remain in the soil along the route of the expedition. Archaeologists have even found Lewis and Clark's campsites. The latrines are loaded with mercury. Talk about a toxic dump!

MUDDY WATER ON THE ROCKS

The Lewis and Clark expedition was scary, amazing, frightening, dangerous, and very exciting. It was also smelly. When they weren't being plagued by constipation, they were dealing with the runs! Everyone had tummy troubles because they were drinking river water. Drink some muddy river water and faster than you can say "thunderclapper," you're doubled over with

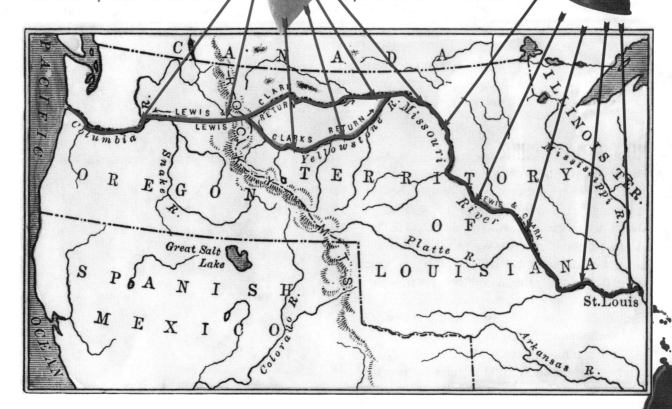

diarrhea, farting up a storm, with booming belches and cramps that can make you a miserable little explorer. Microscopic parasites live in the river mud and carry all sorts of diseases. Captain Lewis complained that for every pint of water he drank, he ended up with a glass of mud. Living on a diet of things like squirrel, horse, dog (which the Corps found quite tasty), and bear also led to some pretty putrid smells wafting along the way West.

Forget grizzlies, storms, and raging river rapids. The greatest danger William Clark ever faced on his journey was the night he took five thunderclappers all at once. As his buddy Captain Lewis wrote in his journal, "My friend, Captain Clark, was very sick all last night but feels himself somewhat better today after the medicine has operated." And I bet you can figure out what the end result of "operated" is!

He writes! He draws! Multitalented Lewis kept an amazing diary of his journey.

MOSQUITO MUNCHING

The first astronauts to walk on the moon had a better idea of what they were in for than the Corps of Discovery did as they set off from St. Louis, Missouri. As their big *keelboat* (which is kind of like a houseboat) made its way up the Missouri River, the Corps faced all sorts of problems. One of the peskiest was the mosquitoes. There were billions of the little buggers swarming in thick black clouds. It was impossible to take a bite of food without swallowing a mouthful of bugs.

In the summer months, Captain Lewis could barely raise and aim his rifle at times because the mosquitoes were so thick. Campsites were chosen based on which were the windiest, in the hopes that a stiff breeze would blow away the bugs. And Seaman, Captain Lewis's big Newfoundland pooch, would howl all through the night because he was being munched on by those bloodthirsty critters.

BABY, IT'S C-C-C-COLD OUTSIDE

Moving up the river through the summer and fall was hard work. The boats were going against the current and often had to be dragged with thick ropes. But that was a cakewalk compared to winter. With the river starting to freeze, the Corps tied up near what is now Bismarck, North Dakota, at the villages of the Mandans and Hidatsas. Some 4,500 people lived there—more than were living in Washington, D.C., at the time.

As you can imagine, Lewis and Clark had no idea what the Mandans and Hidatsas were saying. So they hired Toussaint Charbonneau, a hairy French-Canadian fur trader as an *interpreter* (someone who speaks a lot of languages). His pregnant 16-year-old wife, Sacagawea, was part of the package. Born into the Shoshone nation around 1787, Sacagawea was captured by an enemy tribe when she was a young girl and sold into slavery. Charbonneau won her in a bet (an

Because men are terrible at asking for directions . . . Sacagawea often led the way.

SACAGAWEA: MEGA-MOMMY

It's hard enough to slog through an uncharted wilderness under the best of circumstances. Sacagawea did it with a new baby strapped to her back. And she managed to keep both her infant son and a platoon of gassy explorers happy.

Let's face it. Even a bearded brood of burly adventurers can use a mother. Sacagawea, with her newborn son always in her arms, did a lot to make the journey a success. She tried to help the men eat properly (she was a whiz at finding edible native plants). She sometimes pointed them in the right direction, and she was great at cleaning up their messes. When one of their boats overturned with all of the expedition's journals and scientific equipment aboard, Sacagawea dove into the water *with her baby strapped to her back,* and rescued everything!

Her payoff? A place in the history books, a shiny golden dollar coin (with her baby peeking over her shoulder), and more public monuments in the United States than any other American woman.

But Sacagawea wasn't the only woman that helped make the trip a success. Arikara, Mandan, and Hidatsa women were a constant part of expedition life on the river. They cooked for the Corps and kept the men company. Lemhi Shoshone women helped carry the expedition's gear over the Continental Divide. And a Nez Percé woman named Watkuweis helped keep things friendly between the Corps and her tribe.

---

unfortunate but not uncommon occurrence in those days) and had the good sense to marry her. When Lewis and Clark discovered that the Shoshone, who lived further west, owned many horses, they decided to invite the couple to join the expedition.

The degrees winter temperatures were brutal. It often hit 40° below zero and there was no heat! The Corps spent the winter of 1805 shivering in a makeshift fort. On one particularly freezing cold day, they joined the Mandans on a buffalo hunt and many came home with frostbite. Lewis even had to amputate the toes off an Indian boy without any anesthesia or surgical tools.

Would spring ever come?

AND I THOUGHT BOATS WERE FOR SAILING?

Against the strongest currents, around waterfalls, and over mountains—when spring came, the Corps pressed on! For one terrible two-month period, they actually had to carry their boats over rocks and through forests. They got stabbed by prickly pear cactus. They faced bears. They got lost crossing the Rocky Mountains. They almost starved to death, and then almost died from overeating when they found themselves in a Nez Percé Indian village with an all-you-can-eat salmon buffet. Yet most of the time, the Corps thought themselves the luckiest people on earth to be having such a great adventure!

A COLORFUL GROUP

One of the coolest things about the Lewis and Clark expedition was the melting pot of folks who made the trip. There were a slew of different races, ethnic groups, and social backgrounds all mixed together at a time when most people kept to their own kind. There was a handsome, muscular African American named York, who had been William Clark's slave since childhood. The two became great friends on the trip. The Native Americans had never seen a man with black skin before and often walked up to York, trying to rub off the color! There was a one-eyed French-Canadian fiddler who helped pass the long, boring evenings playing catchy tunes for singing and dancing. Out in the wilderness, rolling on the great river, all men (and woman) really *were* created equal. Especially when it came to being bitten by mosquitoes!

ROLLING ON THE RIVER:

1801: Thomas Jefferson becomes America's third president. The Mississippi River is the western edge of the United States and most Americans live within 50 miles of the Atlantic Ocean. Jefferson decides he needs to know what lies between the river and the Pacific.

Stamp of approval. *President Jefferson told the Corps of Discovery to go west!*

January, 1803: Jefferson asks Congress for big bucks to send a group west to explore the lands on the *other* side of the Mississippi. His aide, Meriwether Lewis, will lead the expedition. Lewis takes a crash course in everything from botany to medicine and invites an army buddy, William Clark, to help him run the show.

July 4, 1803: With the Louisiana Purchase—lands formerly owned by France—America has now more than doubled in size.

Fall–Winter, 1803: Lewis and Clark spend the winter training men for the expedition, and building a keelboat that's 55 feet long and eight feet wide. It will carry almost 10 tons of supplies. There are also two smaller boats, called *pirogues,* for sailing in shallower waters.

May 14, 1804: *Off we go!* The group sets off "under a jentle brease," Clark (an imaginative speller) writes. They cover four whole miles the first afternoon. Only 8,000 more to go! Because they are going upstream, if there is no wind, they will often have to wade along the riverbanks and pull the boats with ropes. On a good day, they will cover about 14 miles.

August 3, 1804: The first official face-to-face with western Indians takes place just north of present-day Omaha, Nebraska. Lewis and Clark hand out little silver medals with Thomas Jefferson's face on them, flags, and assorted small gifts. The Indians are not impressed.

September 7, 1804: Moving into the Great Plains, the crew starts seeing strange animals such as coyotes and antelope. They pass a fun afternoon trying to drown a prairie dog out of its hole with plans to send it back to Jefferson. In the coming months, they will record 178 plants and 122 animals that had never before been scientifically noted.

Fall–Winter, 1804: It's getting nippy. The Corps ties up near what is now Bismarck, North Dakota, at a very large village of the Mandans and Hidatsas. Lewis and Clark decide to winter here. They hire a French-Canadian fur trader and his young Shoshone wife, Sacagawea, as interpreters.

February 11, 1805: Sacagawea gives birth to a baby boy, Jean-Baptiste.

April 7, 1805: Spring is finally coming. Lewis and Clark send the big keelboat and about a dozen men back east with goodies for Thomas Jefferson, including maps and boxes filled with animal skins, skeletons, rocks, and five live animals (including that almost-drowned prairie dog). The same day, the "permanent party" heads west, traveling in the two little pirogues and six small dugout canoes. The expedition totals 33 now, including Charbonneau, Sacagawea, and her baby, whom the crew nicknames Pompy.

June 2, 1805: Uh-oh. A fork in the river. Which way to go? The crew thinks north. Lewis and Clark say south. Lewis makes a couple of 30-mile-a-day walks to explore further and decides to go south. Based on a tip from the Hidatsa Indians, they

A Lewis & Clark Timeline

will know if they guessed right if they hit a big waterfall.

June 13, 1805: Zipping on ahead, Lewis hits "the grandest sight I ever beheld": the Great Falls of the Missouri. But then he sees four more waterfalls just ahead! No way the boats will be able to go over those! They will have to carry the boats around the falls. It is an 18-mile detour. Lewis and Clark think the portage will take half a day. It takes a month!

October 18, 1805: Clark finally sees Mount Hood in the distance. Seen and named by a British sea captain in 1792, it has been the end point on the expedition's map. They are almost to the Pacific! Or so they think!

November 7, 1805: Thinking he sees the end of land in the distance, Clark writes his most famous journal entry: "Ocian in view! O! the joy." (His spelling has not improved on his journey.) But they are still 20 miles from sea. Three weeks of foul, wet, windy weather makes traveling impossible.

November 24, 1805: Winter is here again. The crew needs to stay someplace. Lewis and Clark decide to let everyone vote. In addition to every Corps member, Clark's slave, York, is allowed to vote—nearly 60 years before slaves in the United States would even be freed. Sacagawea votes, too—more than a hundred years before either women or Native Americans can vote. Only little Pompy doesn't get to vote since he is still in diapers! They pick a spot and winter in Oregon.

March 23, 1806: Time to finally head home! Yippee!

May—July, 1806: The team arrives back with the Nez Percé. It is still too snowy to cross the hated Bitterroots. Lewis loves the Nez Percé and calls them "the most hospitable, honest and sincere people that we have met. . . ." Finally, in July, they recross the Bitterroots and the expedition splits up into four smaller groups and fans out to better explore the area.

Late July, 1806: At a sandstone outcropping near present-day Billings, Montana, Clark names the biggest rock Pompy's Tower, in honor of Sacagawea's teeny son. Clark carves his name and the date— the only physical evidence the Corps of Discovery left on the landscape that still survives (besides those mercury deposits, of course).

Lewis and his group are now 300 miles away, near the Canadian border. The next day, Lewis has a run-in with some Blackfeet warriors. He sees the Blackfeet trying to steal his horses and guns. In the fight that follows, two Blackfeet are killed. It is the only violence of the entire trip and Lewis leaves a peace medal around the neck of one of the corpses. He then hightails it out of there, riding for 24 straight hours without stopping.

August 14, 1806: Bye-bye time. The crew has arrived back at the Mandan villages. Everyone says farewell to Charbonneau, Sacagawea, and baby Jean-Baptiste.

September 23, 1806: Their last official day as the Corps of Discovery. They reach St. Louis two and a half years after they left. Folks are shocked. They had been given up for dead!

Fall, 1806: Lewis and Clark and their Corps of Discovery are all national heroes. Everywhere they go folks throw huge parties for them. No one serves them beaver tail, though!

LIKE MEN ON THE MOON

The adventures of Lewis and Clark are a real milestone in the history of America, as important as the day men first hopped around on the moon. It was a great example of people of all colors and genders working as equals for a common goal. I wish I could say that everyone lived happily ever after when they returned home. Sadly, Meriwether Lewis took his own life a few years later. Nothing

EAT LIKE LEWIS AND CLARK

Whip up a batch of Corps of Discovery buffalo jerky. Here's what you'll need:

- Buffalo meat, sliced into thin strips
- Any spice you can get your hands on
- Salt to taste
- Sharpened sticks

Go out and kill a buffalo. Hope that it is not infected with tapeworms. Skin it, scrape off the fat, and slice lean buffalo meat into thin strips. Rub spices and salt into the meat. Thread the meat strips on sticks and dry over campfire. If the meat is not dry by morning, tie the strips to the keelboat mast to dry in the sun as you sail. Leave it flapping there until it looks (and tastes) like shoe leather. Bon appetit!

that followed could equal the joy he had felt as he wrote in his journals, describing all the amazing new things he was discovering. York, William Clark's slave, had tasted freedom out on the trail. It was horrible to have to give it up with his return to "civilization." Sacagawea died at the age of 24. The littlest explorer, Little Pompy, went to live with William Clark. But along with those mercury-filled latrines, the legacy of this amazing expedition reminds us that anything is possible when you eat nine pounds of buffalo meat a day!

Explorers extraordinaire: Meriwether Lewis and William Clark.

M

MISERABLE MEDICINES

Throat sore? G-g-g-gargle and g-g-g-gag. Upset stomach? A spoonful of some pink chalky stuff should do the trick. Cough? Swallow some nasty goop. Medicine may taste bad, but be glad for what we've got. Some remedies have been around for thousands of years, but much of what passed as "medicine" in the past was downright scary. Dirt. Leeches. Maggots. Filthy sawdust. All this was supposed to make you feel better.

THE 5,500-YEAR-OLD MEDICINE CHEST

If you were to zap back in time to ancient Mesopotamia (what's now Iran and Iraq), circa 3500 B.C.E., you'd find that some remedies haven't changed much in 5,500 years.

You'd find saltwater gargles for sore throats, and willow bark, which contains the main ingredient in aspirin, for fevers. Sumerians also had inhalers, suppositories (medicine administered up your butt), enemas (used to make you poop, poop, and then poop some more), poultices (smelly goop to spread on the skin), and all sorts of pills, ointments, lozenges, and sprays. Thankfully, some remedies did not stand the test of time— such as a bracing urine mouthwash to kill bad breath. G-g-g-g-good news, huh?

The ancient Egyptians added more brews to history's medicine chest. They made laxatives from castor oil and senna pods, and antacid from crumbled peppermint leaves and carbonates (a long-ago version of Pepto-Bismol). They developed more than 600 different drugs, and used them to treat everything from baldness to itchy toenails.

For thousands of years, medicines didn't change much. The Greeks and Romans drew on Egyptian and Mesopotamian methods. But when Rome fell to the barbarians in the late 400s C.E., so did the state of wellness all across Europe. During the years that followed—those dastardly Dark Ages—folks were stuck drinking nasty herbal teas, and praying to a whole bunch of saints' thigh bones and other weird relics . . . which, not surprisingly, usually ended up with someone's death.

BLOOD + BARF = ALL BETTER?

During the Middle Ages (1000–1500 C.E.) in Europe, docs thought it made sense to *subtract* body fluids by nicking veins and sucking out blood or by administering drugs that caused the runs or the heaves—or sometimes both! Needless to say, these remedies usually did more damage than good.

Over in the Middle East and Asia, things were a whole lot better. A guy named Ibn Sina (sometimes called Avicenna), who lived from

In the nick of time. Bloodletting was a "get well" cure for centuries.

980 to 1037 C.E., was one of history's greatest medical minds. He wrote a medical book called the *Qanun,* a million-word volume that is still used in parts of the Middle East today. He listed more than 760 drugs, described their use in detail, and tested them to make sure they worked, at least *some* of the time. No wonder he's called the "doctor of doctors." Ibn Sina's book eventually made its way to Europe in 1593 with traveling merchants from the East. His ideas made a lot of sense to people who were sick and tired of dying! Western docs began to study this new way of healing, and were pleased to hear their patients say "I feel so much better" instead of listening to their dying gasps.

GOT BUG GUTS?

Since time immemorial, people have turned to Mother Nature for help when they're feeling icky. Ever since cave-dude days, we've eaten dirt—well, clay to be exact. Turns out white clay, which is still used in Kaopectate—a bestselling anti-diarrhea drug—is a great way to keep you from running to the bathroom every ten seconds when you have the Hershey Squirts!

Our ancestors made tea from boiled tree bark (you may have heard of the stuff? It's called aspirin!) They spread bee vomit on burns (you might know *that* stuff as honey!). But one of the grossest ways to make a guy or gal feel better has to do with bugs—creepy bugs, crawling bugs . . . medical bugs.

During the Civil War in the mid-1860s, docs knew that maggots—newly hatched flies that have not yet sprouted wings—were a good way to prevent gangrene. Gangrene is gross. It's what happens

when a human body part starts to rot away due to infection. By applying maggots, which *love* to eat bacteria and dead tissue, a person's rotting fingers or toes could be saved!

And then of course, there are leeches—those blood-sucking varmints that live in lakes and ponds. They were first used in ancient Egypt about 2,500 years ago to draw out "bad blood," since docs thought that was what made people sick. For thousands of years folks used leech therapy for everything from stomach aches to headaches. Turns out a leech couldn't cure a bad case of the upchucks, but leeches are great for modern-day plastic and reconstructive surgery! They secrete a special slime that helps restore proper blood flow to a surgical wound. They clean away gunk and when they are full they simply fall off the part they were attached to!

YOU'LL FEEL BETTER IN A FLUSH

Things really began to change in the 1600s when healers began learning more about chemistry and what happens when you mix glop A with goop B. Up until that time, most folks just guessed about how much ground-up frog's tongue and snake eyeball they needed in a potion. Now, with Ibn Sina's book as a guide, and a better understanding of the human body, docs began to write down *exactly* how much of what should go into each potion. Folks now knew it was two teaspoons of puréed lark's tongue mixed with ¼ cup of bat blood.

Starting in the 1600s in Italy, docs began doing *autopsies*—cutting up the dead to learn more about human guts and the things that can go wrong with them. But up until the 1800s, getting better when you were ill was mostly a matter of luck, 'cause the docs were pretty clueless.

Hack! Cough! Get the goods on germs in PLAGUES & POXES on page 194!

Take Dr. Benjamin Rush, a signer of the Declaration of Independence and America's top doc in the early 1800s. Dr. Rush's treatment for every disease was bloodletting—draining up to 50 ounces at one bleed. That's almost half the blood in your body! When that didn't work (and, guess what, it never did!), he followed up with pills to purge. Take two of Dr. Rush's Bilious Pills and you'd be glued to an outhouse seat for the next 24 hours. You can see Dr. Rush's handiwork in action by joining LEWIS AND CLARK on their poopy passage through the West on page 148.

DON'T EAT THIS JELLY WITH YOUR PEANUT BUTTER

Bet you've heard of Vaseline. Just about every home has a jar of this greasy, pale yellow jelly.

DOC DITTY

One doctor in colonial America wrote this little ditty:

When patients come to I,
I physics, bleeds, and sweats 'em.
Then if they choose to die
What's that to I?—I lets 'em.

It was invented by Robert Chesebrough in 1859. He learned about it from an oil driller, who was whining about the crud that always built up on the drilling rigs—a disgusting, waxy goop that gummed everything up. The only good thing about it, the worker said, is that it kept his hands soft—and also, it was great for healing cuts and burns. A giant lightbulb went off over Chesebrough's head, and he filled a jar with the gloppy mess and brought it home. Then he started experimenting with it. *On himself!* He cut his arms, burned his hands, and scraped the skin off his body. And each time he hacked at himself, he covered the wounds with the gunky paste. They all healed quickly. None of them became infected. And that's how Vaseline—a combo of the German word for water (*wasser*) and the Greek for oil (*elaion*)—was born.

Soon, everyone was finding a different use for the disgusting goop. Fishermen used globs of it as trout bait. Robert Peary, the first recorded visitor to the North Pole, used it to keep his skin from chapping *and* his equipment from rusting. Down in the Amazon, natives cooked with the stuff, and spread it on bread. It kept car batteries from corroding and burn victims from developing infections. Baseball players rubbed it into their gloves, and long-distance swimmers gave themselves a layer of artificial blubber to help them stay warm in cold water by coating themselves with the stuff.

And Robert Chesebrough? He ate a big spoonful of Vaseline every day for the rest of his life, and lived to the ripe old age of 96! Ick!

I'LL HAVE A COKE

Nowadays, more than a billion people around the world toss back a Coca-Cola every day. And sure . . . the sugar in a Coke can rot your teeth, and the caffeine can make you feel a little wired. But other than that, it's pretty harmless stuff. Well, back in 1886, when John Pemberton, a pharmacist, invented Coca-Cola, it was a whole different drink. Back then, Coca-Cola was sold only in drugstores, and was laced with a hefty dose of cocaine—nowadays an illegal drug. For 17 years, it was sold as a combo refreshing drink and "brain tonic"—and was advertised as a cure for "sick head-ache, neuralgia [muscle aches], hysteria, and melancholy [that means feeling sad]."

You truly got a ZAP when you drank the stuff, and the new drink quickly caught on. Still, plenty of folks realized that drinking it left a person a little *too* buzzed. In 1889, another pharmacist named Asa Candler—the inventor of a yummy medicine called Botanic Blood Balm—bought the rights to Coca-Cola for $2,300. He extracted most of the cocaine to avoid paying a new tax that would penalize patent medicines—those funky concoctions that people sold with claims that they improved one's health (Coke was considered a medicine in those days).

Candler hired a bunch of chemists to figure out how to leave the coca in (that's the part that has the caffeine), but nix the addictive cocaine. Here's how they did it: They ground up the coca plant leaves and mixed them with sawdust, soaked them in bicarbonate of soda, then boiled them with coal-tar solvent and steam. Mmmm-mmmm good!

THE BAND-AID SOLUTION

Until the late 1800s, surgeons packed post-operative wounds with sawdust that had been swept off factory floors and pressed into pads. They were always surprised when their patients died—go figure! But one English doctor named Joseph Lister suspected those filthy pads were killing people. After all, 90 percent of the people who went under the knife in those days died. Lister, however, soaked *his* pads in carbolic acid to kill germs and found that most of his patients lived.

In 1876, a guy named Robert Johnson heard Lister speak about his sterile pads, and he was very impressed! He convinced his brothers to join him in making pre-wrapped sterile bandages for wounds. Johnson & Johnson's dressings caught on and their company grew.

In 1920 Earle Dickson, a guy who worked for Johnson & Johnson, married a clumsy lady who was always cutting or burning herself in the kitchen. The company's surgical pads were too big for her small boo-boos, so one day Earle cut a little piece of the sterile dressing and placed it in the middle of a piece of sticky tape. *Voilà!* The first Band-Aid was born. The folks at Johnson & Johnson liked Earle's little invention and started selling them, but they were a total flop. It was only after they gave free samples to every Boy Scout troop in America that Band-Aids became a must-have in first-aid kits.

IT'S THE PITS

Sweaty people have always smelled *bad,* and many great civilizations have tried to find ways to fumigate putrid pits. The early Egyptians, who lived in a place that could get as hot as a toaster oven, bathed often, then dabbed perfumed oils made with citrus and cinnamon to their smelliest spots. They also found that if you shaved or plucked out all that messy grown-up underarm hair, you wouldn't smell half as bad, so men and women both shaved their pits.

It wasn't until 1888 that someone figured out *why* grown-ups got B.O. Moisture was the culprit! Once they understood that, they figured that if the wetness could somehow be avoided, maybe the stench could be stopped, too. Two chemicals— zinc and aluminum chloride—seemed to do the trick, acting like little corks on the millions of microscopic sweat "bottles" under our arms. That year, Mum, the very first "anti-stinky" hit America's drugstore shelves. Still, for many years people were too embarrassed to buy anti-B.O. creams, since no one wanted to admit that he or she stank. Until 1930 deodorant ads were only aimed at women. Men—usually the ones who smelled the foulest—didn't use them. It wasn't manly!

A DEN OF DRUGS AT THE LOCAL PHARMACY

Cocaine. Opium. Heroin. Nowadays you can go to jail for a very long time if you are caught selling or using these dangerous drugs. But back in 1885 you could walk into any drugstore and buy an item like Cocaine Toothache Drops for 15 cents

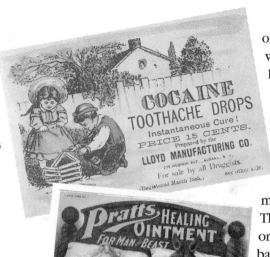

or cough medicine that was loaded with heroin. Dr. Moffett's Teethina Teething Powder, which was meant for teething babies, was full of opium. And the popular One Day Cough Cure featured a bracing mixture of marijuana *and* morphine. The thing is, back then, no one had a clue about how bad for you these drugs were. So perfectly respectable people took dangerous, highly addictive drugs, not knowing what they were doing to themselves. They would gulp down a few spoonfuls of *laudanum* (an opium brew) every day for their "health," then wash it down with various "health tonics," all filled with cocaine. *Yikes,* indeed!

THREE MEDICINE CHEST MUST-HAVES

Open the mirrored doors on America's medicine chests and you'll probably find these:

1. Got Eczema? Even the name sounds gnarly. This red, crusty skin rash itches like crazy. In 1914, a Baltimore pharmacist named George Bunting concocted a soothing cream and started selling it under the name of "Dr. Bunting's Sunburn Remedy." One day, a customer burst into Bunting's shop and raved that the cream had "knocked out his eczema." Dr. Bunting decided that sounded kind of catchy. So he changed the cream's name to Noxzema! (Get it? "Knocks-eczema!") It didn't exactly take off instantly, though: It was touch and go for awhile until World War II, when Dr. B got a deal to supply U.S. soldiers with cooling Noxzema to rub on their smelly, sore, hot, battle-weary feet.

2. Stick a Baby Gay in Your Ear!
Q-tips, the brainchild of a Polish-American named Leo Gertenzang, came along in 1923. He called his invention Baby Gays, but thankfully changed the name three years later. If you've ever wondered what the Q stands for, it's "quality." Quool, huh?

3. Icky Ipecac! For thousands of years, people of the Amazon region in South America had to deal with nasty intestinal parasites and weird poisons, and found that puking was a good way to get well. They powdered the roots of a special shrub, which they called ipecac (*IP-uh-kak*), which means "the sick-making plant." European explorers brought the nasty roots back to Europe, where its use spread as a cure for accidental poisonings.

MOLDY MONEY

What if Uncle Ted and Aunt Hilda sent you a dead beaver skin for your birthday? Suppose you got your allowance in smelly seashells? And what would happen if your grown-ups tried to pay for your burger and fries with a six-foot-high slab of salt? Wipe that smirk off your face, because all of those things were used for money in times past.

So, before you deposit a fistful of sweaty pennies on the candy store counter, read about the coins inside your piggy bank—and the way they have changed history. Hey. Come to think of it . . . I wonder if that's why they call coins "change"?

FORGET PIGS *IN* A BLANKET

How did people get all the things they wanted in the days before money? Simple. They swapped things. It's called *bartering.* Let's say you have a lot of pigs but need a blanket. I make blankets, but I'm dying for a ham sandwich with a side of bacon. We might agree that one pig equals three blankets, and swap. Now you are warm at night, and I get to feast on real pigs in a blanket. Or I might offer to chop wood for you for a week in exchange for a pair of shoes, exchanging labor for something neat-o. Some American Indians were big fans of the barter system and some groups, especially on the West Coast, had huge shindigs called *potlatch ceremonies,* where people brought elaborate and costly things to trade.

THAT'LL BE SIX SLABS OF SALT, A BAG OF FEATHERS, AND A BEAR SKIN

Long ago, money was whatever folks decided was valuable in their part of the world. Nowadays in America, pieces of green-inked paper with pictures of dead presidents are of great value. But long ago, people got paid and did their shopping with useful things such as salt or fur.

Now, if you've ever tried to fit a buffalo pelt into your wallet, you may have noticed that there are a few drawbacks. For one thing, a dead animal is pretty bulky. Smelly, too. Still, animals were probably the very first kind of official money. About 9,000 years ago, people began to use cows, sheep, and camels as cash—not that there was a whole lot to buy in those days. When folks settled down and started farming, bags of grain could buy you the things you needed. But dragging a couple of heavy sacks of flour around while you shop is a real pain.

So some bright soul invented the concept of "money." By money, I mean a special thing that stands for something of value. What makes money "worth" something? It has to be sturdy enough to be traded from person to person and not fall apart. It has to be easy to carry. And it has to be relatively scarce and a little hard to come by—rare enough to be special.

No one knows exactly when money first was invented, but we do know that by 4,500 years ago, shopaholic Mesopotamians were paying for things with weighted bits of silver. They had special weighing stones that were used to check the weight of each silver bit. Picture shops with scales instead of cash registers. A specific weight of silver stood for, let's say, 50 cattle or ten sacks of grain. Soon, they started flattening the hunks of silver to keep them from rolling around. And they also started pressing pictures of famous folks onto the flattened areas to make them even more special.

In the Pacific Islands, money was made from small red feathers glued together and tied to rope—some up to 30 feet long. Brighter feather colors were more valuable. Over in Africa, giant slabs of salt (a *very* valuable item in Africa's hot climate) were used for money. Rare and precious seashells, called *cowries,* were also used in coastal Africa.

The Aztecs of Mexico had "brown gold"—yummy chocolate. Now admittedly, chocolate is fab stuff. But to the ancient Aztecs it was more valuable than real gold. When the Spanish conquistadores searched Moctezuma's palace after his death in the 1500s, looking for gold, all they found were bags and bags of cacao beans.

YUCKY YORE

"**P**aying through the nose" means you've paid way too much. We have the Vikings who conquered Ireland to thank for this expression. Between 800 and 900 they used to slit the noses of any person who didn't pay their taxes on time. Those Vikings sure were swell guys!

Coyote coat, anyone? Animal pelts used to be a form of currency. This sharp-shootin' park ranger is rich!

DOES MONEY GROW ON TREES?

It kind of does! Well, at least the paper it's printed on comes from pulp made from the fibers of growing plants. Since the ancient Chinese were the first folks to make paper, they were the first people to have paper money. It all started because their coins were so darn heavy that people started leaving them with shopkeepers, who issued little pieces of paper stating that they were holding twenty pounds of coins for Mr. Zhou. In 806 C.E., the government took over the note-recording for the merchants and the first official paper money began to circulate in China.

ALL-AMERICAN MONEY:

BEFORE THE EUROPEANS ARRIVED: Besides swapping things, American Indians who lived near the ocean used *wampum*—which was made from quahog clams, conch, and whelk shells in a painstaking process. Wampum means "a string of white beads" in the Algonquin language since the shells were polished down to small bead-like shapes. Black- and purple-colored wampum was rarer, so it was worth the most. The little beads

How many video games can I get for this? Shells used to be used as moolah.

were often woven into beautiful belts and sashes. Not only could you buy things with wampum, but it also helped hold your pants up!

THE 1500s: The arrival of first explorers, and then colonists, from Europe changed everything in the Americas. At first, the newbies used wampum, too. But America's pockets soon started filling with cash brought in by new colonists staking out turf in the New World—especially from Spain. By the mid-1500s the Spaniards had built mints all across South America. After all, they had plenty of stolen gold and silver from which to strike coins. That gold found its way back to Europe, and even to China, as the continents started to connect through trade . . . and piracy. (Pillage your way to PIRATES on page 188.)

In the 1530s the Spaniards gave the world the *piece of eight*—the most successful, most used, most traded, longest-lived coin in history. The cool thing about the piece of eight was that you could actually snap it into eight pieces of smaller value.

THE 1600s: Most settlers in North America used money from Europe (*if* they had any money). But some continued to use wampum. In fact, you could pay for a Harvard education with wampum well into the 1700s! Coins were always in short supply, so folks used commodity money. A *commodity* is something useful—say corn, or oats, or oranges. Back in the 1600s, one bushel of wheat was worth four *shillings* (a kind of English coin) and 48 musket balls were worth four *pence* (kind of like our penny). Nails were also a common form of money. Different lengths of nails were worth different amounts. Even today, you can walk into a hardware store and buy a ten-penny nail (although it'll probably cost you more than ten pennies).

Tobacco was another type of money in colonial America. This money didn't grow on trees, but it sure did sprout from the ground. At first, it was worth a lot. But as more and more folks planted it, its value began to drop. Remember—for money to be successful, it has to be kept in controlled supply.

WORD UP!

How come Granny sends you a few dollars for your birthday every year? Why not pounds, like it was in our mother country, England, or pesos, like it is in Central and South America? The word *dollar* probably came from a German word *taler*, which was short for *Joachimsthaler*—the name of coins made in a town named Joachimsthal in Germany. But it might have also come from the Dutch *Leewendaaler*. All I know is, thank goodness someone shortened the name!

And while we're on the subject of money, we call it money because the ancient Roman temple of Juno Monetas was where the Romans made coins!

162

A Timeline

If it isn't, you end up with *inflation*—a big, fat, bloated money supply that makes your cash worth less and less.

In 1652, the first mint opened in Boston, even though the colonists didn't *exactly* have permission from the king of England to make money. The minters got their hands on silver by doing a little illegal trading with the Sugar Islands in the Caribbean.

The colonists decided to make their coins in English denominations: pence and shillings, but they made them much lighter in weight so that British merchants would not want to use them. Colonial merchants, however, were thrilled to have something easy to trade with—no more dead beavers and heavy sacks of grain! For the next ten years, the Boston mint made coins, but always dated them 1652 because as luck would have it, in 1652, due to a rebellion in England, the king at the time was headless. Since all British coins had pictures of the king stamped into them, this worked out quite nicely!

THE 1700s: European money was commonplace in the Americas. But the English had other ideas and decided that only English money was worth anything. You can bet that ticked the colonists off!

One date everyone remembers is 1776, the year America told Britain to take a hike! During the American Revolution soldiers were paid with coins called *continentals*. After the war, all those coins became worthless because the brand-new United States of America was a financial mess. You know how you can shake all the coins out of your piggy bank? Well, America's piggy bank was empty.

Each state began to print its own money but a dollar in New Jersey was not the same thing as a dollar in Virginia. Finally, the Founding Fathers got together and got to work on a national currency. But first they needed a symbol that would be used on the coins. "Anything but an eagle," said one founding fellow. Poor guy lost *that* request!

1789: THE DADDY OF THE AMERICAN DOLLAR

When George Washington appointed Alexander Hamilton the first Secretary of the Treasury in 1789, there were huge war debts to pay off. The government had to start collecting taxes. Hamilton didn't want folks dragging bales of tobacco or 13 different kinds of state money into his office, so in 1790, he started the first Federal Bank to try to make some sense out of cents. The plan was to make a new national currency. Hamilton was a financial genius and his plan was a good one. (Pssst! Check him out! He's the guy on the $10 bill!)

1792: A HINT OF MINT
Thomas Jefferson, our third president, had another great idea for the nation's new monetary system. Take the old Spanish piece of eight. Call it a dollar. And

divide it into *dismes* and cents. And no . . . I am not a bad speller. Dimes used to be called dismes. But here's a problem. There was hardly any metal from which to make coins. Gold and silver values kept changing. There weren't enough coins to go around. So what do you do when coins just don't cut it? Invent "rag" money! Jefferson gave America its first paper dollar bills.

1800: WILD WESTERN MONEY

As Americans pushed westward, things started getting messy in the money world again. New towns kept springing up and there was no one watching over them, so they made their own laws and they made their own money. There actually *were* wooden nickels. Everyone was making wooden money, from banks to railroads to turnpikes. What a mess!

1850s: YOU AIN'T JUST WHISTLIN' DIXIE

Ever wonder why the South is known as Dixie? Would you believe it's because of money? In Louisiana in the mid-1850s, French was the most commonly spoken language. A bank there issued a beautiful $10 note. It was marked with a DIX on the front and back—the French word for ten. The bill soon became know as a Dix note, called a "Dixie" for short. The name stuck and when a famous song was written about the South, Dixie was here to stay.

No dead presidents on American money in the mid-1800s! Instead, there were chubby milkmaids, noble Indians, African Americans toiling in the fields—even smoke-belching factories.

1860s: WAR!!!

Uh-oh. The Civil War saw America split in two. And boy did that make an even bigger mess of the money! As the war spread, most Confederate states began printing their own money. Up north, the first green-colored money made its appearance, because there happened to be a lot of green ink sitting around. The *greenback* was here to stay.

The Confederate states backed their money up with cotton. But the foundation of their war chest—$1.5 billion in paper money—began to lose its value before the ink had even dried. You wanted a loaf of bread? That'd be $200! Toward the war's end, even Southerners began using Union money to pay for things.

LATE 1800s: KA-CHING!

After the war, America began growing again. New states and new territories were being added. Boatloads of immigrants arrived every day. Cities grew. Factories sprang up all over. A national standard of money

FAKES AND FORGERS

It's always been pretty darn tempting to make fake money, especially paper money. So from the get-go, making counterfeit money was a crime punishable by death. If you knew you were going to be boiled alive, I bet you'd think twice about making a forged ten-dollar note. Still, sneaky Aztecs would hollow out used cocoa beans and fill them with dirt, then reseal them and pass them off as the real deal. Colonists took the white wampum beads of the Native Americans and dipped them in blackberry juice, producing fakes of the more valuable purple beads. And even Ben Franklin, who printed money for Pennsylvania, tried to deter forgers by spelling the name of his state wrong on purpose—thinking counterfeiters wouldn't notice, and would use the correct spelling.

finally began to take hold as American mints began producing pennies, two-cent, and three-cent coins. The disme became the dime. And it was about *tisme!*

EARLY 1900s: SPEND! SPEND! SPEND!

By 1900, the monetary system we use today was beginning to fall into place. Still, all coins were not created equal, especially in the West, where coins were struck from zinc, aluminum, and even rubber.

The early 1900s were a time of easy credit (which means it was easy to get money loaned to you with the promise to pay it back—with a little extra thrown in). People's incomes were on the rise. So were get-rich-quick schemes.

1929: DEPRESSION DAYS

Those good times all came to a crashing end on October 29, 1929. Folks called it Black Tuesday—the day the stock market crashed.

The stock market was a place where people could buy small bits of big companies and own a "share" of the profits. People had invested every spare penny they had and when the companies failed, it was a disaster! Folks lost everything. Banks had invested, too, and many closed. America's businesses couldn't get to their money, couldn't pay their bills, or people's salaries. What a mess!

Out of work and out of bucks. *The Depression bummed out everyone.*

1930s: FLAT BROKE

What exactly is a *depression*? It can be a hole in something. It can mean feeling very blue. And in the case of money, it means not having any. During the Great Depression, which lasted from 1929 to the mid-1930s, lots of businesses went kerplooey. To add to the misery, in the early 1930s the Midwest was hit by a whole mess of truly awful weather—blizzards, tornados, floods, duststorms, and finally draught. People were out of work, they were out of crops, and soon they were also out of money. They went back to using leather, fish skins, even clamshells as money.

How did the nation begin to recover? For one thing, America's government once again took control of the nation's money supply. People turned to the federal government to help bail them out of the mess they were in, and the government responded by creating all sorts of jobs building bridges, tunnels, and dams.

MONEY TODAY

These days the Bureau of Printing and Engraving churns out 37 million notes a day. About 95 percent of those are used to replace worn-out bills. And half the bills printed are $1's. In case you're interested, you can fold a bill about 8,000 times before it will tear. And the paper is made from linen and cotton, so it's actually fabric! (Learn about money's surprising secret symbols in FRIDAY THE 13TH on page 94.)

BYE-BYE MONEY?

Nowadays, more and more people depend on little pieces of plastic in their wallets—credit and debit cards. Money zips and zaps from bank computer to store computer to bank computer without ever passing through human hands. Over in Europe, 12 nations ditched their native monies and all adapted the Euro as their new way to pay. There's talk of no longer minting pennies. What will happen to money in the future?

Well . . . all I can promise you is this: At least you will never have to drag a dead animal skin or 60 pounds of cocoa beans into a store to pay for a pair of socks!

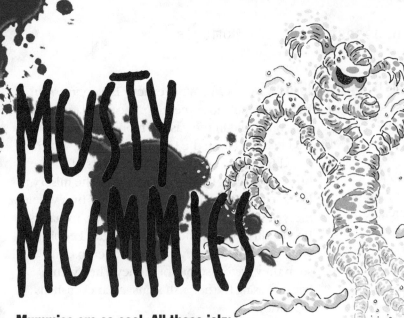

MUSTY MUMMIES

Mummies are so cool. All those icky bandages and those little jars alongside, packed with lungs and guts. And then, of course, there's the whole Mummy's Curse thing—a 4,000 year-old body, dragging one moldy leg behind, ready to crush the life out of the dumb archaeologist who has disturbed the mummy's cozy tomb.

But there's more to mummies than just a bunch of bandaged bodies. Travel from Egypt's Valley of the Kings to the icy peaks of South America's Andes mountains to a creepy carnival in California, and unwrap true tales of murder, mystery . . . and wacked-out twists of fate.

HAPPY MUMMY'S DAY

Life is full of pesky things to deal with: bad luck, stomach flu, and—especially annoying—death. The ancient Egyptians came up with all sorts of rituals that helped them deal with these issues, especially death. The Egyptians believed that when you died, you went to another world, but you still needed a lot of your stuff, including your body. And the best way to keep a body from ending up as an all-you-can-eat buffet for worms and maggots was to mummify it and place it in a big box, called a *sarcophagus.* If you were rich and powerful, your mummy, its box, and *all* your goodies got placed in a very special tomb—a chamber located deep within the Earth, down many long narrow tunnels, sealed shut for all eternity. Dying in Egypt was a very big deal. (Get the poop on pyramids in CRUEL CONSTRUCTION on page 42.)

NOT R.I.P.–ING

For a thousand years, wealthy Egyptians ended their lives as mummies, tucked into their tombs with all their favorite goodies. But the problem with getting buried with all your most precious possessions is this: Dead people cannot yell, shove, or hit a grave robber over the head with a frying pan. The mummies that were being laid to rest along with all their treasures were not laying at rest for very long. Egypt's huge pyramids were always getting robbed.

The kings of the Middle Kingdom (2100 B.C.E. to 1650 B.C.E.) realized that pyramids weren't the smartest of ideas. Hidden burial sites were better, so the thieves wouldn't know where to look. So they moved up the river to a place called Thebes and began to build the City of the Dead—temples with hidden burial chambers, tucked behind false doors and secret passages. But grave robbers are tricky devils, and a job is a job. They *still* managed to find the tombs and rob them. So the pharaohs started leaving warning notes all over their tombs.

Mum's the word.
Many Peruvian mummies were buried all scrunched up.

AND THE MUMMIES CURSED . . .

Walk into the tomb of a guy named Petety in Giza and you'll see a panel with hieroglyphics hanging at the entrance. The panel, very loosely translated, says:

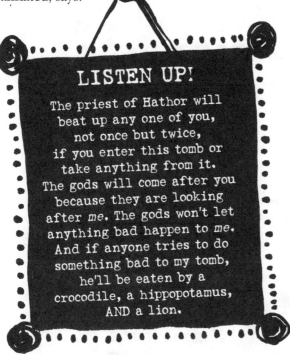

LISTEN UP!

The priest of Hathor will beat up any one of you, not once but twice, if you enter this tomb or take anything from it. The gods will come after you because they are looking after *me*. The gods won't let anything bad happen to *me*. And if anyone tries to do something bad to my tomb, he'll be eaten by a crocodile, a hippopotamus, AND a lion.

Do you think the tomb robbers read that sign and went running out into the night with nothing in their sacks? *Nope!* They just walked right on in and cleaned the place out. That was the fate of most of the tombs of Egypt's kings, queens, and princes. Which finally brings us to a long-forgotten, very unimportant Egyptian pharaoh named Tutankhamen, who, centuries after his death, became one of the most famous people in the world—the man who gave us the tale of the Mummy's Curse.

TUT, TUT, TUT

So just who was King Tut? Well, he ruled in 1362 B.C.E. and became king when he was a whopping eight years old. Tut was then forced to marry his half-sister (now *there's* a major ick), since pharaohs were allowed to have as many wives as they wanted. Little Tut was pharaoh

mostly for show. His "advisors" really ran things. When he died at the age of 18, he was shoved into a tomb, the tomb was sealed shut, and everyone forgot about him.

Fast-forward thousands of years to October 1922. An Egyptologist named Howard Carter had been digging, digging, digging for more than ten years, looking for pharaoh leftovers. He had found absolutely nothing and was close to calling it quits, but decided to try one last time. So one day, over in the Valley of the Kings, digging around an already robbed tomb, he found an odd set of steps, covered with trash, leading downward.

Carter was stoked! He sent a telegraph (the way people wrote to each other when they were in a hurry before the days of e-mail) to Lord Carnarvon, the person who was paying him to dig. "Come quickly!" the telegraph said (you had to pay by the word). In late November of 1922, when Carter and Carnarvon finally cleared away all the rubble that blocked the tomb entrance, they were dumbstruck by what they found: an honest-to-goodness, unrobbed Egyptian pharaoh's grave!

CURSES!

Mystery soon began to swirl up, along with the dust from the tomb, launching tales of a curse. The day the steps to the tomb were found, Carter's pet canary was devoured by a cobra—nothing left but a handful of yellow feathers. And cobras were a symbol of the pharaoh. *Hmmm!* Then, a few months after the tomb was opened, Lord Carnarvon got a mosquito bite on his cheek, which became infected. Within a matter of days, he was dead! *Hmmmm again!* At the moment of his death, the lights went out in the city of Cairo and back home in England, Carnarvon's dog howled wildly and then supposedly dropped dead as well!

Sounds like a curse to me.

But things got weirder still. Not only was Tut's tomb a scary place for the Egyptologists—they found out that poor Tut hadn't been too lucky in life either! After his sarcophagus was opened and his mummy removed for further examination, a mark was found on Tut's cheek in the exact same place that Carnarvon's deadly insect bite had been. There was a chip of bone in his skull and his spine was deformed. There were also two baby mummies wrapped up in his

MUMMY-MAKING MADE EASY

Egyptians were always experimenting with the best way to make a mummy. This method was one of the most popular.

1. Take the dead body to the "place of purification" for a quickie bath in palm wine. Rinse with Nile water.

2. Cut out the internal organs—liver, lungs, stomach, and intestines. Pack them in salt. Scoop out the brain through the nose with a little spoon and toss it to the cats.

3. Pour salt into all the empty body cavities, then cover the entire body with more salt and wait 40 days.

4. After 40 days, wash the salt off and rub oil all over the corpse.

5. Stuff the body with sawdust, leaves, and bits of balled-up linen so it looks plump and lifelike.

6. Rub some more fragrant oils on it. You can never be too greasy if you are a mummy.

7. Either stick the lungs, stomach, intestines, and liver back in the body or tuck each in a special jar, called a *canopic jar.*

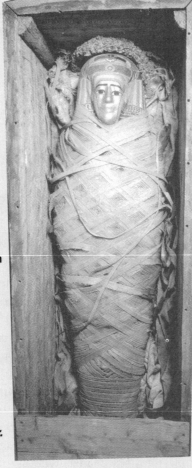

8. Start wrapping the mummy—head and neck first, then fingers, then arms and legs. Add lucky charms to protect the mummy on its journey.

9. Let a high priest read spells and incantations over the body as it is wrapped to ward away bad spirits. Tie arms and legs together and place a scroll from the *Book of the Dead* in the mummy's hands.

10. Wrap the mummy some more. Paint the bandages with special glue that will hold them all together.

11. Wrap a big piece of fabric around the corpse and paint the chief god, Osiris, on the mummy's chest.

12. Place another big cloth on top and tie it to the mummy with strips of linen. Drop a painted wooden board on top of the mummy and pop the corpse in a coffin.

13. Put that coffin in another coffin . . .

14. . . . And a third, a fourth, and sometimes even a fifth coffin, depending on how rich the deceased is.

15. Now it's off to the tomb to begin the journey to the underworld, where the dead person's heart will be weighed and judged. A good, clean heart will get a guy or gal a ticket to the "Fields of Reeds." A black heart? Ugh! You don't want to know!

tomb: Tut's tots, who had not survived past infancy. It looked as if poor Tut might have been murdered! Yikes!

By 1929, eleven people who had been a part of the Tut excavations had died under "strange" circumstances. Naturally, the news media went totally nuts with each death. Headlines screamed of another Mummy's Curse victim. The truth? Just a bunch of hooey cooked up by folks who were trying to sell a lot of newspapers. After all, Howard Carter, who found the tomb and spent years working in it, lived for decades after the discovery. But a few years ago, scientists discovered dangerous spores filled with toxic germs in the tomb. To a person in ill health to begin with, those germs might have proved deadly.

So did ancient high priests load the tombs with bacteria? Zahi Hawass, the head of the Egyptian Supreme Council for Antiquities, and a true man of science, is a big believer in cursed tombs. He's had plenty of weird experiences in Egyptian burial sites—from storms that came out of nowhere to poisonous powders that poofed out of secret crevices. And an article in the *Canadian Medical Association Journal* suggests that poisonous spores may have been deliberately placed in King Tut's tomb. So if you're thinking of poking around in a mummy's tomb, remember—don't inhale!

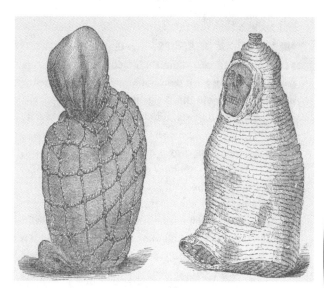

I'm a basket case! These Peruvian mummies were tucked in baskets to protect them.

MORE! MORE! MORE MUMMIES!

Ancient Egyptians weren't the only folks to get in on the mummy action. In 5050 B.C.E., 2,000 years before the first pharoahs began wrapping their dearly departed, the Chinchorro peoples in what is now Chile in South America were preserving their dead. But they had their own unique style.

Mummy's hang-out. These Nazca mummies have their own little nooks. So cozy!

No bandages for these dead dudes. They began by pulling the body apart, limb from limb—even the skull. They then neatly cut off all the flesh, pulled out the organs, and heat-dried the bones, and then reassembled the skeleton by inserting sticks to hold everything together. Fake muscles were made from reeds and grasses and the entire skeleton was then packed with feathers, clay, and more grass. Then, the peeled-off skin-suit was rewrapped around the baked bones. The entire body was painted with an ashy paste and topped off with a coat of shiny black paint made from manganese (a type of mineral), or in later years, bright red ochre. The mummies then donned very cool masks and wigs of long, flowing human hair.

Moche peoples (the granddaddies of the Inca in Peru) were also passionate mummy-makers. Instead of using linen bandages, they wrapped their dead in intricately woven burial cloths. And the Inca made not one, but two types of mummies in the years between 1438 to 1532: frozen, sacrificed little kid-mummies tucked 22,000 feet above sea level on an icy mountain ledge, and their royal kingly types, who were stuffed and seated on thrones. And, in a weird coincidence, the Mayas

(1500 B.C.E. to 1500 C.E.)—who built pyramids, too—also made mummies in a way that was eerily similar to the Egyptians'. Some historians actually believe that adventurers from Africa (where Egypt is) were traveling to the Americas long before Columbus. Could this be proof?

THE MYSTERY OF THE CHINESE MUMMIES

There are plenty of other famous mummies. In about 1000 B.C.E. an unlucky family, now known as the Cherchen Mummies, were laid to rest in the desert-dry, salty soil of western China. Salt (shake on over to SALT ASSAULT on page 225 for more on the white stuff) is a preservative and that's exactly what it did to these dead folks. But the sci-guys who discovered these crusty corpses in the 1980s were stunned by what they found. None of the mummies was Chinese. What was this European family doing in this remote part of China 3,000 years ago? Mystery number one!

Mini mystery mummy. What happened to this babe 3,000 years ago?

The adult mummies (one guy and three women) were all very tall (the man was 6'6"), all had red hair, tattoos, and each was buried with lots of brightly colored clothing, including the man's ten different hats—from a pointy wizard number to a jaunty beret. Mystery number two—how many hats *can* one guy wear?

A sad little three-month-old baby-mummy had small blue stones covering her eyes and was wrapped up with her cowhorn cup and sheep-udder nursing bottle. Mystery number three—what disaster had befallen this traveling family? This particular mummy mystery is still unsolved.

THE WIDE WORLD OF MUMMIES

Here's a shocker. Mummy-making was going on *everywhere*, on every continent except Antarctica.

Everybody loves a mummy . . . A North American Indian says a final goodbye.

World's Oldest Mummy? It's right here in the good ol' U.S. of A.! The Spirit Cave Man of Nevada is a whopping 9,000 years old.

Do-it-yourself Mummies? Starting about 2,000 years ago in Japan, some Buddhist priests began mummy-making their own bodies while they were still alive. They did this by going on a mega-diet for a period of three years, barely eating enough to stay alive. They would surround themselves with scads of large candles as they prayed, which threw off so much heat that their under-nourished skin began to dry up. When the poor monks finally died of starvation, their bodies were already almost dried to the point of mummification. But to make it official, bodies were then tucked in an underground tomb for three more years, surrounded by yet more candles, and dried to a crisp.

Killer Mummy?

John Wilkes Booth was the man who shot Abraham Lincoln back in 1865. But was Wilkes cornered and killed, or did he escape? Rumors ran wild when, in 1903, a guy on his deathbed in Enid, Oklahoma, confessed to his landlord that *he* was really John Wilkes Booth. Naturally, folks went nuts at this news and one guy decided that this was a great business opportunity. He had the corpse quickly mummified. His plan was to display it at carnival sideshows. For years everyone believed they were viewing the body of the assassin, whose mummified state was maintained with generous coats of Vaseline. But the truth is the moldering mummy was not a presidential murderer even though it did, at times, seem to carry a curse of its own. Eight people were killed in the wreck of a circus train in which the mummy was traveling, and almost every showman who displayed the greasy corpse ended up flat broke soon after.

An "Amusing" Mummy?

While filming a TV show in a California amusement park in 1977, a crew member went to move what he thought was a dummy. But when the "dummy's" arm broke off, the truth was revealed. It was Elmer McGurdy, a gunslinger who had died in a duel in 1911.

Heroic Mummies?

They may not be wrapped in bandages, but all these famous folk are considered mummies. Revolutionary War hero John Paul Jones was preserved in whiskey. Eva Perón, the famous Argentine leader, has been preserved since her death in 1952 by being dipped in an infusion of wax. And the preservatives-treated body of Vladimir Lenin, who led the Russian Revolution in 1917, lies in a glass case for all to see in Moscow's Red Square.

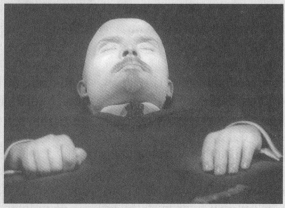

Look! Lenin! Mummified for more than 80 years.

Smartest Mummy?

While dredging at Windover Pond, a bog in Florida, a gruesome discovery was made—dozens of mummified human brains more than 7,000 years old! Turns out, it was an ancient burial site where human smart-parts were the only thing considered worthy of saving.

Aussie-Rules Mummies?

Some aboriginal groups in Australia had a unique way to make mummies. They began by slicing open the body and removing as much fat as they could find, which was then melted, mixed with red ochre, and smeared all over the skin. Eyes, mouths, and those other body openings (such as peeing/pooping holes) were sewn shut. The body was tied into a sitting position, placed on a platform, and smoked over a fire pit for ten days. After several more weeks on the platform, the body was then hoisted up onto a tree branch where it sat—mummified for decades to come.

Over in Melanesia, a chain of islands north of Australia, mummies were made differently. After hangin' out for a few days, the swollen, decomposing corpse was loaded onto a large canoe and sailed out to sea. There, the mummy-makers peeled back the skin and scooped out the internal organs, including the brain, which were tossed overboard. Stuffing with palm pith (soft, gunky stuff inside the stems) gave the body its shape back, and finally the almost-a-mummy was returned to shore. There the dead guy was tied to a wooden frame and allowed to dry. To speed the process, small holes were drilled in the knees, elbows, hands, and feet to help drain any remaining bodily fluids. Finally, the mummy's tongue, the palms of the hands, and the soles of the feet were given to the surviving spouse. A funky inheritance, I think you'll agree. After a number of months, when the mummy was totally dried, it was decorated with seashell eyes, grass, and seeds, and painted in red ochre. The mummy was then tied to the center post of its former house. Mummy's baaaaa-ck!

NOTTY NAPOLÉON

Whack!
Whack!

Whack! What's that? That was the sound of Napoléon Bonaparte's mother following him to school, church, or just about anywhere. She was always smacking him, whacking him, or grabbing him by the ears. And with good cause! That boy could be a real terror. And terror boy grew up to be a terror of a man—one who liked nothing better than to fight, fight, *fight!*

And fight he did, as he took over a whole hunk of the world. But just like you can't blow a giant bubble with chewing gum and not have it explode all over your face, the same thing is true for building empires—as Monsieur Bonaparte found out the hard way. SPLAT!

ONE TOUGH MAMA

Napoléon's mother, Letizia Bonaparte, was a tough-love kind of mom. She was a true believer in the saying "spare the rod, spoil the child." And she sure didn't want to spoil her child! We can be pretty sure that her son, little Napoléon, often walked around with a sore tushy when he was a kid. But then again, he was the kind of lad who always pushed the limits. He was always fighting with his older brother,

Joseph. He made faces at the priests while serving as an altar boy. He was a real handful. Napoléon grew up during the 1770s on the small Mediterranean island of Corsica, which some folks have called the armpit of Italy. (If you look at a map, that's where it is.) Corsica was sold to France by a part of Italy that had run out of money. So the people who lived there weren't quite French, and they weren't quite Italian. And the truth was the Corsicans hated belonging to either country.

BANG, BANG, YOU'RE DEAD!

Even when he was a kid, Napoléon thought soldiers were the coolest. He was always playing at being a general, bossing around his little gang of barefoot buddies. When he was ten, his parents sent him off to military school in France. So there he was, in a strange country, in a strange school. He barely spoke French, and he was surrounded by snooty rich boys who made fun of him. Napoléon sure showed them, though, by becoming even *more* arrogant, *more* tough, and *more* bossy.

One day, after truly ticking off his teachers, Napoléon was punished—he was told to eat his dinner on his knees off a cold stone floor. As he was ordered to drop to the ground, Napoléon went ballistic. He looked up at the teacher and screamed, "In my family, we kneel only before

God!" Then, for further effect, he upchucked on his teacher's shoes.

His meltdown made a huge impression on his classmates. Puking on a teacher will do that! And when a heavy snow blanketed the school and the kids were stuck inside, it was Napoléon who suggested they shovel tunnels, dig trenches, build castles, and wage snowball war. Soon, everyone began to look at the little guy from Corsica with some respect—especially after being pelted with his rock- and gravel-packed snowballs. Ye-ow!

SLEEP IS FOR SISSIES

Napoléon was a workaholic and he always wanted to be the best. He would stay up all night studying. His hard work paid off. In 1774, when he was 15, he was admitted to the best military academy in France. But once again, he faced the same problems. Everyone thought he was too bossy. Didn't this country bumpkin Corsican, who couldn't even speak decent French, know his place? Once again, Napoléon toughed it out, and one year later, he was given a fine uniform and became an officer in the French Army. But because he was very short and really skinny, one of his friends said he looked just like Puss in Boots. Yikes! Comments like that drove Napoléon wild!

Wearing his oversized boots, Napoléon went about doing typical soldierly things until the citizens of Paris went on a rampage in 1789 and, over the next several years, began chopping off the heads of their king, queen, and dozens of other noble folk. The French Revolution and its gory guillotine (hold onto your head and go to page 108 for more on that) changed everything for our little soldier from Corsica.

SHORT BUT SCARY

Napoléon was 20 years old when the French Revolution broke out. He was still small—just 5'3"—and super-scrawny. But that didn't matter. One of the good things

DON'T SCRATCH!

Several famous paintings of Napoléon show him with his hand in his shirt. Why? Well, it wasn't to keep his fingers warm. One popular theory is that Napoléon had a skin condition called *scabies*, which is caused by tiny mites that burrow under the skin, leaving behind itchy patches with oozy crusts. Perhaps his hand was inside his shirt so he could scratch himself when he was holding long poses for the portrait painter? We do know that Napoléon was always soaking in hot baths, sometimes several times a day. Those baths would have soothed inflamed skin. Some docs also think Napoléon had terrible hemorrhoids—big, itchy, swollen veins in the pooping area of a guy's body. Those nasty butt veins made it hard for him to sit in the saddle for long periods of time, and may have caused him to lose an important battle—the battle that ended his career.

about that bloody revolution was that it became possible for a person to be rewarded because they were actually good at something, not just because they came from the "right" family. Suddenly people were talking about equality . . . and quality. And little Napoléon had no equal when it came to war.

173

A NUTSHELL NAPOLÉON

Napoléon lived to fight! fight! fight! Here's a battle history from the time Napoléon took complete charge of the French army.

Age 27 (1796): Becomes commander-in-chief and proceeds to take over Italy while battling Austria. He wins by telling his starving soldiers, "There's lots to eat in that town just up the road apiece. Help yourselves! Do a little shopping, too. It's all free."

Age 29 (1798): Off to Egypt to try to whomp the British, who control much of the Middle East and India. Back in France, the government is a wreck. Napoléon shoots back to Paris, where he seizes control and becomes first consul—the French equivalent of president—in 1799.

Age 31 (1800): Major victories over the powerful Austrians. Napoléon sure does have some good ideas when it comes to war. He always figures out how to cut off opposing armies so they get broken into ineffective pieces.

Age 33 (1802): Bonaparte changes the constitution of France so that he is now consul for life. No need to ever go job hunting again!

Age 35 (1804): Why be consul when you can be an emperor with a throne and a crown and all those extra fun goodies? But when Napoléon claims that he's the King of Italy, too, a bunch of other European countries—Britain, Austria, Russia, and Sweden—say *Basta!* "Enough is enough." Battle after battle follows, leaving Europe in ruin.

Age 39 (1808): Six long years of fighting over all sorts of crummy pieces of land spells the beginning of the end for Napoléon. He's ruling over a massive empire but everyone hates him. And a really stupid move—an invasion of *brrrrrrrrr*-cold Russia in 1812, just before winter sets in—costs him almost half a million soldiers' lives, not to mention most of France's money.

Age 45 (1814): Napoléon has lost his mojo. *Everyone* has had enough. Napoléon is run out of town to the little island of Elba. He tries to regain his throne, but one final battle at Waterloo (fought in tiny Belgium) against arch-enemy England spells the almost-end of our fearless little leader. Off he goes again, sent by the victorious British to live on another even tinier island, St. Helena—a big bleak rock off the coast of Africa.

Age 52 (1821): Napoléon takes his last breath. Nobody knows for sure exactly what caused his death, but what is sure is that the tiny terror is no more. He dies on May 5. But whispers of his murder are the hot topic.

For the next six years, Napoléon led his soldiers in battles big and small. He lost some, but he won a whole lot more. He came up with some really clever battle plans. People began to take notice of the little guy. And when he saved a bunch of highly ranked people from an angry mob in 1795 by calmly ordering his soldiers to shoot cannons at the unarmed crowd, he became downright famous. By the time Napoléon was 27, he was a general, bossing around people who were twice his age . . . and size.

A BAD MOVE . . . AND SOME GOOD ONES

Napoléon was out to conquer the world. To pay for his plans to dominate Europe and parts of Asia, he ended up selling a big chunk of what is now the United States to Thomas Jefferson in 1803. He described the land as one big worthless, swampy snake pit. *Bzzztt!* Wrong! The Louisiana Purchase doubled the size of the U.S.A. and helped it grow into a world power. Oh well, you can't win 'em all . . . .

But, as emperors go, Napoléon wasn't all bad. He dragged France's legal system out of the Dark Ages and modernized it. And he improved schools. But he liked fighting too much to ever stop, and he kept trying to conquer more and more lands. His plans for world domination made a big mess of Europe—a mess that would drag on for years and years.

LOVE AND WAR

When he was 26, Napoléon fell head-over-high-boot-heels in love with a 32-year-old woman. Her name was Rose, but he hated that name, so he called her Josephine. Jo thought he was an obnoxious little man, but she sure did love his fame, so they got married. She pretended to be all lovey-dovey, while secretly having a bunch of boyfriends behind his back. Even her dog didn't really care for the little general, and bit Napoléon on the leg on their wedding night.

When Napoléon finally found out about Jo's bad behavior, he was steamed. Now the tables were turned. *He* hated *her,* just as she was finally falling in love with him. Sheeesh! Love! Eventually, they made up, and everything was hunky-dory, right? Wrong. Napoléon wanted a son and Josephine could not get pregnant, so in 1809 he dumped her and married a younger woman who finally made Napoléon a daddy. But when it came down to it, in the end, Napoléon always said that the only woman he'd ever really loved was Josephine.

DEAD HEAD

Napoléon earns half of his "Yikes!" status because he was a guy who wrecked millions of lives (and let's not forget barfing on his teacher's shoes!). He gets the other half because of the way he died. By 1814, he had been forced to give up his throne, and was sent to live on a little Mediterranean island called Elba. He wasn't the emperor of the world anymore, just emperor of a lump in the Atlantic Ocean with fewer than 30,000 people living on it. Needless to say, this was a big demotion.

However, Napoléon was never one to give up easily. Nine months later, he mustered an army of soldiers still loyal to him and plotted his return to the throne. Somehow he managed to regain power, but after 100 days back on his throne, in June of 1815, he suffered a spectacular loss to the Duke of Wellington and the British (his arch-enemy) at Waterloo. Napoléon was toast. He decided to surrender to the British, thinking they would treat him as a respected guest and maybe put him up in a nice country palace. *Bzzzt!* WRONG AGAIN!

This time he was sent to an even tinier, crummier, in-the-middle-of-nowhere island

I spy with my tiny eye . . . a great place to have a bloody battle.

called St. Helena. In fact, this was more like a speck than a lump. No more palaces for Napoléon, just a little hut perched on a rock. Napoléon lived on this little bump in the sea for five long years. Then he started having terrible stomach pains. No one could figure out what was wrong. He died in 1821, convinced that the British were poisoning him.

A few years later someone got hold of a lock of Napoléon's hair and had it tested. Arsenic, a deadly poison, was found in every strand. Had he been poisoned? Someone suggested that the wallpaper paste in his house was full of arsenic. But why hadn't everyone else exposed to it died? It couldn't have been that! Another theory holds that Napoléon was so bored, miserable, and unhappy that he became a drug addict, with arsenic his poison of choice. A third theory yet explores the possibility that Napoléon suffered from stomach cancer. More locks of hair were produced and more chemical

studies of those strands were done. But were they real? One of Napoléon's aides said later, "I have seen so many locks of hair purporting to be that of the Emperor over the last 20 years, I could have carpeted Versailles with it."

Almost 200 years after his death, doctors are still arguing about what exactly happened to Napoléon. Some want to crack open his spiffy tomb and chop off some more hair to run yet more tests. And that says something about him. He left a big mark on the world. Generals around the world still study his military tactics. To the French, he's still pretty much a hero. The Napoleonic Code, with certain modifications, is still the law of the land in France. The educational system he designed is still one of the best in Europe. People still describe small-ish, bossy people as having "Napoléon complexes." And everyone recognizes the paintings of the little general with his hand in his shirt, scratching away at his oozy, itchy tummy.

O

OOZY OLYMPICS

You know that dream where you're standing in front of the entire school assembly without any clothes on and everybody is pointing and laughing? For athletes in ancient Greece 2,700 years ago, that was a dream come true. Nowadays, Olympic athletes get to wear snazzy uniforms. But back when the Olympics were brand-new, the uniform was a snazzy birthday suit! And if you hate having to strip down to your undies to change for gym, you won't be a bit surprised to learn that the word *gym* comes from the Greek word *gymnos*, which means "naked." Buck naked was how athletes competed.

THE 100-YARD PORTA-POTTY DASH

The first Olympic Games were held in Greece in 776 B.C.E.—more than 2,700 years ago. Every four years for the next 1,200 years, speedy athletes came to the town of Olympia to pay tribute to their gods. So put on your time-traveling shoes and let's jog back to ancient Olympia in Greece. It is now the year 696 B.C.E. and more than 40,000 fans have come to this small town to watch the Games of the Gods. You have been traveling for a couple of weeks just to get there. You need a shower, and a proper toilet sure would be nice! But what's this? For starters, there isn't a single porta-potty in sight, let alone a bathroom, washroom,

OILY OLYMPIANS

Before they set off to compete, each athlete doused himself with perfumed oil from head to toe so that he gleamed and glistened in the hot Greek sun. After a long hot race, there were no showers. Instead, Greek athletes lathered up with *more* olive oil, and then scraped the oil, dead skin, and perspiration off with a metal scraper called a *strigal*. Top athletes then *sold* their scraped-off body dirt and sweat in little bottles to wannabee athletes who hoped that a little all-star magic would rub off when some all-star sweat was rubbed on.

or shower. There's no stadium, either, for that matter. That came about 800 years after the first Games were held. There weren't even many trees or bushes to duck behind if you wanted a little peeing or pooping privacy, since much of Greece is hilly and rocky. So when you had to go, you just found a spot and went.

VIIe OLYMPIADE
ANVERS (BELGIQUE)
AOUT-SEPTEMBRE 1920

WORD UP!

■ "Ouch! Yow! That hurts! I am in *agony*!" Next time you hit your thumb with a hammer, you will have the ancient Greeks to thank for the wonderful word that describes your pain. *Agony* comes from the Greek word for games, *agones*. So let the agony begin!

■ In the early years of the Games, runners competed on an open stretch of level ground with a line drawn in the sand to mark the start, a practice that led to the saying "starting from scratch."

■ The ancient Greeks called amateur athletes who dared to compete in the games *idiotes*, which meant an unskilled person, as well as a . . . well . . . idiot!

other three festivals, winners got crowns of bay leaves, fresh celery, or dried celery. The boy's foot-race winner got a ginormous jar of olive oil. Try wearing *that* on a ribbon around your neck! But there were all sorts of secret prizes. Some lucky winners were given entire houses when they returned home. An Olympic champ became a super-celebrity. And the losers? Those poor guys got laughed at, or flogged with sticks.

The first Olympic sports were simple—mostly foot races, wrestling, and throwing stuff, like javelins, and the discus (which looks a bit like a dinner plate). The rules were pretty simple, too: A guy blew a horn to start the race, and if you were over the line early, you got smacked upside the head.

About 75 years after the first Games began, an event called *pankration* was added—a sport that made boxing and wrestling look like sissy stuff. You could now choke, slap, kick, trip, flip, or punch your opponent. You could squeeze the squishiest, most sensitive parts of a grown man's body as hard as you liked. You could bend fingers back and even snap them if you wished. One brute actually dug out his opponent's intestines! Referees with big sticks or whips made sure you did not poke out eyes or bite. But other than *not* nibbling on your opponent or blinding him, you could pretty much torture a guy limb by limb.

There was also an event called the *hoplito-dromia*, a 400-yard foot race during which contestants wore a suit of armor (try running while carrying an armload of heavy car parts). Then there were the chariot races. A *chariot* is a little two-wheeled cart that is pulled by a team of horses. Now, picture a demolition derby with animals and you get an idea of what happened as up to 40 charioteers tried to make the other guys crash as they raced around in a big circle. And

Now, imagine day after day of steamy, summer weather with 40,000 sweating sports fans who have not showered in weeks, standing shoulder to shoulder, with the pools of pee and piles of poop that surround them growing bigger by the day. Talk about ooze! Seems like breathing without gagging should have been an Olympic event!

DO THE POKEY-POKEY

The Olympics were one of four annual sports events held by the ancient Greeks. Back then there were no gold, silver, and bronze medals. Either you won or you lost. Period. At the Olympics, the winner got a wreath of olive leaves and the right to brag about how super-awesome he was. At the athletes didn't mind driving over a fallen athlete if it meant winning that important olive crown.

NO GIRLS ALLOWED

Naturally, with all those buck naked fellows running and jumping everywhere, allowing women to watch the races was a no-no. Any adult woman caught at the Games could be hurled off the nearest cliff (although that probably never happened). The only exceptions were women who owned the horses that were being used in the chariot races. By 86 C.E. a girl's event was finally added, but until then, maidens had to make do with a separate measly little foot race held before the opening ceremonies for the men's Olympics—the main event.

Why did people put up with the smell, the crowds, the flies, and the heat, not to mention not being able to find a place to tinkle when the need arose? Simple. The Olympics were the most awesome event in that part of the world at that time. All that sweat! All that blood! Such excitement! For almost 1,200 years, those oozing Olympic athletes kept Greek crowds cheering. Then, in the year 394 (after Greece had fallen under Roman rule), a Christian emperor decided that the Olympics were pagan festivals. Good Christians belonged in church, not betting money on who was going to get good and gushy at the next chariot race. The Games were ordered shut down.

FAST-FORWARD 1,500 YEARS

You can't keep a good idea down. In 1896, a French guy named Baron Pierre de Coubertin decided the time was right for the rebirth of the Olympic Games. Since Greece was where the Olympics were born, he decided it made sense to hold them there. Athens, the capital city, hosted those first modern games. Maybe the Baron wanted to make sure there were enough bathrooms for everyone?

Fourteen countries sent teams to Athens: 241 male athletes and a whopping zero female athletes. Winners received a silver medal and an olive branch. And that was that. But things quickly began to change. Four years later, 19 women got the chance to perspire as they competed in tennis, croquet, ballooning, sailing, and golf. And now, more than a hundred years later, the Olympic Games have become a really big deal. Athletes of both sexes can sweat puddles at the summer Olympics, or break off icicles of frozen mucus at the Winter Games. Cool new

What a babe! *Mildred "Babe" Didrikson could do it all when it came to sports. No wonder she took home gold in the 1932 Olympics.*

THE BIRDBRAINED OLYMPICS

1. At the Seoul, Korea, Olympics, in 1988, when the flame was ignited during the opening ceremonies, several sluggish pigeons were caught off guard as they hung on the edge of the giant cauldron. Anyone for a little KFC—Korean Fried Chicken?

2. Speaking of birds, Eddie "the Eagle" Edwards, a British ski jumper at the 1988 Winter Games in Calgary, Alberta, Canada, flew through the air like a ten-ton sack of bricks. He finished dead last in both the 70- and 90-meter jumps. Ironically, the chubby little fella who took up ski jumping as a joke ended up making more money than the real ski jumpers that competed, netting a $65,000 deal to write his story as well as selling movie rights to his tale.

3. And while we're *still* on the subject of bird-brained ideas, an event that was literally for the birds ended up on the docket at the 1900 Olympics—live pigeon shooting. The winner, a Belgian, took first by bagging 21 birds. The losers were the spectators, who ended up with bloody bird parts all over their heads. Yikes!

sports, such as snowboard cross and trampoline are added every year. Along the way there have been some truly dumb events (tug of war, anyone?), some unexpected triumphs (the Jamaican bobsled team's amazing ride in 1988), and horrible tragedy (the murder of several Israeli athletes at the hands of terrorist gunmen in Germany in 1972).

TAKE THAT, MR. HITLER!

One the most famous Olympians of the modern era is Jesse Owens, an African American from the United States. He strutted his stuff in the 1936 Olympics, which earned the funky nickname of the "Hitler Olympics." Those Games took place in Berlin, where evil Nazi leader Adolf Hitler was eager to prove the superiority of the so-called Aryan race—folks with blonde hair and blue eyes, of which Owens obviously had neither.

But no one messed with Jesse Owens—not even the creepiest, vilest dictator to ever walk the Earth. By the end of the Olympics, much to Hitler's frustration, even the German crowds were cheering for this super-cool athlete. Owens won not just one, but *four* first-place gold medals in that single Olympics. Boy, was Hitler steamed! And any guy who could make Hitler look like a fool deserves a thousand gold medals!

The motto of the modern-day Olympics is *citius, altius, fortius,* the Latin words for "swifter, higher, stronger." And even though you may no longer swiftly and strongly rip out your opponent's intestines, the lofty spirit of those smelly hillsides in ancient Olympia still fills the hearts of every Olympic athlete.

Eat my dust. No one could catch Jesse Owens in the 1936 Olympics, much to nasty Nazi Adolf Hitler's dismay.

OUTRAGEOUS OUTLAWS

"Okay. This is a stick-up. Put your hands in the air and give me all your money! Your watch too—and make it snappy. I don't have all day. Whaddya mean you can't get to your money if your hands are in the air? Are you trying to confuse me?"

Ever since people have had things worth stealing, other people have been taking them. And for some folks, robbing a bank, holding up a stagecoach, or just plain-old breaking the law has been their way of earning a living. Alas, those ways of earning a living all too often led to them earning a dying, too.

HIGHWAY ROBBERY

Back in Bible times, a guy only had to glance at those super stone tablets, the Ten Commandments, to see it: *Thou shalt not steal.* And we all know that crime doesn't pay. (Don't believe me? Just do some time in PRISONS AND PUNISHMENTS on page 207.) But the threat of jail—or even execution—hasn't stopped folks from trying to rob their way to riches for centuries. Folks who held up travelers or stole money from a bank became known as outlaws—'cause they lived outside the law.

Some of the scariest thieves were the highwaymen who used to hide out on lonely stretches of road between towns and leap out on weary travelers, stealing everything they owned—even their clothes, every single stitch right down to their underwear! Today, if someone tries to cheat a person, you might hear them say that they were the victim of "highway robbery." Still, it beats showing up in the next town wearing *nothing*.

And then of course there were PIRATES all over the world (ahoy, mee hardies!). So diabolical are these scurvy sea dogs, they have their

own section on page 188. But the "golden age" of the outlaw took place when the United States was still growing and the West was a wild, wild place.

GOLD FINGERS

When gold was discovered in California in 1849, thousands of people flocked there. Who could resist the idea of getting filthy rich by sticking a pan in a river and coming up with fistfuls of gold? But wherever there's a lot of money and not a lot of lawmen, you end up with a lot of crime. Plenty of people figured, why get your pants wet standing in freezing cold water when you could just let other people do the hard work, then point a gun at them and tell them to hand the loot over?

After the Civil War, in the late 1860s, a lot of former soldiers were so emotionally wasted that they found that a life of crime was a dandy way to live. They had all the right skills since many of the West's most outrageous outlaws had fought in the War Between the States. They knew their ways around weapons, and they were a *very* tough bunch.

THINK PINK

Who finally took the first real bites out of crime? Who put an end to the wild ways of the great outlaws? Meet Allan Pinkerton, America's first super-detective. Scottish-born Allan was a super-curious guy. After he helped solve a complex crime in Chicago in the mid-1800s, he started his own detective agency and soon became famous. He helped save Abe Lincoln from an assassination attempt during his presidential campaign and is also the man responsible for the birth of the Secret Service.

Pinkerton eventually built a huge company devoted to stopping crime. Allan was an in-your-face kind of guy. He tacked up big WANTED posters with drawings or photos of the criminals, and offered big rewards for their capture. He studied fingerprints and sniffed for clues. And eventually he helped to bring down some of the country's best-known baddies, from Jesse James to Butch Cassidy.

His Pinkerton Detective Agency grew and grew. Soon his company had a three-story building in Chicago with a big banner that said "We Never Sleep," topped with a huge black-and-white eye. And that is why detectives are called private eyes!

Prez-protector. *Allan Pinkerton saved Lincoln's life once. Too bad he wasn't around on the night Abe went to Ford's Theater.*

There also weren't enough sheriffs to go around in America's new territories. After all, it was a wide-open space with a *lot* of places to hide. So some of the wildest, wiliest bad guys to ever pull a kerchief over their faces decided to say "Stick 'em up!" Some robbed trains. Others held up stagecoaches. Many pinched cattle or horses. And one of the most famous outlaws ever got his start by stealing long johns!

Stick 'em up! *Three little words that led to riches for many a robber.*

BILLY THE LAUNDRY THIEF

Billy the Kid is one of the West's most legendary criminals. He was probably born in New York around 1859, and his real name was William Henry McCarty. He moved out west to Nevada with his mom when her health turned bad, and she died when he was 14. Billy, the teen, was on his own!

Stealing clothes off a laundry line seemed like a good way to get some clean togs. And from there Billy moved up to stealing cattle—or *rustlin',* as they like to say in cow country. He *tried* to earn a living doing odd jobs, but truth be told, Billy was kind of scrawny, and found a lot of those jobs too tough, so he started stealing to support himself.

REWARD
($5,000.00)
Reward for the capture, dead or alive, of one Wm. Wright, better known as
"BILLY THE KID"
Age, 18. Height, 5 feet, 3 inches. Weight, 125 lbs. Light hair, blue eyes and even features. He is the leader of the worst band of desperadoes the Territory has ever had to deal with. The above reward will be paid for his capture or proof of his death.
JIM DALTON, Sheriff.
"DEAD OR ALIVE!"
THE KID

Because he was so puny, he was always getting bullied—especially by a brute named Frank Cahill. One day, Billy snapped. There are only so many noogies a guy can take before losing it! So Billy pulled out his gun and shot Cahill in the gut. By the next day, Billy "the Kid," aged 17, was wanted for murder. He rode off as fast and as far as he could and ended up joining a group known as "the Boys." The "boys" were cattle thieves, and soon Billy was smack dab in the middle of a bunch of nasty range wars—everyone stealing the other guys' cattle. When his boss was killed, the Kid made sure he got revenge. In the next couple of years, he shot a guy or two (or four or six). But did he have 21 notches on his gun—one for every man he killed? Nah! That's just a myth.

Still, Billy was one of the West's best gun twirlers. Folks said he could take two revolvers, one in each hand, and spin one gun away from him and the other one toward him at the same time. Finally, in April of 1881, Billy the Kid was captured and sentenced to death for his part in the range wars. On his way to be hanged, the Kid escaped, killing two guards as he fled. For the next few months, he hid in the hills but his luck ran out when he was shot in the back by Sheriff Pat Garrett on July 14. He was barely 20 years old. Sadly, Billy never got old enough to become Billy "the Man."

THE REAL GANGSTA RAP

In 1919, in America, Congress passed a law, the Volstead Act, which made it a crime to make, sell, or transport alcohol. But that didn't stop people from chugging beer, drinking wine, or selling whiskey. In every town, hidden behind unmarked doors, there were little clubs called *speakeasies,* where people could go to get drunk. But since selling or drinking alcohol was against the law, *bootleggers*—the people making and selling booze—tended to be criminals.

It was time for a new type of crime. Outlaws with homemade shotguns made way for gangsters and vast crime organizations—guys with machine guns hidden in violin cases . . . guys who decided that rules and laws were for sissies. The "Age of the Gangsters" had arrived, and by the 1920s, it had hit its peak.

Of course, there were other ways to be bad besides selling booze. Another crafty crime in those days was *racketeering.* It worked like this. Let's say you own a little restaurant. I walk in and say, "Pay me $1,000 a week, and I will make sure no one ever messes with you." You say, "Oh, that's okay. It's really safe here." So I make sure that a few days later some goons with big sticks come in and smash every window in the place. Then I go back and say, "Pay me $1,000 a week, and I will make sure no one ever

WANTED: Dead or Alive

THE TARGETS

STAGECOACHES

The reason: Picture this: a coach full of passengers and all their valuables on a lonely road in the middle of nowhere, miles and miles from the nearest lawman. Irresistible!

RAILROADS

The reason: In the 1800s trains were so slow! Plus, everyone knew there were gold shipments and payrolls on board. How to start? Simply remove a few railroad ties so the train derailed. Or set fires in the middle of the tracks. Another plan was a member of the gang was on the train from the get-go. He'd point a gun at the engineer's head to get him to stop as the rest of the gang hopped on. Once on the train, the robbers unhitched the car with the safe in it from the engine. Then, the safe was blown open with dynamite.

BANKS

The reason: Why d'ya think? Duh! That's where the money is! Nowadays, security guards, video cameras and panic buttons make banks hard to rob. But in the 1800s to early 1900s all it took was a gun and a hanky to cover your face. You didn't need a lot of people to rob a bank, like you do to rob a train. It was fast and easy to hand the teller a note that said "Fill a bag with tens and twenties."

THE OUTLAWS

"Black Bart" Bowles 1830-ish to 1917-ish (people are a little iffy-ish on his actual dates). Wore a flour sack with eye cut-outs over his head, topped with a dapper black bowler hat and a no-nonsense shotgun in his hand. Robbed the Wells Fargo stagecoach 28 times.

Pearl Heart 1871–1925. The only woman ever caught robbing a stagecoach.

Frank & Jesse James and the Younger Gang (robbing spree: 1870s). Jesse was a bitter ex-Confederate soldier. A lawless type. Joined by his brother Frank and his cousin Cole Younger, his gang robbed and raided from Iowa to Texas. Gutsy guys—they were the first to try to rob a train in 1873. They robbed banks too. Come to think of it, they robbed anything and anyone.

Butch Cassidy, the Sundance Kid, and the Wild Bunch—a group of 17 men and women, each with a special "something" (robbing spree: 1890–1920). The Bunch began by robbing banks, but soon moved on to trains. Sometimes they did well, but one dopey train robbery netted them a grand total of $50.40. Biggest goof? The day they used too much dynamite and sent $30,000 flaming dollars flying all over.

Bonnie Parker & Clyde Barrow (robbing spree: 1931–1935). Clyde started small—his first robbery was a gaggle of turkeys, but he soon moved on to gas stations, stores, and finally banks. And Bonnie just couldn't pick an honest guy. Her hubby was in prison for murder when she met Clyde. Together, the two went on a huge crime spree—a robbery and murder rampage.

Ma Barker & the Kipnis-Barker Gang (robbing spree: 1931–1935). Was that sweet old lady the mastermind behind a brazen group of bank robbers? Did she plan heists that brought home tons of cash? The truth was, Ma "couldn't plan dinner, let alone a bank job." But that didn't stop the FBI from calling her "Bloody Mama."

THE END

Dirty laundry was **Bart's** downfall. A posse found his snotty handkerchief with a stamp on it—FX07—which was traced back to a San Francisco laundry. Wells Fargo agents searched 91 different laundries before nabbing their man—Charles E. Bolton.

After **Pearl** was arrested she made a flamboyant suicide attempt. She swallowed a white powder and then dropped to the floor. A doc was rushed in, took one look at the white powder and said "Stop pretending, Pearl, and get up. No one ever killed themselves by swallowing talcum powder."

When you have a $10,000 reward being offered for your capture, dead or alive, you gotta watch your back. Alas, **Jesse** did not watch his, and was shot and killed while hanging a picture on the wall of his house, by a guy he'd recruited to help him rob a bank.

Butch and **Sundance** escaped to Argentina, in South America, but Pinkerton's, a big detective agency, soon were on their trail. They were caught in Bolivia after stealing a mule loaded with tin from a nearby mine. Butch was shot and Sundance took his own life. They were buried there in 1922.

NOTE TO CRIMINALS: When you steal a car remember to clean your junk out of the back seat before you abandon it on the roadside. **Bonnie** forgot she'd filled a prescription for her aunt. Cops found her aunt and soon Bonnie and **Clyde** were driving through a hail of bullets. The FBI pumped lots of bullets into their speeding car, and that was the end of that.

Who would suspect a sweet old lady of being an evil criminal? As the gang moved from place to place to find new targets and escape capture, **Ma** was a perfect "front man." On January 16, 1935, Ma and her youngest son Freddie were traced to a cottage in Florida. After a four-hour gun battle, Ma was no more.

messes with you." You gonna fork over the dough now?

Then there was *loan-sharking*. I lend you money but you have to pay me back triple what I gave you, and quickly, or—just like after a real shark attack—you'd be a big, bloody mess.

PUBLIC ENEMY NUMBER ONE

The king of the gangsters was a pudgy guy named Alphonse "Scarface" Capone. (Better known as Al.) He got kicked out of school in sixth grade for hitting a teacher, so he headed off to work as an errand boy for a crime lord and eventually became a bartender for an even higher-up crime-wiz. (That's where he got his scarred face: A jealous gangster sliced Al's face up after he made a pass at the gangster's gal.)

Snarl for the camera, Mr. Capone.
Al looked peeved in his official police photo.

Eventually Al moved to Chicago. In the 1930s, Chicago was a bloody city. It was the meatpacking capital of America—a place where tens of millions of cows and sheep were slaughtered every day by butchers wading knee-deep through blood and guts. So what was the big deal with a little more blood? Al's wife thought her tubby hubby was a used-furniture dealer, but the truth was Al was running all sorts of illegal businesses. Protection rackets. Loan-sharking. And of course, the biggest-buck enterprise of all—bootlegging.

Naturally, gangsters were always trying to take over other gangsters' turfs. But there were rules of politeness even for a thug. After a Chicago gangland boss was gunned down in 1924, more than 15,000 people turned out for his funeral.

There were 23 cars filled with flowers, following the hearse to the cemetery. Capone took over this dead bootlegger's turf and soon was the biggest cheese of all the criminals in town. He moved into the best hotel in Chicago—into a huge suite that cost $1,500 a day (about *$16,000* a day in today's bucks). He went to the opera, ran soup kitchens for the poor, and gave money to charity. He was worth more than $60 million, which probably made him the richest man in America. But he was still a "millionaire gorilla" and he knew it. And his clueless wife *still* thought he sold used furniture for a living.

HAPPY VALENTINE'S DAY

It's not easy being a crime kingpin. There were lots of rival gangs to challenge Al's empire. "Bugs" Moran and his boys were one of those gangs. Capone decided Chicago needed to be "de-bugged," so he made one of his most famous moves on February 14, 1929. Four Capone gang members walked into one of Bugs's warehouses, two of them disguised as cops. The seven guys working in the garage thought it was a police raid, so they dropped their guns, put their hands against the wall, and soon found themselves shredded by machine-gun fire. After these loud bursts of gunfire, passersby saw two cops emerge from the warehouse, their guns pointed at two

men with their hands up in the air. Just Capone's guys play-acting a fake arrest while walking away from an absolute bloodbath.

Inside the warehouse seven gangsters lay lined up against a wall—dead, dead, dead! Capone's carnage became known as the Valentine's Day Massacre. After all, it had a kind of poetic twist to it. Bleeding hearts. Lots of red. Get it?

Let's face it: Al Capone was no Mister Nice Guy. His favorite way to dispose of an enemy was to invite the guy to dinner, enjoy a ten-course meal, tell a couple of jokes, beat his guest to death with a baseball bat, then polish him off with a bullet through the head for dessert.

Someone had to stop Capone. But who? And how?

THE UNTOUCHABLES

Eliot Ness was a young man with a mission: to smash Capone and close down every single brewery and speakeasy in town. Ness, who worked for the U.S. Treasury Department's Prohibition Bureau, handpicked nine brawny, brainy, fearless guys to help him, and called them the Untouchables—because touch them, and prepare to go down! Then Ness got to work. He tapped Capone's phones. He began to ram down the doors of Al's breweries with a truck outfitted with a snowplow on the front, and sent thousands of gallons of illegal liquor running through the gutters. You could almost get drunk just from inhaling the fumes in the sewers!

One of Ness's men went undercover (that means he pretended to be a Capone guy) and soon the Untouchables got a lucky break. One of Capone's employees said, "The income tax dicks ain't so smart. They've had a record book of Al's for five years that could send him to jail, only they're too dumb to realize it." Capone had broken just about every law there was. He'd murdered hundreds of people. But if Ness's men, and the FBI, had to send Al to jail on a parking ticket they would do it!

What? No roses? The Valentine's Day Massacre did end with a lot of red.

DUMBER THAN DIRT

Sure, there are brilliant mastermind criminals. But some of them are stupider than a sack of bricks. Here's the proof—five pea-brained outlaws!

1. In Minneapolis, Minnesota, a suspected purse-snatcher was standing in a police lineup. The cops asked him to put on his baseball cap since the thief had been wearing a hat. The guy looked up and asked if he could put his cap on backwards. Said he, "That's the way I had it when I took the purse."

2. A Canadian bank robber got so excited during a heist that he left his car keys on the bank counter as he fled with his bag of cash. Naturally, he didn't get very far.

3. Two crooks in Kentucky had a great idea! They figured if they attached a chain from their car bumper to a cash machine they could pull off the front and grab the cash. Alas, the bumper ended up attached to the unbreakable ATM. The guys panicked and fled, but they left a little something behind—the car's license plate was attached to the bumper.

4. Never mind leaving a fingerprint at the scene of a crime. A man robbing a dry cleaner in Chicago accidentally blew off part of his own finger while waving his gun around. He trotted off with a whopping $10 from the cash register and a missing digit. Police arrived at the scene and found his 3-D fingerprint. Talk about incriminating evidence!

5. Ever seen an armored car? Little tiny bulletproof windows? Guys with guns to protect themselves? Still, somehow, a guy in Rhode Island managed to knock out an armored car driver and then grabbed the closest four bags of money. Bad choice. His bags were loaded with pennies and each one weighed more than 30 pounds. As the robber tried to run away, lugging 120 jingling pounds, he soon discovered that he had been penny wise but pound foolish. He was quickly caught and sent to the slammer.

By now, most of Capone's brewing equipment had been destroyed, thousands of gallons of beer and alcohol had been dumped, and the largest breweries were closed. And failing to pay income taxes was about to send Capone to jail.

On June 5, 1931, a grand jury met and charged Capone with 22 counts of tax evasion. A week later, he and 68 members of his gang were charged with more than 5,000 violations of the Volstead Act.

Just before his trial began, Capone began bribing and threatening jurors. But the government guys were on to him. At the very last minute the judge and the entire jury were switched. Capone found himself being

You're under arrest! That hat is too big for your head!

marched into a totally different courtroom with a different judge and jurors. Capone was sentenced to eleven years in prison and ended up at Alcatraz. (Want to try and escape from that PRISON? See page 207.)

With the end of the laws against drinking in 1933, the era of those colorful in-your-face gangsters came to an end. But there are still plenty of criminals, and there always will be. The FBI, Scotland Yard, and Interpol still stay *plenty* busy tracking down bad guys who live life on the other side of the law. So stick your hands up in the air and give me all your money! And make it snappy! I haven't got all day!

P

PIRATES

MYTH-CONCEPTION

WALKING THE PLANK

Another bit of movie make-believe! No one ever walked the plank. When you think about it, it's pretty stupid. Why waste time dragging out a length of lumber when you can just toss the bloke overboard and be done with it?

YO HO! YO HO! A PIRATE'S LIFE FOR ME!

What was it like to be pirate in, say, the 1600s? Well . . . take a leaky, foul, damp boat. Fill it with 80 guys who never bathe. Make sure they are *always* drunk, *always* swearing, and *always* itching to pick a fight. Got the picture? A pirate's life was dirty, smelly, sometimes boring, and often deadly.

So who in their right mind would want to be a pirate? Well . . . for many folks, it seemed a whole lot better than being an honest sailor in the king's navy. A sailor's life was harsh—a life of foul drinking water, spoiled food, lice, and death from horrible rotting diseases . . . and all for a few pennies a day in pay.

By contrast, a pirate had freedom! A pirate didn't need to work nearly as a hard as an honest seaman in the king or queen's navy (there were about 80 pirates to share the work on the average boat instead of about 30 on a typical naval vessel). As a pirate you also got to vote on where the ship was going and what it was going to do. Best of all, you got to share in all the gold

When you think of pirates, you probably think of Peter Pan and Captain Hook or you might think of that peg-legged parrot-toting dude from *Treasure Island.* You picture a guy in an eye patch and one gold earring and imagine palm-fringed islands and buried treasure chests full of gold. WRONG! WRONG! WRONG! Sure, pirates stole gold and jewels. But for more than 1,500 years, pirates from every corner of the Earth also stole grain, livestock, and ladies' underwear. Anything a ship might carry could—and often was—stolen by pirates.

WORD UP!

Rum is made from sugarcane that's been boiled down to syrup, then fermented and distilled—turning it into flavored alcohol.

Rum mixed with water made a tangy drink called *grog.* A pirate that had drank too much grog and was now face down in a pile of pig poop was definitely *groggy.*

and goodies that were plucked from someone else's ship.

So *what* if you were executed on the spot if you were caught? Being a pirate was one of the few ways to beat the system in the days when the rich were rich and the poor worked 'til they died, making sure the rich stayed that way.

LET'S GET READY TO *RUM*-BLE . . .

The reality is pirates were pretty much always drunk. In fact, during the golden age of the pirates—the 1600s through the early 1800s—pretty much *every* sailor, from the ten-year-old cabin boy to the toothless, creaky old first mate, drank a lot of booze *every* day. But there was a reason for that.

You know when the doctor gets set to give you a shot (*ouch!*) and swabs your arm with alcohol, to kill any germs on your skin? Alcohol was added to the ship's water for the same reason.

Drinking and driving don't mix. A drunk captain could make some very bad choices.

Water, stored in wooden casks, always turned rancid and filled with bacteria. So every time a seaman poured some drinking water, it had a splash of rum in it to kill the germs.

On military or merchant ships, there was someone in charge of measuring out the daily portion of rum. But on board the "one-pirate-one-vote"ships, democracy sometimes backfired when pirates voted to get stinkin' drunk. Then, as the crew snored off the day's drinking binge, it was surprisingly easy for other pirates to pirate a pirate ship. And speaking of democracy . . .

SIGN WITH AN "X"

Pirates had a strict code of honor, which is kinda weird when you consider that they were also ruthless criminals. But when a pirate joined a ship, he or she signed an agreement called *articles*. These were basically a set of pirate rules for living aboard ship, along with the punishments for breaking those rules.

YO HO HO, AND A BOTTLE OF RUM . . .

You know that song little kids love to sing, the one that sounds so funny coming out of their sweet little mouths? "Fifteen men on a dead-man's chest, Yo Ho Ho, and a bottle of rum . . ."? It's a lovely, bloody song, and it was written by Robert Louis Stevenson in *Treasure Island*. But what's it about?

Dead Man's Chest is one of the British Virgin Islands. There's a legend that Blackbeard punished some bad pirates by sending them to this nasty little spot with no drinking water. Nothing but rocky cliffs and snakes. He gave each pirate a knife and a bottle of rum. The hope was they would all get drunk and kill one another. But when a month had passed and Blackbeard sailed by there again, he discovered that 15 of them had actually survived. Guess it goes to show how even pirates can get along in a pinch.

PIRATE
TRUES & FALSES

PIRATE HAT
That Caribbean sun beating down on your head can fry a skull. A hat or scarf to protect a pirate's brain was a must. True.

EYE PATCH
You know how moms always say "Stop! You'll put an eye out with that thing!" Well, they're right! Flying splinters from cannonballs sure do hurt! True.

EXTRA AMMO
You could never have enough bullets on board since high humidity did funky things to bullets and gunpowder. Plus it looks scary. True.

SWORD
Since saltwater-encrusted guns never seemed to fire when you needed them, a sword was a must. True, true, true!

SKULL AND CROSSBONES FLAG
Pirates didn't really fly black flags with skulls on them. False! But many flew red flags as a sign that they were not afraid to spill a lot of blood. The name Jolly Roger comes from the French "jolie rouge" which means "pretty red."

EARRINGS
Pirates believed that pierced ears helped improve their eyesight! Turns out ear lobes are acupuncture points for several eye ailments! True.

PARROT
Would you want a bird sitting on your shoulder all day? Do you have ANY idea how often a parrot takes a dump? False.

DAGGER
A sword is good, but two blades are better than one. True.

A HOOK
When the ship's carpenter was the one doing the operating, most pirates bled to death when a limb was severed. False.

TREASURE CHESTS
Most pirates spent their loot as fast as they got it. A few days of drinking, wooing women, buying silly looking clothes . . . and it was time to go pirate some more. Usually false.

In a bizarre twist of history, the pirates actually created some of the first democracies in the New World. For example, they had the right to vote out a captain who was not pointing them in the direction of enough plunder, and to elect a new leader who promised to do better. And at a time in history when your situation at birth spelled out exactly what your life would be like, any pirate who wanted to could run for captain, even if he or she was the child of a manure-shoveler. It's not President of the United States, but it's something!

Pirates voted on everything—where they would sail to, what ships they would attack, and how to divide the loot. All the plundered loot was shared equally. The captain, cook, ship's carpenter, and pilot got double shares since they generally worked harder. A portion was set aside for ship's supplies and repairs.

THE WIDE WORLD OF PIRATES

What's the diff? And how the heck do you tell them apart?

Pirate—anyone who **robs at sea.**

Privateer—a ship (and the commander and the crew of that ship) with a fancy official letter from a government giving their royal navy permission to **rob at sea.** Yup—official government-issued pirates, except all the profits from their plunder went back to the king or queen.

Corsairs—pirates who did their stealing in the Mediterranean and along the coast of North Africa. These were European and Middle Eastern folks who loved to **rob at sea.**

Buccaneers got their name from the French word *boucan,* which means "barbecue." These New World sea-thieves first hung out on the island of Hispaniola in the Caribbean and got their name because they always smelled like barbecued meat. Soon every pirate in the Caribbean was known as a buccaneer—robbers at sea, Americas-style.

PIRATE SPANKING

Pirate justice could be tough. Let's say you're a pirate who has kept an important secret from the group. This was a big no-no. You would be taken to the nearest scrap of an island and given a small flask of water, a pistol, and enough gunpowder to blow your brains out. Since the island was usually ultra-tiny, you might be up to your gizzard in water by high tide. With no food or drinking water, after a few days of this, a bullet in the skull might seem like a good idea.

If you slugged another pirate on your ship, or carried a lighted candle without a lantern, you received Moses' Law—39 lashes on your bare back. Or you might find yourself tied to the mast, with your pirate buddies throwing bits of broken bottles at you. Another popular punishment was *keel hauling*—being dragged across a barnacle-encrusted boat bottom, then left in the sea until your shredded skin attracted every shark within smelling distance. (For more on this nasty discipline, see PRISONS AND PUNISHMENTS on page 207.)

THE PIRATE HALL OF FAME

Some pirates stole and plundered in secret. Others became world famous. Naturally, one nation's hero was often another's slimy, yellow-bellied cutthroat.

The Most Honored Pirate— Sir Francis Drake: The 1500s

The son of a Puritan preacher, Drake got his start in 1567. He was sailing on a privateer in the Caribbean when his boat was attacked by the Spanish. He lost everything he owned, and almost lost his life. From that moment on, he (along with many important folks in England) flat-out hated the Spanish.

In 1572 he talked his cousin into outfitting him with two ships and set off for Panama. While there, he ran into a group of Cimarrones—escaped slaves who hid in the mountains and lived as outlaws. The ex-slaves hated the Spaniards (who had originally taken them from Africa and sold them into slavery) even more than Drake did. The Cimarrones joined Drake and started harassing the Spaniards' ships.

After scoring a load of loot for Queen Elizabeth I (bow down before her in QUIRKY QUEENS on page 214), Drake set off on an around-the-world plunder-fest. It was a tough journey full of storms, mutinies, and assorted thrills and chills. But he made it! To the Spaniards, Drake was considered a deranged, lunatic pirate. But in England he was a national hero. His greatest score was a Spanish galleon loaded down with so much booty that it took Drake's men four days to move it onto his ship. To celebrate, Drake was knighted. And Queen Elizabeth had a good reason to make this pirate "Sir Francis." After all, she had benefited from the pirating of almost 100 million dollars by today's standards.

The Most Successful Pirate— Sir Henry Morgan: The 1600s

After being kidnapped in Wales as a lad and sent to sea, little Henry ended up in buccaneer territory—the island of Barbados in the Caribbean. Henry grew up to be a real kick-butt pirate, picking up where Sir Francis Drake had left off—tormenting the Spanish galleons that were filled with gold stolen from Aztec and Inca peoples. Because he was ruining Spain's fleet (and Spain was still England's number-one enemy), the British decided to look the other way and honor him by making him the Lieutenant Governor of Jamaica. Who says crime doesn't pay?

The *Almost*-Luckiest Pirate— Captain Kidd: The 1600s

Captain William Kidd was a Scottish sea captain who became a privateer. He was *supposed* to be stealing from French ships and rounding up pirates in the Indian Ocean, all for the British crown, but his crew forced him to go whole hog, so they all became full-fledged pirates. Why turn the loot over to England? It was more fun to keep it!

Alas, after one lucrative run, Captain Kidd was eventually captured. He spent the winter of 1699 in a freezing cold Boston jail wearing 16 pounds of iron manacles and a few tattered rags. He was then taken to an even fouler prison in London where he was held in a rat-infested cell for a year before being hanged. But as the noose was tightened around his neck, the rope snapped! Down Kidd went, still very much alive. They had to re-hang him! This time, just to make sure he was truly dead, they dipped his body in tar, stuffed the corpse in a man-sized cage, and hung it at the entrance to the harbor as a warning to anyone with the same idea. That cage, which had been made to measure by a blacksmith, was tight-fitting enough to ensure that Kidd's bones would stay in place once his tarred flesh rotted away.

The Hairiest, Scariest Pirate— Blackbeard: The 1700s

Little Edward Teach grew up to become one of the most feared pirates ever. He had a huge beard that completely covered his face, growing almost all the way up to his eyes, and down to his chest. He twisted and braided all that facial hair into dreadlocks, and tied them with dozens of ribbons. But just in case you think guys with ribbons are sissies, he stuck smoldering fuses into his beard and beneath his hat so he looked like he was on fire. Add his always-bloodshot eyes, and people swore he was the devil.

Blackbeard's hunting grounds were the waters off the Carolinas and Virginia. By 1718, the governor of Virginia had had enough. He offered a huge amount of money for the capture of Blackbeard, and lucky Lieutenant Robert Maynard of the HMS *Pearl* managed to kill the fuzzy pirate in fierce hand-to-hand combat. Then he hacked off Blackbeard's head and proudly hung it from the front of his ship. Lovely!

PINK PIRATES

Think all pirates were guys? Think again. Some of the wildest "men" at sea were actually women.

Mary Read and Ann Bonny were two gals you did not want to find holding a sword to your neck! They could swear, drink, slice and dice with the toughest men. They walked, dressed—and killed—like guys. In the early 1700s, both ladies ended up sailing on a boat captained by the swaggering pirate "Calico Jack" Rackham. One day after a really big heist, the crew all drank themselves silly in celebration. The men were so plastered, they were unable to fight back when the authorities found their ship and came to arrest them all—all, that is, except Ann and Mary, who were much better at holding their liquor and fought like wild beasts.

All aboard the ship were captured and sentenced to die, including Ann and Mary. But both had a way of saving themselves that none of the men had. They were both pregnant! The law said that a pregnant woman could not be hanged until her baby was born . . . so they were spared, at least for a few months. Mary died before her baby was born. But Ann and her child lived—and then disappeared, never to be heard from again.

RED PIRATES

China's Red Flag Fleet was the biggest pirate fleet in the world—1,500 ships that brought all sorts of misery to people all along Asia's Pacific coast. And for many years, the entire fleet was run by a woman named Cheng I Sao. She was a toughie! Her raids were ruthless and brutal, and in addition to plundering and stealing, her fleet added a little twist, demanding "protection" money from coastal towns. And there was only one punishment for disobeying an order—a swift beheading.

The Chinese emperors wanted to bring Cheng I Sao to justice but they couldn't find her. They even asked the British and Portuguese navies to help. Still no luck! Finally, in desperation, in 1810, the emperor offered complete amnesty to every pirate in the Red Flag Fleet, including Cheng I Sao, if they would simply call it quits. So Cheng I Sao accepted the amnesty, happily (and richly) retired.

WELL... SHIVER ME TIMBERS!

Some putrid pirate highlights!

■ In 75 B.C.E., Julius Caesar, who would become Rome's great ruler, was captured by pirates and held captive on a teeny island for more than a month until a ransom was paid. When he was free again, Julius made sure the culprits were found—and crucified.

■ Over in the Middle East, King Shapur II of Persia (309–379) HATED pirates. He got the nickname Zulaklaf, which means "lord of the shoulders," because (legend has it) he pierced the shoulders of captured pirates, shoved a rope through those bloody holes, and tied them all together, like a string of pirate beads. Yikes!

■ When a French corsair named Murat Rais kept terrorizing the North African coast in the late 1500s, the sultan of Algiers decided to fight back. He rounded up bunches of French citizens, loaded them into the mouths of active cannons, and ordered the fuses lit—thereby inventing the first flying French fry.

■ Chinese pirates had some of the cleanest boats on the seas. No rats on their boats, 'cause they ate 'em for dinner! How does the saying go? There's more than one way to skin a rat?

■ As you might imagine, doctors on pirate ships were few and far between. So when injured limbs needed to be amputated, pirates turned to the next logical choice: the ship's carpenter. At least he knew how to use a saw!

■ A pirate's biggest, scariest enemy was the teredo worm, which lived in warm tropical waters and slithered through a ship's hull. These nasty varmints could grow to 60 cm (about 2 feet) and eat a boat to splinters in a very short amount of time. Boats had to be hauled out of the water and coated with a mixture of tar, sulfur, and tallow in order to keep the worms away.

PLAGUES AND POXES

Don't germs get it? Don't those microbes know not to pick on things that are 10,000 times their size? After all, we humans are at the top of the food chain! They should know better than to mess with us! And yet there they are, always sneaking in when we're not looking, making us heave our guts out or scratch 'til we're raw, or sometimes—wiping out entire cities!

REVENGE OF THE LITTLE GUYS

For as long as there has been life on Earth, there have been teensy little predators around: bacteria and viruses, with the power to kill creatures far bigger than them. But those little predators need a host body to survive. And if they completely *kill* their prey, they will end up starving to death. So it is in the best interest of a microbe to learn to live in harmony with its hosts. Most of the time, they do. But when that balance gets shaken up—by natural disasters, war, or changes in where we live—*lots* of people get sick. *Really* sick. Plagues erupt, and poof! The Grim Reaper is suddenly doing a big business.

THE GOOD, THE BAD, AND THE REALLY UGLY

There are plenty of good-guy microbes, such as the ones that crawled into the guts of elephants thousands of years ago, helping those chunky beasts get big while eating nothing but grass. Bacteria in *your* gut helps break down the food that you have swallowed into smaller pieces so that you can get the vitamins, minerals, and proteins you need to live. Without bacteria, you'd be dead. But unfortunately, sometimes the bacteria takes a deadly turn.

Pick a peck of prickly poxes. *From left to right, scratch away at measles, scarlet fever, and smallpox.*

detects a measles germ and knows that a slight fever and a little rash will do the trick. No need to turn up the heat to 106°F! Now you have an *endemic* disease. That's what happened with things like chicken pox. Endemic illnesses no longer kill us; they just make us itchy and cranky. Finally, a germ can become *systemic,* like the bacteria in your gut that help digest your food.

The trouble starts when we meet germs we have never met before. Every plague that has ever erupted happened because new germs moved into town or people wandered into a new set of germs. When a new microbe sneaks into a body, the immune system goes bonkers! "Get out!" it screams. The body starts to produce weapons to kill the invader: high fevers to burn it out, puking to vomit it out, the runs to squirt it out, or increased blood flow to the skin to drown it out. Unfortunately, sometimes the body goes so overboard trying to kill the new germ that it kills itself in the process.

A brand-new germ can bring an *epidemic*—a widespread sickness. If those epidemics spread to many places, you now have a *pandemic,* such as AIDS. But after a while, our bodies start to recognize each germ and figure out just how to fight it. For example, someone's body

YUCKY YORE

You know all those stupid wars we've fought for centuries? Here's a news flash: Cholera, typhoid, dysentery, and smallpox have taken a bigger toll than guns. Don't believe me? Here's just one example: In Spain in 1489, in a typically idiotic battle, 20,000 soldiers died— 3,000 in battle and 17,000 of typhus.

THE GERM EXPRESS

Germs travel in some pretty disgusting ways. They hop on a sneeze, parachute into puke, take a ride in the runs, or hitch a lift on some other form of public transportation—like rats and fleas.

There are four ways for diseases to get transmitted: by air, by water, by human contact, or by *vectors*— critters like insects and rodents that act as germ jumbo jets.

By the time of the Neanderthals, mankind and disease were no strangers to each other. Our history was going to be closely tied to those billions of teeny little monster microbes whether we wanted it to or not.

PICK-A-PLAGUE

So many diseases, so little time!

Cholera: A "got-your-guts" disease caused by drinking water that has poop particles in it or eating shellfish that has not been properly cooked. It starts with cramps, then moves on to explosive diarrhea and vomiting. Eventually, the body's fluid levels get so out of whack that death follows. In the meantime, all the stuff expelled by the body is loaded with cholera germs, so more people catch the disease.

Diphtheria: A "throat-and-nose" disease. This bacteria makes a poison that spreads through the body and attacks the heart. It used to be one of the most common causes of death in kids. Now there are vaccines given in babyhood to protect you. *Phew!*

Polio: This is a sneaky virus. It enters through the mouth and lodges in the intestinal lining. From there it gets into the bloodstream and finally the nervous system, where it chomps on the muscles and causes paralysis. One of our greatest presidents, Franklin Roosevelt, developed polio in his 20s, and had to wear ten-pound leg braces just to stand up.

Smallpox: Once again, a virus is the culprit. This pox starts with a high fever and an outbreak of the worst case of pus-filled pimples you have ever seen. At its most evil, it can literally make the skin fall off the bone. The good news is, this pox was killed for good in the 1970s, although there are still some live samples of the virus in a few research laboratories.

Typhoid: Why is everyone always nagging you to wash your hands after you poop? Typhoid is why, okay? It's caused by a type of salmonella bacteria and symptoms include high fever, spots on the chest and abdomen, and intestinal problems—either you won't be able to go number two at all, or you will go too much! So wash your hands, already!

Typhus: Don't confuse this with the dirty-bathroom-hands disease above. This one is spread by body lice or fleas. You'll get a skin rash and high fever. Other names the disease has been called: malignant fever, jail fever, hospital fever, ship fever, putrid fever, brain fever, bilious fever, spotted fever, or camp fever. Take your pick!

Tuberculosis: This baddie has been around since the days of Egypt's pharaohs and attacks our lungs. Germs are spread by coughing, singing, even talking! But only about 10 percent of people with TB germs aboard their bodies actually get sick.

THE ANCIENT PLAGUE AND POX PARADE

50,000 Years Ago: Hungry humans decide that just about any living thing can be food. They start catching fish, grinding grasses into flour, and hunting small animals. They dig up clams and mussels. All of these food sources have new and different germs, some of them dangerous.

10,000 Years Ago: People begin settling in villages. But living in close quarters with other humans is even more dangerous than living with wild animals! Where do you put all the townspeople's poop? What do you do with all the garbage? Life expectancy starts to dip from 40 years to 30 years because of disease.

5,000 Years Ago: Empires on the move! Tramping through wild lands disrupts all the happily settled germs. With trees cut down to build houses, viruses and bacteria are looking for new homes. The invention of irrigation brings puddles of water sitting for days and days—like luxury hotels for germs! Fields left to rest after harvest attract new

Swimming with sewage. *Nothing like a bath in a stream filled with garbage like this one was in Korea, 1904.*

visitors, such as ticks and mites and other deadly disease vectors.

4,000 Years Ago: By now people are living in tiny homes, some close to each other, creating cities. Living close together along with their animals nearby equals lots of doo-doo *everywhere*. And tossing trash into the streets and poop and pee into their backyards creates the germ equivalent of an all-you-can-eat buffet. Accidents cease to be the leading cause of death. Now there's a new killer in town: the "crowd disease," or illnesses that spread from door to door.

Biblical Times (around 1200 B.C.E.): You can't read the Old Testament without a reference to a plague popping up every few pages. That's because crowd diseases were everywhere. The high priests tried to do something about it, but sacrificing a sheep at an altar just didn't cut it. What did help was cleanliness, including washing hands, avoiding certain foods that carried particularly awful germs, and not living in a pigsty. A lot of the Old Testament is simply health instructions.

Ancient Greece (500–146 B.C.E.): One of the biggest reasons the Golden Age of Athens came to a screeching halt was because of a plague that hit the city in 430 B.C.E. Over the next five years, so many people died that Athens fell apart. The police were dead. So were the judges and the politicians. Corpses piled up in the streets because people were too sick to bury them. The plague hit young and old, slaves and their owners. To this day no one is sure exactly what it was. All they know is that one day a ship came from the south, and a couple of days later, Athens was dying.

Ancient Rome (753 B.C.E.–476 C.E.): Sure, the Roman Empire was too big. Sure, some of the emperors were real whack jobs. Sure, there was a lot of lead poisoning from the pipes that carried the capital city's water. There were a lot of reasons why Rome collapsed, but the biggest reason was two back-to-back epidemics of measles. And by measles, I'm not talking about a little itchy rash, but a terrible disease that made peoples' skin literally fall off their bodies. Blech!

THE EMPIRE EATERS

Do you see a pattern here? As civilizations grew bigger, people often got flattened by terrible plagues. Sometimes this was caused by people living too close together with poor sanitation. Other times it was because armies went tramping off to parts of the world carrying groups of germs that the soldiers were used to, but the poor invaded people

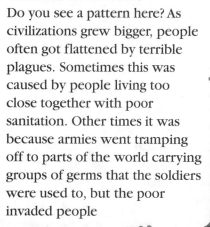

Dropping like flies. *The plague hit ancient Athens hard.*

weren't—and vice versa. People sneezed, coughed, or spit their germs onto one another. People dumped their pots full of pee and poop into the nearest rivers, then drank the water and washed their clothes in it. Killer germs were licked off dirty fingers as people ate without utensils. Even clothing was a way for germs to sneak inside, as lice and fleas crept into the fibers and then under the skin.

THE WORST CENTURY EVER

If there were a prize for the absolutely *most awful* years to ever have been alive, that award would have to go to the 1300s, the century of "the Black Death." This was not just any plague. It was bubonic plague, which made its first appearance in the year 540 C.E. in Egypt, when it sailed along the Nile, across the Mediterranean, and into the beautiful city of Constantinople (in present-day Turkey). In a flash, 10,000 people *a day* were dying. By the time the plague had passed, 40 percent of the city had passed, too. But that was small potatoes compared to what was to come.

For the next 500 years, things sort of calmed down. The plague germs went back to their animal hosts, the rodents and rats and fleas they had come from. The cities were less crowded— after all, half the population had either died or scattered. The weather warmed and crops flourished. Don't get me wrong— life was still pretty bleak. A person who reached the ripe old

Rat-a-tat-tat. Rats and death went hand in hand.

GERM WARFARE

Plague victims make great weapons, as the people of a Turkish city under siege discovered in 1347. One clever but evil general flung dozens of plague-infected corpses over their city walls, using catapults. The guys inside the city flung the corpses right back out. But the damage had been done!

age of 40 was elderly. But it was a heck of a lot better than living among corpses stacked ten deep in the street, as they had during the plague years. Cities thrived once more. Trade between countries began once more.

And then—*poof!*—it all went sour again, in the mid-1300s. Part of the problem was a huge dependence on wheat farming, which drained the soil of its nutrients. Then the weather turned cold and it rained all the time. The crops rotted. The cows got sick. People were forced to eat their pets. And as if that wasn't bad enough, there were all sorts of natural disasters. A volcano erupted in Italy. There were floods and earthquakes. And as if there weren't already enough death and destruction, England and France were at each other's throats in the Hundred Years' War.

Over in Asia, they were facing the same problems—floods and earthquakes in some places, absolutely no rain in others, dead and dying crops and herd animals. So almost every person in Europe and Asia was in "iffy" shape at this point. Then to make matters worse, a germ jumped ship from its host animal—the wild burrowing rodent—and moved to the black rat. Black rats didn't live in wild burrows: They lived in people's garbage and on their sailing ships. And the germ, *Y. pestis,* now happily settled in its new home—a rat's guts— then hopped aboard fleas, which then hopped aboard humans.

The plague began in central Asia and slowly moved west. In 1347, a group of Genoese sailors returned from Turkey to their home port with some stowaways—black rats infected with plague. Within days people in every port the boat had landed in were dying. By the time winter set in, most of the people in southern Europe were sick, and the cold weather helped the disease along by providing another means of transportation: sneezing and coughing.

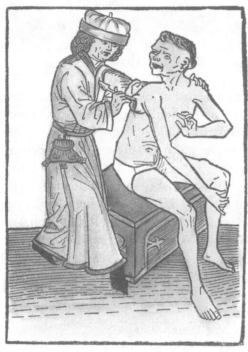

Ring around the rosie? *Some docs tried to drain those nasty black swellings, but it never helped.*

GOT A BUBOE?

This plague was a doozy. It began with apple-sized swellings, or *buboes,* which spread from armpits and groins to everywhere else on the body. Soon those swellings turned black—the reason this plague is called the Black Death. At least no one had to suffer very long. This disease worked fast! You could wake up healthy and be dead by nightfall. Medicine at that time was a complete joke. Doctors didn't have a clue about what to do. They tried bloodletting. They gave drugs to make you puke. They tried poking and burning the buboes and prescribed bathing in pee.

"Ring Around the Rosies" was a plague-inspired ditty: The "rings around the rosies" were the swelling lumps of disease. The "pockets full of posies" hid the smell of rotting bodies. According to some estimates, within a year or two, almost half the people living in Europe died—about 25 million souls. Another 18 million died in Asia. There was no place to bury the millions of bodies, so they were tossed into the rivers. Because of the plague, the Byzantine Empire collapsed. The Islamic Empire lost almost half its subjects. Think about it! Half the people of two continents gone! No wonder it was called the Great Dying.

There were still a few continents where life was still relatively germ-free—including North America. But that would change as the 1400s drew to a close.

LOOK OUT, HERE WE COME!

CREEPY COLUMBUS (see page 37) had a little stowaway aboard ship that he wasn't aware of: germs. The people of the New World were 10,000 years removed from the germ pools of Asia, Africa, and Europe. After Columbus docked, smallpox and measles soon ran through the New World like Olympic sprinters going for the gold.

The Black Death had killed half the people of Europe in the 1300s. Now, in the 1500s, smallpox was about to mow down upwards of 90 percent of the native peoples of the Americas. How did a few cupfuls of little germs change two huge continents? The great civilizations of the Aztec, Inca, and Maya were ruined, most probably because of germs. Because so many natives were sick or dying, they were easy to "conquer." And since there was no one to actually do any work, the European germ-bearers had to find others to do all their heavy lifting. And those "others" were the Africans.

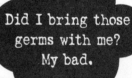

Did I bring those germs with me? My bad.

The people of Africa had been exposed to smallpox for so long that it had become simply a pesky little illness—kind of like chicken pox is for us today. The Africans got smallpox, and it made them miserable, but it didn't kill them. However, the trip across the Atlantic in slave ships was another story. Many millions of Africans died of *other* diseases on the long trip from Africa to America. And those horrifying, degrading ships brought other passengers—like mosquitoes loaded with malaria and yellow fever germs—carrying brand-new plagues to the Americas.

Some 10 million Africans managed to survive the most brutal biological test of endurance ever. And since they had the best resistance to the diseases that kept hammering the Americas, an African was worth three times as much as an indentured European servant. So in a sad twist of fate, their greater physical strength cost them their freedom for hundreds of years.

I FEEL LIKE I'M GONNA HURL

In the 1800s, India was part of the British Empire, and it was there that a new pandemic was born. It started in Calcutta in 1817, a city that had been built by the British, and had grown *way* too quickly. Calcutta was a germ crock-pot—a place packed with merchants and soldiers, religious

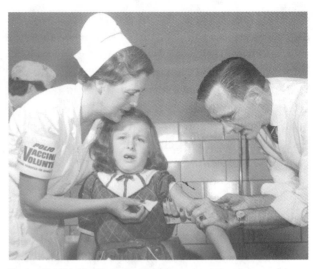

Yowie owie! Old-time shots sure did sting.

pilgrims, and thousands of people flocking from poor villages in hopes of getting rich. It was called "the Black Hole," and with good reason. It was warm, moist, filthy, and crowded—a waterborne bacteria's paradise!

The plague that began in Calcutta was caused by a comma-shaped little wriggler called *V. cholerae.* Cholera attacked the intestinal tract and killed its victims with the worst case of diarrhea and vomiting you've ever seen. And it was highly contagious: Anyone who even tried to clean up the huge mess made by the sick person would quickly get sick, too

Because India was a global crossroads, the disease swept swiftly around the world on the sailing ships and trains that constantly steamed in and out of Calcutta. Because it was such a smelly, horrible disease, several European scientists really hunkered down and tried to find the cause.

I SPY . . . A MICROBE!

Finally, people began to get it. Scientists realized that germs were sometimes a very bad thing. Back in the mid-1600s, a guy named Anton Van Leeuwenhoek improved upon the existing microscopes and was the first to see little creatures called bacteria. At first, sci-guys just thought they

A bacterium, mucho magnified. Critters like this are everywhere.

I HATE SHOTS!

Once you've had an illness, your body usually remembers it, and it knows how to attack the disease without killing you, too. For hundreds of years people in Africa, India, Asia, and the Arab worlds have known that if you break a smallpox blister and transfer a little bit of the fluid into a scratch on the skin of a person who has never had the disease, the healthy person will stay that way. One of George Washington's slaves told him about this way of fighting the pox. When George saw that it actually worked, he ordered all his Continental soldiers to be pricked with smallpox vaccine. It worked like a charm!

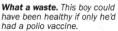

were kinda cool, but by the mid-1800s, Robert Koch and Louis Pasteur were beginning to figure out that there were lots of different *types* of bacteria, and that many of them were killers. And they started to do something about it—developing ways to control or kill the bad germs.

Slap me! Mosquitoes carry malaria, yellow fever, and West Nile virus.

Docs figured out the causes of the major "crowd diseases." Vaccines were discovered to prevent some viruses, and anti-toxins were found to cure others. In America, a fellow named Walter Reed figured out that yellow fever, which was killing Americans in droves, was caused by mosquitoes. And soon there were pills to swallow to kill the little demons who had wrought so much death.

But it turns out, bacteria and viruses are crafty critters. We humans would figure out a way to stop 'em and they'd just *mutate* (change slightly into something new) and reappear, ready to zap us again!

MODERN-DAY MAYHEM

Nowadays we're pretty careful about not throwing the contents of the toilet bowl out the window onto the street. We wash our hands. We eat well. But in spite of all that, there still have been some nasty epidemics in the last 100 years.

"It's just a little flu." Or so it seemed until a flu epidemic took a deadly turn in 1918. Spanish influenza hit even the young and the healthy, and killed more people than all of World War I, which had just ended. It's estimated that at least 20 million died. Kids jumped rope to this sad little rhyme: *I had a little bird, its name was Enza. I opened the window, and in-flu-enza.*

By the 1940s, there was new terror in town. Kids were kept off the playgrounds and told, "Don't go in the pool!" Why? Young people were suddenly getting fevers that lead to a mysterious paralyzing disease. No amount of scrubbing, hand-washing, or general cleanliness could stop this one! Polio became one of the most feared epidemics of the century. Happily, a vaccine was invented by Jonas Salk in 1954. But a few decades later a new virus was in town.

AIDS (Acquired Immune Deficiency Syndrome) made its nasty debut in the early 1980s and although its origins are not certain, it was probably transmitted from monkeys to humans through meat loaded with an animal virus that mutated. That mutated virus was HIV (Human Immunodeficiency Virus). For years, AIDS was a death sentence and by 1997 more than 6.5 million people had died, and 22 million more were infected (that's the equivalent of the entire population of Australia). By 2002, docs finally figured out how to keep the disease under control, with a bunch of very expensive medicines, so expensive that they're out of reach for millions of people. Now, if they can only figure out how to make those medicines affordable, or better still, actually cure HIV/AIDS!

No doubt about it. Plagues and poxes will always be here. Scientists will always have to try to stay one step ahead of those nefarious little critters. And in the meantime, *wash your hands* after you go, for gosh sakes!

What a waste. This boy could have been healthy if only he'd had a polio vaccine.

201

PRICKLY PRESIDENTS

Is it hot in here, or is it just me?

I'm gonna hurl. Former prez George Bush (the first) had the honor of publicly puking at an important dinner.

Grown-ups are always telling us that if we study hard, we can grow up to be the President. The question is, are we sure we want to? At least one of our presidents couldn't spell and could barely read. Another one had to have his wife tell him to stop talking about cow poop in public. And there was one who was so fat, he got stuck in the White House bathtub!

Here's the fun stuff they'll never tell you in history class, about the guys who have fearlessly led America—the folks the Secret Service sometimes calls Mr. POTUS (President of the United States).

PRESIDENTS ARE PEOPLE, TOO

I know it's hard to believe, but those guys in the Oval Office are really just people. They poop. They fart. They burp. President George "Poppy" Bush even barfed in the lap of the prime minister of Japan at a swanky state dinner! And plenty of them have had some pretty strange habits. Take George Washington. You may have already read about his famous fake chompers (if not, brush up on DASTARDLY DENTISTRY on page 54). Even though his own teeth were rotting away, he ordered his stable hands to be sure to brush his horses' pearly whites every morning.

While we're on the subject of odd habits, take John Quincy Adams, our sixth president and an avid skinny-dipper. He liked to start his day at dawn with a nude swim in the Potomac River. One day, a female reporter named Anne Royall decided she had a surefire way to get an interview with the president. She walked down to the river, scooped up Adams's presidential pants, and refused to give them back until he agreed to a chat.

WATCH YOUR MOUTH!

Harry S Truman became president in 1945. Harry was a plainspoken guy, the son of farming people. Harry S was the prez who left us with these heartfelt words: "No man should be allowed to be president who doesn't understand hogs." Since he was such a plain man, you may not be surprised to learn that the "S" in his name didn't stand for anything: That's why there's no period after it.

Truman often gave speeches to farmers. And for some reason he always seemed to veer onto the topic of fertilizer, which he called "manure." (That's cow poop to you city slickers.) His campaign managers cringed every time they heard that word! One of the guys finally went to Harry's wife, Bess, and asked her to help get the prez to stop using the word *manure* in his speeches. Bess gave a long sigh and said, "You'd be amazed how long

WACKY FACTS ABOUT OUR PRESIDENTS

No wars. No laws. No dumb dates. Just the dirt!

President John Tyler was quite a stud. He had 15 children.

Grossest food choice?

President Nixon often ate cottage cheese and ketchup, which looks just like bloody brains!

President Ronald Reagan

had lots of jobs in his pre-POTUS days. He was a sportscaster, a TV host, and a movie star. One day he made $10 for diving into a public pool to retrieve a guy's false teeth.

Celebrity prez. Ronald Reagan played a bad guy in the 1964 movie The Killers.

Secret Service guys are there to protect a president. But President Eisenhower thought they didn't have enough to do. He made his agents trap the squirrels that kept messing up the putting green he had installed on the White House lawn.

Teeniest President? James Madison, a mere 5'4" and barely 100 pounds.

Ever had a Baby Ruth candy bar? It was named after a presidential baby: Ruth, daughter of Grover Cleveland.

Know why Lincoln grew a beard? An 11-year-old girl wrote him a letter saying his face looked too skinny, and told him a beard would make him look chubbier.

Franklin D. Roosevelt

had to wear dresses until he was five. (Head over to **STUPID SUPERSTITIONS** on page 253 and find out why.)

Frilly Frankie. Roosevelt's mom kept Franklin in dresses for years!

Political campaigns

could get ugly in the past—even uglier than today if you can imagine that. When Lincoln was running for president his opponent called him "Honest Ape." Nice talk!

PREZ'S PETS

Those White House families sure did love their cats and dogs! But there were some other strange critters hangin' at the White House, too.

• Andrew Jackson's pet parrot was a real pottymouth. During Jackson's funeral, the bird had to be removed from the room because it was cursing up a storm.

One of the Roosevelt parrots.

• Why waste money cutting the grass, especially in wartime? During World War I, Woodrow Wilson kept a flock of sheep to trim the White House grass.

• Teddy Roosevelt's kids kept a one-legged chicken as a pet. They also had a horse that they would sometimes sneak up to their bedrooms in a White House elevator. Teddy was one of the most pet-friendly presidents. He had a lion, a hyena, a wildcat, a coyote, five bears, two parrots, a zebra, a barn owl, snakes, lizards, rats, roosters, and a raccoon. And let's not forget his six-toed cat, Slippers!

• President Eisenhower's weimaraner, Heidi, was sent packing from the White House. The poor pooch's crime? She would *not stop* peeing on the new presidential carpets.

Johnson and his beagles.

• A major presidential scandal broke when Lyndon Baines Johnson picked up one of his beagles by his ears. The news media went wild and people accused him of being an animal hater. Truth is, he loved dogs!

it took me to get [him] to *start* using the word *manure.*"

While we're on the subject of poop, if President Lyndon B. Johnson had to go "number two" in the middle of an important conversation, he sometimes dragged the people he was speaking with into the bathroom with him. Johnson recalled one guy who "found it utterly impossible to look at me while I sat there on the toilet. You'd think he had never seen those parts of the body before. . . . He was standing as far away from me as he possibly could, keeping his back toward me the whole time, trying to carry on a conversation." Now, who was out of line here? You decide.

DUH TO THE CHIEF

Andrew Jackson, POTUS number seven, was the least educated man to ever live in the White House. He wrote these eloquent words:

It's a damn poor mind that can only think of one way to spell a word!

Not only could he *not* spell, but Jackson also has the honor of being the only man elected president after killing a man in a duel (his victim had said something nasty about Jackson's wife).

Jackson was a colorful character indeed. He fought alongside the pirate Jean Lafitte during the War of 1812 at the Battle of New Orleans. When he inherited some money from his granddad, he squandered it all betting on cockfights and horse races. He was the first president to install spittoons in the White House (special pots used for spitting in). And he was one lucky president! When an assassin tried to kill him in 1848, both of the guy's pistols misfired.

Slob on the job. *Abe Lincoln was America's messiest prez.*

HAIL TO THIS CHIEF

Abraham Lincoln, one of the coolest and funniest guys to ever run this country, was also incredibly sloppy and scatterbrained. He was always losing stuff. You're probably sick of hearing about his log cabin, or the fact that he was a goody-goody who just *loved* to read his books by firelight. So forget about that guy. Think about the Lincoln who loved to wrestle, the riverboat pilot Lincoln, or the Lincoln who worked in a grocery store. And think about the really funny, witty Lincoln. If Lincoln were alive today, he'd probably be a stand-up comic. He had a story for everything! When he was prez, anyone could drop in at the White House. Lincoln would sit down with them, tell them a few jokes, and soon make the poor visitor forget why he or she stopped by.

Lincoln was also the messiest president ever. Back when he was a lawyer in Illinois, his partner found a stack of dusty papers stuffed on the top of a shelf. There was a scrap of paper in Lincoln's handwriting on top of it that said, "When you can't find it anywhere else, look at this." And that tall hat that Lincoln loved? It was the perfect place to keep his most important documents.

THE RAT HOUSE

You think that big, white house with the tall columns would be a cool place to live? Think again! In 1889, when Caroline Harrison, the wife of President Benjamin Harrison, moved in, she found the attic teeming with rats. And after President William Taft's 350-pound body got stuck in a White House bathtub in 1909, all-new—and needless to say, enormous—tubs had to be installed. Actually, Taft was pretty lucky.

HONEST GHOST

Is the spectre of Honest Abe still around? Maureen Reagan, the daughter of President Ronald Reagan, swears that in 1984, she saw the ghost of Abraham Lincoln wandering the halls. And she's not the only one. Several presidents and a visiting queen all insist they have been awakened by visits from the late, great Lincoln.

Maybe poor Abe couldn't rest in peace because his coffin has been moved 17 times and opened up at least five. In 1876, grave robbers almost managed to steal it! Their plan? To hold it for a ransom of $200,000! To make sure that didn't ever happen again, the coffin was re-buried under two tons of concrete deep beneath the foundations of his tomb in Springfield, Illinois.

A tub fit for a tubby prez. *When you weigh 350 pounds a regular tub won't do.*

of throat cancer. Zachary Taylor died of heat stroke at the ripe old age of 84, but his body was dug up after rumors spread that he'd been poisoned. There were also rumors swirling around after Warren Harding's death that he had been poisoned by his wife. And poor William Henry Harrison! He talked so long at his own inaugural speech—which took place on a damp January day—that he got pneumonia and died less than two months later.

When President Millard Fillmore first arrived at the White House in 1850, there was no indoor plumbing at all. When the house was finally wired for electricity in the late 1890s, President Harrison kept getting electric shocks. He finally gave up using the light switches, and just slept with the lights on.

But there were perks to living in the White House, such as having lots of servants. Unfortunately, Herbert Hoover's wife, Lu, didn't quite trust them. She often left a $1,000 bill on her dresser just to see if someone would steal it.

DEAD PRESIDENTS

Sadly, several presidents have been shot and killed while in office. Abraham Lincoln, James Garfield, William McKinley, and John F. Kennedy were all murdered. (Garfield didn't actually die from the gunshot, but from the continued poking of the wound by his doctors with their unwashed hands and unsterilized instruments.) Several other presidents had attempts made on their lives. And some of them did themselves in. Take Ulysses S. Grant. He smoked 20 cigars a day. *Pee-uw!* Not surprisingly, he died

Puffing president. *Grant loved cigars—and they killed him!*

YOU'RE UNDER ARREST, SIR

Presidents can get in trouble, too. President Ulysses S. Grant was once arrested for speeding and his horse and carriage were impounded. He had to pay a $20 fine and walk back home to the White House! President Franklin Pierce was arrested in 1853 for running over an old lady. And Thomas Jefferson and James Madison were arrested by an overeager police officer in Vermont in the spring of 1791, for carriage riding on a Sunday. Perish the thought!

Then, of course, there was Richard "I am not a crook" Nixon, who got into so much hot water he had to resign from office. In June 1972, some of his supporters broke into Democratic headquarters and stole some important papers. Then Tricky Dick lied about it. The president who followed him in office, Gerald Ford, said all was forgiven and officially pardoned Nixon. But the name "Tricky Dick" lives on.

PRISONS AND PUNISHMENTS

Think being grounded is a bummer? Try being marched out to the middle of the town square, tied up, and then pelted with sheep guts as your friends and neighbors gather to watch. Very embarrassing, not to mention smelly! But it could be worse. You could be grounded *for life*—sent to "the big house" (also know as prison, the clink, the pen, the cooler, the joint, the pokey, the slammer, the hoosegow, the jug, and the stir)—a place where the bathrooms have no doors!

A TOOTH FOR A TOOTH

Early man's response to crime was simple. Get even! Revenge was the response to wrongdoing. But as towns grew into cities, things started to get out of hand. We needed some rules! The first person to write down an official set of laws, with punishments for breaking those laws, was a fellow named Hammurabi (*Hahm-uh-ROB-ee*). Hammurabi was a Mesopotamian king back in 1750 B.C.E. and was one of the first to come up with the idea of "an eye for an eye, a tooth for a tooth."

Painful Punishments

The ancient Greeks and Romans figured that an ounce of prevention was worth a bucket of cutoff hands or noses. They

NO NOSE-PICKING

The ancient Chinese and Indians had some interesting ideas about how to punish lawbreakers. In India, thieves had their noses (or sometimes ears) sliced off to broadcast to all that the now-noseless person had stolen something. After all, you could always hide a hacked off hand by stuffing your sleeve in a pocket. But it was hard to hide a big gaping hole in the middle of your face! As a result, the modern day nose job got its start as crafty doctors learned how to rebuild sliced-off schnozzes . . . for a price.

In China, a devious device called a *congue* fit tightly around a person's neck. While wearing it, it was impossible to reach your face with your hands. You could not rub your eyes, blow your nose, or scratch an itchy head. And forget sleeping. After a few days spent wearing a congue, you had learned your lesson. The Chinese were also fond of public spankings with a bamboo pole. Grown-ups had to march into the center of town, drop their trousers in front of *everyone* and bend over. Oh-so-*very* embarrassing.

developed strong governments, wrote laws to protect their citizens, and developed punishments for crime. Do something wrong in ancient Greece and you'd be rowing your little hands raw in a slave galley in the middle of nowhere faster than you can say "Row, row, row your boat." The Romans' solution for folks who misbehaved was a hungry, angry wild beast. Many criminals found themselves face to face with a famished lion. (Read more about battling beasts in GLADIATORS on page 104.)

It's the pits. Underground jail pits make escape almost impossible.

LOCK 'EM UP AND THROW AWAY THE KEY

The Romans were among the first to create prisons—really crummy, nasty places with bars on the windows and doors, and no hope for escape! They were called *carcers* (that's where our word "incarcerated" comes from), and had dungeon-like cages built 12 feet underground. Since people were condemned to death for the teeniest things back then, the *carcer* wasn't used as long-term prison—just a final damp death row.

PAY UP!

Jails didn't become common until the 12th century in England, when King Henry II ordered every county sheriff to build a jail (or gaol, as the English liked to spell it). One of England's scariest "gaols" was called Newgate. Every Monday morning, some of its prisoners were dragged out to the front yard where they were hanged, whipped, or even pressed to death. These public executions were supposed to scare other people away from committing crimes. You can bet it'd make you think twice about stealing!

People sent to "gaol" had to pay to get out, and while they were behind bars they had to pay for their food. Sheriffs figured they had a captive audience, so they charged a lot for the crummy food they served. Visiting friends or family members brought coins to pay. It was either that or starve to death.

WHICH IS WHICH?

Bet you don't know the difference between a jail and a prison. A jail holds people awaiting trial and sentencing. After a person has been found guilty, he or she gets sent off to prison.

THE BIG EIGHT

Being sent to prison is the pits, but the very public punishments doled out for non-prison offenses in Colonial America were pretty bad too—painful, and worse: embarrassing.

1. The Pillory:
Hands and head were held clamped tight between two pieces of wood, always in the center of town, where everyone could see. Folks were encouraged to throw tomatoes or rotten eggs at the pilloried person, which then attracted bugs. With the victim's hands held tight, scratching, or shooing away pests, was impossible. For extra oomph, some folks' sentences included having their ears nailed to the pillory.

2. The Stocks:
The pillory's baby brother. In this version, the lucky victim at least got to sit down on a bench, but his or her feet were held in between two planks of wood. One of the first people to ever be held in the stocks in America was the Boston carpenter who made the first stocks, but then overcharged the town for building them.

3. The Dunking Stool:
Nothing like a refreshing plunge into an icy river or pond on a freezing cold day! That was the point of this punishment. Women often ended up in this not-so-hot seat, being dunked over and over again, for the "crime" of nagging their husbands.

4. The Whipping Post:
Steal a pie, shoot a chicken on a Sunday, throw dirty wash water onto the streets, and you, too, might end up on the receiving end of ten lashes with a whip made from 40 strips of leather.

5. A Scarlet Letter:
Did you tell a fib? You must now stand in a public place for three hours holding up a sign that says, "I am a big fat liar." Sometimes, to make it simpler, one big letter was sewn onto your jacket. For example, a B was for *blaspheming (blass-fee-ming)*, which is an old-fashioned word for cursing, especially if you used the name of the Lord. "D" was worn for being drunk in public. A red letter "A" stood for "adultery" and was worn by grown-ups who had canoodled with someone they weren't married to.

6. Branding:
A real, honest-to-goodness scarlet letter—burned into your cheek, your back, your thumb, or the back of your hand for the rest of your life. So many letters to choose from—an entire alphabet of crime and pain. L for liar, T for thief, F for forger. (And O for ouch?)

7. The Branks:
Take an iron cage. Stick it on someone's head. Attach a spiked plate that clamps onto the tongue. Some models of this torture device even had spikes that pierced the tongue or rang bells to attract the crowd's attention. It was sometimes called the scold's bridle, and many a woman found herself wearing one because she had dared to talk back to her husband.

8. The Bilboes:
A metal bar with two sliding shackles (kind of like big handcuffs for your feet) that was then bolted into the ground. Someone described it as a prison with only one bar! It was impossible to move with one of these on your feet. Drunks and people who spoke out against the government got to hang out from dawn to dusk clamped in these.

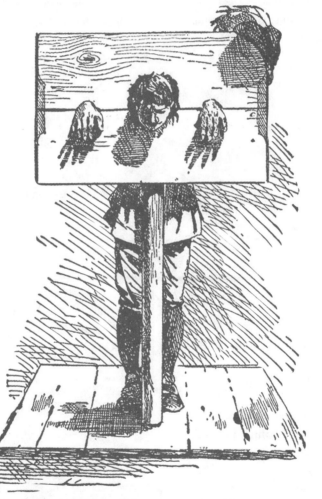

Pain in the pillory. *A day in the public square was a shameful way to pass the time—and it hurt!*

209

SIX JUNKY JAILS

1. Bug jail: The Zindan in Bukhara, Uzbekistan, had pits dug in its cellars that were filled with scorpions, cockroaches, rats, and lice. Soon-to-be-stung prisoners in the 1800s were dipped into the deadly bug pits.

2. I really dig jail: Why build an above-ground prison when you can dig one? 19th-century village prisons in Java, Indonesia, dug their own underground, worm-infested holes which were then covered with logs.

3. Nature's jail: In the late Middle Ages in Central Europe, some villages took hollow tree-trunks fitted with iron bars, then squished as many as six prisoners inside each trunk.

4. Dangling jail: Prisoners in the Italian city of Mantua in the 1500s didn't get prison cells. They got stuffed into big birdcages that swung from a tower 100 feet above the ground.

5. Cruisin' jail: In the 1800s, the English took a bunch of abandoned ships, tied them together, and anchored them in the middle of the Thames River. Prisoners wore heavy leg irons in case they had any ideas about diving overboard and swimming to shore. The boats were rat magnets and one in four inmates died. Shuffleboard, anyone?

6. Don't feed the animals jail: In the mid-1940s, during Word War II, all the animals in the Antwerp Zoo in Belgium died of starvation. The empty cages made great jails for German prisoners of war.

THE TOWER OF TERROR

Picture a place that's part royal palace, part jewelry store (the Crown Jewels are kept here), and part prison, and you have the Tower of London, which is actually a whole bunch of towers, a church, and all sorts of other buildings.

Some of the people who were imprisoned here lived pretty nicely. Take King John Balliol of Scotland, who was sent to the Tower in 1296. He came with two squires, a huntsman, a barber, his chaplain, a chapel clerk, and several assistants to the clerk, two grooms, two chamberlains, a tailor, a laundress, three pages, two greyhounds, and ten other hunting dogs. There are no actual cells here. Prisoners were simply stuffed wherever there was room. But not all the spaces were cushy. One nasty space was called "Little Ease." It was so small that a prisoner could neither stand up nor lie down in it. Try living there for months. And with a name like the Bloody Tower you can bet the people who

spent time locked up in there did not fare well. Over the years, more than 2,900 people were imprisoned in the Tower, and a whole lot of them had their heads chopped off! (For more, check out EVERYDAY EXECUTIONS on page 76.)

Tower power. The Tower of London was the scene of a whole lot of bloodiness.

ATTEN-SHUNNED

Soldiers and sailors had a whole different set of punishments to deal with (and heal from). During the American Revolution, soldiers who were drunk, rowdy, or lazy often had to wear signs around their necks that broadcast their crime. Alas, so many recruits didn't know how to read, that the whole shame-on-you thing was kind of wasted so new punishments were invented.

At Yorktown, Virginia, soldiers often rode *The Horse*. Hmm. That doesn't sound so bad until you realize that the Horse was a narrow plank of wood suspended high above the ground. The soldier climbed on and heavy bricks were then tied onto each of the soldier's feet to add to the pull of gravity. The plank dug into all those delicate man-middle-parts. Ever seen a grown man cry? That "horse" usually did the trick. Sailors were always getting flogged by their commanding officers. But one of the most unpleasant fates was keel hauling. How was it done? A rope was run under the bottom of the boat, from one side to the other. The man's hands were then tied to that rope. His legs were tied together and the poor wretch was tossed overboard and pulled under the boat. We are *not* talking small boats here. If the sailor was pulled too slowly, he would drown. Sometimes the temperature of the water was so cold, it could stop a heart. But usually the thing that did the sailor in was the fact that the bottom of the boat was covered with razor sharp barnacles—perfect for shredding a surly sailor to itty-bits. And then, there was that cutting-kitty-cat . . .

YUCKY YORE

You know how people raise their right hand in a court of law and swear to tell the whole truth and nothing but the truth? That's because in America in the 1600s and 1700s people's thumbs were branded with a hot iron if they were found guilty of doing something wrong. By raising their right hand, a judge could tell in an instant if the person was an ex-convict.

Me-"ow"!

In England's Royal Navy, a favorite weapon of punishment was the cat o'nine tails—a stick with nine strands of braided leather sometimes with bits of barbed wire tied into it. Several hundred strokes with the cat were not uncommon. Afterwards, a bucket of salt water was tossed on the sailor's bloody back, which hurt even worse than the flogging.

The cat had other names. There's a song that is still sung called *What shall we do with a drunken sailor?* It has a verse that goes: "Give him a taste of the captain's daughter." It sounds like fun, until you realize that the "captain's daughter" was really that nasty, bloody cat.

ALL-AMERICAN PRISONS

You would *not* have wanted to go to prison in the 1790s in America. Men, women, and kids were all tossed into one giant cell with piles of straw on the floor for bedding. There was no bathroom.

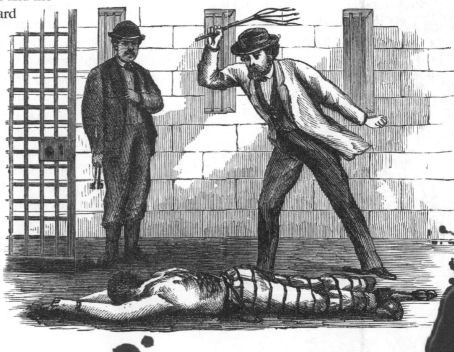

I'll never do it again! Stop hitting me with that cutting cat.

Drunks, crazy people, hardened criminals, and innocent people who happened to be in the wrong place at the wrong time were all packed together. It wasn't until the early 1800s that separate prisons were built for men and women, and kids got sent to junior-jail—"ju-vees"— locked-up live-in schools for delinquent kids.

What was it like to go to prison back then?

Sing-Singin' in the Rain

Sing Sing, one of America's most famous prisons, is just a wee bit "up the river" from New York City. The very first prisoners sent there actually had to build the prison, brick by brick, when they arrived in May, 1825. Until it was finished, they slept outside, no matter what the weather. Each of the 800 cells was teeny—standing in the middle, you could touch the walls without moving an inch! Inmates were given a Bible to read and were allowed no visitors. Talking was forbidden in Sing Sing. The convicts, clad in those funky striped prison uniforms, ate and worked in complete silence. Try and talk and you'd regret it, because punishment was harsh and swift. You might be near-drowned in something called the "bath," tucked into solitary confinement, or "bucked"— hung upside down from a wooden pole between your arms and legs, kind of like a human pig roast, without the tiki torches. And to top it all off, Sing Sing was the place that the electric chair was first used (zap on over to ELECTRIC SHOCKS on page 71 for all the sizzling details). A trip to Sing Sing always proved that crime does not pay.

Shark tale. Legend had it that "Bruce" patrolled Alcatraz.

Welcome to "The Rock"

In 1934, a train car full of America's worst criminals was taken to a rocky bird-poop encrusted island about a mile from San Francisco. The island was named "Pelicans" by the Spanish settlers who first hung out there (*Alcatraces* is Spanish for pelicans), and for 29 years Alcatraz was the place where America's nastiest criminals were sent to live.

It was cold and damp out in the bay and escape was impossible, although over the years 36 prisoners tried. The waters of San Francisco Bay are a bone-chilling 55 degrees Fahrenheit. John Paul Scott, one of only two men ever to make it all the way to shore (he made water wings from pairs of rubber gloves) was so tired from all the swimming that he was immediately recaptured and sent right back. Prisoners were told that the waters around Alcatraz were infested with sharks, including one, named Bruce, that had been specially bred by the Bureau of Prisons with only one fin so that it would swim continually around the island. It wasn't true, but it sure kept prisoners from escaping.

Prisoners who misbehaved were sent to the "dungeons," which had no windows or lights— just fans that blew the cold, damp air off the water. Really bad prisoners ended up in the "hole"—solitary confinement.

In 1962, four prisoners decided they wanted *out.* They made fake plaster heads with real hair swept up from the barber shop floor. They left the fake heads in their beds to

fool the guards and crept through the ventilators in their cells into a corridor and up to the roof. They used spoons stolen from the kitchen and an electric drill made from a fan to make escape holes. One guy was too chubby to fit through the hole and ended up staying behind, but the other three swam off toward San Francisco. The only trace of any of them was a wallet filled with cash that washed ashore a few days later.

No cell-ebrating here. Sing Sing's cells were teeny-weeny.

YOU'RE OUTTA HERE!

There are other kinds of prisons that don't involve high walls or bars— penal colonies in a far-off (usually nasty) place. Beginning in the 1600s, Russia sent prisoners to Siberia—the vast, northernmost part of the country. Freezing cold in the winter and buggy as heck in the summer, it was a gigantic natural prison. Bigger than Canada, Siberia is so vast that a person standing on a beach in Maine is closer to Moscow, the capital of Russia, than a person standing on the eastern coast of Siberia. Between 1923 and 1986, close to 20 million people were shipped off to Siberia, many of them for disagreeing with the government.

Australia, the "Land Down Under," was once nothing more than a giant prison for folks from England. In the 1800s, the first shipload of British convicts—mostly young men charged with forgery, picking pockets, and the occasional murder—landed in what is now Sydney. All in all, about 165,000 prisoners made the long sea journey and one in six was a woman!

Just getting to Australia was a trial. After all, it was a 15,000-mile boat ride. Once there, it was a life of hard labor— building bridges, making salt and bricks, mining coal, and clearing farmland. People lived twenty to a small, hot little hut. Public

floggings were common. Convicts quickly learned that the only relief from a session with the leather cat o'nine tails was to pee on the ground and then lie down, exposing the wounds to the damp soil.

For 400 years, Robben Island off South Africa was a truly hated prison. Its most famous inmate was Nelson Mandela, who was jailed for trying to get equal rights for black South Africans. Mandela spent more than a quarter of a century imprisoned. He was allowed one a visitor a year— but only for 30 minutes. He could only receive one letter every six months. Toilet paper was rationed to eight rough little squares a day. Mandela had no running water and no toilet— just an old iron bucket. Breakfast, lunch, and dinner was porridge—for 25 years! For ten hours every day, he smashed stones. Baths were taken in a bucket of ice-cold sea water. But Mandela never let prison break his spirit. He went on to see his people regain their rights and eventually became the president of South Africa and the winner of a Nobel Peace Prize. Amazing, huh?

Nelson Mandela.

EAR YE, EAR YE

It took centuries of injustice—people jailed with no proof or punished for no reason—to get to where we are today. Nowadays you are supposed to get a speedy trial, a chance to bring evidence on your own behalf, and be judged by a jury of ordinary, everyday folks. So thank your lucky stars you live now, or else you, too, might be splitting rocks 16 hours a day in a silly striped suit, or sitting in your town square with your ears nailed to the stocks and a big ripe tomato dripping down your face.

Q

QUIRKY QUEENS

You think only male monarchs turn into raving royals? When it comes to being a rowdy ruler, women can hang with the kraziest kings. Through the ages, there have been some really wild women running countries all over the world. Some are well-known; some are not. But all of them are truly qu-antakerous!

QUEEN BEES

There have been clean queens, mean queens, keen queens, and beauty queens. But one of the most famous queens of all was a teen queen: Cleopatra.

Cleo plopped down on the Egyptian throne when she was only 17, in 51 B.C.E. Everyone knew Cleo had what it took to be the boss, but girls weren't allowed to rule Egypt at that time, so she had to "marry" her 15-year-old brother. Uck. When her cowardly bro died while running way from an invading Roman army, she had to marry her *next* brother. Finally, tired of getting stuck hitched to her siblings, she set her sights on a really kingly king—Julius Caesar, ruler of the mighty Roman Empire. When he was visiting Egypt, she had herself wrapped in a carpet and carried into his room. Then ta-da!—she unrolled herself into his heart. Everything was hunky-dory until Caesar was murdered by some crabby senators.

When Cleo returned to Egypt with her four-year-old son, the very first thing she did was to have her second brother/hubby killed.

All hail the Killer Kings on page 135 or off to the dungeon with you!

Hollywood hooey. *Cleopatra has been a favorite subject for moviemakers. But you can bet the real Cleo never wore a bra made of snakes.*

She wasn't about to give up having power. Then she settled in and waited to see what was cooking back in Rome. Who was going to end up on the throne? Cleo decided it was going to be Marc Anthony and got romantically involved with him. Guess what? She backed the wrong guy. She was really in the doghouse now. A life without power was a life not worth living, so Cleo found herself a poison *asp* (a deadly kind of snake) and let it bite her. "Better dead than led," thought Cleo.

THE PIG QUEEN

Then there are clean queens. There's a famous saying that a man's home is his castle. So when King Ine, who ruled a part of Germany called Saxony back in the late 600s, started flirting with other women and generally behaving like a barnyard animal that oinks, his wife, Queen Ethelburga, decided that trashing his castle was a good way to get even. The crabby queen got her maids to spread cow poop and other putrid piles of filth all over his room. Then, because the king was *such* a porker, she had her maid place a momma pig that had just had piglets in his bed. When King Ine came home, he found that his castle had become a big, smelly barnyard. Fortunately, he got the message and never made a swine of himself ever again.

DIZZY IZZY

Want to meet a mean queen? Most of us know that Queen Isabella of Spain was the woman who paid Christopher Columbus's way to the Americas. But beyond that, who was she? By the time Isabella was born to a noble family in 1451, Spain had been chopped into three pieces: Castille, Aragon, and Granada. Izzy married Ferdinand, who was the heir to the throne of Aragon. Izzy's brother, who had become king of Castille, hated Ferdy and wanted Izzy to marry someone else. You know how you fight with your siblings? Well, this brother and sister went to war—a big, ugly civil war. Izzy (and husband Ferdy) won. Their next plan was to grab Granada.

Granada was under the control of a Muslim king and the people who lived there belonged to the Muslim faith. Isabella ruled that Catholicism was the *only* permitted religion in the lands she ruled over. Everyone who didn't believe in that faith had to become a Catholic, leave the country, or die. For years and years, Isabella fought to take over Granada. During that time she gave the go-ahead for the Spanish Inquisition, a truly gruesome event that saw thousands of people tortured and burned at the stake if they would not give up their faith. In 1492, the year Columbus headed off to find a new route to China, Granada finally fell to Isabella's army. The Muslims and people of the Jewish faith were all kicked out of Spain—or killed. Mean, huh?

MONARCHS GONE MAD!

Queen Isabella's second daughter, Juana, was born in 1479 (her sister, Catherine, the future wife of Henry VIII, was born six years later). Too bad mommy was busy fighting and hosting the Spanish Inquisition, because her daughter was not the happiest of children. Juana married Philip the Handsome of Austria (I swear, that is what people really called him).

It wasn't exactly a happy marriage since Phil was a bit of a flirt. This made moody Juana *really* cranky and often violent. Still, when Phil died at the age of 28, Juana went bonkers. Phil's coffin was temporarily buried at a monastery in Spain, but five weeks after his death, Juana had the coffin opened because she'd heard a rumor that Phil's body had been stolen. She unwrapped the remains of her hubby and her servants eventually had to pull her off Philip's corpse because she wouldn't stop kissing his former feet.

When the town Philip was buried in was struck by a brief outbreak of the plague, Juana ordered the coffin moved. Throughout the journey, she kept prying open the coffin to gaze at her smelly, rotting, no-longer-handsome hubby. She traveled for months with her decaying spouse. No wonder they called her "the Mad."

HENRY VIII'S RUTHLESS DAUGHTERS

If you've read about Hackin' Henry (and if you haven't, head over to page 116 or off with your head), you know he had two daughters, Mary and Elizabeth. Both became English queens. Both lived in bloody times. But only one got to add the word "Bloody" before her name.

Mary, The Bloody

Mary was once her dad's favorite, but all that changed when daddy dumped Mary's mom for another woman. Suddenly Mary was banished and left to live in rags. Finally she was called back to the palace to become her new baby half-sister's servant. That sort of thing can make a person quite unhappy.

Mary was convinced that her dad was going to kill her. After all, the man *did* have a temper! She began to hate all Protestants—members of the new religion her father had helped put in place in England as part of his plan to divorce Mary's mother. When Elizabeth's mom was beheaded, the tables turned. Mary now had the upper hand. She almost had Liz hanged to get even!

Mary became the queen of England at the age of 37. By then, she was bitter, haggard, and toothless—and with a chip on her shoulder the size of a castle. One of Mary's only buddies was the smallest dwarf in royal service, her page of honor John Jarvis, who was a strapping two feet tall!

Mary ruled for four whole years (1553-1558) in which time she went on an absolute rampage and had 300 people burned alive for being heretics. A *heretic* is a person who believes in ideas that differ from a particular church's teachings. Folks started calling the queen "Bloody Mary." And these days, to honor her, grown-ups can order a drink called a Bloody Mary, which is made with tomato juice. It looks a whole lot like the leftovers of a severed head.

Mary, Mary, Queen Contrary

Just like kings, queens seem to always get stuck with the same name! Take Mary. There have been at least 11 queens in many different countries, all named Mary. The most famous Marys were Bloody Mary and Mary, Queen of Scots, who also had her head chopped off for trying to kill her hubby.

FOUR QU-RANKY QUEENS

1. Queen Boudicca (28–62 C.E.) Sure, the Romans ruled over a big chunk of the world. But they never should have messed with a tall redhead with flaming hair that fell to her hips and a voice like a snarling beast. Boudicca ruled a chunk of what is now England. And when the Romans attacked her land, she went ballistic! She was a phenom as a leader. By the time she was done, her armies had destroyed three Roman-occupied cities, including London. And although she didn't fully succeed in kicking the Romans out of her country, she sure did leave them reeling.

2. Eleanor of Aquitaine (1122–1204)

Women in the 1100s were supposed keep their mouths shut and let men make the rules. Not Eleanor. She was married to not just one king, but two! And not just any kings, but the kings of France and England. Hubby one, Louis VI of France, was too wishy-washy. Hubby two, Henry II of England, was too rude. Eleanor had ideas and opinions, and she wanted them heard. So eventually she moved out and started her own court. Soon her palace became the "in place" to be, and it's there that the legend of King Arthur and his knights first became popular. She was mommy to two kings: Richard the Lion-hearted, one of the most famous kings ever, and King John, who offered little to history. But she outlived them all, dying at the ripe old age of 82.

Outspoken Eleanor.

3. Queen Maria Theresa of Austria (1717–1780)

Maria Theresa had 16 kids. Yikes! How'd she find time to be queen? Turns out being a mother helped her learn how to rule one of the largest and wealthiest empires in the world at the time—the Austrian Empire, which covered one third of Europe. In fact, Maria Theresa called herself "chief mother of my country." She introduced the potato, a crop grown by the Incas of Peru, so there were always spuds for supper. And she made everyone do their homework by making school mandatory for every young citizen. The only flaw was that this queen mom absolutely *hated* people whose religions differed from her own (which makes her a mean queen in my opinion).

Catherine the clever, hardworking—and fun!

4. Catherine the Great of Russia (1729–1796)

Not too many people get to tag "the Great" onto their names. But this super queen earned the right. For starters, she wasn't even Russian, she was German. And her name wasn't Catherine. It was Sophia. But she sure was smart. She changed her name when she was married off to Peter, who became the ruler of Russia. Peter was a slimeball. He treated her terribly *and* he was wrecking his country, too. Finally Catherine had enough. She got a group of her friends to get rid of Peter. Now she was in charge—and she meant to do right by her new country. Working 15-hour days, she helped to make Russia a powerful country, and the equal of the other great kingdoms of her time. And maybe best of all—she installed the world's first roller coaster in her palace!

All dressed up, but oh so hard to turn your head!

Liz, the Lusty

Henry's other daughter was Elizabeth. When Henry got tired of being married to her mom, Anne Boleyn, he made Liz watch her mother's beheading. *Not* a nice thing to do to a child! Then Henry proceeded to ignore her completely. In spite of all that, Elizabeth became queen of England in 1558 at the age of 25. She went on to rule for 44 amazing years and become the greatest queen England ever had, helping her nation grow hugely powerful. And it's good to be queen. Having had a deprived childhood, Elizabeth instantly went on a massive shopping spree. She bought 80 wigs and 3,000 jewel-encrusted dresses. She was the woman who invented the closet.

Liz had lovely pale skin, which she made even whiter as she grew older by using a thick paste of white lead and vinegar. Soon everyone was copying her. There's a reason a certain dwarf-loving heroine

was named Snow White. Snow white was the skin color everyone wanted. Very pale skin said, "I am rich and don't have to work in the fields." But in a cruel twist on the saying "if looks could kill," Liz's lead-based makeup ultimately did exactly that. But before it killed her, Liz's heavy white makeup corroded the surface of her face. To cover the holes that were being eaten into her skin, thicker and thicker applications of lead-makeup were necessary. By the end of Queen Elizabeth's reign, she was spackling on a half-inch of makeup every day.

THE KINGS OF QUEENS

Some queens are really awesome and completely gutsy! Take Njinga Mbande. When the Portuguese invaded her country in the early 1600s (she ruled what is now Angola in West Africa), she was steamed! When she walked into a room where the Portuguese leaders were meeting, she found every chair taken. How rude! Without missing a beat, Njinga snapped her fingers and ordered a member of her entourage to get down on hands and knees and then very regally took a queenly seat on her human throne.

Njinga knew she *had* to show the Portuguese that she was in charge. Wearing a sword necklace and an axe belt, she went to work to save her country. When she took control in 1624, she promptly placed women in positions of power.

And for 40 years, through her bravery and diplomatic skills, she kept the Europeans from taking over her homeland.

India also had a cool woman warrior-queen, Rani Lakshmi Bai. She was born around 1830 and was one of the most fearless people in all the land. She once faced down a charging elephant and jumped onto its tusk at the last minute! But the British had taken over India and now *they* were in charge. Lakshmi decided to lead a rebellion and in 1875, she went to work rousing her people to fight. She rode over 100 miles a day, and fought with horse reins in her teeth, a sword in each hand, and her infant son strapped to her back! She died in battle at the age of 22, but became a legend in India, and with good reason.

OFF WITH ANOTHER HEAD!

Marie Antoinette was another teen queen, and one of France's most famous monarchs. She was actually from Austria, one of 16 kids. She never went to school, and really had no idea how to rule. But she ended up being shipped off to marry Louis, heir to the throne of France, when she was just 14.

Marie Antoinette didn't much care for her life as a queen. For one thing, she was on display for all to see, even as she ate and got dressed. When she gave birth to her first child, a crowd of aristocrats gathered to watch! Marie-Antoinette was mortified that she had absolutely no privacy in the palace. To get out of the public eye, she even commissioned a little pretend village to escape to.

While she frolicked in fine jewels and gorgeous clothes, spending money like it grew on trees, the people of France were eating rats for dinner because they were too poor to afford anything else. So the people of France decided to revolt. And who better to go after than the revoltingly rich royals?

So King Louis lost his head (Chop! Chop! Hurry over to GUILLOTINES on page 108) and Marie Antoinette was tossed in jail. She was no

CAKE FOR DINNER?

There's a famous story about Marie Antoinette. Told that the people of Paris were starving and had no bread, this clueless queen replied, "Then let them eat cake." Actually, she never said this. But even if she didn't, she probably thought it! She wasn't mean—just completely unaware of the world outside the palace gates.

longer called "Your Majesty." She was now known as Prisoner No. 280. On the morning of October 16, 1793, a guard arrived and cut her hair (to better allow the blade of the guillotine to do its business). She was shoved into a horse-drawn cart and paraded through the streets of Paris. And at 12:15 P.M., the blade dropped and her head was held before a cheering crowd. Long die the queen!

"WE ARE NOT AMUSED"

The great days of the quirky queens have come and gone. Queen Victoria of England (1819–1901), who ruled for 64 years, was the last of the diva-queens. She often referred to herself as "we." So with her in mind, "we" must say farewell to these qu-ool, qu-razy, qu-rusty queens.

R

RIP-ROARIN' RAILROADS

DO NOT FLUSH WHILE TRAIN IS IN STATION. There's a reason this sign has hung in many a train bathroom since the days of the early long-distance passenger rail. And it's still hanging in plenty of trains all over the world today. The no-flushing-in-the-station rule was made to protect innocent passengers waiting on the platform from the sudden smelly surprise of butt-pies dropping onto the train tracks. But trains and stinkies often went hand-in-hand as the railroads chugged along, changing the world in a huge way.

THE BOILING POINT

What does a cup of tea have to do with a train? Ever put a pot to boil on the stove and then see the lid bopping up and down like crazy when the water heats up? More than 2,000 years ago, Hero, a Greek inventor, made a little gizmo: a metal ball that could be filled with water and held over a fire until it spun round and round as the steam escaped. It was a cool party trick, but it took centuries for someone to figure out that all that steam could actually move something big—like a train!

By the 1600s, scientists knew steam was powerful stuff and began to experiment with crude steam engines. By the early 1700s, steam engines were being used to pump water out of mine shafts—water that flooded in as the shafts were sunk in deeper and deeper. About the same time, engineers realized that if they laid wooden rails along the rough shafts, the bins filled with coal or tin or whatever they were digging out would roll out more easily. Hmmmm. Sounds a lot like a train to me!

In 1801, a burly Englishman named Richard Trevithick happily showed off the world's first locomotive—a vehicle powered by steam, designed to pull really heavy loads at an ironworks in Wales (a part of Great Britain). Trevithick hadn't quite worked out the kinks, though. In fact, his locomotive, which was difficult to steer, ended up crashing into a house.

ON THE RIGHT TRACK

Trevithick wasn't about to let a little thing like a wreck stop him. Three years later, he won a bet by building a locomotive that pulled a ten-ton load down a ten-mile track. And by 1808, he had built a

RAILROAD CROSSING
2 TRACKS

Are we there yet? Who'd have thought that watching a train go around in circles could be such a treat.

rain poured in. Filthy black smoke did, too. They were deafeningly noisy. And worst of all, the tracks were always breaking, sending passengers flying. But still, a train could move a lot more quickly than a horse. And you didn't have to step over piles of steaming horse manure all the time. By the mid-1800s, trains were everywhere!

Trains shrank the world. People began to travel for fun, to see other places they may have only read about. It also became easier to pick up and move—to follow your dreams or find a better job. So all that boiling water really changed how the world works—in a big way! And one of the places most changed by trains was the very large U.S. of A.

circular train track with a high wall around it in London. Folks paid to watch his train chug around and around. Soon, people were paying to ride on one of these newfangled creations. The era of the railroad was here!

By 1825 the first public rail line began running in England. But the first trains were misery on wheels. They didn't have sides or windows, so the

Trev's train. This 1804 locomotive was Trevithick's pride and joy—the first to run on rails.

THE WEIRDEST TRAIN EVER BUILT?

If you want to cross some water, it's best to go by boat, right? But in Brighton, England, in 1896, some wise guy had the idea of building a train that ran through part of the shoreline of the Atlantic Ocean on track laid along the shore bottom. It was called the Daddy Long Legs and it lasted a whole week before getting toppled in a storm. Daddy was rebuilt, but four years later it got squished for good.

BASIC TRAIN-ING

One of the greatest feats of all times had to do with a little barrier called the Rocky Mountains. How *do* you get a train—something that really can't climb a steep hill—over something that enormous?

A fellow named Judah Washington just *knew* he could do it. In 1860 "Crazy Judah," as everyone called him, finally convinced four of the wealthiest men in California to back him up. Then he headed off to Washington, D.C., and convinced the government to give him the go-ahead. A new bill was passed. Two companies would start laying tracks—one from the West Coast, the other from the East.

The western start of the Great Transcontinental Railroad began in Sacramento, California, on January 8, 1863. But Crazy Judah discovered that his business partners were cheating—taking shortcuts on quality and skimming money. He was shocked! He headed back East to find some new business partners, but the trip back to New York via the mosquito-infested swamps of Panama killed him.

SHOE-SHOE TRAINS

When the first train riders were about to board Tokyo's new trains in the 1870s, they did what every well-mannered Japanese person does before going inside a building: They took off their shoes and got on. The doors closed, and the train pulled out of the station, heading toward the next stop, where the passengers were forced to get off, barefoot!

So now the four West Coast guys had no engineer in charge. No matter! They'd figure it all out, somehow. They ordered some rail cars from the East, which arrived after a six-month trip by boat around the tip of South America. (Too bad the Panama Canal hadn't been built! It would have saved them half a year! Check out the canal's tale in CRUEL CONSTRUCTION on page 42.)

Finally, the railroaders got to work. It was slow going. They laid only 18 miles of track the first year. The second year they added 13 more. It was clear that they needed more workers if they were ever going to finish the job. It was hard to find labor, however, because another West Coast business—gold mining— was distracting all the spare workers.

I'VE BEEN WORKIN' ON THE RAILROAD

A lot of Chinese workers had come to California in the early days of the Gold Rush. But as the gold dried up, the Chinese immigrants needed jobs—any jobs, even damp and dangerous ones. The railroad folks quickly discovered that the Chinese were phenoms! They could lay track faster and smoother than any of the American crews they had hired.

When the crews hit their first obstacle, a 4,000-foot-high cliff, the Chinese guys said, "No problem." They made man-sized baskets; one guy hopped in, and two others lowered him over the sides of the cliff. As the men swung in their baskets, they chipped holes in the rock, stuffed in explosives, lit fuses, and hoped the dudes holding the baskets could pull them up *really* fast. Thousands of gutsy Chinese workers swarmed over that rock face, and eventually blew enough of it away to lay down the track.

Next came the tunnel digging. Such slow going—sometimes only seven inches a day! And, as if crossing a mountain range wasn't enough of a problem, the winter of 1866–67 was a real corker! There were 44 major snowstorms. Snow piled into 40-foot-high drifts. It took 13 months to dig the famous Summit Tunnel. It was so bad, and so

deadly, that the expression "Not a Chinaman's chance" became a popular saying all across America after more than 1,200 men died digging.

Finally the West Coast guys made it across the Sierra Nevada range. By now, people were saying the railroad was a stupid waste. Mountain snows would keep trains from running five months of the year! So the railroaders built roofs over 38 miles worth of track that ran through the snowiest places. It was always *something!*

FEELING HOT, HOT, HOT!

By 1868 the railroad was getting closer to civilization. The crews were only 20 miles from Nevada's big silver mines. The rail owners picked a point along the tracks and decided it would make a sweet spot for a train depot. And just like that, Reno, Nevada, was born. Now the track-laying was moving along more swiftly. As the project headed into the Nevada deserts, the Pueblo Indians worked alongside the Chinese. However, as the snow disappeared, a new foe emerged—the sun. Now it was 120°F. There wasn't a tree for 500 miles. Water and wood had to be carried in from far away.

In the meantime, the Union Pacific Railroad Company was building a railroad from the East, starting in Omaha, Nebraska. Almost 10,000 Irish immigrants were laying that track. They had no huge mountains to tunnel through, but their journey was tough as well. The railroad ran right through the heart of the Plains Indians' most valuable hunting grounds. The government's solution was to push the Indians off their lands and onto crummy reservations where the Indians could not possibly survive. Naturally, the Indians fought back hard to try to stop them, but it was no use. Guns always trumped bows and arrows.

So the Central Pacific Railroad—the West Coast team—was heading east. The Union Pacific—the East Coast team—was heading west. Throughout 1868-69, each laid track faster and faster, taking shortcuts and building rickety bridges that looked like they would blow over if somebody burped. Finally both sides were in Utah, so close they could see each other.

A SWING AND A MISS

A spot was chosen to link the two railroads: Promontory Summit, in Utah. A date was picked: Saturday, May 9, 1869. For a while the East Coast team was getting all the glory in the newspapers, especially after they laid eight miles of track in

CHOO-CHOO CHAMPS

The Longest Railroad: The Trans-Siberian Railroad rolls across eight very chilly time zones in Russia. At almost 6,000 miles (10,000 km) long, it covers more than one-third of the Earth's circumference!

The Fastest Train: China wins this one with Shanghai's *maglev*, which covers 20 miles from the airport to the outskirts of the city in a zippy 7 minutes and 20 seconds. The train actually floats above an electromagnetic track and reaches a top speed of 270 miles per hour. It needs seven miles just to stop!

The Longest Train: Australia has kangaroos *and* the record for a train that, in 2001, stretched for over 4.5 miles (7.353 km) with 682 cars pushed by eight mighty diesel-electric locomotives. Try waiting for the crossing gates to go up on that one!

one day. So the West Coast guys decided to pull a little publicity stunt of their own. They boasted that eight of their guys could lay ten miles of track in one day (an amazing feat)—and they did! And the East Coast team *couldn't* beat them this time, for one reason. They only had nine miles of track left to lay! To add to the East Coast team's embarrassment, their train was held hostage for two days by workers that hadn't been paid in weeks. Once the debts were paid, they chugged off again, but one of their shoddy bridges started to crumble and had to be rebuilt before they could proceed.

So the California guys sat waiting in the middle of nowhere, surrounded by towns with names like Deadfall and Last Chance, bored and hungover

Destination, dirt. *This train not only derailed, it took the track with it.*

from too much partying. Finally, the new "last spike" day arrived. Huge crowds gathered. Bands played. Four spikes had been brought—two made from California gold, and one each of silver and iron, provided by the Union Pacific guys. The heads of both railroads were supposed to hammer in the last spikes. At the key moment, both big shots swung their hammers—and both missed their targets completely! The crowd laughed hysterically! Finally, one of the workers emerged to lend a helping hand, and gave a clanging swing to end the festivities.

America went wild at the news that the country was now linked from sea to sea. Back in Philadelphia, the Liberty Bell was rung! People partied everywhere. Folks tried to steal spikes from the joining spot, not realizing the precious "golden" spikes had been quickly removed and replaced with plain old iron ones. And until men walked on the moon 100 years later, Golden Spike Day was the greatest day in U.S. transportation history.

Ride 'em? I'd rather rob 'em! Grab the train to page 181 and read about some wily train robbers in OUTRAGEOUS OUTLAWS!

SALT ASSAULT

Ever have a dog lick your legs on a hot day? Blech! Now, *you* may have never licked anyone's legs (and please tell me you haven't) but your body is hardwired to need salt, just like that slobbering puppy who's after the salt on your skin. Without salt, you would shrivel up like an old prune. And without enough salt in your diet, you just might end up licking someone's sweaty legs, too. But here's a *news flash!* Salt does not come from the ground in easy-to-use salt shakers. Long ago, finding salt was dangerous work. So grab a headlamp and a shovel. And let's go snooping for salt.

PLEASE PASS THE GOLD

A few billion years ago, getting salt was a snap. That's 'cause the entire planet was pretty much all ocean. As the seas began to shrink and land emerged, the waters left layers of salt trapped beneath the Earth's surface.

In the cave dude days, hunters got their salt by spearing an animal, then eating the raw, bloody meat. (That's because blood is very salty.) But about 30,000 years ago, when our ancestors started depending on grains and grasses for food, they had to find a new source of salt. For the folks who did not live near the ocean, it turned out that one of the best ways to get salt was to dig down deep for it.

THE MAGGOT KILLERS

Imagine that it's about 1,000 years ago. There are no fridges anywhere—no way to keep food germ-free. If you want a steak, you have to go out and kill yourself a big old cow. Meat that sits around for more than a day or so will begin to spoil. Flies are

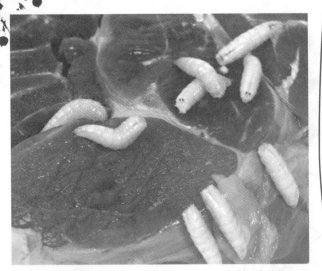

Mmm, mmm, maggots! If this steak had been preserved with salt, these critters wouldn't be having a party.

FOLLOW THE SALTY BRICK ROAD

4,500 Years Ago: Mummy's Feeling Salty

Egyptians needed salt both in life and in death. In their hot climate, they would sweat a lot. And you can't make a proper mummy without salt: The dead body was soaked in a salt bath for 70 days. (See MUSTY MUMMIES on page 166.)

3,500 Years Ago: No MSG, Please

The Chinese were some of the first folks to go gaga for salt. They even fought wars to get control of lands that had salt deposits. They were so desperate to get more food-preserving salt that they tried to figure out how to blast away layers of rock to get to the hidden salt layers. Because of the search for salt, gunpowder was invented.

3,000 Years Ago: Toss Some Salt Over Your Shoulder

Salt is sprinkled all through the Bible, from the story of Lot's wife (who was turned into a pillar of salt—*yikes!*) to the spilled dish of salt at the Last Supper, which came to mean bad luck.

soon laying their eggs on your burgers. Bacteria are throwing a fiesta in your pork chops. Your food has become one big, rotting, stinking pile of bug-infested, germy, bad-tasting swill.

In the days before fridges, burying food in salt was the only way keep it from becoming a maggoty mound of mush. Salt sucks up all the moisture from food. Bacteria and bugs can't live without moisture, so they leave the food alone and the food doesn't spoil. But there's even more to salt. Salt also helps to keep you alive by controlling the balance of fluids in your body. In places where people sweat a lot, it's not uncommon to take salt tablets.

No doubt about it. Salt's a lifesaver.

The Middle Ages: Something's Fishy

Thanks to the medieval Catholic Church, the demand for salt went sky-high in Europe. Meat was a no-no on religious holidays, and holy days took up almost half of the calendar. Catholics could only eat fish on sacred days—and if you have ever smelled day-old fish, you know it stinks! Folks who lived inland depended on fish from far away—fish that had to be heavily salted to keep it from getting gross.

The 1600–1700s: A-Salt With A Deadly Shaker

In France, salt was taxed at twice its value! French kings were growing richer and richer from a pesky salt tax, and the people were getting steamed. French

WORD UP!

It figures that something as important as salt would creep into the way we speak.

■ When you grow up and have a cushy job, you will earn a big *salary*. Back in ancient Rome, that salary was a bag full of salt. *Sal* is the Latin word for salt.

■ Someone who is the *salt of the Earth* is an honest and good person.

■ Not *worth your salt*? That means you're a slacker. Back in ancient Rome, slaves were bought with salt instead of money. A big, strong, burly slave cost a whole lot more salt than a wheezing, skinny slave. But if you paid a lot of salt for a big guy and he turned out to be a wimp . . . well you get the picture.

■ *Rubbing salt in a wound* (OUCH!) means to make a bad thing worse.

■ Long before iceberg lettuce and croutons, there were Romans sprinkling salt onto their vegetables. Salted vegetables became known as a *salad*.

law required every person over the age of eight to buy more salt than he or she could possibly ever use every year. It was one of the reasons the French got sooooooo mad they started chopping off royal heads during the French Revolution (see GUILLOTINES for all *that* gore on page 108).

The 1800s: My Country For A Ham

Ever heard of the Erie Canal? It was built because of the discovery of a salt mine in Syracuse, New York. By 1848, the canal was called "the ditch that salt built." And during the Civil War, one of the first Southern targets was a Virginia saltworks. Salt was as important as gunpowder. Why? You can't make bacon or ham without salt, and that was the South's major source of meat. The North's plan was to starve the South of salt. With no food in your tummy, it's kinda hard to fight a war. The strategy worked!

1900S: A Salty Farewell

When the British took control of India, they took control of India's salt, too. They started taxing Indian-made salt at a huge rate and insisted that the Indians buy salt from Cheshire, England (where, ironically, salt mining had eroded the ground so much that the buildings and houses were all collapsing into the streets). Indians were forbidden to make or gather salt at the seashore. In 1930, Mahatma Gandhi, a very brave man who fought for Indian independence, had had enough. He led thousands of Indians on a 25-day, 240-mile march to the sea and showed the British the meaning of civil disobedience by calmly

Salt of the Earth. *Gandhi protested the mighty British Empire's salt taxes . . . and won!*

(see GUILLOTINES for all *that* gore on page 108).

SCI-FILE

Salt is an amazing little compound (compounds happen when two things are smooshed together and end up as a completely different substance). Salt's two parts are sodium and chloride. Sodium is a metal—so unstable that it can burst into flames just like that. And chlorine is a gas that is so deadly that one sniff can kill you. But put the two things together and you have something yummy enough to lick off your fingers when eating a bag of chips.

Slogging salt. *These workers are harvesting salt extracted from the super-salty Great Salt Lake.*

gathering salt in protest of the stupid tax. His march helped begin the fight for India's independence and the end of British rule—and created a local salt supply for all those spicy foods like like samosas and vindaloos.

LET'S DO THE WAVE

If you've ever gotten smacked in the face by a wave in the ocean, you know that seawater is salty. So why not just guzzle a glass of *real* ocean-spray? Simple. If you drink too much of it, you will die.

Let's say you are stuck in a leaky lifeboat in the middle of the Pacific Ocean. You have a couple of bags of pretzels and nothing else. You are getting *really* thirsty. There's water everywhere—but drink that seawater and you'll be in for a nasty surprise. Your body will go nuts trying to get rid of

TRY THIS!

X-PERIMENT: HOW TO TAKE SALT OUT OF SALTWATER

Think it's easy to get the salt out of saltwater? *Desalinization* (*de-sal-in-uh-ZAY-shun*) plants are expensive to build and run. Here's how to make a mini one! You'll need:

2 two-liter plastic soda bottles, empty

Black spray paint

½ cup salt

4 cups water

12 inches of clear plastic tubing, at least ½" wide (you can find it in any pet store that sells fish products)

Duct tape

Get a grown-up to help you spray one of the two-liter bottles black. Mix the salt with the water. Pour the saltwater into the black bottle. Attach one end of the clear tubing to the opening of one bottle with duct tape, and attach the other end of the tubing to the other bottle. Set both bottles in a sunny window. Place the black bottle higher than the clear bottle. After several days, water will have moved from the black bottle into the clear bottle, and will no longer be salty.

all the extra salt. You'll start to puke. Soon you'll have the runs. Try having to poop in a lifeboat! Worst of all, no matter how much you drink, you'll just keep getting thirstier. So remember, the next time you set out on the open seas, bring some fresh water along. You never know!

THAT MINE IS MINE!

Salt mines are eerie places. Take the salt mine in Wieliczka, Poland, which first was dug in the 1200s. Miners kept dying in gas explosions or in mine-shaft collapses. Things got so bad that

Salty sculptures. The Wieliczka salt mines in Poland have all sorts of surprises, carved from hunks of salt.

they actually carved an entire underground chapel in the salt so that a priest could bless the miners every day before they went digging. Since so much time was spent under the earth's surface, mine workers tried to spruce up the place, and started to carve statues and even immense candelabras all from salt. Don't believe me? You can still take tours of this place!

In the Middle Ages, one of the biggest salt mines on Earth was in Taghaza in western Africa. Salt miners there worked in an oven-on-Earth where temperatures could reach 160°F. No one would willingly work there, so slave laborers were sent to do the digging. While there, they lived in houses built entirely of salt, and slept on salt beds.

And just in case you think salt mining is a long-ago thing, guess again. Detroit, Michigan, is sometimes called the Motor City. But deep beneath the streets lies an eerie ghost city with its own four-lane highways, surrounded by shimmering slab-walls of salt. More than 100 years ago, the first tunnels were sunk beneath the city. Soon, the mega-mine spread over more than 1,400 acres with 50 miles of roads. To build the mine, mules were lowered by rope down narrow shafts into the deep pits. Once the mules went down, they didn't come up again until they were dead donkeys. The workers were a little luckier. They took small elevators for the long ride down and didn't have to wait 'til they were dead to come up. Getting equipment into the cave, however, was a challenge. Trucks, Jeeps, and cars were all taken apart above ground, lowered down the shaft hunk by hunk, and then put together again at the bottom in makeshift garages.

What's shakin' with the Inca? *These ancient salt terraces were built by the ingenious Inca to speed the evaporation of water to get salt.*

That mine has been closed because it was too expensive to get the salt out, but over in Louisiana, there's a big mine still in use—a huge mega-hunk of solid salt that extends eight miles deep, where people drive around in four-wheel drive cars since the salt is as slippery as an ice-skating rink. And there'd be no oil wells in Texas if folks hadn't been drilling for salt when they accidentally struck oil.

Today salt is an ingredient in more than 14,000 products from gasoline to tires to bug spray. Every year we dig up more than 146 million tons of the rock (line up 146 million elephants and you get an idea of the size of that salt pile). So the next time you see a dog licking someone's sweaty legs to get some salt, think about the battles fought, the miners who sweated, and the donkeys who died lugging salt to the world's tables. Salt rocks!

SAMURAI AND SHOGUNS

Think of the absolute coolest guys you can think of—maybe pro ballplayers or rock stars or fearless Marines. Well, being a samurai warrior in Japan was like that. For more than 1,000 years, samurai swaggered all across the land.

But being a samurai wasn't all fun and games. They had it tough, too. Samurai had to deal with a little something called *bushido* (boo-SHE-doe). That meant no whining, ever. No complaining. No screaming if a sharp arrow speared your thigh. You had to be brave— stupid brave. The kind of brave that sends you galloping headlong into an advancing army ten times your size. And if you lost, you had to be willing to cut your own guts out.

WHO'S THE BOSS?

From about 700 C.E. to the 1860s, *shoguns* called the shots in Japan and samurai served the shoguns. They fought for them, and grabbed stuff like castles, peasants, and land for them. They were Japan's knights—the military elite of Japan. Samurai lived by a code called the "way of the bow and arrow." The idea of surrendering to the enemy was the ultimate no-no to them. A samurai warrior always fought to the death. And as hard as it is for us to understand, the samurai really thought of death as something not to fear—like a nice day at the beach. In fact, they believed that the more afraid you were of death, the greater your chances of dying. But that didn't mean they would give up without a fight. Naturally, they wanted to stay alive and kicking in this life for as long as they could, so they tried to make sure they had the skills (and the tools) to send their enemies off to the next life instead.

BULL'S-EYE!

The bow and arrow were the samurai's weapon of choice. But they didn't use just any little bow— their bows were huge. Bows were measured by how many men it took to string them. During one famous battle, a master archer sank not one, but *two* boats with *one* arrow using a seven-man bow. It had taken seven guys to string that sucker!

One of Japan's greatest archers was a warrior named Tametomo (*Tah-meh-TOE-moe*), who lived in the mid-1100s. He was over seven feet tall (too bad there was no pro basketball in those days), and his bow arm was four inches longer than his other arm, so he could pull his bowstring really far back! Folks ducked when they saw him coming. He was the samurai everyone else tried to copy.

IF I CAN'T WIN, I'D RATHER DIE

Unfortunately for Tametomo, his enemy-brother snuck up on him and cut the tendons in his bow arm. When Tametomo realized his samurai days were over because could not fight anymore, he did something *very* weird. He "invented" *hari-kiri,* which means "cutting the belly." He was so distraught that he sliced open his abdomen with his sharpest knife and twisted the blade. His samurai buddies were awestruck. They decided that cutting up one's guts took guts. Tametomo's act became the way many a future samurai would say, "Goodbye, Earth." No being led off in chains or thrown into an enemy dungeon for a samurai! Self-sacrifice was the way to go!

There was an art to committing *sepuko,* or ritual suicide. It had to be done neatly and with style. To insure that the soon-to-be-dead warrior would

Good-bye cruel world. A staged depiction of hari-kiri.

fall forward, not backward, he removed the top of his kimono and tucked the sleeves tightly under his legs as he knelt. A good samurai didn't cry, yell, or even grimace after making the cuts. And when he finally did topple over, for good measure, a witness stood nearby ready to slice off his now-dead head with a super-sharp sword.

Which brings us to the whole sword thing . . .

THE RAZOR'S EDGE

Samurai carried two swords—one long (over two feet!) and one short. Each sword went through an elaborate testing. Sword makers usually tested the blade by cutting up a corpse or two. If there were no corpses handy, a condemned prisoner was trotted out for the occasion. They began by cutting through small bones—a finger, perhaps. Then they moved on to big bones, like a thigh or shoulder blade. Careful records were kept of the time it took to cut through a torso and those results were marked on the *nakago,* the small metal tag that was attached to the sword handle.

Foot soldiers carried a smaller weapon called a *naginata.* It worked wonders when a warrior on horseback was galloping at you, because it was designed to cut the horse's tendons, causing horse and rider to crumble to the ground. It worked well on humans, too. Samurai wives often carried a naginata, just in case. And FYI: Some samurai wives were fiercer fighters than their hubbies.

ARMORED AND DANGEROUS

To protect themselves in battle, samurai warriors put on awesome armor. They wore scary-looking helmets with huge horns and shoulder guards worthy of a football player to deflect arrows and sword-swings. Samurai armor wasn't made of sheets of steel like a European knight's. It was more like fish scales—teeny pieces of shiny iron,

HAIR-RAISING

You might think ponytails are for girls, but think again. Samurai were known for their ponytails. Their hairstyle was probably first worn because it was a good way to anchor a helmet to your skull. Hair was pulled through a hole in the top of the helmet, and it kept the helmet from flying off. But soon, the "top knot" caught on for everyday wear as well. There were all sorts of fun things you could do. You could oil it and form it into a big roll. You could twist it so that little "whisk-brooms" stuck out at the top. You could fold it forward, then chop it straight down the front with a razor so it looked like you had a wall of hair.

By the Edo period (1600–1867) samurai had made ponytails cool. Almost all Japanese men (with the exception of Buddhist priests, who went for the bald-is-beautiful look) wanted to wear their hair that way, and for hundreds and hundreds of years the top knot was in.

copper, and other metals. Silk cords held the "scales" together and thicker cords tied hunks to one another. It was lightweight and easy to move in. The best part of a samurai's armor was his face mask. It was like Halloween all year long! He could look like a monster or a demon—the scarier the better. The masks were not only made to frighten enemies; they also helped to keep a samurai's helmet from flying off, since the helmet was tied to the mask, which was tied to the shoulder pads, which was tied to . . . well, you get it!

DRESS LIKE A
SAMURAI

1. Gotta start with undies. And remember to "go" before you pull on anything more.

2. Next comes a short, padded silk kimono, which looks a bit like a poofy bathrobe. You also need matching baggy silk trousers to go with it.

3. Shoes are next, followed by shin guards—kind of like the ones you wear for soccer.

4. Thighs need protecting, too. So pads like a hockey goalie's get tied on.

5. You'll need metal sleeves to make your arms dagger-proof.

6. Now the midsection of the body needs armor, made of thousands of tiny pieces of metal or thick leather.

7. Next comes a skirt (yeah, a skirt) split into several panels so you can get on and off a horse with ease.

8. Shoulder guards (like a football player's) are a must to deflect arrows.

9. An iron collar is also snapped on. No point in having your head sliced off.

10. Almost there. Pull on a padded cotton cap to pad that thick skull of yours!

11. Face mask. The scarier the better!

12. And finally, your helmet. Careful of the horns! They're sharp!

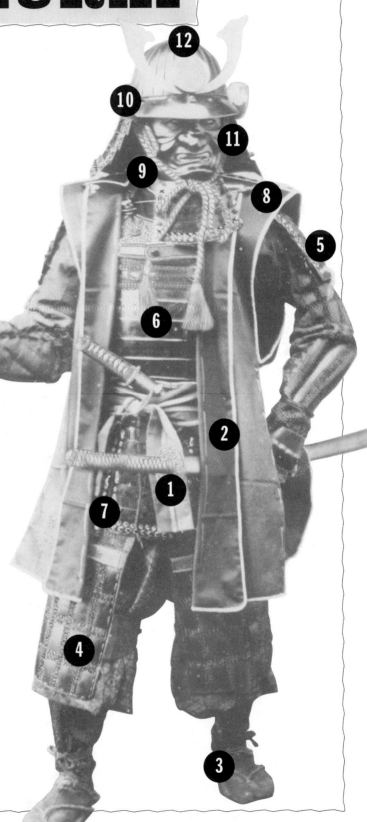

THE OTHER WAY TO FIGHT

For 700 years, shoguns had armies of samurai who fought all across Japan. There were also regular foot soldiers fighting for various emperors, renegade clan leaders, and militant Buddhist monks stirring things up. But there was another kind of warrior learning to fight in the mountains of Japan: the Ninja.

How cool are ninjas? Almost invisible. Almost magical. Ninjas began as small self-defense groups—kind of like those neighborhood-watch associations that look out for burglars. Ninjas weren't about galloping on horseback with arrows a-flying and swords a-swinging. Ninjas were about patience. Surprise. Secrecy. Sometimes they worked to help the samurai. Sometimes they worked against them. And sometimes they set out to kill a particularly whack-job shogun. But they usually worked alone.

Ninjas were not evil killers. They were ordinary folks who had to develop extraordinary skills to survive during very tough times. As warlords fought with other warlords, it was usually the innocent farmers, just trying to eke out a living, who kept getting squished. They needed a way to protect themselves, so they figured out how to use their farm tools to defend themselves against a samurai's bows and blades.

YUCKY
YORE

Being a ninja takes patience. Legends tell that in 1578, one very persistent ninja waited in a powerful warlord's toilet cesspit for several days until the lord, Uesugi Kenshin, finally came to go "number two." As Kenshin crouched down to do his business, the ninja leapt up and killed him.

One weapon the ninjas invented was the *kama,* which was basically a farm hoe. And trust me, if you swing a hoe at someone's head, you *will* do some serious damage. Another ninja weapon was the *shurikan,* a small dagger. Some were star-shaped and thrown like Frisbees, and others were needle-shaped. A shurikan couldn't penetrate armor, but when it was tipped with poison, it was great for catching an unarmed enemy samurai by surprise.

Over time, ninjas came up with lots of ways to fight back. They made spiked iron bands to wear on their hands and feet so they could climb trees and wooden walls. They carried hollow tubes to use as snorkels or as blowguns. They learned about pressure points in the body—places where the squish of a thumb and forefinger would squash a muscle or joint. They adapted Chinese fighting skills and practiced balancing techniques so they could fight on slippery, rocking boats. They learned bone striking and bone breaking—a skill that traveled from Korea to Japan in the 1500s. They also learned how to train their minds to block out physical discomfort so that they could walk through fire or stand beneath a freezing waterfall or hang by their fingernails off the edge of a cliff. And all those neat "hi-yah!" moves didn't happen overnight. It took hundreds of years. Surprisingly, for centuries ninjas didn't even know that anyone had gone to the trouble of describing them. They believed they were just a bunch of nameless folks trying to survive.

GRUNT! Grab onto 589 pounds of pure muscle . . . and some huge rolls of flab. Race over to STRANGE SPORTS on page 248 & read about SUMO!

A real ninja would cringe at these guys. Ninjitsu was all about blending in and being invisible!

SCHOOL DAZE

Pity the poor schoolkid one hundred years ago. Toss one innocent little spitball and before you could say "ABC," you'd be wearing a tree branch on your nose and a sign around your neck that said you were an idiot. And there were even more ouch-y fates. Learning could be a painful and embarrassing event.

I'M AN IDIOT

HEY, MOM? CAN I HAVE A BATHROOM PASS?

The very first teachers were moms and dads who taught their kids the things they needed to know to survive. Intro to cow-milking. Basic stall-mucking. Intermediate pea-picking. Chicken-plucking 101. There were no such things as schools in ancient times. After all, there was no written history to learn. Folks couldn't write, so they didn't need to learn how to spell. No penmanship, either. Heck! How could there be? There were no pens! There was no science. No geography. No foreign languages to learn because no one went anywhere. Math was as easy as: *Bob has two elephants and Mary has two elephants. How much elephant poop do they have to clean up before they can go out and play?* But all that began to change as the world's first mega-civilizations arose.

IT'S ALL GREEK TO ME

Fast-forward to ancient Greece. What you were taught in ancient Greek schools depended on where you were brought up. Grow up in Athens, and you'd study a lot of the same subjects we study today—but grow up in neighboring Sparta and prepare to go to military school from the age of six! Spartan schools were all about pain. Students were always kept cold and hungry, and they were even encouraged to learn to steal—as long as they didn't get caught. There was a class in barefoot marching, and they learned how to wrestle, run, and fight.

There's a famous tale about a hungry Spartan schoolboy who managed to steal a live fox, which he planned to cook and eat. He saw some grown-up soldiers marching toward him, so he stuffed the fox into his tunic. Would he get caught for stealing? The boy let the fox gnaw at his chest, and didn't blink an eye, rather than have the soldiers catch him. Bet his teacher gave him an A for effort!

Sally gets an A+ in milking! In long-ago days, most kids simply did not go to school.

234

PLEASE... HAVE A COW

Starting in the mid-1600s, kids had something new to learn with. It was a little wooden paddle with the alphabet and a prayer nailed to it. It was called a *horn book* because the whole thing was covered by a layer of super-thin cow horn. Here's how to make one: Cut off a sheep or oxen horn. (Careful doing this. Critters don't take kindly to having a body part hacked off.) Leave the horn soaking in water for several weeks until the top layer separates from the bone. Skim off the goopy, gelatinous stuff and boil it in hot water, then toast it over the fire like a marshmallow. Finally, roll it into a thin layer and let it harden. Tack it on your paddle to protect your ABCs and prayers. Kids wore these paddles around their necks. How cool were they?

READIN', WRITIN' ROMANS

Let's graduate to ancient Rome. School began not in September, but on March 24th, the start of the New Year's holiday—and class started before sunrise! Forget notebooks and pencils. Kids had to bring in candles so they could see. There was a lunch break and an afternoon rest, then back to work until late in the afternoon. There were no actual school buildings. Kids gathered at someone's home where a tutor or a highly educated slave did the teaching.

In about 200 B.C.E., wealthy Romans decided to "go Greek" and began sending their sons (and some lucky daughters) to a school outside the home. Kids wrote on wax boards and learned to count with pebbles. They learned their Roman numerals. (Quick—how much is XVI minus VIII? C'mon . . . make it snappy!) And they learned to read the classic writings of the great Greek authors.

At age 12, upper-class boys moved on to "grammar" schools where they learned (duh!) Greek and Latin grammar. At age 16, the smartest boys moved on to "rhetoric" school, where they learned to become *orators*—guys who blab-blab-blabbed for a living. Today we know them as politicians.

OFF TO MIDDLE (AGES) SCHOOL

In the years after the crash of the Roman Empire in the 400s C.E., priests and monks took over as teachers. But they were only concerned with teaching two things: writing enough to copy the Bible over and over and *over* again and reading just enough to be able to read what they

Think these schools are tough? Check out what Aztec kids had to learn in AZTEC ANTICS on page 4.

A NIFTY FUND-RAISER

You know how your school has bake sales or sells candy bars to raise money? Here's a medieval school fund-raiser: Get a huge barrel. Have all the students pee in the barrel until it's full. It might take a couple of weeks. Then sell those gallons and gallons of urine to the local tanneries (where it'll be used to make leather) and wool makers (where it'll be used to soften scratchy wool) and spend the money you earn from the pee-pee sales to buy school supplies.

YOU ARE SUCH A DUNCE!

For many years, kids who didn't quite get what the teacher was trying to teach were sent to the corner with a dumb-looking pointy hat on their heads. That stupid-looking hat was called a *dunce cap* and it was named for a Scottish thinker from the late 1200s named John Duns Scotus. He had noted that wizards often wore pointy hats when cooking up their potions and writing incantations, which led him to believe that cone-shaped hats worked like reverse funnels, sucking knowledge into the brain of the wearer. Eventually Duns Scotus's methods of teaching became uncool, and it was decided that the shame of wearing a dunce cap was the perfect way to make a kid study a little harder.

were copying. Truth was, most kids just didn't even go to school. As Europe wallowed in the murk of the Dark Ages, one of the greatest learning centers was thriving in Mali, in West Africa. There was a mega-university in the city of Timbuktu along with dozens of libraries. Alas, anyone in Asia or Europe who wanted to study there had to take a 400-mile-long camel ride across a toasty desert!

But by the 1200s, Europe emerged from its slumber, and cathedral schools began to spring up. Eventually, the cathedral schools grew into universities where boys (and only boys) around the age of 14 came from far and wide to learn to think. But it wasn't like going to a modern-day college. Even at the best universities, students sat on straw-covered floors. And when day—and homework—were done, that was it. Sports and games were strictly forbidden. There was nothing to do after classes except drink too much ale, get drunk, and start fights.

RECESS FOREVER

For most of history, learning was really only for rich boys. And if you were a girl? Forget about it. You couldn't go to school, and when you grew up, the only job you could get was being a wife and mother. If you were a boy from a poor family, the best you might hope for was an *apprenticeship*—a chance to learn how to make chairs or weave fabric by working for free for someone for years and years *and years!* That's what happened to Ben Franklin, who got *his* education as a printer's apprentice. Paul Revere learned all *he* knew about being a silversmith hunched over somebody else's molten metal. But things began to change in the 1700s—especially in America.

B is for bad. And beating. And bruised bottoms!

236

ONE ROOM. ONE TEACHER. ONE SORE BUTT.

Before the 1700s in America, most kids learned what they needed to know from their parents at home. But that began to change in the eighteenth century. Kids started to go to *dame schools*—like daycare with a little reading and writing thrown in. And by the mid-1800s, many kids found themselves sitting in a one-room schoolhouse along with other much bigger, much older students giving them noogies whenever the teacher turned her back.

In America in the 1800s, school was a "come-when-you-can" event.

School portraits. *This motley group smiles for the camera in front of their one-room school.*

YOU'RE IN TROUBLE NOW!

Think getting sent to the principal's office stinks? Try these old-school punishments.

■ If you misbehaved at school in the Middle Ages, teachers would stick your grubby little hands into a *finger-stock*—a nasty little device. This wooden block, positioned behind your back so your shoulders were twisted, had holes in which your fingers were jammed. There was no way out without the teacher's help.

■ In the 1800s and 1900s, teachers were allowed to *cane* students. This involved the unlucky kid first being sent out to cut a piece of green hickory branch from a nearby tree. The doomed child would then drop his trousers and get a butt-walloping in front of the whole class!

■ Passing notes in a colonial American class? Try wearing a nose pincher made from a two-inch-long split piece of tree branch for an hour or so, and I bet you'd think twice about it.

■ Kids who cried in class (after a stern tongue-lashing from teacher) or bit their nails got to wear wooden signs around their necks that said "cry-baby" or "bite-finger."

Some kids went to school for only a few weeks each winter, when it was too cruddy outside to work on the family farm. There was only one teacher to control upwards of 40 or 50 kids—kids from age six to almost grown-up, who all sat together. A lot of time was spent yelling at, spanking, and humiliating students. Most teachers were poorly trained, and some of them were only 14 or 15 years old themselves. Sometimes a student was older than the teacher! Teachers in remote towns often took turns living in the houses of the families they taught. Can you imagine what it would be like if your teacher lived with you? "Uh . . . Mr. Flynn . . . are you going to be in the bathroom much longer? I'm gonna be late for school!"

SCREEEEEECH!

In 1809, in a school in Philadelphia, something new hit the classroom. A piece of pine lumber was covered with a mixture of egg white and then smeared with blackened, charred potatoes. The whole smelly mess hardened and teachers could write on this stuff with chalk and easily erase it all with a rag when they were done. And soon, they could make horrible squeaky noises with that

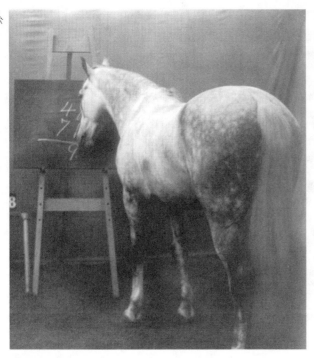

Chalk one up for Prince Albert. *This "educated" horse did sums at the blackboard.*

chalk that would make a kid's teeth hurt! Blackboards had been invented!

By the 1880s, most classrooms had rows of desks bolted to the floor, facing the teacher. There was a pot-bellied stove in one corner. If you sat near it, the warmth made it hard not to doze off. If you sat too far away, you froze and had to wear a hat and mittens to stay warm.

Every desk had an inkwell and it was the teacher's job to make the ink to fill them. In the country, that meant getting tannic acid from oak trees and mixing it with oil. Writing was so messy. The goose-feather quills always leaked. Penmanship was a hard subject to do well in because the pens were always blobbing at the wrong times—but fortunately, you could spell things pretty much any way you wanted. Spelling "rules" really didn't exist until the 1870s. You could spell "quiet" k-w-y-i-t and still get an A!

PADDLES AREN'T JUST FOR CANOES

School sure has come a long way. Screeching egg-and-burnt-potato blackboards have been replaced by quiet green or white ones. Leaky quill pens have been replaced with laptop computers. No one has to take a class designed to teach you how to run barefoot over jagged rocks. Dunce caps have been replaced with snoozing at your desk during detention.

But guess what? In more than 20 states, it is still perfectly legal for a teacher to tell a kid to bend over, grab his or her ankles, and swat that tender tush with a paddle in front of the whole class. We've come a long way, kiddo. But we still have a long way to go!

Bet detention doesn't seem all that bad. *Getting lectured by the principal beats getting whacked!*

SINKING SHIPS

Shipwrecked. Stranded on a desert island. Smashed to smithereens on sharp rocks. Afloat at sea in a lifeboat for weeks on end, or speared by an iceberg and flash-frozen. Anyone up for a cruise?

THAT SINKING FEELING

Cars are cool. Trains are terrific. But there's another way people have been getting around for centuries: boats! Dragon-bowed vessels swept the Vikings across Europe. Giant rowboats, with hundreds of slaves manning the oars, let the Romans conquer their world. Huge Chinese junks helped emperors dominate Asia. And the stocky, sturdy caravels of Spain and Portugal helped blitz the Americas. Pirates pillaged from swift sailing ships. (Go loot a little with PIRATES on page 188.) And where would we be without aircraft carriers? Or the *Mayflower,* come to think of it? But when it comes to the "Oh, Yikes!" factor of boats, nothing beats a good shipwreck. And when it comes to shipwrecks, it's hard to top the tale of the *Titanic.*

A TOO-COOL CRUISE

In the days before planes, boats were the only way to get across an ocean. As more and more people began traveling between Europe and America, the boats kept getting bigger and bigger. After all, the same massive steam engines that pulled trains could propel a boat, too. In March 1909, work began in Ireland on two of the biggest ships ever built. Everything about them was *huge!* The *Olympic* was the first of the pair to be finished. The RMS *Titanic* came

next! The owners crowed that these boats were "*virtually* unsinkable!"

On May 31, 1911, the *Titanic*'s hull was smeared with three tons of soap and 15 tons of animal fat mixed with oil. Then, liked a greased watermelon, the ship slid into the water. Fully loaded, it weighed 66,000 *tons!* How big was it? You could lay more than 25 school buses end to end and still have room to walk around. And it was luxurious, too. Elevators and grand stairways led to opulent staterooms and fancy restaurants. Everyone was awestruck!

The *Titanic*'s maiden voyage—its first trip with paying passengers aboard—began in Southampton, England, on April 10, 1912, at noon, with a thunderous toot of her huge horns. On board were some of the wealthiest, most famous people of the day. But as you traveled

THEY SHOULD HAVE KNOWN BETTER...

How's this for freaky fortune-telling? Fourteen years before the *Titanic* sailed, a novel called *Futility or The Wreck of the Titan* told the tale of a ship trying to cross the Atlantic in record time that hits an iceberg and sinks, losing almost all of its passengers because there aren't enough lifeboats!

And 20 years before the *Titanic* sailed, William Stead had penned a book about a ship that strikes an iceberg in the North Atlantic and sinks. In his book, the survivors are rescued by a ship captained by a character named E. J. Smith. Twenty years later, that author, William Stead, boarded the RMS *Titanic*. The captain—the real captain—was E. J. Smith. That's enough to send some serious shivers down a spine!

down to the lower levels of the boat, the rooms got smaller, the fittings cheaper, the deck more packed with people traveling to America to start a new life.

As the *Titanic* steamed toward New York, it began to pick up warnings of icebergs. "Full speed ahead!" said Captain E. J. Smith, and he was urged on by the ship's owner, who was aboard. *"Captain, Titanic—Westbound steamers report bergs, growlers, and field ice ..."* came another warning telegraph from another ship. Still the mighty ship pressed on. At 11:40 P.M. on a bitter cold, crystal-clear night, a lookout man high up on the crow's nest of the *Titanic* rang the warning bell. Iceberg dead ahead! Now they got the message—but a huge ship traveling at top speed does not stop or turn easily. The

THE SYRACUSE HERALD.

PRICE TWO CENTS — VOL. 36, NO. 10,965 — SYRACUSE, N.Y., WEDNESDAY EVENING, APRIL 17, 1912 — TWENTY-TWO PAGES

TITANIC DEATH LIST GROWS

LINER TITANIC SINKING AFTER FATAL COLLISION WITH ICEBERG

WHAT A WRECK!

Pull on a life vest! Here are three of the most memorable shipwrecks ever!

1. The *Endurance* (1914–1916):

When Sir Ernest Shackleton's crew of adventurers got trapped in the ice of Antarctica, they thought they were doomed. After ten months of trying to break free, they watched ice crush their ship right before their eyes. All they had was three measly lifeboats. Shackleton took a small group and set off on an impossible trip—more than 800 miles in a 22-foot boat across the most dangerous seas on Earth—to get help. It took him 18 months . . . but he *did* return. His 28 men managed to survive for 635 days on a diet of penguins and seals.

Smashed to smithereens. The Endurance was a prisoner of the ice.

A cruise to a coffin. Many passengers on the Empress of Ireland *ended up at an unexpected destination: death.*

2. The Spanish Armada (1588):

The Spanish navy was the best in the world in the 1500s, so when their fleet of 130 ships set out to wipe England off the map, they just knew they were going to win. But guess what? Surprise! The English had huge cannons and they weren't afraid to use them. To add to the misery, gale winds began to blow the ships north toward Ireland. Then came the final wallop—a megastorm that snapped 30 ships into piles of floating twigs. Almost 11,000 Spanish sailors sank along with their ships. No more Spanish navy!

3. The *Empress of Ireland* (1914):

Everyone knows about the *Titanic*. But hardly anyone knows about the sad fate of the *Empress*, which went down just a few weeks later, after a collision in thick fog on the St. Lawrence River in Canada. It all happened so fast there was no time to even get to the lifeboats—just 14 minutes elapsed from the time it was hit until it was sunk! More than 1,000 people drowned, including 840 passengers—eight more than were lost on the *Titanic*.

Titanic slid into the towering mountain of ice, and deep below the waterline, a series of holes were ripped into the hull.

This wasn't the only piece of bad luck Captain Smith had run into. The year before, while he was at the helm of the *Olympic,* it collided with another ship and both were badly damaged. Captain Smith had been blamed for that mess. Now he had a new disaster on his hands. It took him 25 minutes to realize the *Titanic* was in grave danger before giving the order to abandon ship.

THAT SINKING FEELING

The real *Titanic* had never had a full-fledged proper lifeboat drill. So no one knew quite what to do. And some people felt it was crazy to go sit in a little rowboat in the middle of the freezing Atlantic Ocean. For the next two hours, it was sheer chaos on board the *Titanic.* Some people got onto lifeboats and were saved, but others were pushed aside. And the folks down on the lowest levels of the ship were locked behind an iron gate and couldn't get out at all. In the end, more than 1,500 passengers and crew drowned.

A proper prop. The Titanic needed giant propellers like this monster spinner.

To this day, it ranks as one of the worst disasters at sea on record.

Oddest of all, a young girl who was dying in Scotland on the night of April 14, 1912, kept having terrible visions of a sinking ship, people drowning, and a man named Wally who was playing a violin. Just after she died, the beautiful *Titanic* slowly sank into the sea, as Wallace Hartley and his band gallantly played for the doomed souls on the deck of the "virtually unsinkable" ship.

DYING FOR GOLD

There are literally thousand and thousands of wrecked ships still lying at the bottom of the world's oceans. Some are down so deep that a human diver would be squished to death by the water's pressure at those great depths if he or she dared to explore. But nowadays robots and specially built *bathospheres* (little submarine-balls that can withstand great pressure) have treasure hunters licking their greedy little chops. Some of the world's richest wrecks are being explored. Who knows what'll

MOVE IT!

True story. Or so they say.

A U.S. navy vessel received this urgent transmission from a Canadian crew: "Divert your course 15 degrees north to avoid a collision."

Not one to be bossed around, the captain sent a reply. "Recommend *you* divert *your* course 15 degrees south to avoid a collision."

A message came back. "Negative! You will have to divert . . ."

The U.S. ship's captain radioed back, "I say again, YOU divert! This is the aircraft carrier USS *Lincoln* . . . accompanied by three destroyers, three cruisers, and numerous support vessels. I demand that you change your course 15 degrees south or countermeasures will be taken to ensure the safety of this ship."

The radio squawked out this reply. "This is a lighthouse. Your call."

be hauled up along with the sunken skeletons of all those lost sailors in the years to come? Golden treasures? Priceless artifacts? Only time will tell!

Uh, Captain . . . Someone goofed big-time in this shipwreck in Alaska.

SMELLY SHOES

If you've ever almost fainted from the foul stench wafting up from your feet, it is time to consider the things you wear on those little stink-bombs—your shoes. After all, that funky footwear is one of the reasons your feet smell as bad as they do!

BARK-O-LOUNGERS

Imagine if you had to walk outside barefoot in the snow or across a scalding-hot desert. Shoes are a must-have if you're going to walk without sobbing. The first shoes were made when prehistoric hunters peeled off some tree bark, lined the bark slabs with large leaves, and then tied the barky hunks to their feet with vines. In hot places, such as Egypt, those bark-leaf creations soon grew into foot baskets—basically a sole woven just like a basket with toe loops to hold it to the foot. Not the sturdiest of footwear, but cheap and easy to make. In colder places, big squares of animal skins were tied like little bags around each foot and closed with a string at the ankle. In really snowy places, people used bigger skins that went all the way up to the knee. And there you had it—sandals, shoes, and boots were here to stay.

FOOT TO BE TIED

For a long time, shoes were merely practical and comfy, but they soon became a fashion statement—and a flaky one at that! Let's zip back to Europe in the Middle Ages. The Crusaders (you can read about *that* mess in WACKY WARFARE on page 282) were coming back from their jaunts in the Middle East where they had discovered the most amazing shoes: footwear

BABY STEPS

In China, women's feet were considered beautiful only if they were eensy teensy—more like little hooves than feet. Beginning in the tenth century, wealthy women had their feet bound—strapped super-tight until the bones snapped and malformed. That left them pretty much unable to walk. But they got to wear the cutest little baby-sized slippers! Thanks, but no thanks on *this* style!

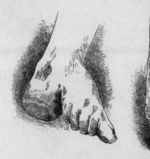

The ideal Chinese woman's foot measured a wee 4 inches long.

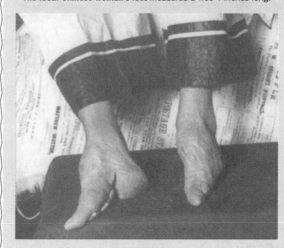

made of silk, velvet, and gold cloth with pointy curving toes. People saw the Crusaders' cool footwear and thought, "*Wow!* I gotta get me a pair of those!"

One of the first places the super-pointy shoes caught on was the town of Cracow (now Krakow) in Poland. Soon every guy wanted *crackowes,* as the shoes were soon called. The toe points kept growing longer and longer—some

Peasants **P**needed sturdy footwear to muck about in the fields. And it wasn't long before a clever person strapped a small log to each foot. Wooden shoes were sturdy. You could walk on a bed of razors and not feel it. Wooden footgear quickly caught on, and soon every peasant worth his or her salt had a spiffy pair of sabots. But in time, the peasants grew tired of always being taken advantage of by greedy lords. One day, a group of them strapped on their sabots and stomped all over the master's fields, trampling His Majesty's crops. Their act—sabotage—is still with us today!

were over two feet long! They eventually got so long that men started wearing chains from their knees to the tips of their shoes to hold the toes up so they wouldn't be tripped over.

In 1344 Duke Leopold II of Austria found himself literally running for his life. Assassins were after him! Unfortunately, it's hard to run fast when you keep tripping over your own feet. Leo's super-long shoes cost him his life. Royalty everywhere took note: POINTY SHOES MAY BE HAZARDOUS TO YOUR HEALTH!

THE SIX-TOED KING

Over in England, King Charles VIII had another problem. He had *six* toes on each foot. No squeezing that many toes into a crackowe! So Charlie decreed that super-wide shoes were now the style. Pointed toes were so "last year." Out went long and pointy. In came *bear's paws.*

Walking in shoes that would fit a duck was a whole new challenge. The bear's paws were just as stupid looking as the crackowes. And soon, they were getting even wider—six, seven, eight . . . even nine inches wide. That's even wider than this book! Some shoes even had stuffed lumps on the ends to look like swollen toes.

Men no longer walked. They waddled!

A (VERY) SHORT HISTORY

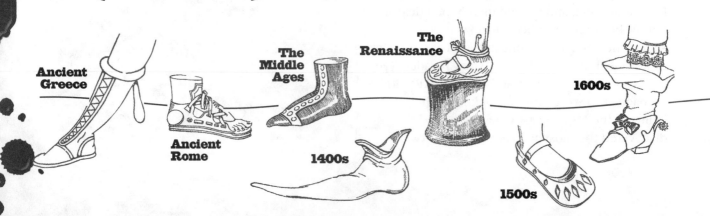

Ancient Greece

Ancient Rome

The Middle Ages

1400s

The Renaissance

1500s

1600s

BOOT-LEGS

These days there are little things like sidewalks and paving. But long ago, there was nothing but mud and horses (who left behind huge mounds of horse poop). It was lovely to have nice shoes, but the things you had to wade through made getting up above the filth super-important. By the 1600s, men and women wore *pattens,* a kind of overcoat for feet that tied on over their pretty shoes. Some pattens had giant iron rings at the bottom to lift the shoes up out of the muck.

In many parts of Europe, people who actually had to work for a living wore shoes made of fabric or hide that had thick wooden soles. In the Netherlands, they wore entire chunks of hollowed-out poplar logs! And speaking of wood . . .

HALF WOMAN, HALF TREE

Women were wearing fairly sensible shoes in the 1500s and 1600s. But over in Venice, a city in Italy that has watery canals instead of streets, it was hard to keep these sensible shoes from getting wet. Someone had the bright idea of adding a high, wooden sole to the shoe to keep it dry. Slowly, the soles started getting

higher and higher until, alas, they were up to 18 inches tall. Go get a ruler and look at how high 18 inches is. These ridiculous shoes were called *chopines*—shoes so weird that women needed someone to walk alongside them to keep them from toppling off their shoes into the mud. In fact, they were so high that someone described Venetian women as "half girl, half wood."

SNEAKY FEET

In the coming centuries more funky shoe styles appeared. In the 1700s rich folks wore dancing shoes made from dog skin. And until 1865, shoes were the same shape for both the left and right foot. But the 1800s were a big century for shoes. Besides shoes for left *and* right feet, the first rubber soles appeared in 1832.

By 1868 someone had made a pair of shoes with canvas (a type of cotton fabric) uppers. By 1873, someone had put the two things together to make sneakers. By 1917 Keds were hoppin' around on playgrounds. The name was a combo of "kids" and the Latin word for foot (*ped*).

Fast-forward to 1971, when Bill Bowerman, the track coach at the University of Oregon, had a brainstorm while eating waffles one morning. Next thing you know, he was pouring molten

OF SHOES

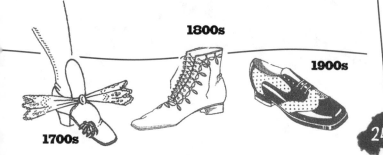

1700s

1800s

1900s

BIG FOOT

The biggest feet on record belonged to Matthew McGrory of Pennsylvania, who wore a size 26. And kicking up her heels right behind him was Fanny Mills—a circus performer, naturally—with size 22s.

SIZE MATTERS

Why do shoes have those weird sizes? Who decided to size shoes from 1 to 13? It began in 1324, when England's King Edward II decided that shoes should have sizes based on barley corn. He took three barley corns and laid them end to end. He then decreed that three barley corns would equal one shoe size unit. The person with the biggest feet around in those days measured 39 barley corns. Thirty-nine divided by 3 equals size 13. How many barley corns do you wear?

latex into his wife's waffle iron to make super-bouncy soles for his team's running shoes. You might have heard of them. They're called Nikes!

STEPPIN' THROUGH TIME
Here's a quick footwear trip through the ages.

Ancient Egypt: How do you tell the difference between a farmer and a pharaoh? Shoes! Egypt's kings made sure their shoes were studded with jewels and gold, and dyed bright colors such as scarlet and purple.

Ancient Mesopotamia: The Babylonians were great leather tanners and they were some of the first to use leather to make shoes. They particularly liked a dye made from sumac leaves, which produced a deep red color. When the Moors (people from North Africa) came to Europe, they brought that color with them. It became known as *cordovan* after the Spanish city of Córdoba, which fell under their rule.

Ancient Rome: How do you keep a huge army of foot soldiers happy? Make sure their feet are comfortable! Soldiers wore *caligas*—open-toed shoes that kept their feet from getting too hot. The soles were completely covered with nail heads to keep the soles from wearing out. And the sound of a thousand soldiers marching into town with those soles was scary! Soldiers who marched north to England had *calceus* and *gallicas*—closed-toe shoes for that dreary, wet weather. This style eventually became our galoshes.

The Dark Ages: Shoes? What are those? Back to bark and animal fur.

The Middle Ages: Shoes are back and they're bigger and sillier than ever. A passion for pointy toes grows and grows . . . and grows.

The Renaissance: With wealthy folks tired of tripping, long pointed toes were replaced with round or square toes. Then shoes got wider and

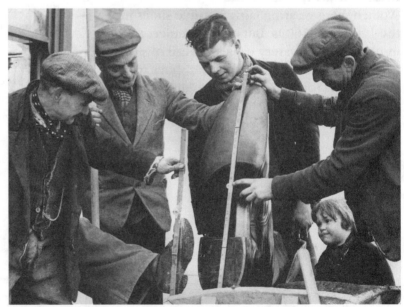

You may take three giant steps . . . *And this giant boot made for a football club in England is just the thing to wear!*

wider until by Henry VIII's time, 6½-inch-wide shoes were in style. Straps and buckles are added to shoes. Soles, too.

This little pig went to market.
This little pig staid at home.
This little pig had a bit of roast beef.
This little pig had none.
This little pig said,—
"Tweak! tweak! tweak!
Mamma, I want some!"

The 1500s: When Europeans came to the New World, they were instantly jealous of the footwear of the Native Americans. Moccasins were made from a single piece of deerskin—oh so cushy and very beautiful when decorated with delicate beadwork or porcupine quills.

The 1600s: Wanna know what men's shoes looked like? Take a look at a pair of your mom's dress shoes today! Men wore high heels!

The 1700s: Left foot? Right foot? Didn't make one bit of a difference. All shoes were exactly the same. Men liked boots—big boots with pouches and pockets and dripping with lace. Men's heels were always higher than women's.

The 1800s: High, buttoned shoes were the style, since ankles were considered shocking. Showing a glimpse of ankle was like mooning someone today.

The 1900s:

Thank goodness! Pain-free, easy-to-walk-in shoes are invented. Sneakers become the biggest thing in footwear. You can now slam dunk like a basketball star!

So pull on your super-comfy shoes. Left shoe on the left, right shoe on the right. And be grateful you don't have to be careful about stepping in piles of horse-poo when you cross the street!

SHOE-PERSTITIONS

■ Ancient Egyptians believed that inhaling the smoke from a burning sandal would cure a headache.

■ During the Middle Ages, people believed that if you wore shoes with pointy toes, witches would have no power over you.

■ In colonial America, placing a heavy boot on your abdomen was thought to be a good cure for a stomachache.

■ An old wives' tale says that putting salt and pepper in your left boot will bring good fortune.

■ In China people toss a red shoe from a roof because it's believed to bring happiness.

■ Among actors, there's a superstition that if your shoes squeak when you walk on stage, it means you'll get great reviews.

■ To this day, shoes are often tied to the car of a newly married bride and groom because in the olden days a dad gave a new hubby one of his daughter's shoes as a symbol of the transfer of authority.

As a last resort . . . *Charlie Chaplin, a great film comic, made a memorable meal from his shoe.*

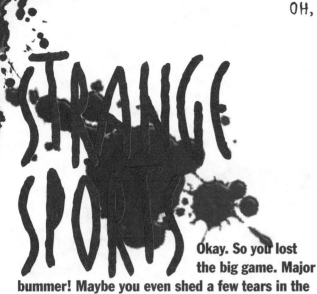

STRANGE SPORTS

Okay. So you lost the big game. Major bummer! Maybe you even shed a few tears in the backseat of the car on the way home. But look at it this way. At least no one got sacrificed to a bunch of angry gods at the end.

SUDDEN DEATH OVERTIME

The Mayas lived in Central America between 200 B.C.E. and 1400 C.E., and they were a "sister" civilization to the AZTECS (see page 4 for their heart-stopping story). The Mayas had a game called Pok-Ta-Pok. It sounds kind of cute, but it was anything but!

To play Pok-Ta-Pok, you needed two huge stone walls, each 26 feet tall. Seven players on each team had to try to get a small rubber ball through a hoop 23 feet above the ground.

AMERICA VS. EUROPE

We owe so much of our modern-day, team-playing ball games to the ancient Americans. While folks in Europe were still kicking around inflated sheep's bladders or skipping around maypoles for fun, America had death-defying pro ballplayers, protective helmets, and true team sports. When the first European adventurers returned from their trips to the Americas in the late 1400s, the bouncy balls they brought back were almost as jaw-droppingly wonderful as gold.

Compare that to an NBA basketball hoop at a measly 10 feet! Now here's the tricky part. Many historians believe that players could not touch the ball with their hands or feet—only the hips, chest, elbows, thighs, and knees. Because the rubber ball was hard and about the size of a bowling ball, players wore thick padding, including chin and cheek protectors and a big leather apron (very handy) instead of that little plastic "cup" Little Leaguers get to wear.

When the games were played for fun, everything was hunky-dory. But sometimes the games were played to honor the gods.

Out of bounds? Not when you played football in the streets of London in the 1300s. No rules, no boundaries. Lots of blood!

There are legends that say that the winning captain would present his neck to the losing captain, who then got to chop off the head of the lucky winner. To the Mayas, winning at Pok-Ta-Pok meant getting a direct ticket to heaven. The Maya athletes who played the game didn't mind dying if it meant *winning*.

The Aztecs in Mexico had their own version of Pok-Ta-Pok. They called it *Tlachtli* (*TLOCH-tlee*)—same hard rubber ball, same two teams, same no-hands-or-feet rule. But the Aztecs sacrificed the losers! You gotta wonder how often someone actually managed to get the ball through that 23-foot-high hoop in the first place!

IN TRAINING

Sports were invented for one reason: to train sluggish, pudgy soldiers. A soldier who could throw a fastball could throw a spear that would skewer an enemy. And a warrior that could hit a ball the size of a baby's fist with a stick while galloping by on a charging pony could do some serious damage when that stick got exchanged for a mace. Ball games were war games, but they were also oodles of fun. Wars were expensive and messy, and people were always getting maimed. Sports had all the thrill of battle without the weeping widows and messy burial services afterwards.

LITTLE BROTHER OF WAR

To America's first peoples, sports were more than just an excuse for a tailgate picnic. So back around 1790, when an argument over a beaver pond had the Choctaw and Creek Indians about ready to kill each other, they decided to resolve the issue with a not-so-friendly game of lacrosse.

Five hundred years ago, the game was a lot different than it is today. For one thing, it wasn't called lacrosse. The Algonquin nation called their game Bagattaway, which means "they bump hips." The Iroquois called their version "little brother of war." And war is a good way to describe the game. (The game was given the name "lacrosse" by French missionaries who thought the Indians' sticks looked like the curved cross of a bishop's staff.)

The only rule was that there were no rules. Games lasted for days, stopping at sunset and picking up again at daybreak. The playing field had no boundaries, and the goals were anywhere from five football fields apart to more than a half-mile apart. And speaking of the goal—it was usually a tree, a pole, or a rock. You got points if you hit the goal with the ball. To add to the fun,

Mega playing field. American Indians played lacrosse with no boundaries.

NOT SO ALL-AMERICAN

Baseball is as American as apple pie, right? Wrong. It got its start as an English children's game called *rounders,* which was played with a bat, a ball, and a couple of bases. In 1904, Al Spalding, a former pitching ace who had become quite rich making sporting equipment, decided that it was very uncool for America's great game to be related to a dumb English kid's game. So he pulled some strings and got a couple of U.S. senators and a few other important folks to look into the history of baseball and give it some real all-American roots.

The committee declared Abner Doubleday, a dead Army general and Civil War hero, to be the inventor of the splendid all-American game of baseball. They did this based on one letter from a very old man in Colorado, Abner Graves, who claimed he had seen Doubleday hanging out on a field in Cooperstown, New York, with between 20 to 50 boys whom he divided into teams of eleven. Graves went on to describe a game with four bases—a game where you "soaked" the runner (hit him with the ball) to get him out. What everyone missed was this: the game Graves was describing had already been played for at least 70 years. Never, never, ever had Abner Doubleday uttered the word *baseball.* But, if Abner in Colorado said it was true, it had to be true. In 1907, Abner Doubleday was proclaimed the inventor of the game of baseball.

each team could have as many players as they wanted. Sometimes more than a thousand players, all waving sticks, would be chasing after that one little deerskin ball. There was no such thing as protective gear. And some of the players didn't even wear shoes! Injuries were a fact of life, especially because, as one French explorer wrote in the 1600s, "almost everything short of murder is allowable."

Lacrosse was serious stuff. It was treated as a religious event. There was a lot of ceremonial "cheerleading" from spiritual leaders on both sides. And the game may have been war's little brother, but every so often, it became grown-up war. Remember the Choctaw vs. Creek game for the beaver pond? The Choctaw won, and the furious Creek made sure that all-out war was the post-game show.

VARIATIONS ON A GAME

People have come up with countless different sports, but many are just variations on a theme.

Going Batty

Grab a stick. Now toss a pig's head up in the air and see how far you can swat it. For extra fun, get a friend to try to catch that flying pork skull as you run from here to there. Thwacking balls with sticks gave birth to all sorts of hit-the-ball sports such as . . .

■ **Polo:** In India and throughout Asia more than 2,000 years ago, folks hopped on a galloping horse or galumphing elephants and began to try to whack a teeny ball through a goal at the end of a large field. They called it *palau.* We call it polo. By 1862, British soldiers in India made it official, with rules and referees. Couldn't afford a horse? No problem! During the British occupation of

Polo ponies. Polo players at a full-tilt gallop.

India in the late 1800s, bored troops would try to keep their polo skills intact by practicing on bikes. It turned out to be fun, and bikes don't leave piles of manure in the middle of the field.

■ **Cricket and Rounders:** In England folks have been playing cricket and rounders (the daddy of our baseball) since 1300. Some say cricket was invented by bored shepherds hitting rocks with their crooks, which are called *cricces,* as they stood in front of the wicket gates in the sheep folds. Both games are a lot like baseball, except cricket games go on for days and absolutely no one outside of the British realm understands the rules.

■ **Hurling:** Don't confuse it with either curling or losing your lunch. This sport from Ireland, which is at least 2,000 years old, fields two teams of 15 players armed with sticks in pursuit of a small leather ball. It was so violent that the game was banned in 1527. But that didn't stop anyone. It lived on as hockey.

■ **Oina:** In Romania, land of DRACULA (read about that bloodsucking dude on page 62), this cross between baseball and cricket was first played in the 1300s. The bat is thinner, the teams are bigger, and the field has no bases. Players have 30 minutes to get as many hits as they can.

■ **Underwater Hockey:** Very popular in Australia. Teams of ten players hit a plastic-coated lead puck across the bottom of a swimming pool using a short wooden stick, trying to get past the other's side goal. All you need to play is a pair of lungs like a whale's.

Ball Bearings

Grab something important. Now run as fast as you can, past 20 guys the size of refrigerators who are coming at you from the other direction. Sound familiar? But before there was NFL football and FIFA soccer, there were some wild move-the-ball-from-here-to-there sports. . . .

■ **Rugby:** A biggie. Imagine football with no helmets and no padding. Imagine no time-outs, no blocking, and plays with names like "maul"

Batter up. *This cricketeer is ready to swat the ball.*

and "spear tackle," and you begin to get an idea of what "unnecessary roughness" *really* means. Rugby has many of its roots in a Celtic sport called *caid.* The word *caid* means the manly part of the bull. (That ought to leave a picture in your mind.) Many other lands had ball-in-hand running games, but the Celts played a particularly vicious form of it. During the Middle Ages, rival villages formed teams and then did everything in their power to move the ball toward their end. It was so deadly that several kings made it a crime to play the game.

■ **Kickball:** Every culture on every continent with people has developed some form of a kicking game. During the Han Dynasty in China (around the second and third centuries B.C.E.), soldiers trained to kick balls into nets—the better to kick a man's private parts into a state of pain on the battlefield. But Britain is the undisputed birthplace of modern soccer, which got its name from "*associ*ation football." Of course, they rest of the world calls it *football,* which makes a lot more sense than American football, which hardly uses feet at all! By the 700s, folks were avid footballers in Britain, but back then it was a war event. There's a famous story that the first football game in England involved a ball made from the severed head of a Danish prince just defeated in battle! GOOOOOOOAL!

Superhuman Feats

No ball. No stick. Just brute human strength to wrestle, climb, or swing around a balance beam better than the next dude. You've heard of gymnastics and wrestling, but try these. . . .

• **Kabbadi:** Ever played Capture the Flag? Try playing capture the other players! Part tag, part tackle football without the ball. In the Middle East, this game has been a huge favorite for centuries.

• **Log Rolling:** What's slipperier than a greased pig? Hop on a fast-spinning log and see how long you can stay up. Fast feet are a must. This funky sport got its start as an actual job in the timber regions of America.

• **Sumo:** Five-hundred-pounders wrapped in black diapers. What fun! Western sports fans just don't quite get this wrestle-mania, the national sport of Japan. By the eighth century, sumo was a hot ticket as entertainment at lordly banquets. By the tenth century, it had become a part of a samurai's fighting technique. And even though the sumos are huge, the sport is all about balance and speed.

Net Gains

Back and forth, back and forth . . . watching the ball, you feel like your head is going to snap off. And sure, you know about volleyball and tennis, but what about . . .

• **Rackets:** What does debtor's prison have to do with a ballgame? This fifteenth-century prisoners' pastime became a well-loved sport in the United Kingdom. Nowadays it's called racquetball or squash. And bet you didn't know that tennis was a big hit with medieval monks, who played so much the Church considered banning the game. They used to hit the ball back and forth with their hands. When their palms started to hurt, they pulled on leather gloves. And one day someone stuck a stick in his glove and a whole new bit of fun was born.

• **Sepak Takraw:** Volleyball played Thai-style. The twist? No hands! Only feet can propel that ball over the net. It's like watching gymnasts play volleyball—somersaulting, spinning gymnasts.

• **Jai Alai:** In Spain they call it *pelota,* but the Basque name has stuck everywhere else. Big wicker baskets strapped to the players' wrists are all that stands between them and a ball traveling at a wall and back at 150 miles an hour. By the 1400s, folks were playing with leather gloves and wooden paddles. But using a basket started in the 1800s when, legend has it, a local Basque man was too poor to afford a paddle and borrowed a basket from his mom's kitchen.

Race Ya!

Hop on a horse or a sled (the first ones were made of reindeer bones) and see who can get from point A to point B the fastest. Mankind has enjoyed racing since time began.

• **Animal Racing:** Saudi Arabians and Bedouin Arabs pride themselves on the speed of their trusty camels, who can travel ten miles in two hours for those of you who are interested. Over in South Africa, where camels are few and far between, folks saddle up for *ostrich racing.* In fact, if there's an animal you can ride, folks somewhere will race it.

• **Cycling:** In Europe, the Tour de France is a huge sports spectacular—a race across the Alps, some of the highest mountains in the world. *You* try pedaling up a steep hill for ten miles without puking! Bikes were invented in France in 1790, but cyclists have come a long way from those first ones. Look, Ma! No steering!

• **Lawn-Mower Racing:** Leave it to those garden-loving Brits to invent a lawn-based race—the highlight of the summer mowing season.

Can't have sports without the OLYMPICS—games so big they have their own section on page 177.

STUPID SUPERSTITIONS

Admit it! When you were littler you believed there were monsters under your bed. And don't even get me started on the creatures that lurk in the darkest corners of your closet (we *all* know they're in there!). A kid needs a little something to ward off all those evil spirits—or maybe a good-luck charm in hand to make sure you pass that spelling test you forgot to study for. So cross your fingers and let's see which superstitions have stood the test of time.

UH-OH!

Superstitions have been around since Neanderthal people first buried their dead with a little snack-pack for the next world. The Earth was a mysterious place back then. Bolts of lightning came out of the sky. Snow poured from the heavens. Glorious rainbows appeared out of thin air. How? Why? People kept looking up at the stars at night and tried to make sense out of life, hoping to explain why stuff happened.

Considering that life was so dangerous back then, it didn't take much to decide that the world was full of big, bad bogeymen. So early civilizations were always on the lookout for things that would repel any evil creatures that were out to do them harm. Trees, chickens, bunnies. *Anything!*

THE EVIL EYE

Ever give someone a "dirty look"? Moms always tell us "it's not polite to stare," and this snippet of

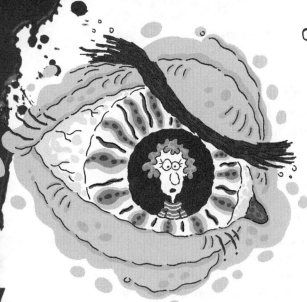

maternal wisdom actually got its start because staring is how the Evil Eye gets its power. Look closely into someone else's pupil (that's the black dot in the middle of the eye). You will be able to see the reflection of a teeny, tiny you. But ancient people believed that creature was an evil spirit—not a reflection. And the evil spirit's favorite "food" was sucking up the soul of a beautiful, healthy baby.

Now, no mother will 'fess up to having an ugly, stupid child. So all across the world, folks tried to figure out ways to protect children from the Eye's horrible gaze. For starters, mothers had to be modest about their kids. If someone said, "Oh, what a gorgeous baby," a mom protecting her child would quickly say, "Yeah . . . but she smells like a sewer."

Many cultures believe that if you tie red ribbons or strings to a child's undergarments or bedding, the red color will freak out the Evil Eye. The ribbon has to be red because in ancient times, red dye was made from worm guts. And what is lowlier and more undesirable than tying something dipped in worm intestines to your baby?

Over in Eastern Europe, moms learned to spit three times between the extended middle and

Smearing your kid with mud—that'll sure fool the Evil Eye!

index fingers of the left hand whenever someone complimented their children. More hygienic moms simply made a spitting noise—a "poo-poo-poo"—to keep the Evil Eye away.

In some parts of India, women lined their eyes and those of their children with dark kohl as a form of protection against the Evil Eye—proof that mascara is a necessary item in every mother's arsenal. In places where male babies were more highly cherished than females, mothers dressed their sons as girls to confuse the Eye. In fact, in Victorian times, many a boy was dressed in a frilly dress for this very reason.

And in Egypt, some of the best mothers deliberately did not bathe their children, and smeared dirt on their little faces to trick the Evil Eye into thinking that the wee one was a worthless beggar. Even today, throughout the Mediterranean, glass charms that look like blue eyes are worn as necklaces and pinned to a baby's clothes.

So deeply rooted is the ancient fear of that old Evil Eye that our traditions of modesty and our dislike of bragging are probably the result of thousands of years of trying to pull the wool over it.

HIP-HOP HOPE

A person could never have enough good-luck charms. Take the rabbit's foot, a promise of good luck (except for the poor bunny, who was now forced to hop around on a little peg leg!). More than 2,500 years ago in Europe, a group of people—probably the Celts, who lived in what is now Ireland—decided that since rabbits lived in underground burrows, they had secret knowledge of another world. And rabbits also reproduce like crazy. People desperately wanted to have as many babies as possible, since so many died in infancy. Folks hoped that if they held onto a piece of an animal that had scads of babies with no fuss and little muss, the animal's mega-fertility would rub off.

Back in 500 B.C.E. any rabbit part—the tail, the ear, even dried intestines—was just fine as a lucky charm. But fortunately, feet were another symbol of fertility, so the rabbit's foot became *the* piece to have.

WHEN YOU WISH UPON A BONE

There's nothing like snapping the clavicle of a piece of poultry to guarantee you'll get an "A" on your next math test! But how did the wishbone get to be a good-luck charm? We have the chicken-loving Etruscans to thank.

The Etruscans, who lived in part of what is now Italy, reached their peak in the sixth century B.C.E. They believed that chickens had special powers. After all, hens always squawked just before laying an egg, and roosters sang cock-a-doodle-doo every morning to

SEVEN YEARS OF BAD LUCK

Mirrors and umbrellas are good things. So why did these things become yucky luck?

Breaking a mirror: Seven years of bad luck for you if you do! The very first mirrors, made of polished metal, were not breakable. But by the sixth century B.C.E, the ancient Greeks were practicing a kind of fortune-telling that used bowls filled with water to show a person's reflection—kind of like a gypsy's crystal ball. Using mirrors, the fortune-teller would study the water and predict the person's future. If the water jiggled in the mirror as the person held it, it was proof that the person's future was SO terrible that the gods did not want it to be seen. So mirrors and the future became linked. In the first century, the ancient Romans added the seven-year twist to the predictions of the future. They believed that people aged in seven-year cycles. Since a mirror reflected a person, it also reflected that seven-year chunk of that person's life. Broken reflections now meant seven years of "uh-oh."

Opening an umbrella indoors: The Egyptians were some of the earliest umbrella users. But they used theirs to keep the sun from frying their brains. And only royalty got to use them, since they were thought of as special gifts from the gods. A sacred umbrella's shade was special, too. If a common person stepped into the shade of a regal umbrella, it was (gasp!) a terrible thing. But over in Mesopotamia, everyone believed the opposite. Standing in the shade of the king's umbrella would bring good fortune. Either way, umbrellas were tied to luck.

Fast-forward to England in the mid-1800s. Our modern-day umbrellas, with their sharp metal spokes, were becoming very common. But the first metal-shafted umbrellas were always springing open, and since that kind of explosive opening could take out an eye, it really WAS bad luck to have an umbrella pop open in a small room!

Walking under ladders: Back in ancient Egypt, ladders were a symbol of *good* fortune, because when a ladder leans against a wall it makes a triangle of wall, floor, and ladder. Triangles were way cool to the Egyptians. After all, their Pyramids are based on them. But by the time of ancient Rome, and the death of Jesus on a cross that had a ladder leaning against it, the ladder had turned bad. By the 1600s in England and France, folks being led to the gallows to be hanged were forced to walk under a ladder. The lucky executioner got to walk around it. Walking beneath a ladder meant someone was going to die. And speaking of dying, old customs die hard!

LUCKY PIGS

Travel around the world and you will find an entire zoo of lucky animals: waving cats in Japan, dolphins in New Zealand, elephants in India, and pigs in Germany. There are bugs for good luck, like the scarab-beetles in Egypt, and bat-charms that bring great fortune, like the fu bat necklaces popular in China.

Hmmm. Not one culture seems to have chosen the skunk as its good-luck animal. I wonder why?

announce the break of day. Clearly, these were critters that knew what was going to happen before it did. So high priests began keeping holy poultry. When the sacred chickens died, their bones were left to dry in the sun. Folks could come by, hold the sacred bones in their hands and pray for something good to happen. The V-shaped clavicle bones became known as *wishbones.*

Why the snapped bones? Some think it was just a case of too many people fighting

Don't miss out on FRIDAY THE 13TH on page 94.

over the lucky bones. The person who got the bigger (and hence more powerful) piece was said to get a lucky break.

NEIGH-SAYERS

The horseshoe is another good-luck charm that has been around since the fourth century. The Greeks are the probable inventors of this particular lucky charm. Horseshoes are made of iron, which is extremely strong. After all, you can stick an entire horse on top of a horseshoe and it will not get squished. The horseshoe shape was also a lot like the shape of the crescent moon, and the moon had been a symbol of birth and good fortune for centuries.

But some of the credit for the spread of horseshoe-shaped good-luck charms goes to a blacksmith in England in the year 959. The story goes like this: Dunston, the town smithy, was approached by a man who wanted to have horseshoes attached to his feet. Dunston thought this was very weird. He noticed that there was something really whacked-out about this guy's tootsies, too. They weren't feet. They were hooves. Dunston realized that the devil was sitting in his shop! He told the "man" that he would have to chain him to the wall before beginning to hammer in the new shoes. Dunston then proceeded to make the job as painful as he could, until the devil begged for mercy. Dunston told him he would not stop hammering until the devil promised that he would never come into a house that had a horseshoe hanging on the door. The horseshoe-shaped door knocker was here to stay.

FOUR LEAF CLOVERS

About 2,200 years ago, a religious group called the Druids were living in England, Scotland, Ireland, and Wales. These were very spiritual dudes who believed in the power of nature. They thought that the trees, forests, rivers, and streams were all filled with special powers. In fact, the name Druid

means "oak-wise." The Druids were the first to think that if you had a four leaf clover in your possession, you were safe from evil spirits. That's because 2,200 years ago, a four leaf clover was a very rare thing. The Druids' lands were taken over by troops from ancient Rome, who then brought the four leaf clover idea to the rest of the empire. A four leaf clover stayed rare and special until the 1950s, when botanists learned know how to breed them by the gazillions. Still, many folks swear by them when they need a little good fortune.

A LUCKY SYMBOL TURNS EVIL

Back in the 1930s, Germany became a terrible place as the Nazis came to power. Led by one of the most evil men to ever walk the Earth, Adolf Hitler, the Nazis began to use a symbol called the *swastika* as their special insignia. They stuck it on their uniforms, flags, and airplanes, and then dragged the entire world into a bloody, deadly war.

When we see a swastika today, we shudder in horror. But that swastika—based on the sun—had been a symbol of good luck for more than 3,000 years, all across the globe. Native American groups decorated their pots with this little sign. In ancient Greece they called it a *tetraskelion*. In China it is called a *wan*. India gave us the name *swastika,* which comes from the Sanskrit language and means "good to be." How unlucky that that lucky symbol became a sign of hatred.

KNOCK, KNOCK. WHO'S THERE? WOOD-N'T YOU LIKE TO KNOW!

A lot of ancient people were in awe of trees. Think about it—a tree could lose all its leaves and look as dead as could be, and then poof!, just like that, one day all the leaves were bursting out once again. Must've been magic! (Of course we now know it was simply spring.)

More than 4,000 years ago, a group of American Indians began to put great faith in sturdy oak trees. They would touch the trees in the hope that some of that solid strength and huge size would rub off. They also believed that any kind of boast or brag would bring bad luck. To counteract bragging, they would touch the base of an oak tree—knocking on the wood—and a new tradition was born!

The same custom also developed in Europe. In fact, just about everywhere there were trees, people were rubbing, knocking, or just plain praying to them. Each culture had a favorite tree—elms, poplars, sycamores. In fact, the custom of Christmas trees began in the 400s when a German monk wanted to get people to become Christians. He told them that evergreen trees were sacred and special—*not* like those stupid pagan ash trees that they were all praying to. That's why folks drag fir trees into their houses at Christmastime, and not elm trees.

TERRIBLE TABLE MANNERS

Johnny . . . get your face off the table! This kid needs some lessons in eating etiquette.

WHAT'S FOR DINNER? SEE-FOOD!

The early hunter-gatherers were so happy to have *any*thing to eat—a maggot-stuffed carcass, some half-rotten fruit—that they didn't give any thought to how that food got to their mouths. Food was shoved in quickly, and in private, before anyone else could steal it. But when people learned how to plant and farm, things started to change. Suddenly, food was more plentiful, and there was enough to share, so an entire subculture developed around eating. If Uncle Ralph's slobbering, drooling, open-mouth chewing grossed everyone out, then it would become a rule that you had to chew with your mouth closed. Table manners were born!

The ancient Egyptians were some of the first to write books telling people how to behave.

"Get your elbows off the table! Stop slouching! I've seen pigs with better table manners than you!" Bet you've heard that a time or two! But, honestly! What's the point of trying to spear a french fry with a fork when your fingers work so much better? Why hack those itty bits of chicken off a drumstick with stupid silverware when your teeth are twice as good?

Pity you didn't live way back when 'cause it's only pretty recently that silverware became common. Until the 18th century just about everyone ate with their hands!

ALWAYS WASH YOUR HANDS . . .

Until as late as the 18th century, regular folks mostly ate with their hands. There was one wee problem with this, however. There was no toilet paper in those days. When people went to the john, they had to wipe their butts with *something*. And at that time, that something was the same hands they ate with. So an absolute "must-do" became to wash your hands after you "doo-doo" and before you eat.

Archaeologists (people who dig up bits and pieces of old civilizations) found an etiquette book from 2500 B.C.E. along with a very well-behaved mummy.

TWEEZE, PLEASE

In ancient China, one of the biggest "don'ts" was serving animals that still looked like animals; they felt it was in bad taste (which is even worse than food that tastes bad!). So, before they cooked, they made their meat unrecognizable by chopping it into teeny little pieces.

There was another reason to chop food up. A great thinker named Confucius *(Kun-FEW-shis),* who lived from about 550 to 480 B.C.E., believed that knives were weapons of death and thought that only barbarians—evil, horrible murderers—would eat with something that could kill. But there was yet another reason, too. Small pieces of food cook more quickly than big hunks. With fuel scarce as the population of China grew and grew, it made sense to cook food as quickly and cheaply as possible. Ta-da! The first fast food!

Folks in Asia needed something special to eat their little food slivers with—something skinny to move their food from bowl to mouth—so they made *kwai-tsze,* "quick-bites," or as we call them, chopsticks.

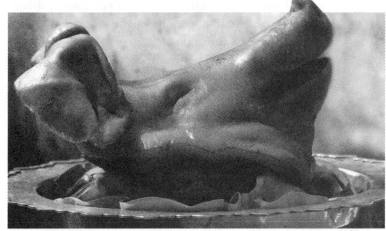

Which fork do you eat pig snout with? *Middle Ages meats were a hands-on feast.*

YORE

Belch! Burp! In some parts of the world, especially the Middle East and Asia, a burp was considered a great way to tell the chef that dinner was deeee-lish. But in Western Europe and America? Better ban that burp!

FLESH-HOOK ON THE LEFT. SPOON ON THE RIGHT

A history of tableware from stones to sporks

Prehistory (before people wrote things down): Sharp pieces of stone are found to be great for scraping and cutting foods. People learn how to make knife-like objects by chipping stone into pointy shapes. Coastal peoples find razor-sharp shells and tie sticks onto them—perfect for stirring hot pots of food. Hollow horns hacked off from dead sheep and goats make great cups. Ta-da! Tableware is born.

10th Century B.C.E.: In biblical times, forks were called flesh-hooks. Now, there's an appetizing name for an eating utensil. Back then, the only folks who actually got to use flesh-hooks were the high priests. They used them to stir up big of pots of sacrifice-stew, then speared up steaming bits of meat with their handy fork-shaped hooks.

500 C.E.: Vikings start using bits of wood to scoop up runny food. They call them *spons* which means a splinter or chip of wood. Creative folks carve their spons from wood, bone, shell, and stone.

Middle Ages: Can't afford a spoon? Use stale bread! Only the rich have utensils. In a practice leading up to the birth of the fork, some people begin to use two knives—one to cut with, and the other to keep the meat from sliding all over.

11th Century: A beautiful princess from the east appeared in Venice, Italy, one day carrying a small case containing a delicate two-tined (tines are the prongs that stab the food) fork, throwing the townspeople into a tizzy. Back then in most of Europe, the clergy—priests, bishops, and the Pope himself—called all the shots. And when they got wind of the fork-carrying princess they went nuts! One priest bellowed, "God in his wisdom has provided man with natural forks—his fingers. Therefore it is an insult to Him to substitute artificial metallic forks for them when eating." And when the princess died shortly after arriving in Venice (of the plague), everyone blamed her fork.

1170: A famous churchman, Thomas Becket, the Archbishop of Canterbury, smuggles some forks into England, but the Brits get confused and several men end up using their forks as weapons.

1533: Catherine de Medici, a rich and powerful Italian, comes to France to marry the future king. She brings forks with her, but the French can't quite get the hang of them. Most of the food slides off halfway between their plates and their mouths. But if the king has forks, then, doggone it, the wealthy aristocrats should too!

1611: A well-traveled Englishman named Thomas Coryate brings a fork back to England. His friends make fun of him and call him *furciferus,* which means a "pitchfork handler," or FURC for short. The name sticks.

1630: Governor Winthrop of the Massachusetts Bay Colony has the only fork in colonial America. Most folks used a spoon to hold their food steady while cutting it. They then put the knife down and picked up the spoon with their right hands—the reason Americans today move their fork from left to right hand before eating.

1690s: Since most people ate with three fingers, fork makers decided to add a third tine to their forks instead of two. They curved the tines a little too, so food would stay put. But people were still spearing their food with their forks, then pulling the food off the fork with their fingers and popping it into their mouths.

Early 1700s: "If three tines are good, four are better," say the Germans, who like their forks fatter. In England, forks still have two tines and are not great for scooping up mashed potatoes, so English knives are made extra wide—the better to eat with.

Late 1700s: The French put a new spin on the fork. There is a revolution brewing and the peasants are chattering about equality. The wealthy aristocrats are freaked and try to create an even greater canyon between rich and poor. They invent individual place settings! Now, if you dine at the home of a wealthy person you get your very own plate, silverware, and drinking glass. Poorer folks still share a single plate and cup—and they still use the finger-and-knife combo.

Early 1800s: Forks start to catch on in America, but are called "split spoons."

1900: All hail that cafeteria favorite—the spork. Half spoon, half fork, all fun.

1920s: Stainless steel is invented. Portable plastic forks and knives follow soon.

CUT IT OUT!

For thousands of years, most men carried a knife with them at all times. Knives were great for slitting an enemy's throat. Then, with a quick wipe on a sleeve, they could be used to slice some fruit for dinner. We can only hope they wiped the dried animal guts off first! Early knives had a really sharp point but you've probably noticed that your table knife is rounded at the tip. Here's why (or so the story goes).

One evening in the 1630s, the very rich, very powerful, *very* famous Duc de Richelieu got skeeved out at the dinner table. One of his guests had taken his dinner knife and was picking the crud out of his teeth with it. Another was cleaning the dirt from under his fingernails. The Duc was horrified and ordered that all the knives in his house have the tips rounded off. Naturally, all of France wanted to be just like the Duc and they quickly did the same. And *voilà*—knives with round ends!

GET YOUR ELBOWS OFF THE TABLE!

Until 1900 most people were lucky to have a fork, spoon, and knife. But suddenly, folks went

If only I had a fork. Or a spoon. Or a bath, for that matter!

MANNERS MATTERED

Moms have been yelling at their kids for centuries about their table behavior. Here's proof—actual rules from European table manner guides that date back several centuries. (Remember—at mealtimes everyone usually shared one big plate.)

- From the 13th century:
    Do not fall upon a dish like a swine, while eating, or snorting disgustedly

    Do not gnaw on a bone and then put it back in the dish

- From the 14th century:
    Do not blow your nose in the tablecloth*

- From the 15th century:
    Do not put back on the plate what has been in your mouth

*Nose blowing at the table was a big no-no. But what if you had to? It was quite acceptable to blow your nose into your fingers. There were no tissues in those days and hardly anyone had handkerchiefs either.

cutlery-crazy, first in Europe and then here in America. It was time when people liked all sorts of fancy and ornate things, so why not do the same at the dinner table. There were special sardine forks, snail forks, jelly spoons, cream-soup spoons, regular soup spoons, cake forks, salad forks, and more.

Sit down to chow-down at a fancy dinner party in the early 1900s and there'd be silverware stretching to the right and left of you. And pick up the wrong fork, and have everyone gasp in horror at how *bad* your table manners were! No one knew which one to use first!

So, lucky you. Your choices are pretty simple. Big fork for dinner. Small fork for cake! No elbows please. And burp at your own risk!

TICKIN' TIME

All day long we stare at those slowly changing numbers on the wall, just waiting for those magic digits to appear—3 o'clock! Yippee! School's out! But what did folks do before there were clocks? How did they know when it was time for recess?

Think about it. Unless you need to catch a train or plane . . . unless you have a dentist's appointment . . . unless you're trying to win an Olympic gold medal in downhill skiing, do you *really* need to know what time it is? Does it really matter if it's 10:47 or 10:56 or, for that matter, 4:42? And who decided what time it is, anyway?

WHAT MAKES US TICK?

People living in early civilizations had it easy. They woke with the light and went to sleep when it got dark. But as religions evolved and rituals grew, as villages turned into big cities, folks began to realize that it might be handy to have *some* way to know exactly when the shops opened or prayer services were about to begin. So they began to try to measure and keep track of the passing of a day. But how do you measure something you can't see?

Think about what makes a clock a clock. First, it has to measure something that doesn't speed up or slow down—something constant. Long ago, in parts of Asia, people tied knots every few inches along a length of slow-burning cord and set fire to the cord. As each knot burned up, they would know that another "hour" had passed. But honestly—try walking around with a burning rope tied to your wrist. Talk about painful!

The second thing you need for a clock is some way to display the measured time. The sun in the sky doesn't work because there are no fixed markings. A burning candle *might* work, if you marked lines in equal places around it. But would you really want to carry a burning candle all day long?

SUNNY DE-LIGHT

Stick a baseball bat in the dirt and watch what happens on a sunny day. The sun casts a shadow that moves in a circle around the bat. By 3500 B.C.E. the Egyptians were very sun-savvy. They also liked to build giant things. Among their favorite structures were huge obelisks, which cast enormous shadows— shadows that moved as the day progressed. The Egyptians made elaborate sets of lines radiating out from around the bases of their

Day clock. *Sundials were how folks told "day" time for centuries.*

obelisks. Now passersby could see that it was six marks past the middle—time to stop for a snack!

By 1500 B.C.E., Egyptian smarties had discovered that small pointy things made a shadow you could "read" just as well as giant ones. These smaller sundial and shadow clocks were cool, because now everyone could have one.

But what about nighttime? And what about cloudy days? How were you supposed to know whether or not you were on time for that big chariot race if the sun wasn't shining?

DRIP, DRIP, DRIP . . .

One day a clever Egyptian noticed that a clay pot with a tiny hole at the bottom dripped water at a very regular rate. Now there was an idea! Draw a series of lines on a pot, kind of like a ruler down the side, and measure the time it takes for all the water to drip out. By 1400 B.C.E. folks were using the *clepsydra* to measure time. Clepsydras were water clocks and the Egyptians quickly moved from the simple—two pots, one of which emptied out to the other— to a much more complicated gizmo

(in which the water dripped onto a wheel that pushed a round dial). Now folks could tell the time, even late at night. Cool!

TRY THIS!

X-PERIMENT: IT'S POTTY TIME

Want to see how some of the first clepsydras worked? Go to your bathroom and lift the top of the toilet tank. Careful . . . it's heavy, don't let it drop! Now look inside and you'll see a stick with a floating ball-thingy on the end of it. Give the toilet a flush. The ball will drop down, then slowly start to rise as the water fills the tank. Now imagine a *huge* toilet-bowl tank in which the water drips in at a very even rate. Some clepsydras worked just like this, using a pointer attached to a rising float to mark the time.

THE SANDS OF TIME

Sand provided another great way to mark the time. No one knows who thought of it or where it first happened, but I'm gonna guess it was a place with lots of sand. People began to make giant hourglasses that used sand slithering through a tiny opening from one end to the other. Hourglasses were a big hit aboard ships, where *watches*—a period of time when a soldier was on duty—were soon divided into six four-hour-long chunks, or the time it took a large hourglass to empty. Ships also had a half-hour glass, and every time that one emptied, a bell was rung as it was flipped over. But if you spent all your time *watching* the time, you were *wasting* time. There had to be a better way!

WHAT'S WITH THE 60s?

Sixty seconds in a minute. Sixty minutes in an hour. Why not 42, or 90, or 27? Well, 4,000 years ago, the folks who lived in Mesopotamia (near what is now Iraq) were some of the very first city dwellers. They sure did like to shop! And because they *loved* to shop and spend money, they needed to count. They needed math.

We use base 10 for our math systems, a system that grew in many different parts of the world for one simple reason. Believe it or not, it's because we have ten fingers. Some civilizations, such as the Inca in South America, used base 20 (ten fingers and ten toes). But the guys and gals in Mesopotamia were big on base 60.

No one is sure exactly why. Some historians think they used their fingers as kind of built-in calculators. Not counting the thumb, each finger has three jointed sections. Count those sections and you have 12 chunks. Using the fingers on your other hand as multipliers, and you get $12 \times 5 = 60$. You can easily count to 60 simply by pointing at one of the 12 parts of the fingers on one hand with one of the five fingers on the other.

Anyway, the Mesopotamians were the ones who came up with the 60-minute hour. They are also the folks who divided a circle into 360 degrees. They divided their money into units of 60. And they were the ones who divided the year into 12 months with 30 days each—360 days. Sixty rocked for these dudes!

By the way, if you want to dazzle grown-ups, drop this smart-bomb on them: We use the decimal system in most of our everyday activities, but we tell time with a sexagesimal (*sex-uh-GUESS-eh-mul*) system.

IT'S TICK-TOCK TIME

Around 1285 C.E., something new popped up on the time-telling scene—the first mechanical clocks. Now instead of water moving the parts, a series of metal springs uncoiled. When the coil unwound, you twisted a little knob to wind it back up again. By 1335, the first public mechanical clock was dinging away the hours of the day, but it only had one hand. You got the hour, and that was all!

Turns out there were other ways to make clocks work, such as *pendulums.* A pendulum swings from side to side, and as it swings, it turns a wheel with teeny-tiny teeth. That turning wheel moves the hands on the clock. Among the first pendulum clock designers was Galileo Galilei, a great sci-guy. (He's the fellow who invented the telescope, then figured out that the Earth was not the center of the universe, which was such shocking news that he ended up getting arrested and sentenced to death for announcing it. But that's another story.) Anyway, in the 1580s Galileo started working on a pendulum clock, but he died before he could finish it.

By the mid-1600s, a guy named Christiaan Huygens had built a pendulum clock that had an error of less than one minute a day—by far the most accurate clock that had been invented. Now that clocks actually kept *accurate* time, you could divide an hour into 60 little parts called *minutes,* and know they'd always be the same length. The clever A.M.s and P.M.s (*Ante* and *Post Meridiem*—Latin for before and after noon) were invented so that a clock dial with only 12 hours marked on it instead of a complicated 24 could be used all day long. Clocks were becoming a must-have—something every town wanted.

MY MAYOR'S IS BIGGER THAN YOUR MAYOR'S

In the 1500s every European town developed clock-envy. Every mayor wanted a big clock in the town square—a bigger clock than the other towns had. Many towns went broke building their clocks. The typical town clock was a four-sided tower with clocks on each side. Extra taxes were paid by the people living on the streets each clock faced. In many towns, it wasn't unusual to see a blank side because that quarter of the town wouldn't fork over their clock cash. Talk about cheap!

By the 1700s most towns had a clock, and each of them was set by figuring out when high noon was in that particular place. Trouble was, noon in Boston came at a slightly different time than noon in Philadelphia. Still, this really wasn't much of a problem until the railroads came to town.

Time for a tumble? This famous movie scene had audiences howling!

WHEN'S THE NEXT TRAIN?

Trains made a mess of telling time, especially when they started covering long distances. For a while every train station had two clocks ticking away, one that showed local time and one that showed "train time." Railroad workers were getting huge headaches trying to figure out when the darn train was due! So the railroad industry began pushing a new idea: standardized time zones.

In 1884, most of the world's countries with rail lines got together and decided that a spot outside London, England, would be the starting point (or the "prime meridian") for the world's "day." The world

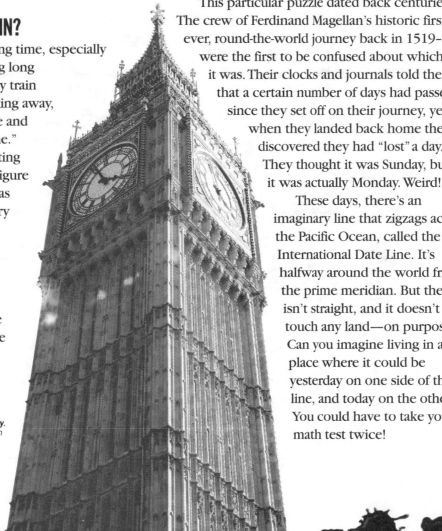

Big Ben bangs boomingly. The most famous clock in the world is in London, England.

was carved into 24 time zones. But there was still one other matter to be decided. Where would today end and tomorrow begin?

This particular puzzle dated back centuries. The crew of Ferdinand Magellan's historic first-ever, round-the-world journey back in 1519–1521 were the first to be confused about which day it was. Their clocks and journals told them that a certain number of days had passed since they set off on their journey, yet when they landed back home they discovered they had "lost" a day. They thought it was Sunday, but it was actually Monday. Weird!

These days, there's an imaginary line that zigzags across the Pacific Ocean, called the International Date Line. It's halfway around the world from the prime meridian. But the line isn't straight, and it doesn't touch any land—on purpose. Can you imagine living in a place where it could be yesterday on one side of the line, and today on the other? You could have to take your math test twice!

SAVING THE DAY (LIGHT)

As winter comes closer, the days get shorter. Is it better to go to school in the pitch dark? Or does it make more sense to "push" time so that you can wake up and not feel like a naked mole rat living in an underground burrow? Daylight Saving Time was first suggested by Ben Franklin in the late 1700s—as a joke. He was a real night owl and often stayed up really late. One *very* late night, he forgot to close his window shutters and was awakened

WHEN BIGGER WAS BETTER

Nowadays we love our teeny timepieces. But way back when? Bring on the giant clocks!

Stonehenge: Many people believe Stonehenge (built in present-day England in three stages between 5000 B.C.E. and 1500 B.C.E.) was a giant clock of some sort. One "time" it definitely told was the first day of summer, since a special stone was positioned to be hit at just the right angle by the rising sun.

Season clock. Stonehenge tells the start of summer.

The Snake Pyramid: The Mayas also had a way of telling when the seasons were changing. On the days of the spring and autumn equinox, the play of light and shadow on the giant Pyramid of the Serpent at Chichén-Itzá in Mexico looks just like a snake slithering down the steps.

The Tower of the Winds: The Greeks needed a clock in their busiest marketplace, so they built this biggie—four stories high—with a giant clepsydra inside it. Gotta wonder if that drip-drip-dripping made the Athenians feel like they had to pee all the time.

Su Sung's tower: By the year 1000, clocks in China were really fancy. One of the fanciest was built in 1088. The Su Sung clock tower was over 30 feet tall. It had a cool, spinning globe on top, and five doors that opened to reveal dolls that rang gongs and held little signs indicating the time.

Big Ben: It's the most famous clock in the world, but "Ben" is actually the name of the 30,000+ pound bell (or the *cloca* if you want to go all ancient on me) that chimes the hour. The actual name of the whole shebang is St. Stephen's Tower. During World War II, as German bombers tried to flatten London, the clock managed to withstand the near-miss attacks of dozens of planes. Didn't even slow it down! But in 1949, a flock of birds parked themselves on the minute hand and stopped time for almost five minutes. That was one of the few times Big Ben went bonkers.

I'M ALARMED

The very first alarm clock was invented in 1787 by Levi Hutchins of Concord, New Hampshire. One teeny problem, though. He could only get his alarm to ring at one time—4 A.M.! Well, at least he was up with the chickens!

by bright sunlight streaming into his room at 6 A.M. He had wanted to sleep late, so he wrote a joking editorial for a newspaper about moving the clocks back an hour. It took more than 100 years, but his joke of an idea eventually caught on after a British dude named William Willet kept yelling that people were wasting valuable daylight by pulling down their shades and sleeping.

Americans first began moving their clocks' big hands back and forth in 1918. We were in the thick of World War I and the government knew that we could save the precious energy that generated electricity to light homes if it stayed light later in the evening. By 1942 we were at war yet again—this time World War II. And again the U.S. Congress ordered us to push the clocks ahead to "save" light. The clocks stayed that way until 1945 and the war's end.

Over in England, they went even further. They pushed their clocks' big hands ahead two hours during the war and called it double summertime (sounds great!). But even in dreary, cold, dark winter, the clocks stayed set ahead.

After the war ended, clocks were all reset back to plain old, year-round regular time. No more U.S. laws about Daylight Saving Time. States and towns could choose to use Daylight Saving Time or not. And what a mess that made! For example, on one 35-mile stretch of highway between West Virginia and Ohio, drivers passed through *seven* time changes as some towns used daylight savings time and others didn't.

Finally the U.S. government stepped in again, and passed the Uniform Time Act of 1966. Keeping time wasn't a local matter anymore. Even so, parts of Arizona and Indiana and Hawaii still said, "No thanks, gov. We'll stick with what we got!" after filing petitions to the government to make them exempt.

WHICH WAY DO I MOVE THAT HAND?

Changing the time at "fall back" and "spring ahead" still creates chaos every year. When our clocks are set back in the fall, every on-time Amtrak train stops running at 2 A.M. and sits on its tracks for one hour to get back "on schedule." What do you do about people who work through the middle of the night? Do they get paid for an extra hour in the fall? Do they get gypped in the spring? And every year, the candy companies tried to get the U.S. government to wait just a few more days before pushing the clocks back. Why? Because Halloween always falls just *after* the time change. Some parents won't let their kids trick-or-treat after dark. So one extra hour would mean more time to go door to door, and a lot more candy corn in those plastic pumpkins!

Did candy win? Starting in fall of 2007, the rules changed again. Daylight Saving Time was extended one month. It begins for most of the United States at 2 A.M. on the second Sunday in March and ends at 2 A.M. on the first Sunday of November. Trick or treat triumphs!

ONE OF THESE POST CARDS FREE INSIDE

"SAVING DAYLIGHT!"

Sign and Mail one of these Post Cards to Your Congressman at Washington and help make it a National Law to SET THE CLOCK ONE HOUR AHEAD

United Cigar Stores Company

Spring ahead. Daylight Saving Time was started in 1918.

WEARABLE CLOCKS

As clockmakers got better at what they did, they learned to make their timepieces smaller and smaller. Soon there were portable clocks called *pocket watches*. Blaise Pascal, a French math whiz, started a whole new fad. He tied his pocket watch to his wrist with string. No wonder everyone says he was a genius!

Wristwatches were considered "girlie" for a very long time. "Real men" wouldn't be caught dead wearing one. It wasn't until the first airplane pioneers started swooping around through the clouds that wristwatches really caught on with men *and* women. After all, when you have both hands on the controls of an airplane, you can't exactly let go and dig around in your pocket for a clock.

Nowadays we have battery-run clocks and atomic clocks that can keep incredibly precise time. Computers and cell phones have time displays. And just about everything we do is controlled by the time, from our schedules at school to when a plane takes off to watching TV to watching the seconds tick down at the Super Bowl. And now, it's *time* to move on to the next entry: Toilet Paper!

TOILET PAPER

We humans are the only species with the ability to wipe our behinds—something that, say, a gerbil cannot do. But do you *really* want to stick your fingers in those places? So, for a really long time, people wiped with whatever was handy—leaves, a branch, or yesterday's very scratchy newspaper.

Read on to unroll the ways the past brought us double-ply, super-soft, comfort-quilted, decorator-colored toilet paper!

WIPE-OUT!

We will never know when the first person decided that having dingly-dangly poo-bits wobbling from his or her backside was *not* cool, and grabbed a stick (or a leaf or a rock) to flick it away. In the old days, where you lived determined what you wiped with. People who lived near the sea used seashells. Folks in the tropics used bits of coconut husk. If you were a king, you might have a royal servant wipe your backside with fine lace or wool. (Wow, what a great job!)

Who needs privacy? This king has his posse waiting on his poop.

BEASTLY BIT

Why do we shake hands with our right hands? Some historians say it's because for centuries, in many parts of the world, the left hand was considered "the wiping hand." Unless you were left-handed, you wiped with your left hand because you did everything else with the right—like putting food in your mouth. And you do *not* want the hand that feeds you to be the hand that wipes. In many places around the world today, it is still considered impolite to use the left hand for eating or for touching others.

ROLLING THROUGH T.P.'S PAST

Here's a Short History of Butt-Wiping!

The Chinese, inventors of gunpowder, the compass, and (fanfare, please) paper—were the very first people to use paper for wiping messy behinds. As early as 200 B.C.E., royals were using toilets with running water and cleaning up the end results with thin pieces of paper. By the late 1300s, the Bureau of Imperial Supplies was producing toilet paper for the emperor and his family. The Chinese, living in one of the biggest countries on Earth, naturally had big toilet paper, too. Each sheet measured a whopping two feet by three feet! You could wipe an elephant's butt with a piece that size!

In Ancient Rome, public toilets usually had a sea sponge tied to a stick that was left soaking in a bucket of salty water. Wealthier Romans preferred a hunk of discarded sheep's wool dipped in rosewater.

During the Middle Ages folks in Arab lands liked to go natural, wiping with small smooth stones or a handful of earth, followed by a rinse of water and a few pats with a strip of linen.

In the Late Middle Ages in France, a clever person invents the *bidet* (*bee-DAY*), a tiny little butt-shaped bathtub that is used for a quick tushy-shower after going number two. The bidet is still a standard fixture in most French homes.

In the 1500s and 1600s, Spanish and Portuguese sailors at sea for months on end found that the frayed ends of old ropes were perfect butt-wipers.

In Colonial America, corncobs were early favorites as wipers, but as newspapers gained in popularity, they become a better choice. By the late 1800s the Sears catalog had become a bathroom favorite, until they started making it with shiny paper in the 1930s. The Sears folks got *major* complaints about the poor wipe-ability of the pages!

TYRANT-PAPER

During World War II, many a patriot wiped with toilet paper imprinted with evil Adolf Hitler's face on it. And after terrorists attacked the World Trade Center and the Pentagon on September 11, 2001, toilet paper with Osama bin Laden's face was a brisk seller.

In 1857, a fastidious fellow named Joseph Gayetty started selling the first paper made specifically for butt-wiping. It came in 500-sheet packets but the product was a failure. Most Americans couldn't understand why you would want to buy brand-new blank paper to wipe your butt when you could just use leftover paper scraps.

After being patented on July 20, 1871, rolled toilet paper as we know it made its debut. By the early 1880s, Albany Medicated Toilet Paper was promising that each wipe with their paper would help cure *hemorrhoids*—pesky swollen veins in the butt area that some grown-ups get from not eating enough prunes. But at 50 cents a roll, it was the same price as a dining-room chair. Sales were as sluggish as a constipated cow.

By the mid-1800s, Ed and Clarence Scott started to make bathroom history by selling *small* rolls of paper wrapped in unmarked brown wrappers. The thing is, even though everyone knows that *everyone* poops, most people do not want to admit that they do. Anyway, the small, unmarked rolls started to catch on (because they were so discreet). But you know the crunchy crêpe paper used to decorate for birthday parties? Try wiping your butt with that stuff and you'll have an idea of the quality of the first Scott tissues.

In the late 1880s, over in Europe toilet paper was still slow to catch on. One dad told his kids to wipe with pages from old books—learning a little poetry with each poop! European toilet paper, *if* you could find it, was sold in squares—splintery, rough, unpleasant-to-use squares. To this day, the quality of European toilet paper is not what it is here in the good ol' U.S.A.

By the 1930s, advertisements in America's magazines were singing the praises of something new! Splinter-free toilet tissue! One popular magazine ad read, "They have a pretty house, Mother, but their bathroom paper hurts." We were on our way to squeezable, huggable potty paper.

In 1964 one of the high points in toilet paper history arrived with the creation of Mr. Whipple and his "Please don't squeeze the Charmin" ad. Mr. Whipple became the third most recognized name in America—behind President Nixon and the Reverend Billy Graham.

A LITTLE SOMETHING FOR "THE HELP"

Here's a great moment in the annals of toilet hygiene! When Peter the Great, the czar of Russia, visited Paris in 1717, he wanted to leave a tip for the men's room attendant. Now mind you, there were no flush toilets in those days. After taking a dump, Peter had asked the attendant for something to wipe with. Alas, there was nothing

A NASTY NOTE

According to the makers of Charmin, the average person uses 8.6 sheets per trip to the can—a total of 57 sheets per day for an annual total of 20,805 sheets. And an unofficial survey of 109 people found that most folks take a look at what they have wiped before depositing the paper in the potty. Pee-yew!

available, so the czar pulled out a 100-franc note (like our $100 bill) and wiped with that. He then offered the used bill to the attendant as a tip. The attendant didn't want to touch it, so he said he wasn't allowed to take tips. In disgust, Peter the Great threw the poop-smeared bill on the floor. What would *you* do? (P.S.: The guy picked it up—without touching it directly, I hope!—after his boss pointed out that when it was washed and dried, it would buy some pretty nice stuff!)

PAPER CUTS ON THEIR BUTTS

War is a messy business, no doubt about it. And for Lt. Commander James Coe of the USS *Skipjack,* a submarine on patrol in the South Pacific during World War II in the early 1940s, it was also getting very embarrassing. He had written to the supply office at a naval base near San Francisco requesting toilet paper for his crew. *Eleven months later* he received a letter back saying that his requisition was being returned because the item in question (toilet paper, for gosh sakes!) was a material that "could not be identified."

Lt. Commander Coe wrote back, this time attaching a precious square of toilet paper to his letter, along with this note: ". . . cannot help but wonder what is being used in Mare Island in place of this unidentifiable material . . ." Coe's "toilet paper" letter reached the Mare Island Supply Depot and news of the toilet paper snafu soon spread throughout the fleet, even reaching President Franklin D. Roosevelt. When the *Skipjack* came in from her next patrol, Jim Coe and his crew were greeted by an amazing sight. Toilet paper streamers waved from the lights along the pier. There was a seven-foot-high pyramid made from toilet paper rolls. Two men carried a long pole with rolls of toilet paper fluttering in the wind. There was a band wearing toilet paper neckties instead of the usual Navy neckerchiefs. The brass players had stuffed squares of toilet paper into their horns, and

every time they played, puffs of paper showered out. It was a TP bonanza! The crew of the *Skipjack* had spent almost a year without toilet paper. But that "21 toilet-roll salute" almost made up for all the paper cuts on the sailors' once-tender tushies.

YOU DON'T KNOW WHAT YOU GOT 'TIL IT'S GONE

Some of the scariest moments in recent history have occurred when toilet paper—that stuff we all take for granted—has disappeared. Don't think it can happen? Read on!

During World War II there were lots of products in short supply: tin, paper, nylon, wire. It was all going towards the war effort, being used to build ships and planes and parachutes. Folks had to learn to do without a lot of things, including TP. And if they tried to hoard it, they were accused of being unpatriotic!

Let's zip to 1973—a time when there were gasoline shortages and people had to line up to buy gasoline. One of the most popular TV shows at the time was *The Tonight Show with Johnny Carson.* (Almost 20 million people watched every night.) One night, Johnny began his opening monologue by saying that there was terrible shortage of toilet paper in the United States. By the following day, supermarket shelves had been stripped bare. You could not find a single roll to buy! It got so bad that Johnny had to go back on the air and explain that there was no shortage ("It was a joke!"), but the public still wasn't convinced. Scott Paper had to air filmed footage of its factories spewing out paper as fast as they could, but the panic continued for weeks.

If you are reading this in the bathroom (and it *is* perfect bathroom reading), as you wipe, think about all those who have wiped before you with corn cobs and catalogs and leaves! And remember to wash your hands!!!!!!

U

UGH! UNDERWEAR

I see London. I see France. But ick! What's with your underpants?

Itchy, woolen union suits. "Tighty-whiteys." BVDs. Bikinis and thongs. Undies have had a pretty amazing past. In fact, you won't believe some of the things folks have pulled on under their clothes. Or NOT!

LOINCLOTHS AND SUBLIGACULUM

As far back as cave-dwelling times, folks have been covering up their private parts. But no cushy, comfy cotton for them. Way back when, folks wore leather *loincloths.* (Loins are the part of the body that starts at the bottom of the rib cage and goes to the tops of the legs, including your very juicy rump area.) Loincloths were lengths of material that got wrapped around that mid-part, kind of like a grown-up diaper. For 7,000 years, loincloths ruled (and they still do in parts of the world today). But *leather* underwear can get a little warm and sticky, and no one really wants sweaty loins. So when the Egyptians figured out how to make linen fabric, folks sighed a breath of relief. Ancient Egyptian loincloths were shaped like a big triangle, with strings coming off the long ends that then got tied around the hips or waist. The hunk of linen cloth hanging down in back was brought forward between the legs and tucked over the tied strings from the outside in.

Women in Egypt went underpant-less. By gladiator times in ancient Rome, the panties of choice were called *subligaculum,* which means "little binding underneath." Subligaculum were shorts or loincloths worn under a toga or tunic. But macho Roman guys decided that wearing absolutely *nothing* under their tunics was much cooler than wearing loincloths. As for Roman women, well, they went underpantless for quite some time, too.

At first, folks wore long robes over their braies, but in the 1300s, the styles changed. *Chausse* (kind of like really high knee-socks) became popular, and showing off a lot of leg became the style. So now, you have men in stockings, pulled over braies. In the meantime, men's tops kept getting shorter and shorter. Suddenly, the tops were so short, they weren't covering a man's loins, and you could see parts of a person that most people consider very *private*. Which leads us to one of the weirdest bits of underwear ever invented.

ATHLETES IN UNDERPANTS

Sumo wrestlers grunt, groan, shove, and push in underpants (and they are *not* sitting on the potty while they are doing this). Sumo wrestlers wear a loincloth called a *fundoshi,* a rectangle of cotton that is between 6 and 10 inches wide and 8 feet long. Until the 1940s, these were the traditional underpants of Japan—what *every* guy wore under his kimono. It's tough to pull on a fundoshi. You actually need to use your teeth to hold the fabric ends! (Sprint on over to STRANGE SPORTS on page 248 for more on sumo.)

LETTING IT ALL HANG OUT

And so it went in Europe for 1,000 years. Finally, around 1200 C.E., the first underpants that sort of look like the ones we wear today were invented in Persia (modern-day Iran). Men started to wear large baggy linen pants called *braies* under their robes and tunics. Braies were eventually called "drawers" because a guy *drew* on first one leg, then the other. For the next 800 years, drawers were what fellas in Europe wore. Imagine really baggy pajama pants that tie at the waist and have a little opening for peeing.

IF YOU'VE GOT IT, FLAUNT IT! (IF YOU DON'T, PAD IT!)

Okay. This is going to be a little . . . ahem . . . delicate. You know how many athletes wear a hard little cup to protect the part of a guy's body that needs the most protection? Well, by the 1400s, men's tops were so short, they weren't even covering their undies. Beginning

Jock strap on the outside, aka codpiece: 'Cause you never know when someone is going to make a sudden move.

in the 1300s, men started wearing cups called *codpieces,* over their braies. At first these cups were just big enough to fit over the parts they were covering. But naturally, since folks like to brag, the codpieces started getting bigger and bigger. Flashier, too! In 1482, King Edward IV even passed a law that men *had* to cover their peeing parts. It was actually against the law to go without a codpiece if you were a man in England. For the next 200 years, the codpiece was a big fashion *must.*

Most codpieces were padded. Some even had pockets sewn into them—a handy place to

WORD UP!

Long johns are cozy on a chilly day. But they got their name from a sweaty boxer named John L. Sullivan, one of the most famous fighters ever, who threw his punches in the late 1800s. John boxed in his underwear— long wool drawers—and that's why they're called "long johns." After Sullivan called it quits, American boxers started showing up to fights in, yup, you guessed it, boxer shorts.

keep coins and candy. Jewel-studded codpieces also were a hit among the rich. As the years went by, the codpieces got bigger and bigger, and really silly-looking. Finally, in the late 1500s, priests started speaking out about the stupidity of all that padding. In the meantime, braies grew pouffier and pouffier and grew into *breeches,* which soon were dubbed *pantaloons.* And the codpiece went bye-bye, but not completely. After all, where would male athletes be today without their handy jockstraps? Probably in a lot of pain!

GREAT MOMENTS IN UNDERWEAR

■ We salute Eli Whitney. His invention of the cotton gin in 1793 helped make it easier to produce cotton fabric. Kudos also to Elias Howe, who unveiled his spiffy sewing machine in 1846. Factories full of his sewing machines could mass-produce things like panties and briefs.

■ In the late 1800s, "union suits" were all the rage. Grown-ups and kids alike wore these one-piece garments that covered folks from wrist to ankle, complete with a handy drop-down butt-flap so the wearer could go number two without having to take off every stitch of clothing. They were called "union suits" not because there were worn in the North or produced in unionized factories, but because the top and bottom pieces were *united* into one piece. They were a huge hit! Union suits came in rusty red and dirty beige, and eventually, in knee-length, short-sleeved versions.

■ It wasn't until the 1930s that the word *underpants* entered the dictionary. About the

same time, the creation of elastic meant the end of underpants that buttoned, snapped, or tied shut. A company called Jockey started to make undies with a clever little Y vent, to make it easier for guys to "go." In fact, when the first pairs of Jockey's hit a department store in Chicago, they were such a sensation that they sold out almost instantly even though there was a major blizzard on the day they arrived.

■ "Day of the Week" underpants were a craze in the 1950s. Each pair of underpants in the set of seven was labeled with a different day of the week. Woe to the girl who wore her Thursday panties on Monday!

■ Have you ever owned a pair of Underoos? In 1978 kids discovered the thrill of wearing super-power undies. Mom might make you dress like a dork, but underneath you knew you were cool in those Batman or Wonder Woman briefs!

■ Today some people like to go *commando,* which means they are not wearing any underwear at all. It's very historic when you think about it, but still, rather *eee-uw.*

Waist not, want not. *The ideal gal in 1900 has a waist the size of a kindergartner's.*

WHY SHOULD GUYS HAVE ALL THE FUN?

What about girls? Ladies may not have worn underpants in times gone by, but they had a whole lot of other dumb underthings to wear. Painful, itchy, scratchy, and even downright dangerous things.

Take corsets, a super-tight garment that was laced around a woman's middle to make her a size and shape she was never meant to be. It all began in the 1500s, when Queen Elizabeth I started wearing a flat board-shaped accessory called a *busk*.

Busks were made to flatten a woman's front. Now, if you have ever looked at a grown woman, you will probably notice that most ladies are curvy and round. Busks made women's chests look like planks of wood, and they were one of the original undergarments to introduce women to the idea that being beautiful requires *pain*.

Soon women were getting laced up like too-tight sneakers, in corsets made of whalebone, animal bone, wood, and even steel. By the 1550s, royal women were yanking on steel *stomachers*—metal cases, hinged on one side, and fastened on the other by clasps, encasing a gal's entire mid-section. In the 1700s, a tiny waist was *the* symbol of beauty, and corsets were laced even tighter than in previous centuries. Tight corsets made it difficult to breathe. They squished a woman's internal organs and could, on occasion, even snap a rib!

HIP, HIP, HOORAY!

One way to make your waist look teeny is to make your hips look huge. But can you imagine being so hippy that you couldn't walk through a door? In France in the 1700s, that was the in style. But how do you get hips the size of a car? Underwear! French women (and soon wealthy women all over Europe) began to wear giant hoops under their skirts called *farthingales.* Less well-to-do ladies simply added a fat, round, padded pillow, called a *bum roll,* around their hips to make their skirts stick out and their waists look smaller.

Around 1750 an undergarment called the *pannier* (which means "basket") came into style for women. Some were funnel-shaped, and others were just super-wide—with the largest ones reaching a circumference of 18 feet! Some were called elbow panniers because women could (and did) rest their elbows on them. It was like walking around with a kitchen counter attached to you. And forget about sitting down!

And there was more torment ahead! In 1780, dress designers decided that big butts were the next *big* thing, so the first *bustles* (BUS-elz) were strapped on. Women no longer had rear ends; now they had shelves! Picture a birdcage made of wire and whalebone trapped to a women's derrière, and you will have a picture of a bustle. It took the French Revolution, the Reign of Terror, and that gory GUILLOTINE (see page 108) to stop this particular bit of under-silliness. And for a few years in the early 1800s, women were actually woman-shaped. Naturally, though, that did not last.

UNDER-WHAT?

By the 1800s women were *still* not wearing underpants. They wore a *shift* (kind of like a giant cotton nightgown) under their clothes, along with several petticoats and stockings. It wasn't until the 1830s that the first women's pants, called *pantalets,* appeared. Even then, they were frilly bits just for show that covered the legs but nothing else.

In the 1840s, skirts started getting wide again. At first women would wear five or six petticoats under their dresses to give them fullness. Then came the *crinoline,* which got its name because it was made of *crin*—the French word for horsehair. Imagine wearing a cactus under your clothes. That's what crin feels like!

By the 1860s, women were wearing lace-trimmed cotton drawers under a cage-like frame of steel hoops, and skirts that were mega-wide. It was not unusual to have a skirt that needed more than 10 yards of fabric. Try walking around in something the size of a circus tent! One strong gust of wind, and a gal could end up airborne.

FOR THE SAKE OF THE SOLDIERS . . .

World War I was called the "War to End All Wars." Unfortunately, it didn't. But it did change underwear. For one thing, all the metal that had been going into corsets and bustles was needed for the war effort. In 1917, the United States War Industries Board pleaded with women to stop wearing heavy metal, and in one year alone,

WHAT IS UNDER THOSE KILTS?

Is it true that a kilt is worn without underpants? Originally Scotsmen wore *trews* underneath their kilts—a Celtic garment consisting of loose-fitting breeches and hose, knitted into one piece. But as many a brisk breeze on the Scottish Highlands has revealed, many real Scotsmen don't wear diddly beneath their plaids!

managed to free up 28,000 *tons* of steel—enough to help build two battleships. So the enemy was beaten, and women could finally breathe.

During World War II, there was a shortage of rubber to make elastic, so buttoned-up undies came back into use. And underwear started being produced in colors for the first time when soldiers found that hanging out their "tighty-whiteys" was a bad idea—they attracted enemy fire! The military declared olive drab the official men's underwear color. And finally, in another war-and-panties connection, the bikini was invented in 1946 by two Frenchmen who named it after the Bikini Atoll in the Marshall Islands, site of the first test of the atomic bomb. Was it because bikinis were "da bomb"?

V

VICIOUS VIKINGS

SCREAMING MEANIES

Maybe it's the bleak, cold weather in northern Europe. Maybe it's because it's night practically all day long up there for three months of the year. But for whatever reason, between 750 and 1050 C.E., a lot of folks who lived in modern-day Denmark, Sweden, and Norway were downright cranky a lot of the time.

Some of them dealt with the fact that they were living in an icebox for half the year by getting the heck out. They learned to build amazing sailing ships, and they were outta there! The Norsemen ("people of the North") who sailed on these vessels were called Vikings. Vikings lusted for loot and plotted pillage. Think pirates, minus the eye patches.

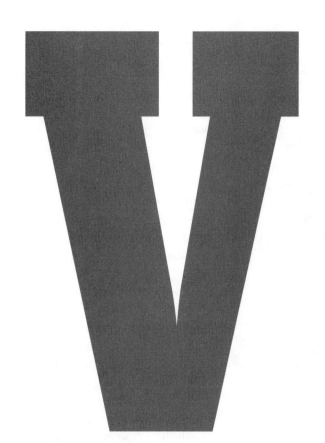

Are you the kind of kid who likes to run screaming through the streets, yelling at the top of your lungs, waving your arms like a wild thing? If so, you would have made a fabulous Viking. So sharpen an axe, grab a dead animal head—complete with eyeballs and tongue hanging out—and find out if you could have hacked it as a Viking. And I do mean *hacked*.

THE PEE-PEE FRIDGE

Why did these folks take to the water? Well, life was pretty rough in the typical Norse village. The land wasn't great for farming or grazing animals. There weren't many natural resources. The average Norse family lived in a one-room house with no windows and a dirt floor. A fire pit in the center of the room was a combo stove, light, and heat source. A hole at the top of the ceiling was *supposed* to draw the smoke up and out, but a lot of the time all it did was let the snow in. It was dark and chokey-smoky inside. When it was cold outside (which was much of the time), the animals moved indoors with the rest of the family. To top it all off, almost everyone had *lice*—a biting, itch-making parasite that sucks human blood.

Many houses kept a big barrel of the family's pee in a corner. Human pee was so useful! It was collected and saved to clean sheep fleece. (That's because the alkali in human urine reacts with the lanolin in the sheepskin to make a kind of natural soap.) And some archaeologists believe that Norse moms may have stored the family food in barrels of urine to keep it critter free, then rinsed it off when it was time to cook it. Pee-*yew*!

Life was brutal. Life was unpleasant. So the Vikings took to the seas.

CRUISIN' FOR A BRUISIN'

The Vikings were master boat builders. They learned to build sleek, strong sailing ships that were able to handle the roughest oceans *and* the shallowest rivers. In their travels, they

WORD UP!

Ever gone *berserk*? That's a word that means going super-nutsy. Our word *berserk* comes from the Berserkers, a group of *really* wild Viking warriors who wore entire wolf skins—head and all. They worked themselves into such horrible, screaming frenzies that they almost had super-human strength. With eyes rolling, biting the edges of their shields, howling at the tops of their lungs, they were *very* scary dudes. Sometimes their rage was so out of control that they attacked their own friends. Our Wolfman legends—the hairy guy howling at the moon, then chewing other people to shreds—are based on the antics of these truly wild and crazy guys.

LORD OF THE RINGS

J.R.R. Tolkien's *Lord of the Rings* is set in a place called Middle Earth, but he based his stories on a very real time and place—that of the Vikings. Tolkien's characters were based on the Celts (Irish), Anglo-Saxons (British), and, of course, our dear, devilish Vikings.

quickly discovered that one of the best places to stage a raid was at a church or a monastery—places where monks hung out, living peaceful lives of prayer.

Take poor St. Cuthbert's. In the year 789 C.E., three Viking ships appeared on the horizon off the coast of England. A local gentleman went out to greet them and was promptly hacked to pieces. The Church of St. Cuthbert was sacked, the golden crosses and jeweled cups stolen. The priests were sliced to smithereens. And so began the Vikings' trail of terror across England, Scotland, Ireland—and soon, the rest of Europe.

The Catholic Church (the big kahuna of churches in those days) was rich—filthy rich! Although the Vikings had never heard of the Christian God, they soon learned that holy priests and monks—gentle men of prayer—weren't the best fighters.

SHOCK AND AWE

One of the most famous Viking raids came on a summer day in 793, when the monks at England's Lindisfarne monastery looked up from their prayers to find themselves staring at the wrong end of the Vikings' broadswords. What was shocking to everyone was not the fact that the Norse raiders were stealing and murdering. That was pretty common. But attacking

THE VIKING NAME GAME

Every Viking name told a story. And what stories they told! Would *you* wanna mess with someone named Eric Bloodaxe? How about Thorfinn Skullsplitter? There was also Sigurd Sow, a king with a thing for pigs. Then there was Ivar the Boneless, a double-jointed fellow *and* a wicked warrior. There was the peg-legged Onund Treefoot. And let's not forget the ginormous Hrolf the Walker, who was so big that even the dumbest horses ran away when they saw him coming.

Vikings could also be quite mean when it came to naming their slaves. One famous Norse poem told of a slave family where the boys were named Lump, Foul, and Thickard. The girls were called She-Lump, Clump, Beak-nose, and Thicklegs. Nice talk!

churches again and again? That was a whopping no-no!

Now, to be fair, these were pretty whacko times all across Europe. Going a few months without an attack by robbers or raiders was a rarity. Kings from the next realms were always galloping through towns and villages with their soldiers, taking whatever they wanted by force—and always trying to make *you* their newest subject. Kings changed all the time. The only thing that didn't change was the fact that in another year or so, someone else was going to sweep in and make a big mess for the poor peasants to clean up.

The Vikings' war skills were pretty darned impressive. They could actually catch a spear that had been thrown in mid-flight, then hurl it right back at the person who had tossed it. But they were really just one more band of *brigands* (a fancy word for bullies)—the only difference was that they didn't think twice about killing *anyone* that got in their way. And if that anyone was a priest, a nun, or a little baby—well, *hmmph*! Too bad!

For the next hundred years or so, no place was safe from the Vikings' bloody blades and wild ways. Towns were attacked, and anyone who fought back was killed. Any survivors of a Viking raid ended up as some grumpy Norsemen's personal property— his slaves. Slaves were treated just like farm animals. The ones who outlived their usefulness were actually "put to sleep." Permanently!

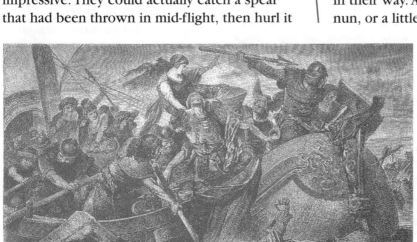

Excuse me while I slaughter you. *Viking raids were truly vicious.*

RING AROUND THE INTESTINES

After a while, a lot of people got sick and tired of the Vikings' bullying. Some fought back and won. After a battle between the Vikings and the Irish army on Good Friday in 1014, some 7,000 Vikings were left dead. The Irish, with only 4,000 dead, did the math and declared themselves the winners. Alas, the Irish could not truly celebrate because their leader, the legendary Brian Boru, had been smashed with an axe and killed. The Irish soldiers were so steamed, however, they took a revenge worthy of the Vikings. They found Boru's killer—a Viking named Brodir—then sliced his belly open, nailed his intestines to a tree, and forced him to march around the tree trunk until he died. That was the last time a Viking fleet messed with the Irish!

In time, even the Vikings got tired of fighting. It was easier to simply threaten to wipe out a town unless money (and lots of it) was forked over. Some towns (wisely) set aside huge sums of money to offer Viking raiders in exchange for being left alive. This seemed like a great idea to the Vikings—sparing the hard work of killing and maiming. Just cold, hard cash. It's kind of like doing that big bully's homework in exchange for being allowed to eat your lunch in peace. Pretty soon, the Vikings were collecting money from towns all over Europe.

THE GOOD WITH THE BAD

Sure, the Vikings were barbaric and brutish. But they were also very smart and totally fearless. As they hacked their way across Europe, they began to build cities, such as York in England and Amsterdam in Holland. They traveled east to Baghdad (in what is now Iraq) and gave Russia its name. They went west to Iceland, Greenland, and started the first European settlements in North America. They also wrote beautiful poetry, and set up vast trading networks.

The Vikings seemed to turn up everywhere. They helped to reconnect a continent that had been plunged into total chaos when Rome fell. Because they were traveling all over the place, picking up ideas at every port, and then moving those ideas all over the continent, they were slowly pushing the world into a new phase. The Vikings helped to strike a giant imaginary match that soon began to light up the Dark Ages.

In time, the Vikings accepted Christianity. After that, the church-looting and much of the killing stopped. And, in a surprise twist, these super sailors actually helped spread Christianity across Europe. How ironic!

MYTH-CONCEPTION

HORN-SWAGGLED

Ever seen the *Hagar the Horrible* comics? You know those goofy curving horns that stick out of his helmet? (If you need a reminder, check out the guy on the left.) Make-believe! The horn-head idea originated as a nineteenth-century opera costume based on archaeological findings at earlier Celtic (Irish) sites. Wrong guys!

BAD TO THE BONE

Just how bad were the Vikings? Here's a taste.

Ivar the Boneless was a master at "carving a blood eagle." He put this skill to good use in 867 C.E., when he and his gang captured King Ella of Northumbria (a part of Britain) and cracked open his rib cage. They then ripped his lungs out of his back, leaving the two lobes flapping like wings every time the dying king took a breath.

One famous Viking chieftain was wild even as a wee lad. When little Egil was just seven, he killed a playmate. By the age of 12, Egil was leading raids across the seas. When his bones were discovered generations later, everyone noticed that the skull was really big and very heavy. So they decided to conduct a little experiment. The skull was set on a churchyard wall and someone started swinging at it with the reverse side of an ax. But as the saga goes, "the skull neither dented nor split." How's that for hard-headed?

A favorite Viking raider "sport" was baby skewering. After the Vikings conquered a town, the helpless little infants were rounded up, then tossed in the air. The object of the "game" was to catch the baby on the point of a spear.

When opportunity knocks, open the door! One Viking sailor named Lika-Lodinn had a great job! He collected the bodies of seamen who had died far from home, then boiled the flesh from their bones to make for lighter transportation back to Viking settlements for a decent burial. For his efforts he was dubbed Corpse-Lodinn.

COLUMBUS, MY FOOT!

Five hundred years before Christopher Columbus "discovered" the Americas, a fellow named Leif Eriksson became the first European to set foot in the "New World" (which was every bit as old as the "Old World") in about 1000 C.E. His dad, Erik the Red, had been exiled for killing a guy, so Leif's family ended up on a hunk of land that the Eriksson's jokingly dubbed "Greenland." Truth is, it was covered with ice and snow. In fact, Greenland was so miserable that Erik's son went looking for some *real* green land. He found it!

Sailing along the edges of the northern coastlines, the Vikings ended up in what is now Newfoundland, a part of eastern Canada. They called this new region Vinland because there were tons of wild grapes growing there—perfect for making *vin,* or wine, as we call it.

Why didn't Leif Eriksson's band of bullies stay in America? Because they ran into an even scarier group: the Indians, or as the Vikings called them, *Skraelings.* One day, the natives attached a huge, black blob to a pole and sent it flying over the heads of Leif's guys. The blob landed with a terrifying screaming noise. It was just an inflated moose bladder, but it really panicked the Vikings. Although they lingered in America for two more years, they finally left because they were worn out by the Skraelings' endless harassment. They could dish it out, but they couldn't take it!

Where the heck are we? *Leif Eriksson wades ashore in a strange new place: America!*

W

WACKY WARFARE

"I saw that wild boar first." "Gronk's cave is drier." "My fabulous sun god is better than your stupid moon goddess." Sadly, folks have been fighting with one another from day one.

Mostly these fights have been about stuff. Land. Castles. Gold. Wives. Sometimes people have fought over ideas. Freedom. Equality. No freedom. No equality. And of course, there have been plenty of "I want to be the king!" battles, too.

You'd think that over the course of centuries, we could find a better way to work out our differences. But noooo! At least not yet.

FIGHT! FIGHT! FIGHT!

Imagine a football game. There are two teams, one on each side of the field. The goal of the game is to get your team onto the other guy's turf, while he tries to keep you out. That was the way armies fought most battles for thousands of years. The warring parties would meet at an agreed-upon time, as rows and rows of foot soldiers with sharp spears lined up. Behind them were guys on horseback with bows and arrows. And way up on a hill somewhere, there were generals calling the plays instead of quarterbacks. They also had some special super-nasty weapons to help them scare the bejeebus out of the other guys.

Now imagine a football game in which one team has the usual pads and helmets, but the other team comes onto the field with giant flamethrowers that can turn a team into actual toast with one explosive launch. Who do *you* think is going to win?

Well, sometimes brains beat back the big guns. But all too often, the guys with the bigger, better weapons have had their way.

282

SUPER SCARY DUDES

You probably think of American Indians when you hear the words *war paint*. But plenty of folks all over the world knew that painting yourself to look wild and crazy can really freak out the enemy. The Visigoths (the guys who helped trash the Roman Empire in the 400s C.E.) dyed their hair blood-red. The Saxons (the early English) preferred blue hair; they grew long, droopy moustaches that they painted blue, too. And the early Gauls (who lived where France is now) wore blue body paint and horned helmets—and nothing else—into battle. Stark, blue naked!

One of the reasons America's first peoples became known as "redskins" was because of one tribe, the Beothuks, who lived in northeastern Canada. They covered every square inch of their bodies and their weapons with red paint made from powdered ochre (a kind of mineral), mixed with fish oil or animal grease. They were so over-the-top with the whole red thing that the Micmacs, another group, called the Beothuks the "Red Indians." These Indians were some of the very first people European fisherman met up with in the 1200–1400s and were the reason Europeans referred to the American Indians as red men.

Other groups had their own unique styles: black circles around one eye, white around the other, stripes everywhere else. Almost every Indian nation had its own unique style—kind of like a painted uniform. Helpful so you didn't attack your own guys!

Some folks took the warpaint thing one step further, to permanent warpaint. We have the folks of Tahiti to thank for the word *tattoo*. In their language, *tatua* means "to mark the skin." People of the Pacific Ocean islands—especially warriors—decorated their bodies with all sorts of zigs and swirls. Native New Zealanders, the Maoris, had some of the fiercest decorations. And they went a step further. Their markings were cut deep into their skin and left raised, ridged scars. To a Maori warrior, a tattooed face was considered groovy. It made a guy extra-fierce in battle.

In the Americas, many a wild warrior tattooed his body. Using animal-bone needles or thorns to pierce the skin, folks would draw eagles, serpents, and dragons on their bodies. Then, while the wounds were still bleeding, they would rub charcoal into them to permanently stain the skin. It was a rite of passage for young warriors that showed how tough they were. Ouch!

GENTLEMEN, CHOOSE YOUR WEAPONS . . .

Every battle, big or small, needs something to battle with: weapons. These gory gadgets started out simple, but grew more complex— and deadly—over time. Bows and arrows got bigger and bigger: Some were almost six feet tall and could launch close to 20 arrows a minute. Those mega-bows gave way to muskets with sharp bayonets on their ends. And *those* made way for semi-automatic

Top gun. *When it comes to weapons, bigger is usually better.*

rifles that could spew out a slew of bullets in a split second. Cannons the size of elephants could shoot cannonballs the size of hippos. And bombs dropped from swooping aircraft could wipe out entire cities in seconds. And then, every so often, someone dreamed up something *so* whacked out that the other army could only shudder and say, "Uh-oh. We're in big trouble now. . . ."

Here are some truly odd ways to scare the enemy into saying, "I give up!"

HOLD YOUR HORSES!

The ancient Greeks were always fighting with their neighbors. Legends tell of one of the world's most famous battles between Greece and a city called Troy (which is in modern-day Turkey). In 1180 B.C.E., something pretty grim happened there—and before you could say "neigh," Troy was totally trashed.

For nine long years, as the story goes, the Greeks and the Trojans kept fighting, fighting, fighting. Then, just like that, the Greeks packed up their ships and sailed away. The Trojans rushed down to the beach to see what had happened. Had the Greeks given up? All they saw was one lonely guy left on the beach moaning about having been left behind. Oh . . . and something else. Something really *big*.

It was a huge statue of a horse, built from the wood of several abandoned ships. The lone leftover soldier kept whining about how he'd been deserted. Still, he assured the Trojans that the horse was meant as a good-luck gift from the defeated Greeks. So the happy Trojans dragged the horse into their city, past the thick walls and the brave guards that had protected them so well from the Greeks. Then everyone partied like crazy and drank way too much wine. They had won! They had beaten off the Greeks. Hooray!

That night, as the Trojans snored, the "left-behind" Greek soldier opened a secret door in the belly of the giant horse. Dozens of Greek warriors tumbled out and went around hacking at the drunk, sleeping Trojans, pretty much wiping out the entire town. To this day, a "Trojan horse" is an expression that means the worst possible kind of surprise.

SIEGE CITY

What do you do when your enemy is tucked happily away inside a castle, with huge walls and smelly moats protecting them? How do you get inside a heavily fortified town with towering gates and highly trained soldiers aiming their weapons right at you? Easy! Just be patient. Sit there and wait. Eventually the people living behind those high walls have to come out to get food and water. Or die!

When armies surrounded a place and set up camp, just far enough away so that the people inside the town couldn't reach

Oh look! Someone left us a present! The Trojan horse turned out to be a nasty surprise.

them with *their* weapons, it was called a *siege* (*seedj*), and warring countries still use this strategy today. Still, sometimes the armies got tired of sitting around, just waiting. It felt better to be able to take action. Here's how they engaged the enemy:

1. Batter Up: Battering rams were huge logs that swung on chains. As they were pulled back then let go, they gathered a ton of force. All the better to blow that door down! *BAM!*

2. Porta-Stairs: Castle walls too high? The Huns (Go, ATTILA!—see page 1 for more on that wily dude) were the first fighters to build siege towers. They were like those old-fashioned airplane stairs—the kind that get rolled out to planes. Except these stairs-inside-a-tower rolled up to castle walls so that soldiers could scamper up, over, and in.

3. The Head-Hurler: Take a slingshot. Now make it big enough to hurl a refrigerator. You're staring at a *catapult* or *trebuchet* (*treh-boo-SHAY*). You

could sling all sorts of things over a wall with one of those suckers. In 1100, short on ammunition during a siege in Turkey, the Crusaders cut the heads off their prisoners and then shot them over the fortress walls. Trebuchets could hurl large boulders that could break a stone wall to smithereens. If you ran low on ammunition, you could hurl all sorts of other goodies, too. During the Middle Ages, trebuchets tossed hives of sting-happy bees, filled-to-the-brim cartloads of doo-doo, or plague-infected corpses.

4. Greek Fire: Imagine a fireball coming at you at full-speed ahead. This hot-as-heck ball first made its flaming appearance in the 600s C.E. when the Byzantines used it to keep the Muslims from taking their capital in Constantinople. It was so top secret that eventually even the Byzantines forgot how to make the stuff. Flaming weapons had been around since the fourth century B.C.E., but Greek fire could not be put out. Throwing water on it only made it burn more and spread faster, and it stuck to whatever it landed on. *Very* nasty stuff!

HAIR TO GO

So what's the deal on scalping? Some historians think fierce guys in Scotland were some of the first people to do it; others point to the Americas, where capturing a warrior's hair in combat was said to destroy his spirit. But a lot of native tribes say the colonists did it first! The whole thing may have started when the English settlers in Connecticut paid a group of Indians to bring them the heads of a rival tribe. Since heads are a real pain to cart around, scalps were collected instead. You know how you return empty soda bottles in exchange for five cents? Many towns offered "scalp bounties"—money for a head of Indian hair.

In the town of Salem (the witch-hunt capital of America), people cashed in scalps, which were then hung along the walls of the town courthouse, where they hung for many years in full view of the public. One historian tells a story about his great-great-great-great grandfather, who was scalped and left for dead during the American Revolution. He woke up without his hair, but lived to be a very old man . . . a very old, VERY bald man!

Just take a little off the top. . . . This man (right) survived being scalped.

285

THE ANIMAL ARMY

About 2,200 years ago, a fellow named Hannibal, who lived in Carthage in northern Africa, decided he'd had enough of the Romans and their empire-building. Hannibal was a think-outside-the-box kind of guy. He scored a big victory against the Romans by tying flaming torches to the horns of herds of cattle and sending those soon-to-be-steaks-on-a-stick stampeding into the enemy camp. Hannibal decided that the "horn" thing really worked, and next turned his attentions to elephants—really *big* animals with sharp pointy tusks—perfect for spearing and stomping.

Hannibal's first battles with elephants worked pretty well. Watching one stampeding in your direction is pretty scary. But there are two basic problems with elephants. One, they get spooked easily and become impossible to control. (And no one wants to be around an out-of-control elephant.) Two, they *hate* cold weather. So when Hannibal tried to cross the freezing cold Alps and

WORD UP!

When we are *civil* to one another, it means that we treat each other nicely. That's where our word *civilized* comes from. But civil can also mean "of or about citizens." Still, it's kind of odd that we call wars in which people in the same country fight with each other "civil wars." There is absolutely nothing civilized about them! And when it comes to civil wars, America's Civil War gets the prize for the most soldiers killed in one battle. At Gettysburg, Pennsylvania, a staggering 51,000 were killed and wounded in three awful days. A very uncivil battle!

sneak into Rome with 34 elephants, most of the herd froze to death. But some other armies have had better luck putting Mother Nature's creatures to work for them.

BIRDBRAINS

Many centuries later, more than half a million pigeons were drafted for military service, and they helped the Allies win World War II. They were packed into teeny little parachutes and dropped into occupied areas, then gathered up (the parachutes kept them from flying away) and kept in pigeon rooks until it was time to send a message back to home base. Then tiny notes were taped to their legs. When they were released, the pigeons did what pigeons do: They headed straight for home. Back home, soldiers read their messages and took action accordingly. It was one of the few times in history when birdbrains were a really good thing!

A WORM WELCOME

Imagine an earthworm the length of a car and you can begin to understand how giant worms helped win a war in the early 1800s in South Africa. During a battle between rival South African chieftains, something weird happened. One side was just marching happily along, not

*"**Snow way!** I'm not going up those mountains!"* But that's what Hannibal's elephants thought.

A WAR BY ANY OTHER NAME...

The Children's Crusade Sounds like a good thing, right? A way to raise money for kids who need help? Fund-raising for local schools, maybe? No way! In 1212, two very religious boys (one French, the other German) decided that children should walk from France to Jerusalem (that's a few *thousand* miles) and kick the Muslims out. This was the kiddie part of a dumb-dumb war called the Crusades, which was the nastiest religious war ever fought. More than 9,000 kids left home—some as young as age six— to make the trip. Many never made it to their destination, but instead got sold into slavery by seedy sea captains.

The Hundred Years' War (1337–1453) For a very long time, the French and the English flat-out hated each other. A group from France called the Normans (whose great-grandfolks were Vikings), headed by a guy called William the Conqueror, grabbed most of England in the 1060s. Naturally, the English were steamed. By 1337, they'd had just about enough.

So Edward III and his mysterious son, the Black Prince, decided to take England back for the English. One hundred years later, his great-great-grandkids were still going at it!

The War of the Roses (1455–1484) Roses are pretty. They smell good, too. But *these* roses were smelly soldiers, and the only thing red about them was the bloodshed. This stupid war broke out because two families both wanted to rule England. One family, the Lancasters, was led by King Henry VI (or King Henry the Sometimes Crazy). England's Parliament (where legislators write the laws) decided Henry was a rotten ruler. They gave Richard, the Duke of York, the thumbs-up to rule. And boom! Before you knew it, the Lancasters, who had a red rose as their emblem, and the Yorks, who wore a white rose as their sign, were going at it. This family feud dragged on for almost 30 years! (By the way, the red team won. As if it matters anymore!)

---

paying much attention to anything. Suddenly, out of nowhere, out popped the enemy. In fact, they seemed to rise right out of the center of the Earth! Turns out they had been hiding in giant tunnels that had been dug by huge earthworms.

During World War I (1914-1918)—the first war between many countries from a bunch of different continents—soldiers found themselves having to dig the equivalent of those giant earthworm tunnels. With both sides evenly matched in terms of weapons and the will to win, soldiers from both sides ended up living in muddy tunnels called *trenches.* Every soldier carried a shovel along with his guns.

Living in a trench became a way of life. The German soldiers' trenches were like little mud houses, complete with shutters and even doormats for wiping muddy feet. The Allies (English, French, Belgian, Canadian, and, eventually, American soldiers) lived in cruddier

Home, sweet trench. *Remember to wipe your feet when you come in.*

trenches. Their officers didn't want them to get too comfortable. During the day, soldiers hung in their trenches, then crawled out at night for surprise raids. They had lots of "pets" in the trenches, though. Rats and lice loved them!

TO THE BAT CAVE!

Even though it is sometimes called "the good war," World War II (1939–1945) was probably the worst war ever fought—a war that spread to every continent except Antarctica. Cities were bombed, boats were torpedoed. Fifty-five million people died! Things were very awful.

One of the weirdest weapons ever dreamed up was a kind of "mad scientist meets Mother Nature" device—the Bat Bomb, which a team of Americans developed in 1942. The plan was to fit millions of bats with tiny explosive devices and drop them on the enemy—in this case, the Japanese. At 1,000 feet, a mechanism would release the bats from their bomb-like containers, which were attached to parachutes. The bats would then scatter and roost in the eaves and cracks of all the enemy houses, setting hundreds of thousands of fires. Alas, their first stateside test run burned an entire brand-new military airfield to the ground, so the bats were banned.

FOOLED-YA FOOTPRINTS

World War II saw a lot of strange tactics. One of the oddest was used in the Pacific, where a lot of the fighting was on islands with sandy beaches. Undercover agents got special foot-shaped rubber soles that strapped onto their boots. That way when they landed on a beach, they left behind "bare feet" footprints instead of boot prints, making it appear as though some local folks had gone for a stroll along the shore.

The first humans to come face-to-face with a beached whale, thousands and thousands of years ago, must have seriously freaked! What *was* this huge creature? Still—a meal is a meal. So ancient man took his sharpened flint knife and began to slice . . . and slice . . . and slice . . . *and slice* through up to nine inches of rubbery blubber. Turned out, the blubber tasted pretty good—kind of like eating sticks and sticks of salty butter. But there was another discovery. Whales had lots of stuff that was useful for us humans. Good for us . . . but bad luck for the poor whales.

Where there's a whale, there's a way. These guys had to figure out how to de-beach this poor critter.

THAR SHE BLOWS

Turns out, whales were a one-stop shop for all sorts of useful things. Their blubber melted when it was heated up and made great oil—perfect for lighting oil lamps in the days before electricity. There were also long strips of plastic-like stuff called *baleen*. Folks figured there had to be *something* useful to do with that stuff! That poor, dead whale turned out to be a mega-meal and energy source all rolled into one. And all those

WHALE MOST-WANTEDS

Whale hunters were after four things:

Baleen is often confused with whalebone, but it's made of *keratin,* the same stuff that fingernails, hair, hoofs and claws are made of. Baleen hangs in long, skinny strips from the roof of a whale's mouth and it's used to strain *krill* (tiny, shrimp-like critters) from the gallons and gallons of seawater the whale swallows. During the nineteenth century, baleen was used to make buggy whips, carriage springs, women's corsets, fishing poles, hoops for women's skirts, shoelaces, hat brims, collar stays, and umbrella ribs. Can you imagine tying your shoes with whale-mouth bits?

Eau du Parfume

Whale Oil was another biggie. Before we discovered *petroleum* (the stuff we pump into our cars and home heating systems these days), most people lit their homes with whale oil, made from melted blubber. Sperm whales have the finest oil, since it burns with no smoke or smell. It also doesn't turn into a blobby ooze in cold weather. It was used to light lighthouses, help keep machines running smoothly, and even to make soap.

Ambergris is a black, semi-liquid, *really* foul-smelling substance located in a sperm whale's bowels. You know how sometimes you can see a hunk of corn or a bit of carrot in your poop? That's because it didn't get digested. Sperm whales eat a type of fish called a cuttlefish, which has a beak the whale cannot digest that irritates the whale's gut. When the whale poops, out comes that slimy mass of crud. But when the disgusting hunk is exposed to air, it hardens and begins to smell quite nice. Once this property was discovered, ambergris became a much-wanted ingredient for expensive perfumes.

Dragon drool. The ancient Chinese knew all about ambergris. They called it dragon spit fragrance and thought it was the drool of sleeping sea dragons that had dribbled into the ocean.

Spermaceti is yet another valuable sperm whale product. It's a waxy substance found in their brain which makes a super-fine lubricating oil for watches and really delicate machines.

All of this meant that the sperm whale soon became a dead duck.

whale species blissfully splashing out in the sea were about to become Wanted: Dead or Alive.

HARPOON-HAPPY

At first, people waited for their whales to wash ashore, already dead. But many people, such as the Inuit up in Alaska, learned to depend on the whales to survive in their frosty lands. Besides using whales for food and light, they built their houses out of whale ribs. Jawbones made great sled runners. Shoulder blades made sturdy shovels. Baleen made strong fishing line and sewing thread.

The Japanese were also serious whale hunters. More than 2,000 years ago, the Japanese had a big whaling fleet. By the year 700, over in Europe, the Vikings were also on the lookout for whales. Soon folks all over the globe were sailing off to see if they could spear themselves a *cetacean* (the scientific word for whales). By the 1800s whaling had grown into a huge business, especially in America.

Slaughter at sea. Onlookers admire the whale hunters' haul.

MOBY ICK

By the 1720s, whales in coastal waters were becoming hard to find. Whalers had to go search farther out at sea. When that happened, the era of the great whale ships was born. Folks set out on journeys that could take them everywhere from the steamy African coast to the freezing cold Arctic Sea.

All along America's coasts, especially in New England, fleets of whaling ships set off to search for that elusive blubber. Whalers lusted after sperm whales and right whales, which got their name because they were the "right" whale to hunt—slow swimmers with so much blubber that they rarely sunk.

Being a whaler was a hard, dirty, smelly, icky business. One of the most famous books of all time is about a mysterious giant white whale named Moby Dick, and the captain that went nuts trying to catch it. And he wasn't the only one. . . .

OH, STOP BLUBBERING!

How *did* you catch a whale? First off, you had to find one, and that is easier said than done. Lookouts would get to spend a two-hour shift standing at the tippy-top of a ship's mast ten stories up, in search of a whale's spout. When a whale was finally spotted, an experienced lookout could tell what kind it was simply from the way the whale blew! And when a lookout saw a sperm or right whale, he'd yell, "Thar she blows!" and the entire ship would zip into action.

Smaller boats were lowered over the side of the ship, and groups of six men would set off. Whales have excellent hearing, so the whaleboat crew had to sneak up very quietly. When they got close enough, they launched a *harpoon,* a long pole with a *really* big hook on the end that slid into the blubber and held fast. The aim was not to kill the whale, simply to attach it to the whaleboat.

The harpoon was connected to a coiled line as long as three football fields. The rope had to be able to uncoil quickly without any kinks because the whale, when hit, did what any smart critter would do: try to get away ASAP! Sometimes the whale swam so fast, and the line uncoiled so quickly, that it caught on fire.

The whale usually dove down, taking the harpoon (and the swiftly uncoiling rope) with it.

Hopefully, there was enough rope to keep the boat from being dragged down, too. Now came the fun part for the boat's crew. The whale swam like mad, trying to get away, and the attached whaleboat was taken for a wild ride. Imagine being on a roller coaster with gallons of cold salty water hitting you full on! Gurgle . . .

In time, the whale would get tired and the whalers would start to play tug-of-war with the line, pulling in closer and closer to the exhausted cetacean, until one of the crew could plunge a lance into the whale's heart or lungs. Blood would spout out—a "fire in the chimney," they called it. The dying creature would lurch around in smaller and smaller circles, until it gave one final slap of the water with its huge tail and flopped on its side—dead.

The *very* tired men now had to row back to their ship, towing 50 tons of dead whale behind them, sometimes miles from the mother ship. In rough seas or in bad weather, some crews never made it back.

Rub a blub-blub. *Flaying blubber was a messy, smelly job. This fellow is being helped by a steam winch pulling a cable attached to a blanket of blubber.*

HARD LOADS OF GREASY LUCK

Here's what happened when the small whaleboat got back to the ship. The whale's head was cut off and hoisted onto the deck. Spermaceti was poured from a pocket in the whale's brain into barrels. A cutting spade sliced the blubber at three-foot

BLUBBER BATH

What smells worse than a dead fish? Try sniffing a rotting 45-foot-long dead whale! So when the folks of Florence, Oregon, came face-to-face with 16,000 pounds of stinking seafood that had washed up on their beach, they had to do something. They couldn't bury the creature. It'd be easier to bury a bus! A plan was hatched. The highway department decided to blast the blubber into bite-sized pieces so that hungry seagulls could finally get their beaks around the chunks. Sounds like a plan, huh? Well . . . here's what happened.

Almost half a ton of dynamite was placed around the whale as a large crowd of onlookers gathered in the dunes to watch. The dynamiters counted down, then pushed the plunger. There was a deafening noise, and suddenly it was raining blubber. Chunks of fat were flying everywhere. One hunk the size of a washing machine crushed a car that was parked more than a quarter of a mile away. People were coated with a stinking slime of whale guts.

Just recently, over in Taiwan, a dead 60-ton sperm whale washed ashore. The folks there, perhaps having learned from the Oregon experience, loaded their whale onto a flatbed truck to move it. They were driving it through the streets of a nearby city when the decaying body, full of expanding internal gases, exploded, showering the streets with blood and whale intestines (which trust me, are *very* big). Talk about a whale-size fart!

Moby goes to the movies. One of the most famous films ever featured a giant white whale, named Moby Dick, and a sea captain with a peg leg who was obsessed with him.

intervals, rolling the whale around as it was cut—a bit like peeling an apple. The seamen sliced a hole in the end of the strip of blubber sections called "horse pieces" (because they were almost the size of a horse), and those were cut into "Bible leaves." Another crew member used a blubber fork to load the minced Bible leaves of raw blubber into a cast-iron try-pot, which was used to boil the blubber down into whale oil. "Hard loads of greasy luck" were what ships full of whale oil were called. Bet you can guess why!

As weapons improved later in the 1800s, the whales' chances of survival grew even dimmer. Harpoon guns replaced the manual throw. Then explosive harpoons came along. It was not a good time to be a whale. But times change. Hoop skirts and corsets and horse-drawn buggies fell out of favor (thank goodness). Petroleum was discovered in Pennsylvania in 1859. It was much easier to pump natural gas out of a hole than to roam the seas looking for hard-to-find whales.

The great era of Yankee whaling came to a quick end with the invention of the electric lamp in 1879. By 1906, the development of spring steel ended the need for baleen. But sadly, the poor whales' world has never been the same.

WICKED WITCHES

What are you gonna be for Halloween this year? A ninja? A space alien? A pirate? Well, you can always paint your face green, stick a pointy black hat on your head, grab a broomstick, and then head off in hot pursuit of 15 pounds of cavity-causing candy.

And if you think witches are a girls-only costume, you'd better think again. Men and women, young and old, rich and poor—anyone, *anyone*—could be accused of being a witch in times past. And many a person fried, then died for it!

ALWAYS GOOD TO HAVE SOMEONE TO BLAME . . .

Witches and witch-like folks—people claiming supernatural powers—have been around forever. Way back in ancient Egypt, witches and sorcerers were a "must-have" for the pharoah. In ancient Mesopotamia, the very first written laws included one to protect people from witchcraft, and another to protect people from being accused of witchcraft. How thoughtful! But during the biblical period, starting around 1000 B.C.E., witches started to get a bad rap. After all, the Hebrews believed in only one all-powerful God. How could anyone else have special powers?

By the Middle Ages, accusing someone of being a witch was a pretty common way to get even with someone you didn't like, or to explain bad luck that befell you. All over the world, everything and anything that went wrong was blamed on a witch, or a sorcerer, or *soothsayers* (people who could "predict the future"). If a baby died soon after being born, people believed it was because of witchcraft. If a farmer's crops failed? Witches. If there was someone you didn't like? All you had to do was shake like a crazy thing, roll your eyes around in your head a few times, point a finger at your enemy, and yell, "*witch!*"

And let's face it. You really didn't want to blame a big brute of a guy—someone who could punch your lights out. So most of the time it was easier to blame women—especially older women.

YORE

Until 1951 there were still witchcraft laws in England. After the Witchcraft Act was repealed, a woman named Sybil Leek came forward and confessed to not only being a witch, but to being a spy for the British government during World War II. She said she had cast horoscopes for evil Nazis who believed in astrology (the ability of the stars to tell the future). Supposedly, she convinced a leading Nazi that the stars said he should fly to England; once there, he was captured and taken to the Tower of London.

The years between 1400 and 1800 were the peak of witch hysteria in Europe. Anywhere from 50,000 to 100,000 people were burned at the stake or hanged for being witches. Another 100,000 were banished or punished by having a useful body part hacked off. Some countries paid no heed to sorcerers and spell casters. But the lands under Germanic rule seemed to be the place where witch hunting reached a peak. Switzerland, Holland, Poland, Scotland, and Scandinavia also were witch-hunt hot spots. Eighty percent of the victims were women—especially poor, old widows. But being a guy didn't guarantee your safety. Over in Russia, more men than women were burned as witches. A witch could be anyone. A witch could be *you!*

WHICH WITCH?

Witch hunting came to the Americas in a *big* way —to a little village called Salem, Massachusetts— in the late 1600s. The winter of 1692 had been a doozy. It was *so* cold! The crops were a mess. The farmers were fighting with the townies. Church leaders were fighting with the village leaders. There was talk of the town splitting in two. Rumors were spreading like wildfire.

The largest family in town decided they needed a new minister to take their side on political matters,

A witches' convention? Nah, just a bunch of old biddies who like tall hats!

so they hired a man named Samuel Parrish, who arrived with his 9-year-old daughter, Elizabeth, and his 11-year-old niece, Abigail. Some stories say that the girls decided to make a fake crystal ball to see who their future husbands were going to be. They did this by dripping egg whites into a bowl of water. A young woman named Tituba, the family's slave, joined in the little game. They decided the egg white looked like a coffin. The girls went a little nuts with their game, and Elizabeth knew her preacher-dad would have whipped her if he knew she was playing around with fortune telling. That was a big no-no in Puritan America. So the girls kept on spazzing until Reverend Parrish called in the local doctor, who decided that the girls were under "an evil hand."

Tituba's husband decided to cook up a West Indian potion to rid the girls of that evil hand. He made a little cake out of rye flour and the "bewitched" girls' pee, which he then fed to the dog. The rye may have had some sort of fungus in it, because the dog got sick—proof of witchcraft!

The girls continued to twitch and jerk. Was it a game? Maybe. But it stopped being funny when they accused Tituba and two old women in the village of being witches. The girls were getting a lot of attention. Soon other girls in town started getting twitchy. Whatever "it" was, it was spreading!

WHICH END IS UP?

Over the following few months more girls got the "spazzes" and more than 60 people were accused of being witches. By May, the jails between Salem and Boston, 20 miles away, were packed. Every ache and pain, every wilted cabbage plant, every cow with bad gas was proof that witches were doing their evil work.

Finally a new governor, William Phips, arrived from England and called a special court to order. The court decided that there were only a few types of evidence that were admissible. They

looked for strange birthmarks or weird freckles on people that might be a witch's mark. Suspects' houses were searched for dolls or puppets (even children's toys). After all, those could be used for black magic by thrusting pins into them or twisting the limbs. And if a witness remembered that shortly after an argument or disagreement with "a witch," a cow died or an ankle twisted on the way home—that was allowed as evidence.

Between June and September, 27 people went on trial. Among them was a 71-year-old devout churchgoer named Rebecca Nurse. Forty people signed a petition saying that she was a kind old lady who had never harmed a fly. The jury found her innocent. Upon hearing the news that she was spared, the old lady let out a cry. The judge decided her cry sounded devilish. Old Lady Nurse was quite deaf, and when the judge asked her a question and

WHICH DOCTOR IS THE WITCH DOCTOR?

In the Zulu culture of South Africa, *inyangas*—witch doctors—were people hired to cure patients who had been put under the spell of a witch. They themselves were not the witches! I feel better already!

she did not answer, he decided she was a witch after all. She was ordered hanged.

By the time Governor Phips had returned to Salem after a skirmish with Indians in the surrounding areas, things were really out of hand. There were now 100 people accused of witch-craft, awaiting trial. Phips finally realized that things had gotten crazy. "No more!" he said.

MY BAD!

People began to realize just how stupid and deadly everything had become. The colony's leading minister, Increase Mather, spoke out saying, "It were better that ten suspected witches should escape, than that one innocent person should be condemned." Duh!

A lot of people started apologizing, even though it was too late. Reverend Samuel Parris, whose daughter Elizabeth had started the madness, said he was sorry he'd gotten carried away. Five years after the witch hunts began, he was finally fired and sent packing. There were no

What to do with wicked witches? *Lock 'em up and toss the key.*

more witch trials. But for the next hundred years, most New Englanders still believed in witches.

But next Halloween, when you have a run-in with someone in a pointy hat dressed all in black, you'll know that witches are a whole lot of hype.

WHAT WOULD YOU DO?

Let's pretend you are a Salem resident. It's 1692 and a couple of hysterical girls have just pointed their fingers at you and accused you of being a witch. Now what? You have five choices: Circle the correct answer.

A. You can leave town.

B. You can protect your own butt by accusing someone else and saying, "THAT witch over there *made* me put a spell on the hysterical girls."

C. You can confess to being guilty even though you know you're innocent. At least that way you won't get killed, just tossed in jail.

D. You can tell the truth—you are totally innocent and the girls are giant fibbers—and stand trial.

E. You can refuse to listen to those nut-jobs, shrug your shoulders, and not give them the time of day. After all, who's going to believe a hysterical 11-year-old over a respected member of the community?

Now, let's see how you did.

So how did you do? Still alive?

E. An elderly tavern owner who thought the whole witch thing was ridiculous tried this approach. He refused to go to court! His punishment was the dreaded peine forte et dure—slowly being crushed to death with heavy weights piled on his chest.

D. Ooooh. Big mistake! That's how 19 people ended up swinging by their necks from the gallows. After all, every time you walk into the room, the possessed girls start acting like crazy people. Clearly, it's you! Proof that you are lying. GUILTY!

C. A very shrewd move. Of the original three women accused of witchcraft, the only one to live was Tituba, the family slave, who admitted to being a witch. Fifty-five people confessed during the Salem trials. Those confessions had to be proof that the crazy, spazzoid girls were telling the truth, right?

B. Not a bad idea! Some daughters even accused their own mothers of being witches. It sure shifts the blame!

A. Yeah, you can leave town, but where are you going to go? Into the wilderness? And what about your house and your family?

OH, YIKES!

X

X-FILES

Ever shuddered through a scary sci-fi movie? The kind where a vile creature from outer space with creepy tentacles and seven eyeballs slimes some poor guy—or worse? Books and movies have brought us all sorts of gooey, goofy space creatures, from E.T. to that awesome giant cockroach-dude from *Men in Black* who landed his flying saucer in the middle of a cow pasture.

But the truth is even weirder. There are *things* in the skies above us—and things right here on Earth that simply cannot be explained. Things that have been driving some folks nuts for centuries!

So let's X-plore the X-citing, the X-traordinary . . . the un-X-plained.

GREAT X-PECTATIONS

Are we alone in the universe? Maybe, maybe not. After all, the universe is pretty big—bigger than any of us can imagine. In 1992, NASA, the government space agency that sent astronauts to the moon, began to build ginormous radio telescopes in Puerto Rico and New Mexico to listen for signs of life in other galaxies. They were trying to find out if we truly *are* all alone by studying outer space with huge telescopes— some as big as ten football fields (well . . . round football fields if you want to be picky).

After a few years they gave up and turned that project over to a private group called SETI, which stands for Search for Extraterrestrial Intelligence. Today, dozens of SETI radio telescopes

Sci-fi-guys.
From E.T. to Men in Black,
we love our space critters.

296

scan the skies, listening like giant pairs of ears for the noises of other galaxies. So far, nothing—but you never know!

HEADS UP!

Right now, there are no other life-forms that we are aware of, but there sure are lots of *other* things flying around out in space. Some of them occasionally end up zooming our way. *Meteors* (large space rocks) and *asteroids* (imagine a small, all-rock planet) have made some pretty big dents on Earth in times long past. Absolutely massive, destructive dents! In fact, one such event 65 million years ago—a direct hit by a six-mile-wide asteroid—is probably the reason you don't have to fight with a dinosaur for a parking space.

But more recently, at just past 7 A.M. on June 30, 1908, something went *boom* in Siberia. In an instant, an enormous explosion flattened a 20-mile circle of forest in northern Asia. Eighty *million* trees snapped like twigs, all laying in the same exact direction except for the center of the blast, where a circle of trees stood unharmed. What in the world (or out of the world) had happened?

Eyewitnesses reported seeing a "a flying star with a fiery tail." Was it a spaceship? For a lot of years, plenty of people sure thought so! Turns out, it was a probably a *comet* (a huge frozen slush ball) that smacked into the Earth. Imagine getting hit in the head with a snowball the size of a shopping mall! That's gonna leave a mark!

THE SKY IS FALLING! THE SKY IS FALLING!

For thousands of years, comets like the one that crash-landed in Siberia made people seriously freak out. Most comets pass by the Earth without ever hitting it. But just the sight of a comet in the night skies was enough to make many ancient people, from the Egyptians to the Aztecs, think the world was coming to an end.

Comets meant that the crops were going to fail, that war was brewing, or that death was just around the corner. And why wouldn't they have thought so?

WHAT THE HALLEY?

Edmund Halley (1656–1742), an English astronomer, had a brainstorm one day. He had been studying a huge streaking ball in the sky with a long, glowing tail—what we now know is a comet. He also noticed that there seemed to be a pattern as to how often such celestial bodies appeared. The first written record of a comet in the sky dated back to 240 B.C.E., but folks had also written about long-tailed celestial bodies recently, in 1531 and 1607, and had painted pictures of them. Now, here it was 1682 and the long-tailed comet seemed to be back! Could it be the same comet, going round and round and round the sun? Could it be that it took 76 years to make the trip?

In 1682, Halley made a prediction: that the long-tailed comet would be back again in 1758. And he was pretty close. In March 1759, it returned. Today Halley's Comet still spins around the sun, passing by the earth every 76 years. It'll be back again in 2062, so be there or be square!

After all, the sky literally did look like it *was* falling! More than one very smart person looked up at these huge flying slush balls and decided that they were carrying visitors from other planets—visitors who were out to harm us. And in the late 1880s, as authors began to write a new type of story called science fiction, folks started to get extra-spooked at the thought of little green guys from space.

THE REAL X-FILES

So what's the story on UFOs? Are there really such things as Unidentified Flying Objects? Believe it or not, 90 percent of

Captured on film. *Are those ghostly white saucers really UFOs? The photographer who snapped this in 1954 thought so.*

alien spaceship sightings can easily be explained. After all, there's a lot of stuff up in space these days: satellites, space stations, weather balloons, comets, meteors, and other things that actually belong there. So what accounts for the other 10 percent? The most likely explanation is overactive imaginations, optical illusions, and practical jokes. But still, there have been some pretty convincing tales told, and one of the weirdest took place right smack dab in the middle of World War II.

What happened? Pilots kept coming back after their missions with the same strange story. They kept seeing weird lights and silvery blobs! One pilot reported that he had seen more than 150 wobbly silver things, grouped in lines of 10 or 12 each. Others told of orange lights that followed them wherever and whatever they did, even when they did swoops and nosedives and barrel rolls to lose the blobs. The pilots were a little freaked. Was the enemy up to something? Still, no one had ever been hurt by the blobs so the pilots eventually gave them the cute little name of "Foo Fighters."

These unidentified flying lights were named after a really popular comic strip called Smokey Stover. Smokey was a firefighter and used the syllable *foo* a lot. There were "foomous" people. People had "foolings." Smokey's thoughts were his "foo-losophy." So the funky little lights that followed the World War II pilots around became "Foos."

After the war, a bunch of pilots admitted they had been sure the enemy—the Japanese

CLOSE ENCOUNTERS OF WHICH KIND?

Just in case you ever have a run-in with an extra-terrestrial, or just want to pretend you do, here's how to describe it. We can thank Dr. Hynek of "swamp gas" fame (see page 299) for these cool expressions.

1. Close Encounter of the First Kind:

You just saw a very funky cluster of swirling pink and green lights in the night sky.

2. Close Encounter of the Second Kind:

You just saw those funky lights touch down on a field just outside of town.

3. Close Encounter of the Third Kind:

You and the space dudes in the pink and green swirly-light spaceship are sharing a pizza together.

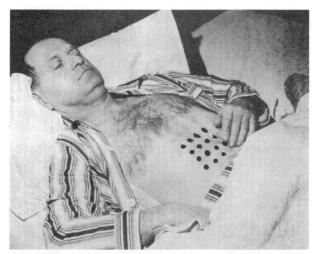

A real grid iron? This poor fellow got too close to a landed UFO in Manitoba, Canada, and ended up with this bizarre burn—or so he says.

and Germans—had some sort of secret flying weapons. But it turns out, Japanese and German pilots were being "foo-ed," too. Smokey Stover always said, "Where there's foo, there's fire." And maybe the world's most terrible war ever needed a few "foos" to put an end to the foo-lishness.

FLYING SAUCER DEAD AHEAD

The thing that really kick-started the whole UFO craze in America took place in June 1947, near the little town of Roswell, New Mexico. A rancher found some strange debris on his property—shiny foil strips and odd-looking tape with weird floral designs on it. A few days later, a pilot told reporters he had seen nine strange objects flying in excess of 1,200 miles per hour, zipping over the Cascade Mountains. The pilot described the airborne "things" as stones skipping across the water. And that is how the stories about the "flying saucers" were born.

The rancher heard the pilot's stories and handed his crash-trash to a U.S. Air Force official,

who released a statement saying a flying saucer had been found near Roswell. There was also talk of strange "corpses" found amidst the crash remains. Pretty soon everyone was going nuts with stories about aliens. So what really happened?

The official story is this: In the late 1940s, the government was testing spy equipment because America and Russia were not getting along very well. (That's an understatement: in fact it was the beginning of the almost 50-year-long "Cold War.") The Russians were threatening to "bury" America by dropping an atomic bomb or two on us. What the pilot saw, and what the farmer had picked up as trash, were actually high-altitude spy balloons. The crashes (and the "corpses") were nothing more than surveillance aircraft and the poor stuffed dummies that had been used for crash-testing and flung to Earth. Still, to this day, a lot of people believe that the U.S. Air Force is hiding something.

DID SOMEONE JUST FART?

Michigan became another famous UFO-y place in March 1966. Frank Mannor and his son called the local sheriff with the news that they had seen a flying saucer landing in a nearby swamp. They (bravely? stupidly? you decide!) followed the weird object to the bog and watched as a bright light rose up over their heads before vanishing into the night sky. A local patrolman saw the same light a few minutes later and some folks even snapped photos of the mysterious glowing blob.

Out came Dr. J. Allen Hynek—an astronomy professor, UFO investigator, and a member of the U.S. Air Force's Project Blue Book team. At first he thought the Mannors

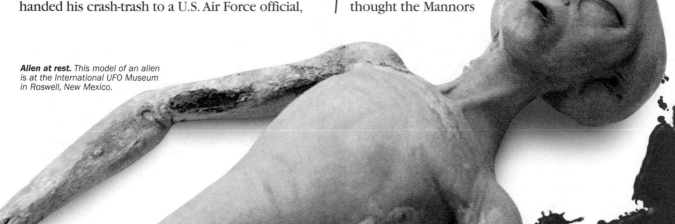

Alien at rest. This model of an alien is at the International UFO Museum in Roswell, New Mexico.

DID YOU SEE THAT?

It was January 6, 1969. Night was falling in Leary, Georgia. No wind. Really cold, too. And the governor of the state—a man who would one day become president of the U.S. of A.—was craning his neck looking skyward. There was definitely something funky in the sky!

Former President Jimmy Carter is a man of science, and a graduate of the United States Naval Academy. He has won the Nobel Peace Prize. Clearly, the man is not a whack job! But there he was, standing outside the Lions Club with a bunch of other guys, pretty sure he was staring at a UFO. In the report he filed with the International UFO Bureau, Carter wrote, "It seemed to move towards us from a distance, stop, move partially away, return, then depart. Bluish at first; then reddish—luminous—not solid. At times it was as bright as the moon, and about as big as the moon—maybe a bit smaller." But Carter's letter was filed away—another unexplained, unsolved UFO sighting.

had seen the real thing. But he soon said, with a snort, "It's swamp gas." To this day, sci-guys use that term—"swamp gas"—to make fun of silly spaceship sightings.

And what of Project Blue Book? From 1947 to 1969, the U.S. Air Force recorded 12,618 UFO sightings and explained all but 701 of them. And of those unexplained sightings, no one was hurt and nothing was damaged—not so much as a blade of grass. Whatever "they" were, they were totally harmless, so Project Blue Book was shut down. No more tales of swamp gas.

UFO RUNWAYS?

There have been reports of some pretty weird things happening up in the skies. Here's one that happened when a guy looked down. In 1926 a pilot was flying over the deserts of Peru, looking for signs of water. Instead of water, he saw huge, football-field-sized drawings of monkeys and spiders and birds spread out for miles and miles! The Nazca Lines, as they were named, are completely *amazing!* And here's the woo-woo part: *You can only see them from the air!*

They were made by the Nazcan civilization, which existed between 200 B.C.E. and 700 C.E.—long before there was any way to fly high enough to see these carvings. Why would someone draw pictures that you could only see from way up high if there was no way to get up there to view them? "Made by space men!" some said. "Landing strips for alien spaceships," said others. "Bah, humbug!" say I.

For one thing, why would you want to land a space ship on a drawing of a monkey? And who says the Nazcans didn't know how to fly? Recently, several historians have come to believe that the Nazca built primitive hot-air balloons and that they may have been the first human fly-guys ever. Or perhaps the Nazca lines were made as religious offerings to a god—something really nifty for an all-powerful heavenly being to look down upon from above.

Feel like flapping around some more? Head over to FREAKY FLYERS on page 87 for some real funky flying objects!

DO NOT FEED THE HUMAN!

ZANY ZOOS

I'll bet you collect something. Trading cards. Stuffed penguins. Headless Barbies. *Something!* It's human nature! So it's probably no surprise to hear that the first civilizations collected stuff, too. And one of the first things they collected were totally awesome animals. Oh . . . of course there were other, funkier critter collections, too. Deformed animals. Dead animals. And I will bet you've never seen a zoo filled with real live humans—behind the bars!

ZOOMIN' 'ROUND THE ZIGGURAT ZOO

If you're just an average person, your ability to collect animals is going to be limited. Looking around outside, I could collect, oh, maybe mice or ants. But there's nothing special about any of those. So rich and royal types in ancient Egypt started collecting rare animals as a way to show off. Some wealthy people had their own private zoos with lions, leopards, gazelles, baboons, giraffes, and even porcupines hanging around on their properties. It was how you bragged if you were a rich Egyptian. And since you can't exactly stick a lion in your backyard and just hope he'll be happy, they had to build special places to show off their critter collections.

Over in Mesopotamia, the Sumerians came up with a towering animal collection—a man-made "mountain" built in 562 B.C.E. It sat in the splendid city of Babylon, right in the middle of the very flat Tigris and Euphrates River valleys. The "mountain" was called the Hanging Gardens of Babylon, even though it didn't actually hang

301

and it wasn't all garden. Part of it was a zoo. Picture a pyramid with lots of flat terraces cut into the sides, and ramps and stairs leading higher and higher, and you have a *ziggurat*. Now grow all sorts of plants and water them like crazy so it's just dripping with vines and giant plants and trees. Add exotic birds and lots of adorable animals in cages. Add little paths going up, and you have a zig-zaggy ziggurat zoo (and one of the Seven Wonders of the Ancient World at that!). Now say "zig-zaggy ziggurat zoo" ten times fast!

WANNA SEE MY HYENAS?

The ancient Romans had their own goofy ideas of what to do with wild animals. They put their collections of animals on public display, except they often didn't bother to keep the lions away from the hyenas, or the tigers away from the jackals. Crowds came to huge stadiums and paid to watch the animals rip each other to bloody shreds. For extra fun, they'd toss some people in with the animals. (Want to know what happened? Go hand-to-beast with GLADIATORS on page 104 to find out more.)

About 1,000 years ago, the first real zoo opened in ancient China; it was called the Garden of Intelligence. No silly plants and flowers to get in the way. No animals ripping each other to bloody shreds. Just a bunch of different critters, kept safe in enclosed spaces, hangin' out and doing typical animal things. Built by the emperor Wen Eang, this zoo was a cool place to study animals up close.

But other monarchs had different ideas about what to do with *their* wild beasts. Take William the Conqueror, for instance. . . .

A-HUNTING WE WILL GO...

Remember Bill the Fat? (Bop back to KILLER KINGS on page 135 to get the scoop on what killed Big Bill.) One day, ol' Bill decided to set up a hunting forest around his castle and fill it with wild things. He built really high walls around a large part of his estate, then dumped his collection of animals inside. He had some typical barnyard animals, such as sheep and rabbits, but he also kept lions, leopards, lynx, camels, and rare owls. Most of the time they lived in pens, but when Bill and his buddies felt like hunting a leopard, for example, the animal was released, and off Bill and his buddies went in hot pursuit of the poor creature, who was later served up for supper.

In 1235, Bill's animals (the ones that hadn't already been caught and cooked, that is) were moved to the Tower of London, where wild animals got to hang out for the next 600 years. But only the king or queen and his and her buddies got to visit.

Then there was Ivan the Terrible, who ruled Russia from 1530 to 1584. He loved bears so much he had his own little bear zoo. He adored watching his furry beasts play, and when that got boring, he loved taking his vicious dogs out to hunt them! When the bishop of Novgorod really ticked Ivan off, Ivan got even. He had the bishop sewn into a dead bear's skin, thrown into a bear pit, and then set his hunting dogs loose. *Grrrrr-ross!*

WOW! CHECK OUT THE THREE-ARMED KID

The Aztecs, whose civilization peaked in the 1500s, had several lovely little zoos, with living reptiles, birds, and fish. Cute! But they also had a zoo with live deformed humans—unfortunate people born with three legs, two noses, or no arms. And over in Europe, the very rich also collected misshapen human specimens, but they preferred their deformed people to be dead. Sick!

THE WORST ZOO IN THE WORLD?

It was called the Exeter Exchange, but folks called it the 'Change for short. Between 1800 and 1828, this squat brick building in London was where you went if you wanted to see the animals. With nasty little cages crammed with unhappy critters, it was a smelly, smelly, smelly place. Did I mention it was smelly? *Pee-eew!* There were sad llamas, grumpy gnus, miserable emus, and bored-to-tears kangaroos. And then there was a big bull elephant.

One day he got a terrible toothache and got so cranky that he broke through his cage and ran wild through the building. It took 152 badly aimed musket balls fired by inept guards to kill him. But the best story about the 'Change is this. It's said that if you didn't have enough money to pay for admission, you could pay with a live dog or cat, which was then fed to a zoo-dweller while you watched.

FOR ME? YOU SHOULDN'T HAVE!

Rich people had a habit of giving each other exotic animals for gifts beginning in the Middle Ages. It was the kind of gift that said "Am I rich, or what?"—because catching wild animals was difficult and very expensive. And moving them from say, India or China or Ghana to Europe was even more difficult and expensive. Exotic and rare animals were caught by being driven into deep pits lined with nets, from which they could not escape. They then were moved over great distances and into very different climates. It was tough to keep them alive. In 1770, one animal collector loaded a ship with 400 live sheep just to feed the two tigers he planned to capture on the return voyage. Hippos were carried across the desert in huge animal-hide slings that rested between the backs of camels. More camels followed right behind carrying huge tubs filled with bathwater to keep the hippo moist.

Most captured animals made the zoo-bound trip by boat. Most never made it. Forget seasick. Try sea-dead! When an animal conked en route, the ship's crew saved its skin and bones to sell, and usually ate the meat and internal organs. During the long journey home, the fur would often begin to rot or get chomped on by bugs or rats. The hides stretched, which distorted the measurements of the animals. An iguana, captured in the Americas, died en route and was so altered by the time the boat docked in Europe that scientists thought they were dealing with a serpent with wings! But there was another solution to the "whoops, they're dead" situation in the years between 1400 and 1600. Something absolutely, deliciously yucky: the Cabinet of Curiosities.

I wanted a watch . . . but all I got was this baby monkey.

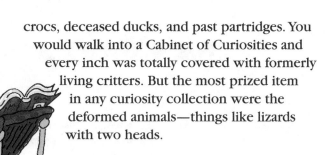

OH, YIKES!

crocs, deceased ducks, and past partridges. You would walk into a Cabinet of Curiosities and every inch was totally covered with formerly living critters. But the most prized item in any curiosity collection were the deformed animals—things like lizards with two heads.

ZOOMING ZOOS

By the 1700s in Europe and America, there still were no actual zoos. Instead, *menageries* (*men-ADJ-ur-eez*)—traveling collections of animals crammed into little cages—went from town to town. Nowadays if I say "tiger," you immediately form a mental pic of an orange-ish creature with stripes. But 300 years ago seeing a tiger was like seeing a ghost or a fire-breathing dragon—something you'd heard of but weren't sure really existed. Audiences went nuts!

Don't believe me? People in Paris in 1774 went absolutely bonkers trying to see a rare *gangan*. "It has the eyes of an elephant, the ears of a rhino, the neck of a snake and the tail of a beaver," said the breathless folks waiting on long lines to see the fabled creature. What was it? Try a camel.

So by the late 1700s, we had private animal collections. We had traveling menageries. But when it came to public zoos, we were still clueless—and zooless! It took the French

PUDGY PACHYDERM

Do elephants ever look in the mirror, pat their hips, and decide they need to drop a few pounds? Or in the case of Maggie, a pudgy pachyderm at the Alaska Zoo, a few thousand pounds? Nowadays, zoos really care about the health of their animals and a lot of people were angry that Maggie was not getting enough exercise. After all, Alaska, with its long cold winters, was keeping Maggie stuck inside for months at a time. So in 2005, her clever zookeepers bought her a $100,000, 20-foot-long, 16,000-pound treadmill that could zip along at eight miles an hour. Too bad elephants can't ride exercise bikes!

CROCODILES ON THE CEILING

With so many animals not surviving the trips from afar, many well-to-do Europeans started a new kind of collecting—dead-animal decorating. They collected stuffed creatures of all kinds, literally covering the walls and ceiling of their dens with hundreds of former foxes, conked

The wildly weird. Some zoos had displays of malformed animals.

Pachyderm for dinner. *During the Franco-Prussian war, zoo animals were killed for food.*

PLEASE DON'T FEED THE HUMANS

"Wow . . . look at that. See the fella in the fur parka? The cute one with the blond hair and blue eyes? That's Sven. He's from the same part of the world as those reindeer!"

Welcome to ethno-zoos. Here, folks could watch fur-clad Eskimos with their reindeer, natives of Tierra del Fuego hangin' with their llamas, and Australian aborigines with their kangaroos. The very funky human zoo-biz first began in Germany in 1874, when a group of reindeer were displayed with six people from Lapland, complete with their tents, sleds, and other objects of daily life.

Ethno-zoos were the brainchild of a fellow named Carl Hagenbeck, who pretty much invented the style of zoos we visit today—zoos with no bars or cages, where the animals can "think" they are in their homelands. Hagenbeck's huge zoo, which was in Hamburg, did things on a big scale. He didn't just have one monkey; he had 10,000. He had 1,000 bears and 700 leopards. Hagenbeck believed that zoos should teach people about the world. And he absolutely would not dream of hurting an animal if he could help it, which was a far cry from the way other zoos had been treating *their* animals up to then.

Hagenbeck's animal and people displays were a huge hit. The humans hung out in the exhibits and did things their "native" way. They

Revolution in 1792, with its guillotines (slice on over to page 108 for more on those) and rolling royal heads to lead to the creation of the first public zoo. The king of France had a royal plant and animal collection called the Jardin de Plantes. After the Revolution, with the royals gone bye-bye, the park was opened to the public. It was a huge hit, and led to the birth of something new all across Europe: zoological gardens. By 1847, people were tired of saying such a mouthful. From then on, we got to go to the zoo.

France's new zoo came in handy in 1870 when some of the animals in the Jardin de Plantes ended up as the main course at dinner for starving Parisians. With their city under siege by Prussian armies (from part of what is now Germany), the choice was simple: eat some elephant or eat air. You can't pour ketchup on air. (March on over to WACKY WARFARE on page 282 to learn how sieges and grumbling tummies went hand in hand.)

Who's watching who? *This lion lover is doing ballet for her big cats.*

GIFT SHOP GUNK

No visit to a zoo would be complete without a trip to the gift shop for a chubby pencil and an eraser shaped like an elephant. But many zoos have something even better for sale! Bags of animal poop with catchy names like ZooDoo, which is exactly what it sounds like. The manure from animals with hoofs (such as giraffes, zebras, elephants, llamas, and rhinos) is collected, shredded, and put into piles. Then the whole mess is covered with black plastic, which helps the piles of doo-doo get very hot. The heat kills any germs and sterilizes the gunk. Every two days, the stuff is pitch-forked and stirred, and after two and a half weeks you are left with *compost,* which is a plant's favorite thing to eat. Isn't Mother Nature thoughtful? And aren't you glad you are not a plant?

cooked, played games, napped after lunch, did crafts, and occasionally pretended to hunt. And so it went for the next 50 years, until it became harder and harder to find enough people who wanted to be zoo exhibits. Gee, I wonder why?

Unlike the animals, the humans *did* get to leave the zoo every night after it closed. They quickly adapted to life in Europe—the clothing, the language, and the way people lived and worked. And after a mellow night spent hanging out in a café, sipping espresso and eating chocolate mousse, it was really hard to be "wild and savage" the next morning.

Think the whole humans-in-zoos idea is too weird for modern times? In 2005, the London Zoo tried something new and different. Eight volunteers, wearing nothing but fig leaves, were displayed for the crowds for three days under a sign that said, "WARNING: Humans in their Natural Environment." The humans were fed and cared for by animal keepers and given games and music to keep them entertained. Of course, at the end of the day, the humans got to go home.

But it kind of makes you think a little bit harder about the whole zoo-biz. Sure . . . zoos today are all about educating the public about nature and helping endangered species survive. But sometimes I wonder who's really looking at whom? If lions could visit the London Zoo and stare at the humans, safe behind bars, what would *they* think of *us*?

Well, that does it for us. Thanks for hanging out and reading!

PHOTO CREDITS

Despite extensive research, it has not always been possible to establish property ownership/copyright. Where this is the case, we would appreciate notification.

Front Cover: *left, top left,* Graham French; *bottom right,* Mary Evans Picture Library; **Spine:** Graham French; **Back Cover:** *top left,* Superstock Inc./Superstock; *top right,* The Granger Collection, New York; **page v:** Mary Evans Picture Library; **page vi:** *left,* Mary Evans Picture Library; *right,* Bridgeman Art Library; **page vii:** AP/Wide World Photos; **page viii:** *left,* Photofest; **page x:** *camels,* Library of Congress Prints and Photographs Division; *Mosque,* Library of Congress Prints and Photographs Division; *knight,* Superstock Inc./ Superstock; **page xi:** *top middle, bottom middle,* Library of Congress Prints and Photographs Division.

ATTILA AND THE HUNS—CUSSIN' COWBOYS

page 2: Mary Evans Picture Library; **page 4:** *left,* Bettmann/ Corbis; **page 4:** *right,* The Granger Collection, New York; **page 5:** Library of Congress Prints and Photographs Division; **page 8:** Mary Evans Picture Library; **page 9:** *top,* Library of Congress Prints and Photographs Division; **page 10:** Mary Evans Picture Library; **page 12:** Library of Congress Prints and Photographs Division; **page 15:** Index Stock Imagery; **page 16:** *top,* Library of Congress Prints and Photographs Division; **page 18:** *top,* Mary Evans Picture Library; **page 20:** The Granger Collection, New York; **page 22:** *bottom,* Petrified Collection/Getty Images; **page 22:** *top,* Archive Holdings Inc./ Getty Images; **page 24:** Library of Congress Prints and Photographs Division; **page 25:** *bottom,* Library of Congress Prints and Photographs Division; *middle,* Index Stock Imagery; **page 26:** *bottom & top,* Library of Congress Prints and Photographs Division; **page 27:** *left & right,* Library of Congress Prints and Photographs Division; **page 29:** *bottom,* Photofest; **page 31:** Mary Evans Picture Library; **page 33:** *main,* Library of Congress Prints and Photographs Division; **page 34:** *bottom main,* The Granger Collection, New York; *bottom detail,* Library of Congress Prints and Photographs Division; **page 37:** Library of Congress Prints and Photographs Division; **page 38:** Library of Congress Prints and Photographs Division; **page 40:** Library of Congress Prints and Photographs Division; **page 41:** *bottom,* Library of Congress Prints and Photographs Division; *middle,* Library of Congress Prints and Photographs Division; *top,* Library of Congress Prints and Photographs Division; **page 42:** *top & bottom,* Library of Congress Prints and Photographs Division; **page 43:** *bottom main,* Library of Congress Prints and Photographs Division; *top,* Bridgeman Art Library; **page 47:** *bottom, top left,* Library of Congress Prints and Photographs Division; *top right,* Library of Congress Prints and Photographs Division; **page 48:** *bottom,* Library of Congress Prints and Photographs Division; *top,* Photography Collection, Miriam and Ira D. Wallach Division of Art, Prints and Photographs, The New York Public Library, Astor, Lenox and Tilden Foundations, Lewis W. Hine, NYPL Digital Gallery; **page 50:** Library of Congress Prints and Photographs Division; **page 52:** Library of Congress Prints and Photographs Division.

DASTARDLY DENTISTRY—HUMONGOUS HOAXES

page 57: Library of Congress Prints and Photographs Division; **page 60:** Library of Congress Prints and Photographs Division; **page 61:** Library of Congress Prints and Photographs Division; **page 62:** The Granger Collection, New York; **page 63:** The Granger Collection, New York; **page 64:** The Granger Collection, New York; **page 67:** Library of Congress Prints and Photographs Division; **page 68:** Fox Photos/Getty Images; **page 70:** *bottom,* The Granger Collection, New York; *top left & top right,* Library of Congress Prints and Photographs Division; **page 72:** Mary Evans Picture Library; **page 74:** *bottom,* Library of Congress Prints and Photographs Division; *top,* Mary Evans Picture Library; **page 77:** Mary Evans Picture Library; **page 78:** Mary Evans Picture Library; **page 80:** *bottom,* Mary Evans Picture Library; **page 83:** *bottom,* The Granger Collection, New York; *top,* Mary Evans Picture Library; **page 85:** *bottom,* Getty Images; *top,* Mary Evans Picture Library; **page 87:** The Granger Collection, New York; **page 88:** *middle,* Library of Congress Prints and Photographs Division; **page 90:** *bottom,* Library of Congress Prints and Photographs Division; *top,* Hulton Archive/ Getty Images; **page 91:** *bottom left, bottom right, top left, top right,* Library of Congress Prints and Photographs Division; **page 92:** Bettmann/Corbis; **page 93:** Library of Congress Prints and Photographs Division; **page 96:** Dale O'Dell/ Superstock; **page 98:** *bottom,* Library of Congress Prints and Photographs Division; *top,* Mary Evans/Roger Mayne Photographs; **page 99:** *bottom,* Library of Congress Prints and Photographs Division; **page 102:** *bottom,* Mary Evans Picture Library; *top,* Library of Congress Prints and Photographs Division; **page 105:** *top,* Mary Evans Picture Library; **page 106:** *top,* Mary Evans Picture Library; **page 107:** Library of Congress Prints and Photographs Division; **page 109:** Mary Evans Picture Library; **page 110:** Mary Evans Picture Library; **page 111:** Superstock Inc./ Superstock; **page 112:** *top,* Photofest; *1900's,* Library of Congress Prints and Photographs Division; *1920's, 1940's,* Library of Congress Prints and Photographs Division; *1950's,* Photofest; *1960's,* Superstock Inc./Superstock; **page 113:** *top,* The Granger Collection, New York; **page 114:** Mary Evans Picture Library; **page 115:** *bottom,* Library of Congress Prints and Photographs Division; *top,* Mary Evans Picture Library; **page 117:** *left & right,* Mary Evans Picture Library; **page 118:** *top,* Mary Evans Picture Library; **page 120:** *bottom,* Photofest; *top,* The Granger Collection, New York; **page 122:** New York State Historical Association; **page 123:** Mary Evans Picture Library; **page 124:** BBC; **page 125:** The Granger Collection, New York; **page 126:** *screen image,* Museum of Hoaxes.

IDIOTIC INVENTIONS—OUTRAGEOUS OUTLAWS

page 128: Hulton Archive/Getty Images; **page 130:** Library of Congress Prints and Photographs Division; **page 131:** Angus McDonald/Index Stock Imagery; **page 132:** *left & right,* Library of Congress Prints and Photographs Division; **page 133:** Library of Congress Prints and Photographs Division; **page 136:** *main,* Library of Congress Prints and Photographs Division; **page 137:** Mary Evans Picture Library; **page 138:**

Mary Evans Picture Library; **page 139:** Mary Evans Picture Library; **page 143:** *detail left,* Bridgeman Art Library; *main,* Superstock Inc./Superstock; **page 149:** *bottom,* North Wind/ North Wind Picture Archives; **page 150:** *left,* The Granger Collection, New York; *right,* The Granger Collection, New York; **page 152:** The Granger Collection, New York; **page 156:** *top,* The Granger Collection, New York; **page 157:** The Granger Collection, New York; **page 159:** *bottom & top,* The Granger Collection, New York; **page 161:** Library of Congress Prints and Photographs Division; **page 164:** Library of Congress Prints and Photographs Division; **page 165:** Jack Novak/ Mary Evans Picture Library; **page 166:** Bridgeman Art Library; **page 168:** Ashmolean Museum/Bridgeman Art Library; **page 169:** *bottom,* Bridgeman Art Library; *top,* Michele Burgess/ Index Stock Imagery; **page 170:** *left,* AP/Wide World Photos; *right,* Library of Congress Prints and Photographs Division; **page 171:** AP/Wide World Photos; **page 173:** *left,* Mary Evans Picture Library; **page 174:** *figures & photos* by King and Country, supplied by the Sierra Toy Soldier Company; **page 176:** Mary Evans Picture Library; **page 178:** The Granger Collection, New York; **page 179:** Library of Congress Prints and Photographs Division; **page 180:** Library of Congress Prints and Photographs Division; **page 182:** *bottom,* Library of Congress Prints and Photographs Division; **page 183:** *left,* AP/Wide World Photos; *right,* Bridgeman Art Library; **page 184:** *bottom left,* Photofest; *bottom right,* Library of Congress Prints and Photographs Division; *middle left,* Photofest; *middle right,* Library of Congress Prints and Photographs; *right,* Library of Congress Prints and Photographs Division; **page 185:** *left top, left bottom, right,* Library of Congress Prints and Photographs Division; **page 186:** Library of Congress Prints and Photographs Division.

PIRATES—RIP-ROARIN' RAILROADS

page 189: The Granger Collection, New York; **page 192:** *top left & bottom,* Library of Congress Prints and Photographs Division; **page 193:** Library of Congress Prints and Photographs Division; **page 195:** Mary Evans Picture Library; **page 197:** *bottom,* Library of Congress Prints and Photographs Division; **page 197:** *top & bottom,* Library of Congress Prints and Photographs Division; **page 198:** *bottom,* Graham French; **page 199:** *left,* The Granger Collection, New York; **page 200:** *top,* AP/Wide World; **page 201:** *bottom,* AP/Wide World Photos; **page 202:** AP/Wide World Photos; **page 203:** *left,* Photofest; *right,* AP/Wide World Photos; **page 204:** *bottom left,* AP/Wide World Photos; *bottom right,* Library of Congress Prints and Photographs Division; *top,* Library of Congress Prints and Photographs Division; **page 205:** Library of Congress Prints and Photographs Division; **page 206:** *bottom,* Library of Congress Prints and Photographs Division; *middle,* Philip Lief & Marcel Feigel; *top,* The Granger Collection, New York; **page 207:** Bridgeman Art Library; **page 208:** Mary Evans Picture Library; **page 211:** The Granger Collection, New York; **page 212:** Library of Congress Prints and Photographs Division; **page 213:** *top,* Library of Congress Prints and Photographs Division; **page 215:** Photofest; **page 217:** *left,* Library of Congress Prints and Photographs Division; **page 217:** *right,* Mary Evans Picture Library; **page 218:** Library of Congress Prints and Photographs Division; **page 219:** *main,* Mary Evans Picture Library; **page 221:** *top,* Mary Evans Picture Library; **page 224:** Archive Holdings Inc./Getty Images.

SALT ASSAULT—TOILET PAPER

page 226: *top,* IT Stock Free/Superstock; **page 227:** *bottom,* The Granger Collection, New York; *middle,* Library of Congress Prints and Photographs Division; *pretzel,* Comstock/Superstock; **page 228:** Henryk T. Kaiser/Index Stock Imagery; **page 230:** *bottom,* Pacific Press Service/The Granger Collection, New York; *top,* Bridgeman Art Library; **page 232:** Pacific Press Service/ The Granger Collection, New York; **page 233:** *left,* Photofest; *right,* age fotostock/Superstock; **page 234:** Library of Congress Prints and Photographs Division; **page 235:** The Granger Collection, New York; **page 236:** The Granger Collection, New York; **page 237:** The Granger Collection, New York; **page 238:** *bottom,* The Granger Collection, New York; *top,* Library of Congress Prints and Photographs Division; **page 240:** *book,* Mary Evans Picture Library; **page 240:** *top,* Mary Evans Picture Library; **page 241:** *left,* Bridgeman Art Library; *right,* Library of Congress Prints and Photographs Division; **page 242:** *bottom,* Library of Congress Prints and Photographs Division; *top,* Library of Congress Prints and Photographs Division; **page 243:** *bottom,* Library of Congress Prints and Photographs Division, Mary Evans Picture Library; **page 245:** *top,* Mary Evans Picture Library; **page 246:** Hulton/Getty Images; **page 247:** *bottom,* The Granger Collection, New York; **page 249:** *bottom,* Mary Evans Picture Library; *top,* A. Forestier/The Illustrated London New Pictures Library; **page 251:** Library of Congress Prints and Photographs Division; **page 254:** Keith Alstrin/Index Stock Imagery; **page 258:** Index Stock Imagery; **page 261:** Hulton/ Getty Images; **page 263:** *bottom,* The Granger Collection, New York; **page 265:** *top,* Photofest; **page 267:** *bottom,* Library of Congress Prints and Photographs Division; *top,* Library of Congress Prints and Photographs Division; **page 268:** Library of Congress Prints and Photographs Division.

UGH! UNDERWEAR—ZANY ZOOS

page 273: *bottom,* Mary Evans Picture Library; *top,* Mauritius/Superstock; **page 274:** Mary Evans Picture Library; **page 275:** Library of Congress Prints and Photographs Division; **page 276:** Library of Congress Prints and Photographs Division; **page 278:** Mary Evans Picture Library; **page 279:** The Granger Collection, New York; **page 280:** Mary Evans Picture Library; **page 281:** Bridgeman Art Library, London/Superstock; **page 283:** *top,* Library of Congress Prints and Photographs Division; **page 284:** Mary Evans Picture Library; **page 285:** *left,* Library of Congress Prints and Photographs Division; *right,* Library of Congress Prints and Photographs Division; **page 287:** Library of Congress Prints and Photographs Division; **page 288:** Library of Congress Prints and Photographs Division; **page 290:** Library of Congress Prints and Photographs Division; **page 291:** Library of Congress Prints and Photographs Division; **page 292:** Photofest; **page 293:** Library of Congress Prints and Photographs Division; **page 294:** Mary Evans Picture Library; **page 295:** Library of Congress Prints and Photographs Division; **page 296:** *left,* Photofest; *right,* Photofest; **page 298:** AP/Wide World Photos; **page 299:** *bottom,* AP/Wide World Photos; *top,* Mary Evans Picture Library; **page 300:** *bottom,* Photofest; *top,* AP/Wide World Photos; **page 302:** Mary Evans Picture Library; **page 303:** Library of Congress Prints and Photographs Division; **page 305:** *bottom,* Library of Congress Prints and Photographs Division; *top,* The Granger Collection, New York; **page 306:** Library of Congress Prints and Photographs Division.